READINGS IN ABORIGINAL STUDIES

Volume 2

Identities and State Structures

Readings in Aboriginal Studies is a series of volumes spanning the full range of contemporary interests in Aboriginal Studies. The books are intended to provide basic readings in the discipline of Aboriginal Studies for undergraduate students and interested laypersons. Each volume covers a specific topic, presenting selected articles from scholarly periodicals, reports and other documents in the field. Each brings together a range of description and analysis by the most distinguished writers of the day, specialists in particular areas of Aboriginal Studies. Each volume, edited by one or more recognized scholars, includes both the original notes accompanying the papers and a comprehensive bibliography of references cited. Introductions provide the context for these significant papers in Aboriginal Studies.

This series is published by Bearpaw Publishing, a division of the Department of Native Studies of Brandon University, Brandon, Manitoba, Canada.

General Editor: Samuel W. Corrigan

Editorial Board: Robert C. Annis
                    Arthur W. Blue
                    Colleen Cutschall
                    B.A. Nicholson
                    David Pentland
                    Joe Sawchuk
                    Paul Voorhis

Design and Typeset: Pat Evans

Volume 1: Human Services
          Edited by Samuel W. Corrigan
Volume 2: Identities and State Structures
          Edited by Joe Sawchuk

READINGS IN ABORIGINAL STUDIES

Volume 2

Identities and State Structures

Edited by

Joe Sawchuk

Bearpaw Publishing

Canadian Cataloguing in Publication Data
Main entry under title:

Readings in aboriginal studies

Contents: v.2. Identities and state structures.
Includes bibliographical references.
ISBN 0-9695498-2-2 (v.2 : bound) – 0-9695498-3-0
(v.2 : pbk.)

1. Indians of North America – Canada. 2. Métis.
I. Corrigan, Samuel W. (Samuel Walter), 1939–.

E78.C2R42 1991   971'.00497   C91-097171-4

Printed and bound in Canada

Much of the material contained in this volume is reprinted with permission.
Full credit for each selection reprinted is listed in the Acknowledgements
section on pages vii-viii.

Bearpaw Publishing
Department of Native Studies
Brandon University
Brandon, Manitoba
Canada, R7A 6A9

TABLE OF CONTENTS

Acknowledgements vii

PART I   Introduction: State Structures and Imposed Identites:
          the Invention of "Indian."   1

PART II   Canada: State Definitions of Aboriginality

          Introduction 7

          1)   Ethnostatus Distinctions in the Western Subarctic:
               Implications for Inter-Ethnic and Interpersonal
               Relations
               James B. Waldram 9
          2)   Indians, Métis, Native: Some Implications of
               Special Status
               Noel Dyck 24
          3)   The Absurd Little Mouse: When Eskimos Became
               Indians
               Richard J. Diubaldo 39
          4)   The Reification of Ethnicity and Its Political
               Consequences in the North
               Graham Watson 51

PART III Canada: The Reclamation of Aboriginal Identity

          Introduction 68

          5)   The Métis, Non-Status Indians and the New
               Aboriginality: Government Influence on Native
               Political Alliances and Identity
               Joe Sawchuk 70
          6)   Redbaiting and Racism On Our Frontier: Military
               Expansion in Labrador and Quebec
               Peter Armitage and John C. Kennedy 87
          7)   Who Are the Métis?
               David Boisevert and Keith Turnbull 108

Part IV   Canada: Individual Responses to State Definitions of
          Aboriginal Identity

          Introduction 142

          8)   Underground Policy: An Essay on Identity and the
               Aboriginal Victims of Non-Aboriginal Structures
               Samuel W. Corrigan 144

9) Judicial Preservation of Ethnic Group Boundaries: the Iroquois Case
Sally M. Weaver 165

10) Sexual Equality and Indian Government: An Analysis of Bill C-31 Amendments to the Indian Act
Joyce Green 176

Part V   Canada: Sovereignty, Nationhood and Identity

Introduction 188

11) Tribal Traditions and European-Western Political Ideologies: the Dilemma of Canada's Native Indians
Menno Boldt and J. Anthony Long 190

12) Internationalization: Perspectives on an Emerging Direction in Aboriginal Affairs
J. Rick Ponting 207

Part VI   Some Comparisons: United States

Introduction 235

13) The Situation of Indigenous Populations in the United States
Ward Churchill 237

14) Federal Indian Identification Policy: A Usurpation of Indigenous Sovereignty in North America
M. Annette Jaimes 245

PART VII Some Comparisons: The Fourth World

Introduction 263

15) Aboriginal Identity: The Management of a Minority Group by the Mainstream Society
Deirdre F. Jordan 265

16) The Sami Law: A Change of Norwegian Government Policy Toward the Sami Minority?
Oystein Steinlein 301

References 314

ACKNOWLEDGEMENTS

Preparing this volume of readings was an informative and enjoyable task, made so primarily by the high standards of the authors of the many previously published papers included in this book, and the editors of the journals that were consulted for possible works. We appreciate their willingness to provide permission, often on very quick notice.

In particular, I would like to thank Sheila Somers, who tracked down and secured the copyrights and permission for the papers, and who also completed the herculean task of standardizing the bibliography and references, and S.W. Corrigan, who conceived the idea for this series, and this volume.

The following are the copyright holders, authors and publishers of the contributions contained in this volume, whose assistance we gratefully acknowledge:

Canadian Ethnic Studies, Faculty of Social Sciences, University of Calgary, 2500 University Drive N.W., Calgary, Alberta, Canada, T2N 1N4. Jim Frideres and Anthony Rasporich, Editors.

Noel Dyck: Indian, Métis, Native: Some Implications of Special Status. *Canadian Ethnic Studies/Etudes ethniques au Canada* 12(1):34-46, 1980.

J. Rick Pointing: Internationalism: Perspectives on an Emerging Direction in Aboriginal Affairs. *Canadian Ethnic Studies Journal* 22:85-109, 1990.

Canadian Journal of Political Science, The Canadian Political Science Association, Suite 205, 1 Stewart Street, University of Ottawa, Ottawa, Ontario, Canada, K1H 6H7. John McMenemy, Managing Editor.

Menno Boldt and J. Anthony Long: Tribal Traditions and European - Western Political Ideologies: The Dilemma of Canada's Native Indians. *Canadian Journal of Political Science* 17(3):538-553, 1984.

Culture, the Journal of the Canadian Anthropology Society, Department of Anthropology, McGill University, Montreal, Quebec, Canada, H3A 2T7. Margaret Sequin and Jean-Claude Muller, Editors.

James B. Waldram: Ethnostatus Distinctions in the Western Canadian Subarctic: Implications for Inter-Ethnic and Interpersonal Relations. *Culture* 7(1):29-37, 1987.

Issues in Radical Therapy: New Studies on the Left, Saxifrage Publications Group, 1480 Wicklow Street, Boulder, Colorado, U.S.A. 80303. Ward Churchill, Editor.

M. Annette Jaimes: Federal Indian Identification Policy: A Usurpation of Indigenous Sovereignty in North America. *Issues in Radical Therapy: New Studies on the Left* 13(3&4):26-36, 1988.

Journal of Canadian Studies, Trent University, Peterborough, Ontario, Canada, K9J 7B8. Joy Manson, Managing Editor.

Richard J. Duibaldo: The Absurd Little Mouse: When Eskimos Became Indians. *Journal of Canadian Studies* 16(2):34-40, 1981.

National Museums of Canada, Ottawa, Ontario, Canada, K1A 0M8.

Sally M. Weaver: Judicial Preservation of Ethnic Group Boundaries: The Iroquois Case, pp 48-65. *Proceedings of the First Congress of the Canadian Ethnology Society.* National Museum of Man, Mercury Series, Canadian Ethnology Service, Paper No. 17.

Native Studies Review, Department of Native Studies, University of Saskatchewan, Saskatoon, Saskatchewan, Canada, S7N 0W0. James Waldram and Frank Tough, Editors.

Joyce Green: Sexual Equality and Indian Government: An Analysis of Bill C-31 Amendments to the Indian Act. *Native Studies Review* 1(2):81-95, 1985.

Studies in Political Economy, Box 4729, Station E, Ottawa, Ontario, Canada, K1S 5H9. Emer Killean, Editorial Administrator.

David Boisvert and Keith Turnbull: Who Are The Métis? *Studies in Political Economy* 18:107-147, 1985.

The Canadian Journal of Native Studies, Brandon University, Brandon, Manitoba, Canada, R7A 6A9. Samuel W. Corrigan and Don McCaskill, Editors.

Dierdre F. Jordan: Aboriginal Identity: The Management of a Minority Group by the Mainstream Society. *The Canadian Journal of Native Studies* 7(2):271-311, 1986.

Oystein Steinlien: The Sami Law: A Change of Norwegian Government Policy Toward the Sami Minority? *The Canadian Journal of Native Studies* 9(1):1-14, 1989.

The Canadian Review of Sociology and Anthropology, Room 039, MacKinnon Building, University of Guelph, Guelph, Ontario, N1G 2W1. James Curtis and Gail Pool, Editors.

Peter Armitage and John C. Kennedy: Redbaiting and Racism on our Frontier: Military Expansionism in Labrador and Quebec. *The Canadian Review of Sociology and Anthropology* 26(5):798-817, 1989.

Graham Watson: The Reification of Ethnicity and its Political Consequences in the North. *The Canadian Review of Sociology and Anthropology* 18(4):453-469, 1981.

Wicazo Za Review, Route 8, Box 510, Rapid City, South Dakota, U.S.A., 57702. Elizabeth Cook Lynn, Editor.

Ward Churchill: The Situation of Indigenous Populations in the United States. *Wicazo Za Review* 1(1):30-35, 1985.

PART I _____

Introduction:
State Structure and Imposed Identities:
the Invention of "Indian"

Aboriginal. Native. Indigenous. Tribal. These are some of the terms that have been used to lump together the original inhabitants of North America, South America, Africa, Asia and Australasia as "them" or "other" in contrast to Western or European society. In North America, this dichotomy between Western and other has resulted in a varied group of peoples being collectively referred to as "Indians," a classification authorized by force of law in both Canada and the U.S.A. In Canada, over 50 nations have been reduced to the concept of Indian. Cree, Innu, Chipewyan, Huron, Kwakiutl, Gitksan, Siksika, it matters not—they are all the same as far as the Canadian government is concerned. Even more humiliatingly, these people are further designated as "Status or non-Status," "Registered or non-Registered," "Treaty or non-Treaty." It is the effects of such legislated and imposed identities that this collection of readings is designed to explore.

The stage of colonialism where European capitals controlled vast empires may be over, but the effects of colonialism, particularly the imposition of outside concepts of identity, are not. Imposed identity was part of a world-wide classification that diminished all peoples with the false dichotomy of primitive or civilized; Native or non-Native. It is a phoney distinction, because it developed a mythic Western ethnic identity to contrast with the rest of the world even though "Whites" or Europeans are no more homogeneous a group than are "Native" peoples, and it imbued Europeans with a spurious sense of superiority over the rest of the world.

This fusion of peoples into a single Native collectivity is so long-lived and pervasive that it has entered into our sub-conscious, where it is unlikely ever to be excised, existing independently of historical, political or social reality. I should stress that this view of Native as an undifferentiated mass is quite different from another concept shared by most of the writers in this volume, that there is a perceivable commonality and shared world view of Aboriginal peoples around the world. The very existence of the discipline of Native Studies rests on the idea that there is a separate, identifiable, and world-wide distinction between western and Native thought. While this may well be so, we should not forget that a vicious cultural imperialism has been at work for many years, trivializing the cultural differences among Aboriginal peoples and creating distinctions of status between them and the dominant states.

Of course, *all* people, not just Europeans, have terms which are used to represent "the other"—people who come from distant lands, speak different languages, and share a different culture. It is part of the process of ethnification—defining one's own social boundaries and individual identities in contrast to other societies. The First Nations of North America[1] are no exception—they distinguished themselves from other Indigenous North American societies, and from Europeans as well. Native as well as non-Natives tend to have an ethnocentric or condescending attitude towards outsiders...it is one of the most universal, although least estimable, of human emotions.

Yet there is a fundamental difference between the practice of ethnification, or contrasting one's own group from others, and what Europeans did with Aboriginal identity in the context of colonialism. Indigenous peoples were never able to impose their concepts of self and other (and the often implicit concept of inferiority of the outsider) onto European society. But through the process of domination and colonialism, Europeans were able to force their concepts of inferiority and superiority onto Native people. This process has long been known and analyzed (Fanon, Memmi, Mannoni, Wolf, etc.) Europeans typically would characterize the different races they encountered as "savage" or "primitive," which justified the process of colonialism as part of a world-wide march towards "civilization." Memmi, for example, demonstrated that the colonizer would not only characterize the colonized peoples as inadequate by European standards, but could further manipulate the situation so that the colonized would eventually accept these concepts of inferiority as true (Memmi, 1967).

Of course, this process is more than simply institutionalized ethnocentrism, or a rationale for exploitation by the colonizer. Racial terms are part of the political and economic process which turn the Native populations of the colonized areas into suppliers of coerced surplus labour; ethnic categories reflect the ways that particular segments of the population relate themselves to specialized aspects of the economy (Wolf, 1982:380-381).

Much of Canadian history regarding the interaction between Aboriginal people and Europeans can be seen in the light of Wolf's observation. The Métis, for example, came into being as a separate group through participation in the fur trade as buffalo hunters and in other mercantile endeavors; later in the 1960s, as they were forced into a marginalized position, they used that as a means of mobilizing force as well (Sawchuk, 1978). One should also recall that many of the contemporary "tribal" or national group-ings of Aboriginal peoples found in Canada today are probably relics of Canada's early colonial development: Fried makes the point that "tribes" if they exist as real sociopolitical groups at all, are usually secondary phe-nomena brought about by the intervention or existence of state societies, which often coerce previously independent bands or groups into a new political unity for the purposes of trade or forced tribute (Fried, 1975:114). Wolf uses this thesis to suggest that many of the groupings we take for granted today — Ojibwa, Salteaux, even the Six Nations — are secondary phenomena of the fur trade (1982:158-194.)

However, this volume is not concerned with the historical antecedents of colonialism so much as with the contemporary manifestation of that process; the effect of state structures upon Aboriginal. As noted above, Memmi suggested that acceptance of the colonizer's terms is one of the possible responses of the colonized. In Canada, there has been a certain acceptance of the state as arbiter of identity, both by Native people and the public at large. This has had many repercussions, both in the imposition of identity and the denial of it. Two illustrations will suffice for this introduction. The most obvious example of *imposition* of identity came with the concept of "Status Indian." The idea of the state arbitrating who was and who was not an Indian, and the concept of Status Indian itself, was first proposed by the Canadian government in 1850.[2] There are two possibilities that can occur when a dominant society imposes new groupings and/or names on people under its domination: the members may continue to struggle to maintain their separate identity and culture; or they may come to *accept* and institutionalize the new identity, and even defend it. This is what has happened to the concept of "Status" Indian in Canada. Native people today not only accept the state-imposed classification of Status and non-Status, but fight over such recognition, and treat it as an official acknowledgment of their Aboriginal heritage (Dyck, 1980; Sawchuk, this volume).

Not content with the concept of an official Indian status, the government then imposed rules on how membership in this group was to be passed on. Status was to be inherited patrilineally, despite the fact that many First Nations used matrilineal forms of descent (Weaver, this volume). Even today, after the passage of Bill C-31 which was intended to remove this and other discriminatory aspects of the *Indian Act,* arcane rules define group membership, arbitrarily dispensing Status to some, denying it to others (see Green, this volume).

The invention of "Indian" and "Status" also involved the *denial* of identity for some Aboriginal groups in Canada, particulary the Métis, who had to struggle for years before they got constitutional recognition of their Aboriginal status, and to convince the government and the general public that they were different from non-Status Indians. For the greater part of this century, their political organizations were ignored by both provincial and federal governments, and all attempts at dealing directly with government were rebuffed on the grounds that they were "just another ethnic group." Even today, there is disagreement over what their Aboriginal status may be (Flanagan, 1983a).

One should not assume from these two examples that state imposition of outside concepts of Native and non-Native is confined to Canada. The effects of colonialism are world-wide, and comparable for Aboriginal peoples everywhere. Therefore, although the general perspective of this volume is definitely Canadian, readings which explore Aboriginal identity in the United States, Australia, and Norway (Churchill, Jaimes, Jordan and Steinlien) have also been included.

As the articles in this volume illustrate, the state can affect Aboriginal identity in many ways, injecting confusion in terms of individual identity (Corrigan) or group identity (Sawchuk, Waldram, Watson). The reader may well ask if the effects of imposed identities can be countered in any way, and if so, how? The only obvious solution at this time seems to come from the reclamation of power by Indigenous peoples themselves. As identity has been imposed or taken away through power, it can only be reformulated or regained by taking power back. Native people in Canada are now claiming the right to self-government (or more precisely, are claiming that they never gave up that right). There has been some definite progress towards having the right to Aboriginal self-government recognized in the Canadian Constitution. One specific responsibility of self-government is the right to determine criteria for citizenship, and by extension, group identity. There are already the beginnings of such governments in Canada. The Gitksan Wet'suwet'sen for example, are developing a limited community self-government package in consultation with the Department of Indian Affairs[3] wherein group membership is determined by "traditional means," that is by membership in Clans and Houses (matrilineages). Other First Nations are engaged in similar negotiations. But taking back determination of group identity in that limited sense does not mean the end to controversy, even if First Nations develop such structures all across Canada. All that is settled is Band membership; Indian Status itself remains in the hands of the federal government. And the short history of Bill C-31 in Canada has already illustrated the difficulties inherent in changing the rules of conferring Status after the concept has become institutionalized among Native peoples. Some Indian politicians and commentators have argued that the reinstatement of Indian women's Status through Bill C-31 violates the right of a people to determine their own identity, while others have suggested that the exclusion of other Aboriginal peoples from Status, which the Bill also does, equally intrudes upon this right. Self-government will undoubtedly give some Native people more control over their own identities, at least on the local or community level; but whether even this will be enough to heal the divisions, breaches, and inappropriate groupings that government has imposed is hard to say. Five hundred years of being classified as "Indians," Status or otherwise, will be difficult to overcome in a short time.

In closing, I would like to say that this collection of readings is not intended to attribute blame or impose solutions to the subject of state structures and Aboriginal identities. It is simply an attempt to bring together many of the articles and discussions relevant to the subject in a primarily Canadian context — one that I hope will prove useful for students in Native Studies and related disciplines. If the reader finds the articles as stimulating and interesting as I did when collecting them, I will judge this volume to be a success. Unfortunately, space, copyright and/or cost considerations have made it necessary to omit several important papers which I would have liked to include: in particular I recommend those interested in further reading to consult Hedican (1991), Flanagan (1990), Waldram (1986) and Chartrand (1991).

NOTES

1. Given the history of cultural imperialism, it is difficult to isolate a value-free term to identify Aboriginal peoples. "First Nations" is a term that many — though not all — of the original peoples of Canada are using at present to describe themselves. I will be using that term as well, but following current practice I will also occasionally use "Indigenous" "Aboriginal" and "Native" to refer to the original peoples of Canada and the U.S.A., even though it is difficult to use these terms in a value-free sense. They are loaded terms, constructed categories deriving from a specific history of colonial domination (Hiller, 1991:4). However, these are the terms most in use at the present time. At any rate, styles change and these terms are likely to pass in or out of acceptance of "political correctness" in defiance of any attempt to predict their future use.

2. *An Act for the Better Protection of the Lands and Property of the Indians in Lower Canada,* and *An Act for the Protection of the Indians in Upper Canada,* both passed on August 10, 1850, defined "Indian" in terms of blood, membership in a particular band or tribe, marriage and/or adop-

tion. An amendment passed on August 30, 1851: *A Bill to Amend the Indian Lands Protection Act for Lower Canada* (14-15 Victoria, chapter 59) which prevented Whites married to Indian women from having the same legal and land rights as Indians, was probably the first enactment that differentiated between "Status" and "non-Status" Indians (Moore, 1978).

3. This is being developed through the federal government programme "Indian Self-Government Community Negotiations," administered by the Department of Indian Affairs. The rationale for this programme comes from the so-called "Penner Report" on Indian Self-Government (Canada, House of Commons, 1983b) which stated that in the event the right to self-government was not entrenched in the Canadian Constitution, negotiations should begin with the First Nations to develop as many self-government structures as possible without constitutional reform. None of the structures developed under this programme are to curtail any existing treaty or Aboriginal rights, nor are they intended to affect the outcome of future constitutional discussions. While there are many problems and shortcomings with the programme, several First Nations across Canada are engaged in negotiations with the government of Canada to develop their own versions of this limited self-government.

PART II _____

Canada: State Definitions of Aboriginality

INTRODUCTION

Canada is not the only country that imposes Eurocentric definitions of "Nativeness" on its Aboriginal population, but it does maintain an exceptionally complex and oppressive structure of legal and quasi-legal terminologies which determine many Native peoples' rights and affiliations. There are many categories of "Native" in Canada, including Status Indians, non-Status Indians, Métis, and Inuit or Eskimo. These are almost all government-defined rather than Native-defined, and are broken down into complex and often confusing subdivisions. For example, "non-Status" can refer to either Métis or non-Status Indians, but often the term is used to refer to both, treating them as a single unit. "Status" can include Treaty and non-Treaty Indians, C-31s, on-reserve Indians, or off-reserve Indians. Some Inuit or Eskimo have "disc numbers", some do not. What all these terms have in common is that they are *legalistic* distinctions rather than cultural or national distinctions, and have evolved as expediencies for federal and provincial governments, and even the Native organizations themselves. Although these terms have little to do with cultural affiliation, many, especially the term "Status," have become reified for Aboriginal populations, and now bear considerable emotional and cultural significance.

Waldram's article in this section investigates some of the ramifications the Status/non-Status distinction has for Native people living in Canada's Western subarctic regions, where the cultural distinctions among Indians, non-Status and Métis may not be clear-cut, but the legalistic distinction between Status and non-Status are. Waldram uses the concept of "ethnostatus" to discuss the fact that while there are few cultural differences between those people labled Status, non-Status or Métis, differential treatment in terms of social assistance, housing, education and health care in the northern part of Saskatchewan and Manitoba is routinely accorded Aboriginal peoples due to government-imposed differences in Status.

It is not only the state that has imposed outside ideas of Aboriginality upon people; academics and the media have done it as well. Dyck explores the tendency of some social scientists to downplay the differences between Status and non-Status, and explains why Status Indians have fought efforts by government and others to redefine registered Indians as simply another class of "Natives." Dyck, in contrast to Waldram, argues that the distinctions between Status, non-Status and Métis are very real, and of cultural significance to the actors themselves.

But as Waldram points out in another work (1986), the distinction Dyck sees may be due to the fact that Dyck's work is concentrated in the southern prairie regions, where the distinction between Métis and Plains Indians has a historic and cultural basis as well as a political one. When Dyck discusses the more northern parts of Saskatchewan, for example, it is clear that any significance that exists has surfaced fairly recently, and in response to political expediency. Dyck shows the importance of the distinction between Status and Métis, but fails to distinguish between non-Status and Métis, possibly because when the paper was written (1980), the distinction had not yet become politically significant, and the two sectors were joined in one political union. However, since then the political organization that represented both the Métis and non-Status Indian population of Saskatchewan has split up, and the distinction is quite important today (see the readings in Part III of this volume).

Perhaps the ultimate in state effrontery and arbitrariness in imposing identities came in 1939 when the Supreme Court of Canada decreed that "Eskimos were Indians!" This surprising decision came about because of a long-standing feud between the federal government and Quebec, regarding the responsibility for Eskimos living within Quebec. Richard Diubaldo describes the events which led to the Supreme Court decision, and which made Eskimos the responsibility of the federal government. Given the deliberate neglect of the Eskimo by the Canadian government at that time, the decision may have been a necessary and even welcome one, but it also serves as another example of how government has disregarded the conception which Aboriginal peoples have of their own identity.

In the final paper in this section, Watson discusses how scholars have tried and failed to come up with a list of traits that would clearly differentiate Métis from Indian. He demonstrates how these categories may better be demonstrated through the processes of self-identification, showing us some of the interpersonal bargaining which differentiates the identities of "Indian" and "Métis" in the Northwest Territories. This consideration of self-identity versus identification by others makes this paper a good transition to the next section on Native conceptions of identity.

ETHNOSTATUS DISTINCTIONS IN THE WESTERN CANADIAN SUBARCTIC: IMPLICATIONS FOR INTER-ETHNIC AND INTERPERSONAL RELATIONS

James B. Waldram

The study of inter-ethnic and interpersonal relations in subarctic Native communities owes a great debt to the pioneering work of John Honigmann (1952; 1957; 1962; 1975), whose examination of the nature of relationships between non-Natives and various Native groups in multi-ethnic northern communities inspired a great deal of research. Recent research on inter-ethnic relations in the pre-contact, historic post-contact and contemporary periods has focussed on relations between members of different Native cultures (e.g. Barger, 1979; J.G.E. Smith, 1981; Jarvenpa, 1982a, 1982b). Indeed, a special issue of *Arctic Anthropology* (Volume 16, Number 2, 1979) was dedicated to this important area of study. However, it is evident that the study of inter-ethnic and interpersonal social relations has consistently avoided addressing the implications of legal Indian and treaty status. Relations among Native people who are distinguished according to such status would seem to be a logical area of investigation, yet very few studies addressing this issue exist. The purpose of this paper is to explore the manner in which legal status plays a role in the formation, maintenance and expression of individual identity, and the manner in which it governs or influences social, economic and political relationships and interactions. The ethnographic context of this discussion will be the western Canadian subarctic, although the basic principles should be transferable to Native Canadians in other areas.

NATIVE IDENTITY: CULTURAL AND LEGAL PERSPECTIVES

It is evident from the literature, and from personal communication with various subarctic ethnologists,[1] that the distinction between those subarctic Native people with legal "Indian" or treaty status and those without has rarely been a topic of investigation.[2] While in some cases virtually no mention has been made of the existence of a non-status population, in others this population has been lumped together and labeled "Métis", and in an even cruder form, "other Natives". Labelling seems to have caused a great many problems, and we are often faced with such confusing and overlapping terms as "Indian," "status Indian," "registered Indian," "treaty Indian," "non-status Indian," "non-registered Indian," "non-treaty Indian," "Métis," and "Native." These terms have frequently been applied very loosely, without proper attention to the very specific meaning of each. Noel Dyck first brought this to our attention when he wrote the following:

> [Some academics] use terms such as 'Indian' and 'Native' quite interchangeably and without qualification. Since individual authors seldom offer any explanations of why they follow this practice — even though they may note that they do follow it — one is left uncertain about the basis of their disinclination to distinguish between registered Indians and other peoples of aboriginal ancestry in circumstances where such distinctions are appropriate and sometimes even essential. It may be that they are not aware of the significant nature of the legal and — in some parts of the country — social distinctions that exist between registered Indians and other indigenous peoples. On the other hand, it may be that they subscribe to a school of thought which denies that such distinctions are either 'meaningful' or warranted (Dyck, 1980:36).

Further, where these terms are used locally by Native people themselves, there has been a tendency for ethnologists to assume cultural differences because of the existence of separate terms. Even the contemporary, seminal work on the subarctic, appearing as volume six in the *Handbook of North American Indians* (Helm, 1981), failed to consider the implications of the legal distinction in any coherent fashion, although a few authors did address the issue briefly in their submissions.

From those ethnologists who have grappled with the complex legal and cultural issues affecting social relations in the subarctic, three basic approaches are discernible. The first approach has been to describe the non-status residents as culturally synonymous with their status Indian relatives and friends, and describe both groups as culturally "Indian." In the treaty areas of the western subarctic, the distinction has occasionally been made between "treaty Indians" and "non-treaty Indians" (e.g. Smith, 1975; 1978; Jarvenpa, 1980; 1982b). Such a distinction has served to define to some extent the somewhat different legal position of the two populations, although treaty status is not a legal status in the same sense as status under the *Indian Act*. Making the distinction according to treaty status, while accurate (since Natives lacking Indian status cannot be treaty Indians), may shroud the issue somewhat by failing to clearly distinguish "treaty" rights from those rights flowing from legal Indian status under the *Indian Act*. So, for instance, when J.G.E. Smith (1978:46) discusses the "differential treatment accorded by the federal and provincial governments to treaty and non-treaty Indians" in northern Manitoba, he is likely describing a situation which is primarily the product of the different legal position of segments of a culturally homogeneous population with reference to the *Indian Act*, and not the result of the treaties. Similarly, Jarvenpa also does not make the distinction between treaty and *Indian Act* rights in his discussion of the Cree and Chipewyan in northern Saskatchewan. In this case, he notes that,

> Differential rewards and expectations of government-imposed policies makes the categories "Treaty" and "non-Treaty" increasingly significant dimensions of identity and sources of tension in everyday life (Jarvenpa, 1982b:297).

For the most part, these "government-imposed" policies are a product of the legal status of the client group, and not their status under treaty.

A second approach has been to view subarctic Native people in the context of ethnicity. Sawchuk (1978), for instance, clearly distinguished the "non-status Indians" from the "status Indians" in the legal context in his discussion of the Métis of Manitoba, yet he condemned any attempt to define the Métis in cultural terms as separate from the Indians. For him, being Métis was primarily a product of ethnic self-identification. One is Métis because one identifies oneself as Métis. However, this definition is little better than the circular *Indian Act* definition of "Indian,"[3] and fails to deal with the fact that some non-status Indians have adopted a Métis identity as a result of their incongruous legal position. Nonetheless, Sawchuk anticipates the present analysis when he writes that, for the Métis,

> ...it would be the height of folly to attempt to generate ethnic entities using cultural criteria such as language, territorial contiguity, or any such marker, without a consideration of the

politicalprocesses (or boundary maintenance) which in reality defines the unit [emphasis added] (Sawchuk, 1978:13).

Sawchuk (1978) also viewed Native (and especially Métis) ethnicity as adaptable and manipulable to the particular socio-political situation. A similar view has been expressed by Watson (1981) in his discussion of ethnicity in Yellowknife. According to Watson (1981:460), Native ethnic "categories" are "essentially amorphous, proteanly flexible, and inherently prone to manipulation in the course of social transactions." He too eschews the practice of employing cultural criteria to distinguish Native ethnic groups, but offers little in replacement. Largely absent from his analysis is the impact of legal status on the development and manipulation of Native ethnicity.

A third approach has been to distinguish those subarctic Natives with legal Indian status and those without by creating a category of "white-status" persons to contrast with those of "Indian-status." Driben (1986:17), for instance, has noted that in the northern Ojibwa community of Aroland, those who are legally "non-status Indians" are "Indians culturally but legally white." Both Hara (1980) and Acheson (1981), in their use of this concept, have attempted to grapple with the legal status issue in a similar manner, but in so doing have implicitly assumed the cultural synonymy of the non-status Indian and Métis populations by failing to distinguish them. While it is true that in many instances those Natives with legal status and those without are culturally synonymous, as in the case of Aroland, it is also true that throughout the subarctic there are culturally distinct Métis communities and individuals. While the concept of "white-status" Native persons deals adequately with the differential legal status of the status Indian population in contrast to the non-status Indian and Métis populations, it fails to take into consideration cultural similarities and differences as well as self-identification.

It is clear that ethnologists have had some difficulty in dealing with the complex issue of legal Indian and treaty status in their investigations of subarctic Native communities, when they have considered the issue at all.[4] It is my argument that the dynamics of social relations in these communities cannot be adequately understood unless both the varying cultural and legal identities, and the contexts in which they come to the fore, are investigated.

ETHNOSTATUS DISTINCTIONS

In order to accurately understand the implications of legal Indian status for subarctic inter-ethnic and interpersonal relations, we must first be convinced that such status distinctions are a legitimate avenue of inquiry. Despite the dearth of literature in this area, it is possible to piece together case material that establishes the broad dimensions of such inquiry. I refer to this broad area as the investigation of "ethnostatus distinctions" (Waldram, 1986).

Ethnostatus distinctions are those distinctions which an individual or population makes concerning themselves, and the significant others in their lives, in which the factors of legal status and cultural affinity play a varying role. Ethnostatus distinctions can also develop as a product of ascription to a particular cultural group or legal category by individuals or agencies external to the community. In the western Canadian subarctic, government legislation and policy implementation at both the federal and provincial levels have probably played the most prominent role in the development and maintenance of such distinctions. The product of these distinctions is the development of separate ethnostatus identities which may shift and surface from time to time in different socio-political contexts or situations. In this sense, the concept of ethnostatus precludes the identification of "ethnic" groups as defined in the anthropological literature.

Barth, in his classic essay on "ethnic groups and boundaries," argued that membership in a particular ethnic group effectively governed all behaviour in virtually every social situation, and further "that it cannot be disregarded and temporarily set aside by other definitions of the situation" (1969:17). As I shall demonstrate, ethnostatus distinctions rarely produce "ethnic groups" in this sense, since, according to my conception, the identities formulated tend to govern behaviour only in certain contexts and can be readily set aside or altered as the situation dictates. Further, it is evident that a concentration on boundaries between ethnic groups, as Barth suggests, would not prove fruitful in understanding ethnostatus distinctions precisely because such boundaries are too amorphic. While ethnostatus distinctions have the potential of forming ethnic groups, the existence of such groups must be demonstrated and cannot be presupposed.

In a similar vein, ethnostatus groups are not the equivalent of "factions," as defined in the literature. Nicholas (1965:27-29) has presented five characteristics which define "factions": they are political groups; they are conflict oriented; they are not corporate groups; members are recruited by a leader; and recruitment occurs according to a variety of criteria, such as religion and kinship. As Nicholas (1966:52) notes, factions are primarily involved in political activity, "the organized conflict over public power." As I shall demonstrate, ethnostatus distinctions by-and-large do not reflect groups organized by a leader to achieve a political goal, and certainly there is no active recruitment. This does not mean that factions cannot develop along ethnostatus lines, especially since legal distinctions and certain cultural variables, such as kinship, would seem to be the substance from which factions could develop. But, once again, this is not necessarily the case and must be empirically demonstrated. Ethnostatus distinctions are truly distinctions," and they operate in many different spheres. Group formation, even on an informal level, around a political cause is only one possible expression of such distinctions.

In the context of the Native subarctic, it is evident that a number of somewhat different ethnostatus identities may exist, and that an individual's identity is not always fixed. As the concept "ethnostatus" implies, identity can be derived from a combination of cultural and legal factors (unlike "ethnicity," which develops primarily from cultural factors). In the purely cultural sense, we can distinguish two categories: "Indian" and "Métis." In both cases, such a cultural identity has no relationship to legal status. The "Métis" as a group may also contain non-status Indians who, in search for a more positive identity, have gravitated toward the Métis cultural group. However, while these individuals might declare themselves as "Métis," an objective examination might reveal a cultural pattern more congruent with "Indian." In some contexts, non-status Indians are clearly pariahs, fitting in with neither the Indian nor the Métis cultural groups. Some Métis may also find themselves in a similar situation, since they too frequently suffer from a negative identification: "They are Métis because they are not somebody else" (Sawchuk, 1978:10).

In the legal sense, two broad ethnostatus categories exist: the status Indians, or those Indians registered as such under the *Indian Act*, and all others of Aboriginal ancestry having a "white-status" designation. This latter category would include the legally-defined "non-status Indians," and the culturally-defined "Métis." The inclusion of a treaty status compounds the issue further, since not all status Indians are necessarily treaty Indians, and certain rights are afforded to treaty status Indians as a result of the treaty which are not afforded non-treaty status Indians, non-status Indians or Métis. Hence, treaty status would properly form a related component of the legal status category, or perhaps even a third separate category.

As we can see from this discussion, a variety of ethnostatus identities are possible, and can be invoked or imposed at specific times for specific reasons. Figure 1 outlines in summary form these identities. Interactions which cross the identity boundary, as demonstrated in Figure 1, are those which are most likely to result in tension or conflict in certain socio-political contexts, though conflict based on ethnostatus distinctions may occur within each category. In properly understanding these interactions, or the signifi-cance of social, economic or political events, the ethnographer should distinguish from amongst these identities those which have come to the fore and are being expressed (either overtly or covertly). While for some

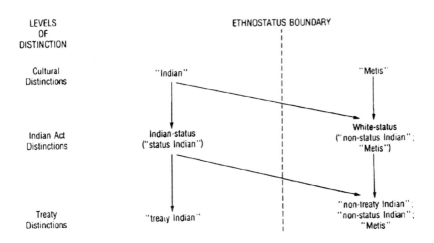

Figure 1: Schematic Presentation of Ethnostatus Distinctions

interactions, two role players may express themselves as "Indians" in the cultural sense, in other interactions one may clearly define himself as a "status Indian" in contrast to the other's position as a "non-status Indian." Likewise, a "Métis," culturally defined, may find himself at odds with a relative or co-resident because of the latter's treaty status. The following sections of this paper will detail to a greater extent the various dimensions in which each of these ethnostatus identities are most likely to be invoked or imposed.

SOME DIMENSIONS ETHNOSTATUS DISTINCTIONS

Cultural Distinctions

This dimension stresses two broad cultural categories: "Indian," and "Métis." It is argued that in certain spheres of community life, cultural considerations are the most important in the formulation of ethnostatus identity and the governing of social interaction. Further, it is apparent that these considerations are mostly internal: that is, they have developed from the people themselves, usually demonstrate cultural continuity with the past, and have not been greatly affected by external considerations (particularly the legal definition of "Indian," the treaties, and federal and provincial government policies and programs). Also, it must be noted that the historic cultural differences between the Indian and the Métis cultural groups have diminished to the extent that, in some communities, virtually no cultural distinction can be made between the two (despite the persistence of the label "Métis").

In cultural terms, ethnologists and other writers have frequently found it difficult to distinguish between those Indians with status and the other Native residents of their communities. This seems particularly true of the Cree and Ojibwa areas in northwestern Ontario (Sieciechowicz, 1984; Molohan, 1984), and among the Dene in the Northwest Territories (Asch, 1984a). Driben, in his discussion of Aroland in northwestern Ontario, noted that those Indians lacking legal Indian status nonetheless "[thought] of themselves as Indians" (1986:8), are "Indians culturally" (1986:17), and are viewed as such by those residents of the community who are status Indians. According to Asch (1984a), the Natives of Wrigley and Fort Good Hope in the Northwest Territories "regard themselves as Dene rather than Métis/Status/non-Status, etc." Hara elaborated on this point for the Hare Indians in her description of the process of "native categorization" whereby individuals are culturally identified:

> ...if an individual is born of Indian parents, he is "dene" regardless of his legal status. If an individual is born of a mo'la [white] father and dene mother, and if he leads a hunting and gathering life, he is designated as dene (Hara, 1980:20).

In the subarctic regions of the provinces, a similar situation prevails. Frequently, the only way in which those Indians with legal status and all other Indians and Métis can be distinguished is by their location in the community: treaty status Indians, having been granted reserves, are usually resident there, with most others occupying fringe or adjacent areas (although exceptions are common) (Kew, 1962:16; Card *et al.*, 1963:187; Jarvenpa, 1980:61). For non-reserve communities where there have been no government-sponsored housing projects, distinct status and non-status areas are rarely evident.

In some subarctic Native communities, it is also the case that the cultural distinctions between those calling themselves "Métis" and "Indian" are difficult to determine. Over the years many non-status Indians have abandoned this negative identity for a more positive "Métis" identity, yet they have retained for the most part their Indian cultural characteristics. J.G.E. Smith (1981:267), for instance, notes of the "Métis" who live among the Cree in northern Manitoba, that "many are linguistically, culturally, and genealogically identical" to the status Indians. The converse can also be true, as demonstrated by Kew (1962:16), who argued that the small treaty status Indian population at Cumberland House, Saskatchewan, was "socially and culturally part of the larger Métis group."

We can define some areas in which cultural considerations are predominant in the ordering of social relations within subarctic Native communities. These areas would include: kinship, marriage, friendships and economic partnerships.

In terms of kinship and marriage, it is evident that any possible legal distinction among residents of subarctic communities plays little or no role. As J.G.E. Smith (1981) described above, frequently the genealogies of all Native residents are indistinguishable, a fact which has also been noted by Sieciechowicz (1984), Molohan (1984), and Driben (1986) for Cree and Ojibwa communities in northwestern Ontario, and Brightman (1984) and Waldram (1986) for Cree communities in northern Manitoba. Further, in the selection of marriage partners, legal status considerations seem not to be an issue.[5] Hence, kinship and marriage, operating along essentially Indian cultural lines, presently serve the important function of cross-cutting legal boundaries and thus integrating the two broad legal categories found in the communities. Friendships also cross-cut legal status boundaries, further promoting community integration.

Kinship obligations remain the primary factor in the ordering of social relations in subarctic communities, and hence carry over into other spheres of activity. For instance, individuals involved in various hunting, fishing and trapping activities usually form "partnerships" with their relatives, regardless of legal status. This is most significant in treaty areas since certain of these activities, such as hunting, may at times of the year be illegal for the "white-status" member of the partnership. Yet, these units persist.

Legal Distinctions

This dimension stresses two legal categories: "status Indian," which is precisely defined under the *Indian Act*, and a more general category of "white-status" individuals encompassing non-Status Indians and Métis. In certain spheres of community life, legal considerations become dominant, frequently submerging cultural considerations. In other words, while two individuals may be both "Indian" in the cultural sense, in other spheres they may be separated into "Indian-status" and "White-status" categories. The development and maintenance of these categories constitutes a largely external process: they are the product of British and Canadian colonial policies, the enactment of federal and provincial legislation, and agreements between the two levels of government concerning jurisdiction over such areas as natural resources, health care, social services, education, and taxation. In many cases, these legal considerations have been super-imposed upon culturally homogeneous populations, resulting in a process of "ethnic dichotomization" (Sawchuk, 1978:43). The new, arbitrary legal identities frequently become internalized and begin to manifest themselves as if they were cultural identities. The Native population is administratively separated for purposes of federal and provincial government program implementation, and such separation occasionally leads to the actual physical relocation and separation of some residents. The legal distinction between Indian-status and White-status individuals and populations is most easily discernible within the context of government-Native interaction, and the inequities that develop are frequently sources of tension and conflict in subarctic Native communities.

One of the most visible indicators of the legal status of subarctic people is the condition of communities and houses and the location of residences. While it is true that only Status Indians may legally reside on a reserve, and others with band permission, it is a fact that many White-status Natives often also reside unopposed on reserves, and further that some Status Indians can be found living on lands adjacent to the reserves. In these cases, cultural considerations as described previously have been invoked, partic-ularly traditional kinship and post-marital residence patterns. However, as the impact of the development of separate identities based on legal status spreads, hostility often develops. Hence, Sawchuk writes that,

> Indians have the right to close the reserve to any non-status person, and there are many cases of Métis who have grown up on a reserve being forced to move off (Sawchuk, 1978:43).

Beyond these cases, housing often demarcates the legal status of the resident since, as in most other programs, housing for the Status Indians is the responsibility of the federal government, while housing for the White-status Natives is the responsibility of the provincial governments. Jarvenpa highlighted these issues clearly in his description of a Chipewyan community in northern Saskatchewan:

> An offshoot of the recent house building boom has been the division of Patuanak into distinct Treaty and non-Treaty Indian settlements. Because the federal housing money was ear-marked for registered band members on reserve land, the non-Treaty or Métis families have had the burden of paying for and constructing their own houses...Formerly, Treaty and non-Treaty Indians lived side-by-side in the log cabin villages at Dipper Lake, Primeau Lake and Knee Lake, and there has never been any reason for these groups to segregate them-selves spatially in bush camps while moving about the country

hunting and trapping. The spatial segregation of otherwise closely related peoples must be attributed largely to the legal technicalities bound up with the possession of reserve land granted by treaty. The fact that such possession derives from the purely arbitrary legal circumstances extending back to the signing of the treaty is generally appreciated by the people: it is illustrated by the fact that several non-Treaty Indian families recently lived on reserve land in Patuanak with little noticeable resentment by band members (Jarvenpa, 1980:61).

Differences in housing conditions, and the quality of housing programs, for Indian-status and White-status individuals do not go unnoticed, and frequently contribute to feelings of unfairness by the disadvantaged group (Sawchuk, 1978; D.M. Smith, 1981; Waldram, 1986).

Inequities in the delivery of social assistance have also been the cause of much grievance and tension. D.M. Smith (1981:692), writing about Fort Resolution in the Northwest Territories, noted that the "treaty" Indians received more social assistance, and that, "This form of governmental discrimination has exacerbated bitter feelings on the part of some members of both groups toward the other group." J.G.E. Smith's (1978:48) observation among the Chipewyan of northern Manitoba corroborates this view, and he notes that, "The non-treaty Indians were fully aware of their differential treatment, which was both resented and a matter of pride in their independence."

Education provides a context in which more overt hostility has been known to erupt between ethnostatus groups. This is especially true with the recent trend toward local control of schools. Prior to this process, both Indian-status and White-status children usually attended the same school with little controversy. As local political bodies developed, the control of educational programs became an important part of their increasing self-determination. While the schools were under federal or provincial jurisdiction, parents were essentially content. But when the schools came under the jurisdiction of members of one or the other of the ethnostatus categories, this attitude changed. Hence, in some subarctic communities, such as Cross Lake and Easterville in Manitoba, separate schools were eventually constructed at the behest of estranged parents who resented the control of the opposing ethnostatus category over the education of their children (Waldram, 1980; 1986).

Community economics is another area in which differential treatment by federal and provincial governments, and the application of somewhat different laws to Indian-status and White-status individuals, fosters an inequitable situation, some tension and occasionally overt conflict. Government sponsored economic development or make-work projects are invariably targetted to the particular group for whom the initiating government is responsible. For instance, Hara (1980:8) noted that among the Hare Indians, "...if there is a construction project administered by the Indian Affairs Branch, the 'Treaty Indians' are given priority for the job over the 'Non-Treaty Indians.'" Bone *et al.* (1973:76) noted a similar situation among the Chipewyan of northern Saskatchewan in the context of federal logging projects. The corollary is also true where provincial governments target the White-status residents in their programs.

Those Status Indians who are under treaty generally have the right to hunt and fish for food at any time of the year, in contrast to all others who must adhere to a myriad of federal and provincial regulations. This often creates problems since, in most subarctic communities, economic units are formed along kinship lines. Hence, invariably an economic unit (often referred to as a "partnership") will be involved in some activity that is illegal for one or more members of that unit. This fact rarely prevents the continuation of these units, but occasionally arrests and convictions ensue. The likely impact of the differential legal position of these units *vis-à-vis* hunting and fishing is largely contingent upon the actions of the local conservation officers. For instance, Jarvenpa (1980:62) has noted that the "non-Treaty" Chipewyan of Patuanak, Saskatchewan, were treated throughout the 1970s as "treaty Indians" for purposes of the enforcement of hunting regulations. He also notes that, "This lumping is atypical. In most areas the Métis are subject to white game laws" (Jarvenpa, 1980:177). In recent years, even the situation of these "non-Treaty" Chipewyan has changed as the Saskatchewan government has attempted to enforce greater control in all areas of resource utilization.

A related problem pertains to the tensions that frequently develop within communities where some members have an unequal access to the wildlife resources compared to other members. Explanations for poor hunting or an apparent decline in animal populations may be explained by the White-status residents as the product of over-hunting by the treaty status Indians (Waldram, 1986).

Other economic problems have arisen from time to time which relate to the issue of differing legal status. For instance, businesses established on reserves are immune from taxation, and hence may provide some perceived advantage to Indian-status entrepreneurs over their White-status, non-reserve counterparts. Band councils also have much more control over the economics of reserve territory, and can legally bar the reserve to rival businesses, such as White-status taxi services (Sawchuk, 1978:43).

At the individual level, provinces such as Saskatchewan exempt Status Indians from provincial sales tax, while all White-status individuals must contribute. Significant differences in disposable income can result (Reid, 1984:336-337). Further, in small communities where members of both the Indian-status and White-status categories cohabit, such a system seems patently unfair.

Probably the sphere of community life with the greatest potential for conflict between Indian-status and White-status groups is that of politics, broadly defined. Since politics is, in essence, the mechanism whereby relatively scarce resources are allocated, it has the potential of affecting most other areas of community life. As I have demonstrated elsewhere (Waldram, 1980), the development of ethnostatus distinctions in one particular Manitoba Native community resulted in political conflict which manifested itself in other areas such as economics, education, and law enforcement. Clearly, the potential for conflict in other spheres is self-evident.

In general, the Indian-status residents of subarctic Native communities, through the actions of the federal government, have a much longer tradition of political organization than the White-status Natives. Band councils to represent the Indian-status people have been around for many years, while the development of political bodies to represent all other Natives is much more recent. As Jarvenpa (1984) indicates for Patuanak, "Non-status families have felt somewhat subordinate to the status community for many years, because their own political council is a relatively recent development." While political bodies which have incorporated both Indian-status and white-status individuals have been attempted, they frequently have met with great opposition from government. Driben (1986) has described the problems experienced by the Aroland Indian Association, a body which sought to represent all members of the Aroland community. Such representation was denied them by the federal government, with then-Minister of Indian Affairs and Northern Development Jean Chrétien dismissing the white-status residents as "non-Indian" (Driben, 1986:117). A division subsequently began to appear between the Indian-status and White-status members of the Association.

The case of the non-reserve Native community of Brochet, Manitoba, provides an excellent example of the local level dynamics of ethnostatus distinctions in the political context. In the 1960s, the "non-treaty Cree" formed a separate local government to address their specific concerns. However, according to J.G.E. Smith (1975:185), "The non-treaty council has no basis for legal recognition by the provincial government, and its activities have consequently been limited." Subsequently, in 1968, a local government was established by the Manitoba government to represent the interests of the "Chipewyan, treaty Cree, non-treaty Cree and Euro-Canadians" of the community (Smith, 1975:185). However, a variety of tensions, including the "differential treatment of those with treaty status," paralyzed the organization. Finally, in 1976, the Chipewyan left Brochet to form their own settlement at Lac Brochet. J.G.E. Smith described the reasons for the move:

> The shift to the new settlement is unanimously attributed to "the trouble" — the problems arising from alcohol and interethnic hostility, particularly that of the nontreaty Cree (Métis) who are coming onto the reserve proper (Smith, 1978:47).

CONCLUSION

In much of the western subarctic, social relations are presently governed by two broad factors: cultural affinity and legal status. While cultural considerations play a predominant role in many areas of community life, specifically those that reflect a cultural continuity with the past, in other areas, broadly political in orientation, legal status plays a significant role. Hence, the ordering and expression of social relations can be seen to be a product of both cultural and legal factors. The concept of ethnostatus distinctions accommodates this fact, and argues for a careful examination of social relations in order to distinguish the impact of these cultural and legal factors.[6] Only through such analyses will the true nature of social relations in modern western subarctic Native communities be known.

NOTES

1. In the course of the research for this paper the author contacted and received comments from the following: Michael Asch; Robert Brightman; Paul Driben; June Helm; Robert Jarvenpa; Kathryn T. Molohan; Robin Ridington; Henry S. Sharp; Krystyna Z. Sieciechowicz; Richard Slobodin; James G.E. Smith; and David H. Turner. Their contributions were greatly appreciated. The views expressed in this paper are solely those of the author, and do not necessarily reflect the views of these individuals.

2. For purposes of this paper, the term "Native" is used to describe all people of Aboriginal descent regardless of legal status.

3. According to the *Indian Act*, "'Indian' means a person who pursuant to this Act is registered as an Indian or is entitled to be registered as an Indian." *Indian Act*, R.S.C. 1985, c.I-6, Section 2(1).

4. To the best of my knowledge, the only ethnographer to grapple directly with the ethnostatus issue has been Paul Driben (1986). No other such case studies are evident.

5. The author has not uncovered any cases in which legal status was an important factor in selecting marriage partners. It is quite likely that such cases do exist, especially in light of the potential benefits to be gained or lost through marriage prior to the 1985 amendments to the *Indian Act*. I would argue, however, that at this point the available evidence suggests that legal status was not a predominant concern, and was subordinate to other factors.

6. In the spring of 1985, the *Indian Act* was amended in an attempt to end discrimination against Indian women, who previously lost Indian status when they married a "white-status" person. While these amendments ensured that such women will no longer lose their status, and have resulted in the reacquisition of Indian status by many women, men and children, these facts do not alter the significance of my argument in this paper. There remains an undefined number of "non-Status Indians" and Métis in the Subarctic, and indeed throughout Canada.

INDIAN, MÉTIS, NATIVE: SOME IMPLICATIONS OF SPECIAL STATUS

Noel Dyck

INTRODUCTION

The *British North America Act* of 1867, which brought the Dominion of Canada into existence and serves as its constitution, refers to two types of Canadians: citizens and Indians. The B.N.A. Act did not specify which people were Indian and which were not, but merely stated that, "Indians, and Lands Reserved for Indians" fell within the exclusive legislative and administrative competence of the Federal Government (Section 91:24). In subsequent legislation, notably the Indian Act,[1] it was firmly established that an individual was either an Indian,[2] in which case he was subject to the Act, or a non-Indian, in which case he was not.[3] Upon this constitutional foundation was erected a framework for the administration of Indian affairs that has effectively segregated Indians from the mainstream of Canadian society for over one hundred years.

This paper investigates a contingent but, nonetheless, important aspect of this administrative experience. Specifically, it considers the empirical utility and analytical implications of "Indian," "Métis" and "Native" as descriptive categories and as identities. It takes as its starting point the common practice in the mass media and among some social scientists of treating the legal distinction between registered Indians and other peoples of Aboriginal ancestry as being arbitrary and, therefore, as a factor of purely nominal significance. An examination of contemporary social science literature reveals that some writers base their use of broad and loosely defined categories such as "Indian-Métis" and "Native" on assumptions that there are no substantial social, political or cultural differences among various peoples of Aboriginal ancestry. This paper undertakes a critical evaluation of these assumptions and draws attention to the political implications they entail. The situation of Indian and Métis peoples in Saskatchewan provides an ethnographic focus for discussion of these issues.

THE PREMISE OF "NATIVENESS"

The widespread use of terms such as "Indian-Métis" and "Native" is a relatively recent development in Canada. In the immediate post-war period there was far less public interest in and media coverage of indigenous peoples than there has been during the past decade. The confusion generated in many quarters in the 1960s and 1970s by the appearance of organizations such as the National Indian Brotherhood, the Native Council of Canada, the Inuit Tapirisat of Canada, the Métis Society of Saskatchewan, the Alberta Native Communications Society, the British Columbia Association of non-status Indians and many others representing different peoples of Aboriginal ancestry created a demand not merely for explanation but also for a streamlining of terminology. The term "Native" that was employed by some urban and provincial organizations provided a convenient single category that was soon being used to subsume a variety of other terms that different indigenous peoples used to identify themselves. The adoption of the term "Native" also served to cognitively combine peoples who, from a Euro-Canadian perspective, were essentially similar.

The response of social scientists in Canada to these developments has been varied. Several writers have dealt with the manner in which particular peoples such as Inuit, Métis and registered Indians are distinguished not just from Euro-Canadians but also from other peoples of Aboriginal ancestry as a significant matter that deserves careful consideration. Thus, Slobodin in his stimulating essay on Indian identity asks, "what segment or segments of the present Canadian population are identifiable as Indians" (Slobodin, 1971:287). Cumming and Mickenberg address the fundamental question of who is entitled to be registered as an Indian and who is not (Cumming and Mickenberg, 1972:6ff); Hatt (1971) devotes a section of his paper to a consideration of various definitions of Métis; Sawchuk reports the discussions about who is and who is not Métis as an important and controversial topic in Manitoba Métis communities (Sawchuk, 1978:3); Brantenberg (1977) provides a fascinating account of the complex internal and external dynamics of defining Inuit status in a contemporary Labrador community and Larsen documents discussions amongst reserve residents in Nova Scotia about "what an Indian is" (Larsen, 1977:57-60).

A reflective way of coping with these concerns is demonstrated by Justice Thomas Berger in his report on the Mackenzie Valley pipeline inquiry:

> Throughout this report I have referred to the land claims of the native people as *native claims.*
>
> Often I have referred to native people meaning all of the people of Eskimo and Indian ancestry, whether they regard themselves as Inuit, Dene or Métis. They are, of course, distinct peoples, yet they have an identity of interest with respect to many of the issues dealt with in this report and have often, in such instances, been referred to collectively as *native people.* Where only one of these peoples is meant, that is apparent from the text (Berger, 1977:209).

This practice of employing the term "Native" along with other specific terms when and where these are required is also evident in the writings of academics such as Sally Weaver (1977; 1978) and Joseph Krauter and Morris Davis (1978) and the Indian politician Harold Cardinal (1977). Nevertheless, an increasing number of social scientists (e.g. Nagler, 1970; Schmeiser, 1974; Stymeist, 1975; Whiteside, 1977) use terms such as "Indian" and "Native" quite interchangeably and without qualification. Since individual authors seldom offer any explanation of why they follow this practice — even though they may note that they do follow it — one is left uncertain about the basis of their disinclination to distinguish between registered Indians and other peoples of Aboriginal ancestry in circumstances where such distinctions are appropriate and sometimes even essential. It may be that they are not aware of the significant nature of the legal and — in some parts of the country — social distinctions that exist between registered Indians and other indigenous peoples. On the other hand, it may be that they subscribe to a school of thought which denies that such distinctions are either "meaningful" or warranted.

An early statement of this position was provided by A.K. Davis who stated that he had not found differences between the terms "Treaty Indian," "Métis" and "non-Treaty Indian" to be of any great significance for describing the "Indian way of life" on Indian reserves and in Métis hamlets in Saskatchewan (Davis, 1968:219). His second reason for treating the legal distinction between registered Indians and other peoples of Aboriginal ancestry as being unimportant was that treaty Indians, Métis and other non-Status indigenous peoples living in towns face basically the same range of problems, life prospects and living conditions. Implicit in other authors' rendering of this argument is the suggestion that there is no reason to retain "legalistic" distinctions between "Status" and "non-Status" indigenous peoples since the majority of registered Indians will in the future be urban dwellers (Dosman, 1972:11; Nagler, 1975:xiv).

A third proposition in favour of ignoring the distinctions between registered Indians and non-Status peoples is that, "the distinction...cannot be made visually" (Frideres, 1974:5). This same line of reasoning – that to the larger society somebody who looks "Indian" is an Indian – led Dosman (1972) to endeavour to account for the situation of registered Indians *and* Métis people in Saskatoon almost exclusively in terms of the structure and administration of Indian reserves. There is also reason to suspect that studies relying heavily upon statistical data made available by government agencies may indirectly be compelled to accept this assumption; for example, the inability of prison classification officers to distinguish between Indian and Métis inmates effectively obliged Schmeiser (1974) to employ the broader category of "Native" in spite of the fact that he had available to him only very speculative estimates of the size of the "non-Status" population in each province.

A fourth argument for not observing the distinctions inherent in the special legal status of registered Indians is that, "those in power are aware that making such nominal distinctions between Canadian natives has a "divide and conquer" effect" (Frideres, 1974:3-4). Implicit in this position is the suggestion that these legal distinctions are "illegitimate" since they provide governments with the means to exercise control over Aboriginal peoples. One author has even taken this approach to the point of accusing registered Indians who believe in the importance of maintaining their special legal and cultural status as having been duped, presumably by the government (Whiteside, 1972:5-6).

Notwithstanding these sentiments, the Federal Government has recently begun to express support for the contention that the maintenance of legal distinctions between registered Indians and other peoples of Aboriginal ancestry may be without "meaning," validity or equity. In May 1976 a review of Federal "Native" policy was prepared by a steering committee comprised of representatives of the Prime Minister's Office, the Treasury Board, the Federal-Provincial Relations Office and the Departments of Indian and Northern Affairs, Justice and the Secretary of State. In contrast with the 1969 White Paper, which concerned itself almost entirely with registered Indians and did not even mention "Native" peoples, this document concludes

> (1) that the special problems and needs of all 'classes' of 'Native' peoples are similar and

(2) that the Indian Act is arbitrary, anachronistic and harsh in excluding certain 'classes' of indigenous peoples from its provisions.

The memorandum goes on to suggest that these legal distinctions and the separation of Federal and Provincial jurisdictions which these inspire now serve to prevent governments from meeting their moral obligations to all peoples of 'Native' ancestry.

The steering committee's memorandum indicates that its recommendations were informed by previous discussions between Federal representatives and the leaders of non-status and Métis peoples. This might conceivably be interpreted as evidence not only that Federal officials are finally listening to "Native" peoples, but also of the essential correctness of the arguments outlined above in favour of ignoring the legal distinctions between registered Indians and other indigenous peoples. Both of these readings have, however, been explicitly and emphatically rejected by at least one provincial Indian organization, the Federation of Saskatchewan Indians (F.S.I.). Some explanation of the basis of this rejection of the premise of "Nativeness" is clearly in order since it runs counter to positions taken by urban "Native" organizations, several of the provinces, the Federal Government and some social scientists.

Legal Status and Social Identities

The conceptual approach to be employed here is derived largely from the work of Frederik Barth (1969). Barth's contribution to the analysis of ethnic groups and identities consisted of directing attention to the processes by which members of a group or category are distinguished from non-members. He contends that the most important characteristics that members of an ethnic group have in common are those which set them apart from "others." In his approach the particular criteria that symbolize and, in so doing, maintain the social separation of groups and of individuals assume crucial significance, for these criteria serve as the elements of social boundaries which constrain social interaction between and within groups.

The most salient feature of the boundary between registered Indians and non-Indians is that it is one that is and has been decreed by Canadian law for more than one hundred years. In Saskatchewan the legal distinctions set out in the *Indian Act* reflect historical realities that extend back to the events surrounding the signing of treaties between Indians and the Crown in the 1870s. The only people of Aboriginal ancestry who were prohibited from "taking treaty" were those who had previously declared themselves to be Métis by receiving halfbreed scrip. The rule applied in all of the numbered treaties was, with the above exception, that all persons of mixed blood who lived as Indians had the option to be dealt with as "full-blooded" Indians (Cumming and Mickenberg, 1972:200). The initial establishment of band lists and enumeration of registered Indians was, therefore, based upon socio-cultural considerations and the choice of peoples of Aboriginal ancestry either to be treated or not be treated as Indians. It should be noted that while treaties were negotiated at particular places and at particular times, those Indians who had either been absent from these proceedings or unwilling to accept the terms offered immediately were subsequently permitted to sign adhesions to these treaties (Dyck, 1970). As late as the 1920s halfbreeds who had not accepted scrip were allowed to apply for membership in bands in Saskatchewan and to be registered as Indians.

Yet, whatever the socio-cultural distance between Indian and Métis peoples prior to the signing of the treaties, it was exponentially increased thereafter by the system of reserve administration to which registered Indians were subjected.

Under the terms of the *Indian Act* and the accompanying sets of regulations established by the Minister of Indian Affairs, Indians were subjected to a range of prohibitions: they were denied the franchise; they were not allowed to leave their reserves without obtaining a pass from the Indian agent which specified the destination, purpose and period of their travel; they were unable to purchase or to sell stock, personal possessions or any other commodity without the written permission of the agent; and, they were forbidden to possess or to consume alcohol. Appropriate punitive means for the enforcement of these and other prohibitions were contained in the *Indian Act*. This roll call of legal disabilities is, however, only a partial outline of the "reserve experience" that in Saskatchewan was uniquely the lot of registered Indians.

Following the Rebellion of 1885 the administration of Indian affairs in the Prairie Provinces assumed a format that endured with few changes until the 1950s. In implementing government policies and in enforcing the *Indian Act*, Indian agents enjoyed considerable authority and vast personal discretion. The agent distributed rations and other forms of relief, and supervised the bands' economic activities. The power to determine the suitability of individual Indians as candidates for offices as band chiefs and councillors rested with the agent. All non-Indians were required by law to obtain permission from the local Indian agent prior to entering a reserve. While the Royal Canadian Mounted Police provided policing services for reserves and various Christian denominations operated schools for Indian children both on and off reserves, personnel of these agencies were subordinate to the authority of the Indian agent on reserve lands. In short,

The (Indian Affairs) Branch was a quasi-colonial government dealing with almost the entire life of a culturally different people who were systematically deprived of opportunities to influence government, a people who were isolated on special pockets of land and who were subject to different laws (Hawthorn 1966:368).

Prior to 1970 there were relatively few Indians in Saskatchewan who had not lived the greater part of their lives within the confines of more or less strict variants of this "reserve experience." The impact of the reserve as a "total" social institution upon Indians' social and cultural organization was nothing short of enormous. It is hardly surprising that their legal and administrative status became a central feature of their social identity as well as the major component of the boundary between themselves and non-Indians. Similar processes of social and cultural change, which are not accurately described as mere "acculturation," have been reported on reserves outside Saskatchewan (Dunning, 1959b; Hawthorn, 1966; Inglis, 1971; Colson, 1971). However arbitrary the operation of reserve administration, the fact is that over a period of time such a system leaves indelible marks on the people who have been subjected to it, and becomes a vital aspect of their reality and self-identity. Because of the reserve system (which continues, albeit in a rather different form today), registered Indians in Saskatchewan are neither ordinary nor typical "Native" people.

It might be argued that the harsher side of reserve administration vanished in Saskatchewan along with the Indian agent in 1969. This line of reasoning leads to the supposition that since Indians have been freed of the heavier burdens of Indian status that they *should* suddenly become virtually indistinguishable from other peoples of Aboriginal ancestry. In fact, some younger urban Indian politicians in Saskatchewan have declared their solidarity with Métis and non-Status peoples. But on the reserves there is still a strong sense (and in some instances a growing sense) of the differences between Indians and non-Indians, be they Euro-Canadian or Métis. Moreover, there are many people who today are prepared to call themselves Métis or "Native" who yet prefer not to be identified as Indians. In her autobiography, *Halfbreed,* Maria Campbell notes that, "There was never much love lost between Indians and Halfbreeds. They were completely different from us..." (Campbell, 1973:26). In the minds of many Indian and Métis people in Saskatchewan today the situation has not changed.

The salience of legal status for Indian social identity is especially evident in the activities of past and present Indian associations in Saskatchewan. Since the 1920s successive district and provincial Indian organizations have struggled against heavy odds to maintain and protect their peoples' treaty rights: indeed treaty rights are seen by Indians in Saskatchewan as an essential basis of their continued survival as Indians. In the 1950s when the prohibition on consumption of alcohol was removed and in 1960 when Saskatchewan Indians received the federal and provincial franchise, there were serious fears expressed that the acceptance of these liberal measures might jeopardize treaty rights. Similar suspicions prevailed when amendments made to the Indian Act permitted a limited degree of band self-government; in consequence, bands in Saskatchewan were exceedingly hesitant to involve themselves in local administration.

In 1965 the provincial government assembled a conference of Indians and Métis people to hear the plans which had been drawn up in Regina to "help" the "Native" people. The premier and his cabinet were somewhat surprised when informed by Indian delegates that registered Indians were the responsibility of the federal government and, thus, would have to eschew participation in provincial programs if they were to maintain their treaty rights. When the newly elected Trudeau government unveiled its White Paper on Indian Administration as one of the first planks in its crusade for a "just society," the response of Saskatchewan Indians was immediate, articulate and uncompromising. In the eyes of Indians in Saskatchewan and elsewhere in Canada, the implementation of the White Paper would have constituted "cultural genocide," for these proposals were seen to threaten their treaty rights, reserve lands and special legal status.

Being a registered Indian has, on a number of planes, involved a great deal more than merely being poor and non-White—features that form a basic definition of "Native" for many Canadians. The legal status of Saskatchewan Indians subjected them to a form of Indian administration that has spawned social and cultural changes that have resulted in what some have referred to as "neo-Indian cultures" (Inglis, 1971; Colson, 1971; Fisher, 1976). Even in the northernmost part of the province where a modified version of reserve administration was introduced only quite recently, the distinction between those who are registered Indians and those who are not have become important and objective facts of life for Indian people.[4]

THE IMPLICATIONS OF "NATIVENESS"

To understand why organizations like the Federation of Saskatchewan Indians view efforts to redefine registered Indians as merely another "class" of "Natives" as a serious threat to the rights and, indeed, to the existence of Indian people, it is necessary to return to the federal steering committee's recommendations about federal "Native" policy. The report of this steering committee includes in its general conclusions several of the arguments cited above in favour of ignoring distinctions between registered Indians and other indigenous peoples and presents these as reasons why the Cabinet ought to develop a policy toward "Native" people in general. There is, in other words, a correspondence between assumptions that have become fashionable in social science circles and government policy in the making. Moreover, the report recommends the participation of all segments of the "Native" community in revising the *Indian Act.*

It is unlikely that the *Indian Act* could have the same significance for non-Status "Native" peoples as it has held and continues to hold for registered Indians in Saskatchewan. Yet, the federal government now proposes to establish general "consultative frameworks," supposedly to permit the resolution of important questions which the report says affect the lives of "Native" people – such as the revision of the *Indian Act.* In view of the increasingly subtle tactics adopted by federal officials since the White Paper controversy of 1969 (Manuel and Posluns, 1974; Cardinal, 1977; Marule, 1978), it is understandable that registered Indians in Saskatchewan diagnose this current initiative as merely a more sophisticated and better disguised method of pursuing the same ends. While the report recommends to Cabinet that reassurance should be given to registered Indian leaders that the position of Status Indians will in no way be compromised or diminished by measures envisaged for non-Status peoples, it then goes on to restate what was the central aim of the now officially recanted White Paper: "to develop a general strategy for obtaining greater co-operation of provincial governments in native affairs." If an undertaking is made to revise the *Indian Act* into a form that adequately meets the legitimate aims of other peoples of Aboriginal ancestry, its probable end result would be the outright abolition of the *Indian Act.* In its place a series of cabinet commitments would be made to the newly homogenized "Native" community – commitments that would last as long as is administratively convenient.

The Chief of the Federation of Saskatchewan Indians has outlined the concerns of registered Indians in that province quite clearly:

> If government succeeds in reclassifying status Indians as just another category of 'Natives,' it will then be only a small step to reclassifying all of us – status Indians, non-status Indians, Métis and Inuit – as simply part of the 'disadvantaged sector' of Canadian society.
>
> All of us will then be dealt with on the same terms and by the same agencies as all other disadvantaged groups.
>
> If non-status groups co-operate in the erosion of our rights and status, they will be inviting governments to eventually sub-

merge them, along with us, into the Canadian multicultural mosaic.

We will be left with welfare programs, beadwork, powwows and very little else.

The proposed 'Native' policy uses the cover of improving government effectiveness in dealing with non-status groups, but it really has the effect of making substantial changes in government policy toward registered Indians (Ahenakew, 1976).

There are people of Aboriginal ancestry both in Saskatchewan and elsewhere in Canada who would consider the adoption of the term "Native" and the possibility of their being included under the provisions of a new federal "Native" policy as desirable developments. But this does not alter some social scientists having placed their stamp of factual authority and academic impartiality upon ideas, propositions and terms that are the objects of intense political debate. Whether or not these actions have any immediate impact outside of academic circles is not, in the first instance, the issue. What is of concern is that we should recognize the complexity and sensitivity of matters such as these before we inadvertently become partisans. It should be noted here that the social scientists who have in effect argued in favour of the premise of "Nativeness" apparently were not aware that they had come down squarely on one side of what is an escalating controversy.

Having introduced these broader implications, let us now turn to an evaluation of the various arguments and assumptions that in the social science literature at least make up the premise of "Nativeness." The first of these is that since the legal definition of people entitled to be registered as Indians within the provisions of the *Indian Act* is the result of unilateral decision-making on the part of government that such legal distinctions are "meaningless" and without any "real" basis. Yet, taking into account the manner in which treaties were signed and band lists were originally drawn up on the Prairies, it is simply not correct to characterize the current registered Indian population there as being solely the product of arbitrary government action. Moreover, the choice of individual Indians to give up their Indian Status either through elective enfranchisement or by virtue of marrying a non-Indian was a voluntary act that presumably was taken with prior knowledge of the consequences.[5]

Granted that the form Indian administration subsequently took in Saskatchewan and elsewhere was most definitely arbitrary and unilateral, this hardly renders it any the less "real" or "meaningful" for those who have experienced it. The reality and meaning of Indian Status past and present may not be well known or immediately apparent to non-Indians, but it scarcely behoves us to deny the validity of registered Indians' understanding of their situation and identity. To dismiss the "reserve experience" of Indians in Saskatchewan as something that is no longer relevant is to obliterate the history of a people, an activity that social scientists should avoid.

The least convincing of the points underpinning the premise of "Nativeness" is the suggestion that special status is becoming less important since Euro-Canadians are unable to distinguish between registered Indians and other indigenous peoples. Of course, whether or not they happen to possess a distinctive legal status, different peoples of Aboriginal ancestry are commonly deemed by mainstream society to possess stigmatized identities and are in their everyday lives constantly made aware of the distance between them and other Canadians. In order to comprehend the nature of the stigma borne by peoples of Aboriginal ancestry within Canadian society it is necessary to consider the various types of situations in which this stigma is operative. Suffice it to note that the range of locales, situations and types of people subsumed in the convenient term "mainstream Canadian society" includes tiny northern settlements, small towns in rural areas and large urban centres. Yet, for reserve residents in Saskatchewan the formal relationships entailed in the experience of being directly administered by a federal government department have been of undeniable importance. In this respect their dealings with Canadian society have been and still are significantly different from those of non-Status peoples.

The difficulty with using the term "Native" to refer to all peoples of Aboriginal ancestry in any and all situations is that this practice tends to homogenize and eviscerate historical and contemporary realities. On reserves in Saskatchewan and elsewhere in Canada, "Indian" relates to a special legal status that is and has been embedded within the structure of federal Indian administration. Inasmuch as this legal status was a creation of Parliament, we might with some justification speak of Indian status as being originally the product of "others" rather than the handiwork of "self." But if, as a result of almost one hundred years of reserve life, Indians in Saskatchewan see themselves as being different and distinct from other peoples of Aboriginal ancestry, then is this not an important consideration? Euro-Canadians and governments may for their purposes choose not to distinguish between registered Indians and non-Status peoples and while these practices certainly ought to be taken into account, in no sense do they provide anything like a sufficient reason for social scientists to follow suit without considering the matter carefully.

There are also problems with the argument that there is little reason to retain legalistic distinctions between status Indians and non-status peoples since the majority of registered Indians will in the future be urban dwellers. Few of the apparently "urbanized" Indians I have met during the course of fieldwork in two Saskatchewan cities are prepared to cast off their special legal status merely because it is not presently a predominant feature of their life in town. Moreover, the observation that increasing numbers of registered Indians are now living in urban centres has been combined with an assumption that once they leave their reserves they will become permanently settled in cities. A preeminent aspect of Indian migration to Prairie cities is the frequency with which people move between reserve and town and from one city to another, a pattern that can be expected to continue as long as cities offer the vast majority of Indians little more than unemployment, welfare, slum housing and increasing hostility. Whatever their deficiencies, reserves are Indian communities that offer their members a place to return to when attempts to relocate in the city have failed. Indians in Saskatchewan are in no hurry to have their reserves converted from communities into blocks of land.

The final argument in support of the premise of "Nativeness" is that the socio-economic needs of Métis and non-Status peoples are equal to the needs of registered Indians and that the maintenance of "inequitable" legal distinctions prevents governments from meeting their moral obligations to all peoples of Aboriginal ancestry. The trouble with this type of argument is that it combines objective observation — namely, that non-Status indigenous peoples are by and large miserably poor — with an *ad hoc* prescription for rectifying this situation. There can be little doubt of the validity of the first part of this statement; but the solution implicit in the second part — that to improve the situation of non-Status peoples it is necessary to abrogate the special legal status and rights of registered Indians — is specious.

The suggestion that the only way that non-Status peoples can expect to receive recognition and assistance from the federal government is at the expense of registered Indians flies directly in the face of the events of the past decade. The recognition and the as yet admittedly meager resources that Métis, non-Status and Inuit organizations have received to date has usually come in the wake of similar concessions ground out of the federal government by Indian political organizations at the local, provincial and national levels. In effect, registered Indians have served as pacemakers in reshaping the relationship between peoples of Aboriginal ancestry and government. The very fact that Indian organizations have achieved these successes has provided the precedent and rationale for non-Status groups to demand and to receive similar treatment. The "good" fortune of Indian organizations has been based primarily upon the legal status, administrative history and treaty rights of their constituents. It would be of no material benefit to non-Status peoples – let alone registered Indians – to have the rights and legal status of registered Indians eroded and replaced with the "programme elements" of a new "Native" policy, a policy that could be wound down as hastily as it has been devised.[6]

CONCLUSION

This paper has investigated the assumption that there are no substantial social, political or cultural differences between registered Indians and other peoples of Aboriginal ancestry and has argued that for a number of reasons it is a misleading assumption. A final task is to identify some of the analytical considerations that emerge from this discussion. Perhaps the most obvious is that the history of a people is vitally important for understanding their present situation. In the case of registered Indians in Saskatchewan, this means that a knowledge of the history of their relations with the federal government is crucial. Until such time as we endeavour to know as much about Indian administration as the people who have lived with it, we will be in a poor position to study and explain their place in society. A second point is that Canada is geographically a large country and we can expect significant variation in social life from one area to another, variation that ought not to be buried under gross and overly simplistic generalizations. It may be that registered Indians in Saskatchewan are absolutely unique in holding these sentiments, but the current social science literature that speaks not of different regions, but of "typical" situations and not of "Indians," "Métis" and "Inuit" people, but of "Natives" does not provide sufficient empirical data to inform us of this.

A final consideration is that a lack of ethnographic awareness may well constitute a lack of political sensitivity. If registered Indians in Saskatchewan or elsewhere insist that they should not be lumped in conceptually with non-status peoples, then we ought to take note of such occurrences. Surely our principal task as social scientists is to understand situations and not to become the unwitting accomplices of federal policy who inadvertently become engaged in redefining and, thereby, managing the people whose situation we profess to study.

NOTES

1. See Tobias (1976) for a brief but comprehensive account of the evolution of the Indian Act.

2. The *Indian Act* provides precise definitions of who is and who is not an Indian. At the time of the signing of the treaties in Western Canada, band lists containing the names of all persons who "took treaty" were established. In other parts of the country where treaties were not made, but where the "Indianness"of Aboriginal peoples was recognized, provisions were made for the registration of these people as Indians and they too became subject to the Act. In 1951 these band lists were consolidated into a central registry of people of Indian status. The descendents of persons whose names were entered in this register make up the legally defined Indian population of Canada, with a few exceptions. First, any Indian woman who marries a non-Indian automatically loses her Indian status and children born of the marriage are not legally considered to be Indians. Second, any non-Indian woman who marries an Indian male automatically gains Indian status and her name is added to the central registry; children of such a marriage are also registered as Indians and their names are added to the father's band list. Third, any band has the right to admit halfbreeds and other non-Status people of Aboriginal ancestry to membership in the band (and thus to Indian status) subject to approval by the Department of Indian Affairs. This provision was exercised on several occasions prior to 1920 in Western Canada. Finally an adult Indian has the right to surrender his Indian status or to "enfranchise" himself, his wife and their dependent children, subject to approval by the Department of Indian Affairs.

3. The general point here is correct, notwithstanding the fact that certain provisions of the Indian Act are applicable to Indians only when they are resident on their reserves. See Lysyk (1967:541-542).

4. There has been some variation in the form of Indian administration practised within different parts of Saskatchewan at different times. For example, Indian bands in the area North of the Churchill River were never subject to prohibition to travel and, in some cases, have not yet even been granted formal reserve lands. The point is that historical and geographical variation in types of relations which Indians have had with their administrators is likely to be the rule rather than the exception.

5. In the 1920s Indians could be involuntarily dropped from band lists but it is not known how many times this actually happened. In any case there was a general consolidation of band membership lists in the early

1950s and those who were not formally registered as Indians were entitied to apply to have their names added to band lists at that time.

6. It has been suggested by some observers that the lack of equity between registered Indians and other peoples of Aboriginal ancestry could be remedied simply by broadening the legal definition of the former. It is further argued that this could be enacted without abolishing or otherwise jeopardizing the rights and special status of registered Indians. Although a thorough evaluation of this argument is beyond the scope of this paper, given the nature of federal government policy and practice during the last ten years, it is difficult to accept this proposal uncritically.

THE ABSURD LITTLE MOUSE: WHEN ESKIMOS[1] BECAME INDIANS

Richard J. Diubaldo[2]

On 5 April 1939, the Supreme Court of Canada ruled that Eskimos were Indians (Canada, Supreme Court, 1939:104-124),[3] a rather astonishing pronouncement since everyone knows that Eskimos are not Indians but Eskimos. Or are they? Diamond Jenness, one of Canada's most respected anthropologists, described the decision in the following erudite fashion: *Parturiunt montes; nascetur ridiculous mus* ["The mountains are in labour. From their womb will issue an absurd little mouse"—Horace] (Jenness, 1964:40). Despite Jenness' obvious scorn, the judgement represented a landmark decision in Eskimo relations with the federal government.[4] Until 1939, however, there appears to have existed only a limited moral obligation toward the Eskimo on the part of Ottawa; certainly it was not a legal one. This condition becomes clear when one examines the central government's denial of any formal responsibility for the well-being of the Eskimos living within provincial—as opposed to territorial—boundaries, particularly in Quebec. Nevertheless, it was this anomalous situation which brought about a confrontation between the Government of Quebec and the Government of Canada in the 1930s. The way in which the matter came to a head and the legal grounds which led to the Supreme Court's decision are the subjects of this short study.

The immediate cause of the disagreement was the refusal of Quebec to reimburse the federal government for relief measures provided the Eskimos living within Quebec, mainly along the shores of Hudson Bay and

Hudson Strait. The problem, however, went deeper: the federal government simply did not wish to involve itself in Eskimo affairs.

From the late decades of the nineteenth century into the first quarter of this century, contact between Whites and Eskimo increased considerably, and with that greater contact there was a departure from the traditional way of life of hunting and fishing. The Eskimo began to engage in the whaling industry and, later, fur trapping, thereby becoming dependent on southerners for supplies and wages. In the process many of them began to lose their traditional skills of hunting and fishing, and their ability to survive in a harsh, unrelenting northern environment. As long as either the whale or fur economy continued to be productive, things looked after themselves. Should economic dislocation occur, however, the Eskimo faced the prospect of being left to his own resources for the simple reason that no agency, be it private in the case of the fur companies or public as in the case of the government, accepted a legal responsibility for their well-being. This is precisely what happened to the Eskimo of Quebec in the late 1920s and early 1930s.

Aside from a general survey of Eskimo activities undertaken by the North West Mounted Police, which began its high northern duties after 1903, little was done federally or provincially by way of exercising actual responsibility. In 1922 the Department of the Interior recognized a duty to check the high mortality rate among Eskimo infants by appropriating $1,500 "to be expended in the purchase of wearing apparel, flour, needles, thread and similar articles, which will be distributed by the R.C.M.P. to Eskimo parents with children under five years of age, as an inducement to retain and bring up their children" (Canada, Department of the Interior, 1921-22:19). Despite this measure, unlike the case of the Indians, no one government department assumed consistent responsibility for the Eskimo:

> Prior to the year 1924 the Indians located in the North West Territories were governed and came under the Department of Indian Affairs by virtue of the Indian Act. The Eskimos, however, were not looked upon as Indians, and though aborigines residing in the North West Territories, they were apparently considered wards of the Dominion Government but not the responsibility of any one department. The case of the Eskimo, though not authoritatively so, was assumed by the commissioner of the North West Territories (Public Archives of Canada, 1939).

The confusion continued, primarily because the *North West Territories Act* of 1905 did not make any provisions for the administration of Eskimo affairs, nor did the Territories Council pass any ordinances between 1905 and 1930 which discriminated between the Eskimo and other inhabitants of the Territories. In 1921 the Department of the Interior created the Northwest Territories Branch to deal with northern Canada, and before long the Branch assumed that the Eskimos—of the Territories at least—were wards of the federal government. In 1924 an amendment to the *Indian Act* brought the Eskimos in the Territories under the Superintendent General of Indian Affairs. Unofficially, the Department of Indian Affairs had been looking after destitute Eskimos from about 1880 (Jenness, 1964:32). Between 1918 and 1923, $31,000 had been spent by the Department, mainly for education at mission schools and medical attention at Herschel Island (Jenness, 1964:32-33). The Department extended its medical services into the Eastern Arctic and by 1926 provided a full-time physician for Baffin Island. Within a few years, however, confusion again prevailed as to who was responsible for the Eskimo; by then the Commissioner of the Northwest Territories conducted Eskimo matters. Yet on the eve of the Depression certain aspects of their status were not resolved. For example, it was illegal to sell liquor to Indians; yet if Eskimos were considered ordinary citizens of the realm such laws should, theoretically, not apply to them. Technically, the Eskimo was entitled to all the liquor that a White man was legally allowed in the Northwest Territories; but in actual fact this was not so:

> ...the question of the status of the Eskimo with respect to the issue of liquor permits was brought before the North West Territories Council in session of the 11th December, 1929 ...Parliament has declared that the Eskimo is neither an Indian nor is he a ward of the nation. It has always been felt that he should enjoy the full status of a white man in the Territories. However, for the present it is not considered to be in the best interests of the Eskimo to issue liquor permits for medicinal purposes...(Director of the Northwest Territories O.S. Finnie to Dr. Unquhart 21 February 1930, quoted in Jenness, 1964:37).

The problem sharpened as the twenties gave way to the Depression. Throughout the 1920s the northern fur economy experienced a decline; as well, the caribou upon which the Eskimo depended were disappearing. Lacking money to buy food and the means to hunt effectively the rapidly diminishing game, the Eskimos found themselves on the verge of starvation, especially in the province of Quebec. By early January 1929, arrangements had been made between Quebec and Ottawa whereby the latter would provide relief for Quebec Eskimos; Quebec would then reimburse the federal government for the expenses incurred. Supervision of the relief was carried out through the Northwest Territories administration "which was familiar with Eskimo affairs in other parts of Canada" (Canada, Department of Justice, 1932a). For a period of three years the government of Quebec did reimburse the central government to the tune of $54,660.16 or $9 per person per year (Jenness, 1964:40). By mid-1932, however, Quebec, under the Taschereau government, adopted a new and stubborn position. For reasons of economy, the province began to question its responsibility toward Eskimos within its boundaries. Thus, the Deputy Minister of Justice wrote to Ottawa:

> Will you [*i.e.* Ottawa] please let us know on what the Federal Government bases its contention that the Province is responsible in the matter (of relief to destitute Eskimos). Are not Eskimos included in "Indians" in number twenty-four of section ninety-one of the British North America Act? (Canada, Department of Justice, 1932b).

Section 91 of the *British North America Act* enumerates the exclusive powers of the central government; number 24 of section 91 states simply: "Indians and Lands reserved for the Indians." To the query Ottawa replied in the negative, stating that Eskimos were ordinary Canadian citizens, hence ordinary citizens of the province and not wards of the Crown, as were Indians (Canada, Department of Justice, 1932b). After a further exchange of "views," Quebec informed Ottawa that it would make a final payment in the ongoing scheme but that such a payment "must not be taken as an admission of our liability in connection with Eskimo relief in this Province. This moreover will be the last payment we will make until the question of liability has been definitely settled..." (Canada, Department of Justice, 1933). There the matter lay until both sides agreed to have the issue referred to the Supreme Court of Canada.

Both sides prepared their cases during 1933 and 1934. In this period Eskimo relief was minimal and their situation unimproved. No long-range plans were forthcoming to better their circumstances. In the absence of policy there was only *"ad hocery"* and a general evasion of responsibility. For example, in 1934 the government initiated the infamous Dundas Harbour colonization experiment in which responsibility for the Eskimo was placed squarely on the Hudson's Bay Company without expense to the government (Jenness, 1964:54-64). The latter's avowed policy was as follows: if a trading company wished a licence or permit to establish posts, the Department of the Interior "stipulated that all applicants must assume full responsibility for the welfare of the countries who trade with them and the destitute natives must be maintained without expense to the Department."[5]

As the federal case was being prepared, a number of weaknesses became apparent. In August 1934, Alaskan Indians were given extended rights which included educational and business opportunities, namely the development of Indian lands and resources. For the purposes of this *American Act* the term "Indian" was to encompass all Alaskan Aborigines, thus including the Eskimo (Canada, Department of Justice, 1934a).[6] The Act suggested a precedent for the Canadian case. As 1934 wore on the federal position seemed hopeless. The deeper the Department of Justice's researchers dug, the more the Quebec position seemed to be confirmed. The Department's major external legal counsel, James McGregor Stewart of Halifax, was inclined "more and more to the view that the Courts will find that the term 'Indian' as used in...the British North America Act includes the Eskimos" and felt Quebec would "win the day" (Canada, Department of Justice, 1934b). As the federal case was not strong enough to win, Stewart questioned the wisdom of pursuing the matter: "on the whole I would seriously consider whether it is wise to incur the expense incidental to bringing this matter before the Court" (Canada, Department of Justice, 1934c). Despite the warning Ottawa went ahead, mainly, one suspects, because it had to. The status of the Eskimo had to be defined. By not going to court the issue would never be resolved.

The case finally reached Supreme Court in June 1937. The federal government led off, its goal being to demonstrate that there was a basic difference between Eskimos and Indians:

> In preparation of the Dominion's Case, Council for the Dominion have collected considerable material relating to, 1. The ethnological, anthropological and sociological aspects of the question, with a view to showing that in a scientific sense the Eskimos are not Indians, although there may have been or was a remote common stock; and that at the time of Confederation the consensus of scientific opinion was against even a remote common stock. 2. Popular usage, with a view to showing that in the common understanding of mankind in 1867, the term "Indian" did not include "Eskimos" and 3. Governmental or departmental usage, with a view to showing that the Governors, Colonial Secretaries, legislatures and other bodies making treaties, appointing committees and passing legislation dealing with "Indians," never had in mind "Eskimos" (Canada, Department of Justice, 1935).

The federal government lost, despite an impressive array of anthropologists, including Diamond Jenness,[7] a wealth of evidence including history and geography books, dictionaries, and a scattering of nineteenth century political and administrative practices. Quebec was successful in disproving exactly what Ottawa had tried to prove.[8]

Anthropological and ethnological testimony from some of North America's most noted authorities was largely ignored and played virtually no role in the Court's decision. The Court would rely on evidence which would outweigh conflicting academic theories and ideas.

The Government of Canada had claimed that, at the time of Confederation, there were no Eskimos within the boundaries of the newly created Dominion, especially Quebec. Technically speaking that may have been correct, given the truncated nature of Quebec in 1867; her boundaries were not extended until 1912. The Court, however, ruled otherwise. At the time of Confederation, the territory in question — Rupert's Land and the North Western Territory — was under the administrative control of the Hudson's Bay Company. In this territory was to be found ninety percent of the Eskimo population, some 4,000 to 5,000 souls. Canada acquired these areas in 1870. As well, there were Eskimos to be found on the coast of Labrador, east of Hudson Strait, under the control of Newfoundland. The Court pointed out that one of the most reliable authorities of the time, the Hudson's Bay Company, considered Eskimos in its domain to be Indians. In 1857, a decade before the passing of the *British North America Act*, an investigation was conducted into the affairs and future of the venerable Company. A committee of the British House of Commons was charged with the probe, which had been sparked by charges of mismanagement and dereliction of duty. The Canadian government of the time was present at these meetings in London, represented by Chief Justice William Draper. The United Provinces of Canada had a vested interest in the proceedings, as it hoped that adverse findings would lead to the transfer, without any compensation, of Hudson's Bay Company territory to itself. The committee also wished to discuss the Company's relations with the Aborigines. Partly to this end, a census — along with a map — was drawn up by the Company to show the Indian population under its control throughout North America. Both the census and the map included Eskimos under the general heading of "Indians." In the margin of the HBC map, printed and published by authority of the British House of Commons — which made them official documents — appeared two significant tables which included "Esquimaux" with such Indian nations as Blackfeet and Sioux, Cherokee, Algonquin and Iroquois. The census itself concluded that the total number of "Indians" in Hudson's Bay Territory amounted to 147,000, 4,000 of which were "the Esquimaux."

Seven years after the investigation, the *Quebec Resolutions* (10 October 1864) declared that provision should be made for the admission of Newfoundland, the North West Territory, and British Columbia. Section 146 of the *British North America Act* (1867) made specific provision for the acquisition of Rupert's Land as well as the North West Territory. By 1870 these vast territories became part of the Dominion and were brought under the jurisdiction of Parliament. For the most part this area was populated almost entirely by Aborigines. The Court ruled that the latter term included both Indians and Eskimos alike and placed much weight on the findings of the 1857 Select Committee of the British House of Commons, "the principal source of information as regards the aborigines in those territories until some years after Confederation" (Canada, Supreme Court, 1939:109).

As for Eskimos living along the Labrador coast beyond Hudson's Bay territories and within Newfoundland's jurisdiction, the Court believed there was conclusive evidence, from about 1760 to Confederation, that Eskimos were known and referred to as Indians. Such evidence could only strengthen Quebec's case. In 1762, for instance, General Murray, then Governor of Quebec and later first Governor of Canada, officially reported on the "Indian nations residing within the government." Dealing with the "savages" along the North Shore, he included "Esquimaux" and Montagnais in the same group. In fact, from this time until the 1880s a succession of governors, commanders-in-chief of the navy, missionaries and traders in the region consistently referred to the Eskimos as either "Esquimaux Indians" or "Esquimaux Savages."

The word "savages" was used interchangeably with "Indians" (Canada, 1939:109-115). As well, the official French translation of the word "Indian" was not "Indien" but "Sauvages." This could be found in the official French translation of the *Quebec Resolutions* and in the official French version of the *British North America Act.* In fact, when Champlain visited the New World in 1625 he wrote of discovering "une nation de sauvages qui habitent ces pays, qui s'appellent Esquimaux." Throughout the many reports of missionaries and official correspondence between France and New France, Indians are referred to as "sauvages" and the Eskimos as "sauvages esquimaux." The French regime had viewed, or considered, Eskimos as Indians (Canada, Supreme Court, 1939:118-119).

In addition to this official usage of interchangeable terms and perceptions, the Court placed much stock in contemporary books known to the Fathers of Confederation and the British Parliament of the day which indicated that "the Eskimo was considered as one of the Indian tribes." The 1855 edition of *Webster's American Dictionary* defined the Eskimo as: "A nation of Indians inhabiting the northwestern parts of North America" (Canada, Supreme Court, 1938b: Exhibit #37:178). Other contemporary works with a similar view were Adrien Guibert's *Geographical Dictionary* (1855) and Charles de Wolf Brownwell's *The Indian Races of North and South America* (1856).[9] Despite the Dominion government's evidence to the contrary, the Court sided with Quebec in this particular argument, citing from the 1934 edition of *Webster's International Dictionary* which defined "Indian" as:

> ...a member of the aboriginal American race; an American or Red Indian; an Amerind*** About 75 linguistic families or stocks are recognized in North America, and about 75 more in South America and the West Indies. Some stocks comprise many tribes speaking distinct, but related, languages. The 16 stocks listed below occupied more than half the area of the continent and comprised a large majority of the Indians at the time of the discovery of North America, Algonquin, Athapascan, Eskimauan, Iroquoian, Mayan, Muskhegean, Siouian, and Uto-Aztocan (Canada, Supreme Court, 1939:121).

On another point the Court did agree that Eskimos had never been mentioned in any legislation until 1924. In that year the *Indian Act* was amended to include a subsection which stated that "The Superintendent General of Indian Affairs should have charge of Eskimo affairs." This was repealed and the repeal could be considered, said the Court, as an explicit denial of responsibility by the government of Canada. *But,* this belated action would count for naught, because Quebec possessed a trumpcard: 1879 correspondence between Hector Langevin, then the Postmaster General and first minister to act as Superintendent of Indian Affairs (from 1 July 1867 to 7 December 1869), and Sir John A. Macdonald, Prime Minister and Superintendent General of Indian Affairs — both Fathers of Confederation. The Court considered this evidence especially as "conclusive as to what was in the minds of those responsible for the drafting of the [Quebec] Resolution (1864) leading to the passing of the British North America Act" (Canada, Supreme Court, 1939:123).

In 1879, there existed a serious food shortage amongst the Quebec Natives of the north coast of the St. Lawrence River below the Saguenay. Langevin felt something had to be done:

Ottawa, 20 January 1879

My dear Sir John,

The enclosed letter from the Very Reverend Edmond Langevin, Vicar General of Rimouski, calls my attention to the position of the Montagnais and Esquimaux Indians on the north coast of the St. Lawrence below the Saguenay. He says that the amount that used to be given to these Indians was seventy eight cents a head, and that now it is only thirty eight cents. These poor people are starving; they can't cultivate the land, which in that region is hardly cultivable, and have had no provision made for them by the Government, and he requires on their behalf that we should come to their help. Will you kindly see that they are treated as well as we treat the Indians of our new territories. Of course I leave the whole matter in your hands.

Yours truly,
Hector L. Langevin[10]

The matter was commented upon by the Deputy Superintendent General of Indian Affairs.

To the Right Hon. Sir John A. Macdonald, K.C.B. Supt. General of Indian Affairs

Ottawa, 27 Jan'y, 1879.

With reference to the letter of the 20th Instant (placed herewith) from the Honorable Hector Langevin, enclosing a letter of the 13th Instant, from the Very Reverend Edmond Langevin, of Rimouski, in the province of Quebec, relative to the insufficient relief given to the Montagnais and Esquimaux Indians of the Lower St. Lawrence the undersigned has the honour to report that frequent representations to the same effect have been made to the Department and that last year he endeavoured to induce the then Superintendent General of Indian Affairs to ask Parliament for a larger grant. But that when the proposed estimates for the year 1878-79 were submitted to Council for revision, the proposed increase of $2,000 to the Parliamentary Grant for these Indians was struck out.

The present Government has however sanctioned the Supplementary Estimates for 1878-9 which will be submitted to Parliament at the approaching Session being anticipated by granting the said sum of $2,000.00, and the undersigned has moreover increased the grant for those Indians by that amount in the proposed estimates for the year 1879-80 with the hope that the Government will sanction and Parliament confirm the same.

All respectfully submitted,

L. Van Koughnet,
Deputy Supt. General of
Indian Affairs.[11]

"Where," asked the counsel for Quebec, "could be found better contemporaries than Mcdonald [sic] and Langevin to understand the meaning of the word Indians in the British North America Act" (Quebec Canada, Supreme Court, 1938d, *Factum*, p.60). The point needed little elaboration: the actions of these Fathers of Confederation in 1879 made their intentions of the 1860s crystal clear. The Court could not but agree. The word "Indians" in the *British North American Act* was meant to include Eskimos.

The matter should have ended there. It meant, though, that the federal government would have to bear new costs and responsibilities. The Minister of the Interior tried to have the decision overturned by the highest court in the Commonwealth, the Judicial Committee of the Privy Council in London.[12] Cooler and obviously more humanitarian heads prevailed and discouraged such an appeal. As well, war had just broken out and it was considered wise to leave matters where they were (Jenness, 1964:40). With the war's end it was too late to turn back the clock, and Canada began to live up to its long belated obligations toward its far northern inhabitants with a score of programs. In retrospect, the Supreme Court's decision—the absurd little mouse—had not been so absurd, given the deliberate and cultivated neglect of the Eskimo by the Canadian government.

Perhaps the last word belongs to the respected Professor of Anthropology at Harvard University, Dr. Ernest A. Hooten, who testified on behalf of the Dominion but who nevertheless was disturbed by Ottawa's position. In light of today's concern over Native land claims, his views of almost a half century ago have considerable application today:

> [I] cannot refrain from a comment upon the sociological and ethical principle involved in any attempt to deprive the Eskimo of Dominion support on the ground that they are a people racially distinct from the American Indians. The Eskimo, whether or not he may be called an Indian, shares with the so-called Indian the honor of being the original and rightful owner of the soil of the Dominion. The Europeans who have dispossessed the original occupants, whether legally or illegally, are normally obligated to provide for descendants of the aboriginal settlers. The Eskimo is as any much of a veritable American [and Canadian] as any Indian of whatever tribe, and should not be excluded from equality of treatment on the specious plea of racial difference (Canada, Supreme Court, 1938a: Exhibit #51:379-380).

NOTES

1. Although the term "Inuit" is more acceptable today, I have used the word "Eskimo" because it was the expression universally accepted during the period which this article covers.

2. The author is indebted to Mr. Bryan Zand who aided in the primary research.

3. They are not, however, to be included in the *Indian Act*.

4. There are exceptions, however. When Newfoundland entered Confederation in 1949, it insisted that Eskimos within her boundaries be treated as citizens of the new province without special status, and not be considered a federal responsibility. Also, and somewhat ironically given the background to the 1939 decision, Quebec has moved in the last two decades to enlarge its role and jurisdiction *vis-à-vis* the Eskimos within its domain.

5. Excerpt from a letter written by the Director of Lands, N.W.T. and Yukon Branch, to the Deputy Minister of the Interior, February 1936, as cited in Jenness (1964:54).

6. The *American Act* was dated 8 August 1934.

7. Appearing for the government of Canada, Jenness made a rather bold statement at the proceedings and one that, probably in this day and age, goes without further comment. When asked the difference between Eskimos and west coast Siwash Indians he replied, "I should think the difference between them would be about as great between say, the Englishman and an Italian or Greek..." Canada, Supreme Court, *In the matter of a reference asked whether the term "Indians" in Head 24 Section 91 of the British North America Act, 1867, includes Eskimo inhabitants of the Province of Quebec. Case on Behalf of the Attorney-General of Canada* (Ottawa: King's Printer, 1938). Testimony of Diamond Jenness, 18 June 1938, page 20.

8. Rather than present in detail both sides of the argument, for the sake of brevity the author has decided, at this point in the essay, to relate the opinion(s) of the Chief Justices themselves who found in favour of the Quebec contention (see Supreme Court, 1939:104-24). For those interested in how the case proceeded and the arguments put forth by both governments, see the *Case on Behalf of the Attorney General of Canada* [the *Canada Case*], and the *Case on Behalf of the Attorney General of the Province of Quebec* [the *Quebec Case*], and their respective *Factums*; all in all, some 1447 pages of testimony, exhibits and arguments.

9. See Canada, Supreme Court, 1938b; the *Quebec Case*, Exhibit numbers 131, p. 394; 132, pp. 397-398; 133, pp. 399-400; 134, pp. 407, 409; 135, p. 418; 136, p. 410; 139, pp. 446-447; 141, p. 451; 142, p. 461; for others see Canada, Supreme Court, 1938d:46-53.

10. See Canada, Supreme Court, 1938b; the *Quebec Case*, Exhibit 144, pp. 466-469.

11. See Canada, Supreme Court, 1938b; the *Quebec Case*, Exhibit 144, pp. 466-469.

12. It remained the highest court of appeal for Canada until 1949.

THE REIFICATION OF ETHNICITY AND ITS POLITICAL CONSEQUENCES IN THE NORTH[1]

Graham Watson

This paper deals with the means whereby Native peoples in Yellowknife manage their ethnic identities within constraints imposed by their biographies and Euro-Canadian power, and explicates the political consequences of this management. It is guided by Pollner's (1974b:27) programmatic "Where others see 'things,' 'givens' or 'facts of life,' the ethnomethodologist sees (or attempts to see) process: the process through which the perceivedly stable features of socially organized environments are continually, created and sustained."

Ethnicity is neither, *pace* Abner Cohen (1974(ed):xv and xiv) "a variable" which "manifests itself" nor pace Pierre van den Berghe (cited in Frideres and Goldenberg, n.d.:8)) something we are born with whether we like it or not: these are reifications. Ethnicity, like age and gender, is, rather, an emergent property of an ongoing inter-personal bargaining process. Claims, implicit or explicit, verbal or non-verbal, are made, made by somebody, and assessed, accepted, rejected or shelved by somebody else. While all of us continually achieve ethnic identities, most of us, like the Lue (Moerman, 1968) experience little tension in the process. In the Northwest Territories, on the other hand, the labels "Indian" and "Métis" are often hotly contested because the implications of making them stick are so consequential. So for many in the North, as for Cape Coloured Pass-Whites, (Watson, 1970) the achievement of ethnic identity is consciously problematic: they must struggle to exhibit and maintain it.[2]

INDIANS AND MÉTIS: THE OBJECTIVIST APPROACH

One scholar after another has attempted to identify clusters of traits whereby Métis might be unambiguously differentiated from Indians and Whites. All have failed. Card (1964:116), who has made a determined attempt, admits ultimate defeat. After dismissing physical characteristics as reliable diacritica because "since earliest fur-trade days Indian heredity has been diluted by liaisons with Whites..." he observes that "it is the style of life and plane of living, the standard of housing, dress, consumer behavior, drinking and 'morals' which appear to be the elemental criteria used..." But even these "elemental" criteria he finds "ambiguous for distinguishing between Métis and Indian..." And problems encountered in efforts to differentiate Métis and Whites are illumined by Lagassé's remark (1959:56) that while conducting a field survey, "At every third or fourth name, the person would say, 'You don't want to visit this person. He is no longer a Half Breed.'"

A survey of Yellowknife uncovered no single objective criterion or set of criteria which would unfailingly identify a person as an Indian or a "breed." There are people in Yellowknife who attend tea dances at Detah (Yellowknife's "Indian village"), who have a Treaty number, and who live in houses intended by the Department of Indian Affairs for Status Indians, but who nevertheless are normally identified by their acquaintances as "breeds." Conversely, there are Indians who lack Treaty status and who do not attend Detah tea dances. (A local chief's son turned up his nose at the mention of a Detah tea dance, refused to drive his father there, and chose instead to attend the Friday night teen dance at the Legion Hall.) The only differences between "Indians" and "breeds" are of a general nature and inconclusive in any particular instance. For example, Métis are more likely than Indians to have a command of French (25 per cent of those surveyed), and more likely than Indians to have English as their sole language (28 per cent); but there are Indians who speak French (10 per cent of those surveyed) and there is one Indian who speaks only English. Both Indian and Métis males formed unions largely, but not exclusively, with their own kind, while a large proportion of both Indian women (32 per cent), and Métis women (55 per cent), are married to or (rarely) "shacked up with," White males.[3]

It might be contended that while there is indeed no Platonic form of an Indian or Métis there nevertheless exists a cluster of objective traits no single one of which is possessed by all and only Indians or Métis but most of which all Indians or Métis have. In this formulation ethnicity is part of the natural world, encountered rather than accomplished, and the arguments I advance appear to apply only to those exceptional individuals in the grey areas where paradigmatic clusters of ethnic traits overlap. But it seems to me that we can no more discover what a Métis or Indian is by examining the objective attributes of those who are called Indian or Métis than we can discover who the good are by examining the attributes of those who are called good. Not all who are "objectively" Indian are called Indian, and not all who are called Indian are "objectively" so. *The objective properties of persons said to be Indian or Métis are of consequence only insofar as they render the assertion that persons are Indian or Métis more or less plausible, more or less easy to sustain.*

THE INTERPRETIVE APPROACH

The interpretive approach to ethnicity may be traced to Weber (1968:389) who defined ethnic groups as "those human groups that entertain a subjective belief in common descent...", but is most closely associated with Barth's seminal *Ethnic Groups and Boundaries* (1969:14), in which he observes that "we can assume no simple one-to-one relationship between ethnic units and cultural similarities and differences. The features that are taken into account are not the sum of 'objective' differences, but only those which the actors themselves regard as significant." But even Barth failed to fully capture the intrinsically negotiable, diffuse, shifting, and indeterminate quality of ethnicity. Handelman (1977:187) remarks that when Barth (1969: 13-14) writes, "[T]o the extent that actors use ethnic identities to categorize themselves and others for purposes of interaction, they form ethnic groups in this organizational sense," he "appears to confuse the idea of 'group' with the ascription of social categories that are ever present features of the process of interaction, and which are not necessarily associated with bounded groups." Ronald Cohen (1978:386-387) observes that in Barth's writing "Terms like 'group,' 'category,' 'boundary,' connote an actual entity, and Barth's concern with maintenance tends to reify it still more," and "[T]he important point is that ethnic boundaries are not, as Barth implied, stable and continuing."

The situational approach advocated in his paper is less in accord with Barth than it is with Vincent (1974:376), who asserts that "We tend to seek the embodiment of ethnicity in overly corporate forms" and that it has a fluency which evades analysis if we attempt to stop it dead and reify it. It is also in accord with Lyman's and Douglass' (1973:350) observation that "[T]reating ethnic identity strictly as a group phenomenon in which recruitment of membership is ascriptive forecloses study of the process whereby individuals make use of ethnicity as a manoeuvre or strategy in working out their own life changes in an ethnically pluralistic social setting." It is an approach which may be identified with Moerman's (1968:160) celebrated paper on the Lue, in which he notes that each of us is simultaneously identifiable by a large number of identifications and that the "objective correctness" of an identification is never sufficient to explain its use. He writes, "the preferring of any identification should be a problematic phenomenon, not a comforting answer. The question is not, 'Who are the Lue?' but rather when and how and why the identification 'Lue' is preferred."

The Lue seem little preoccupied with ethnicity, and Moerman doubts that they would employ ethnic categories with the frequency they do were it not for the presence of the ethnographer known to be researching ethnicity. In this respect the Lue are in marked contrast with Canada's "Native" peoples who seem perennially concerned with the process of self-definition.

INDIAN ETHNIC REDISCOVERERS

The National Indian Princess Pageant, held in Yellowknife in the centennial year of the Northwest Territories was an occasion used by Indians to address themselves to the question of their identity. Few events could illustrate more strikingly that current Indian ways of life owe less to a remote Aboriginal culture than to an overwhelming Euro-Canadian presence. An Indian legend was composed for the event:

> A beautiful princess dies suddenly, plunging her father's people into sorrow. The Chief plans to choose another daughter from among the princesses of surrounding tribes. The choice he leaves to a wise old man, giving him from sunset to sunrise in which to make up his mind. Ten beautiful girls are brought before him. Each one has some special merit, so he cannot decide between them. At dawn, when he goes to meet the Chief, the 'true answer' comes to him: no princess possesses all possible virtues; each possesses some particular virtues; the Chief should therefore take them all for his daughters and so bring his people joy.

This legend was fastidiously narrated in English by a lady of Indian ancestry in a full-length white evening dress to an audience which, on the opening night of the Pageant, consisted largely of middle-echelon White civil servants in dark suits and stiff white collars. The event was advertised as "'Choosing a Princess,' a fashion show in story form for the whole family. Indian princess candidates modelling fabulous fashions for Team Products Ltd., Edmonton," was held in the Roman Catholic school hall, in the White part of town. The princesses of the legend were represented by competitors who were chosen on a provincial, rather than a tribal basis. One of them, according to *The News of the North*, "stepped forward in a green maxi eskimo parka and a beautiful smile. Under the parka she wore a black leather formal with a thigh high slit on the side." The wise old man of the legend was replaced by a multi-racial committee charged with assessing competitors' "poise, talent, and knowledge of Indian customs and language."

On the second night of the pageant, Johnny Yesno, hailed as the "popular star of CBC'S Indian Magazine," introduced George and Joe Saddleback, who were clothed in exceedingly colourful buckskin and feather regalia of a kind not seen in the north outside the cinema. They performed a dance which was described for radio listeners with the words, "There's a guy there doing a sort of an eagle thing on the floor." White dignitaries sat with Indian brotherhood workers on the cordoned-off front rows but were eventually invited on the stage. An apprehensive-looking White commissioner smoked "the pipe of peace," engaged in a grave "pow-wow" with George Saddleback and, to the merriment of Dogrib and Métis, was dubbed "Chief of the North Setting Sun." He declared the evening a noteworthy example of Indian-White co-operation.

Some of the competitors for the title of Indian Princess, being required to demonstrate their "knowledge of Indian life, customs and language," essayed to identify that which made them "Indian." One reported that a friend had advised her to "paint your face brown," and, indeed, the appearance of the competitors was sufficient to render implausible any lingering impression that complexion might be the crucial criterion of Indianness: of the eleven competitors only four had complexions which could not be taken for anything but Indian, while four appeared incontestably White.

That there was a vital Indian culture to be identified and preserved went unquestioned, as was the assumption that that culture was significantly rooted in the past. History was frequently invoked, but selectively: moccasins, baby carriers, bows and headbands were celebrated, as was the capacity to survive a harsh environment, to be close to nature, and to share; but the scalping of enemies and the competitive wrestling for wives went unremarked.

Competitors implied that there is some underlying notion of an ideal Indian against whom concrete reality might be measured. But if that ideal represents continuity with an uncorrupted precontact past it is nowhere to be found in the empirical world. The label "Indian" is itself not Aboriginal. Richmond (1970: passim) questions the relevance of current tribal designations such as "Dogrib" and "Slavery" to autochthonous social organization. Mason (1946:33) notes that "[w]hatever authority is possessed at present by the Chief is generally vested in him by the fur traders and the Canadian government, who find it advisable to deal with an established representative." Tales are told of how in the past a chief might be appointed by Whites against the wishes of his band: "My father was the spokesman for the Indian people," reports Johnny Beaulieu. "...The Treaty people told my father that since he was a Métis he was not to represent the Indian people...So this is how we got somebody who was nothing"[4] When Helm and Leacock (1971:370) conclude a scholarly historical survey of the cultures of subarctic Canada with the hope that "the Indian" will be able to hold on to "his ethnic identity," and when McFeat (1979:222) observes that "it has been an incredible accomplishment by Indians that they have changed so much yet maintained a convincing identity," one wonders what is the unit whose continuity in time is assumed.

All Indians are in an important sense creatures of Euro-Canadian society, and are to be understood primarily in terms of a massive adjustment to the Euro-Canadian administrative structure, participation in a cash and welfare economy, and the pervasive presence of Euro-Canadian technology. To characterize the Dene, who helped organize the pageant and who participated enthusiastically in it as "hunters and gatherers", as they were characterized at the Conference on Ethnology and Canadian Realities (29 March-1 April 1981) in London, Ontario, is seriously misleading. But the fact that Indian claims may involve historical and social fictions does not render them any the less real in their consequences: that much Barth has taught us.

THE MÉTIS

Indians, of course, are not the only people exercised by the question of their identity. In Alberta the Métis organizer of a series of seminars entitled "Is there a Métis culture?" maintained that the Métis have borrowed from both Indians and Whites. From Indians they had acquired beadwork, leatherwork, pemmican, a migratory life-style, an easy-going attitude to time and money, and an aptitude for hunting, trapping and fishing; the White contribution to Métis culture was acknowledged as no more than the Welsh horse, the Red River cart, and a passion for fiddling and jigging.

"A Métis person, he don't give a damn for nobody. He's a hard drinker, a hard fighter, a hard worker. But the best way of identifying Métis in any community is by fiddling and dancing," declared another participant in the seminar. But he also admitted that at Smoky Lake "most of the Métis boys up there can talk to you in Ukrainian, and some of the Ukrainian kids is just as good at fiddling as the Métis kids." It seems that no one objective criterion suffices to identify a Métis.

FOLK NOTIONS OF ETHNICITY AND THEIR CONSEQUENCES

Informants insist that they encounter no difficulty at all in differentiating Indians, Métis, and Whites in Yellowknife. They note a stranger's complexion, enquire after his reputation, and observe the company he keeps ("A guy comes into town and goes to the pool hall and meets somebody there, say a white guy, and that's the only guy, he knows. And the white guy says 'let's go to the bar,' and when they get there they sit down with a bunch of whites. If he's a breed he will only stay a couple of minutes and then go. He doesn't feel right.") In case of doubt informants rely on verbal instruction. A person wishing to declare himself an Indian might, for example, intimate that he relishes bannock but detests whoever is Minister of Indian Affairs. A Métis might joke about being all mixed up.

The folk notion that sharp differences exist between "Indians," "red apples," and "breeds," is preserved intact, in the face of evidence to the contrary, by dismissing as not "true Indians," etc., those who apparently breach the category, or by having recourse to an indefinitely extendable list of diacritical features. Even if the validity of each and every particular feature be challenged, the list can be expanded so as to maintain the sense that "in general" the contrast holds good. Moreover, diacritical features are seldom held to be the exclusive property of any one group; instead, they are said to be *typical* of one group rather than another. *Typical* is an inconclusive and indeterminate word, and hence in everyday discourse it is difficult to refute. For all practical purposes it is nonfalsifiable. All the "objective" procedures employed by laymen and anthropologists to differentiate Indians and Métis are of this kind: they are infinitely adaptable and inherently inconclusive.

Informants claim that ethnicity is lodged "in the heart." "An Indian person is one who feels deeply as an Indian," pronounced a candidate for the title of Indian Princess. Her words were to be echoed at the Métis seminar in the declaration that "One is not a Métis unless he identifies as such: I speak of spirituality. Some Métis live like Indians and others non-Indians, but if it is not in their hearts and their minds they are not Métis within the true and full meaning of the word. It's what a person feels and thinks that basically makes him what he is."

The arguments that, on the one hand, ethnicity is *au fond* a matter of moral attachment and, on the other, that ethnicity is based on ever-changing self-interest, are both so ductile and open-ended that there seems to be in principle no way to decide between them. It can be argued plausibly that those Indians and Métis who were able to renounce their stigmatized identities did in fact do so—Lagassé (1959:77) estimates that "80 per cent of the people of Métis ancestry in Manitoba...have integrated to the point of not being recognized by their neighbors as Métis"—and that those who retained their identities had no choice. It could further be argued that the renaissance which Indian and Métis identities are undergoing may be traced ultimately to the bait of land rights, suddenly of enhanced value, which has lured backsliders to return to the fold. On the other hand, it might be contended with equal plausibility that we cannot assume that the advantage gained by people constitutes their motive: it may well be that the identities "Indian" and "Métis" are still with us precisely because people clung to them out of moral conviction through long periods when it could not have seemed to them to be to their advantage to do so.

Informants accept it without question that ethnic characteristics are intrinsic to those said to possess them.[5] A participant in the Métis seminar expressed a popular sentiment when he observed that "Our people migrated to follow game. That is still in their blood. They don't know what keeps them going. If they have a good job they still go some place else without even a sod of a chance."

Beliefs, whatever their origin, have consequences, and may have a profound effect on political and economic groupings. Clyde Mitchell writes (1970:97-98), "It is not ethnic differences that lead to political divisions. Political oppositions, rather, are phrased in ethnic terms and in so doing provide the sentiments in terms of which social actions might be justified." But it would be an error to dismiss lay beliefs as merely epiphenomenal: to believe that ethnicity is innate is to give ethnic identities a sense of permanence and to make transformations seem contrary to nature; to believe that ethnicity is a matter of the heart is to make cynical transactions of ethnic identity seem unthinkable; to believe that ethnicity has a basis both in nature and in sentiment is to furnish the bedrock of a moral community in which trust might thrive.

The popular ideology of a durable ethnicity rooted in nature and in sentiment obfuscates the reality of ubiquitous and continual interpersonal negotiations, over which it may be appropriate to employ ethnic categories in a given situation, over which rights and disabilities might attach to these categories, and over whom might rightfully be included in which category. Nevertheless, a meeting of, say, the Indian Brotherhood is not merely a shareholders' meeting, for there exists among participants a diffuse trust which rests not merely upon the common ownership of land rights but upon a belief, however misplaced, that in unforeseen and unforeseeable circumstances all who are "Indian" will stand together. Trust is at the heart of the matter. Abner Cohen (1974:91-98) reports that the successful Hausa monopoly of the Nigerian cattle trade depends upon implicit trust between distant Hausa traders: if Hausa ethnicity were to be seen as an instrument of advantage then fellow Hausa would be perceived as unreliable, there would be no grounds for confidence, and no monopoly. Not that a trusting relationship need be durable or concern matters of much consequence. A civil servant winked conspiratorially at me from behind the back of a chief who was engaged in making a plethora of demands which the Federal Treaty party visiting Yellowknife's "Squaw Valley" thought exorbitant. In spite of the fact that I was a total stranger, the civil servant trusted me not to disclose his reaction to the chief. It was enough that I was a fellow White.

Trust is predicated upon the belief that fellow ethnics share an essential identity which is both durable and constraining. The constraint derives partly from popular beliefs that overt changes in ethnic identity are monstrous, and partly from persons' commitment to their own ethnic identities. This commitment in turn derives partly from socialization and partly from the fact that people continually underwrite their informal bargains with their ethnicity. Should a Hausa trader prove untrustworthy then, presumably he would suffer a loss of reputation, and a severance of ethnic relationships built up over the years. That is, the social capital which people sink into their ethnic identities constitutes a side bet, and the possibility of having to forfeit it will act as some guarantee of acceptable behaviour.[6] An Indian has a stake in his Indianness which is implicitly placed at risk every time he solicits credit on the basis of his ethnicity.

It is my contention not merely that ethnic categories are seldom precise classifications: that point is well established (Le Vine and Campbell, 1972:81-113; Gulliver 1969:5-35). I contend that ethnic categories are essentially amorphous, proteanly flexible, and inherently prone to manipulation in the course of social transaction. Further, I argue that it would be futile, indeed perverse, to decry the inconclusiveness of techniques employed to accomplish a contrast between Indians and Métis, Dene, Northerners, Natives, and Whites; futile to advocate a sharpening of conceptual tools in the hope that we should see more clearly the "true" differences. That would be to complain that if the walls of a building were only gotten out of the way one could see better what was keeping the roof up.[7] It is because the means are inherently inconclusive that the assigning of ethnic labels to people is always tentative, good only in general, and held only until further notice; and precisely because they are tentative they are manipulable and, hence, of utility. Were the means of assigning labels to others and to oneself of a conclusive nature then whoever did the assigning would have options foreclosed and would be deprived of room for manoeuvring in the light of changing circumstances.

CONSTRAINTS ON THE MANAGEMENT OF ETHNICITY

Of course an individual is not always able to lay successful claim to whatever identity he fancies. His capacity to manipulate his identity is severely constrained not only by his biography, but also by persons with whom he engages in social transactions. Wealthy Ganda in 1950 may indeed have classed themselves as "Europeans" and referred to members of other tribes as "Natives," as Audrey Richards (1969:45) reports, but they would never get away with that in South Africa. Similarly, Yellowknife Indians, especially those in search of employment, must contend with the constraining effects of White stereotyping. It requires no great effort to elicit from some Yellowknife Whites pronouncements indicative of extreme hostility (e.g. "Indians are talking animals"; "A white prostitute could never make a living here as the promiscuous Dogrib women can always be had for half a bottle of beer") or of unctuous paternalism (e.g. "Merv Hardie raised his voice in the House of Commons on behalf of his Indian constituents...[He said] it was wrong to supply the native with nets and a fishing hut out on the lake ice without supervision and guidance. He can easily be duped of his catch with $5 and a bottle of rye..." [*News of the North:* 2 June 1956]).[8] The coercion exerted by means of such stereotyping is a significant component of the interpersonal bargaining process under examination. Being a reliable worker (or a White, or an Indian, or a Métis) is not a state but a status that can sometimes be withheld by the powerful. However, the constraints of stereotyping and of biography are not so onerous as to prevent persons known to the writer as Métis from achieving office in the Indian Brotherhood of the Northwest Territories, or to prevent persons known to the writer as Indians from being employed by the NWT Métis Association.

The most powerful constraint on peoples native to the north is what Carstens (1971:130) has called "administrative determinism." I want to dwell on one aspect of this determinism and attempt to show that, formidable though it is, there nevertheless remains ample scope for the transaction of ethnic identity.

Yellowknife Whites typically express despair at their inability to coax Indians to conform to their wishes. A free trader declares, "Indians can never be assimilated. They are timid and do what you say, but when you go away they are back to the old ways." He is echoed by the game warden who grumbles, "They only say 'Yes, yes, yes,' but when you talk to the chief next day he says 'What was that about?'"; also by the outraged social worker who animadverts, "Indians treat game more considerately than they treat Government."

An incident which caused civil servants exasperation occurred in the summer of 1971 when representatives of the Canadian Federal Government paid their annual summer visit to Yellowknife's "Squaw Valley" to distribute treaty money and to "take the temper of the people." The local Dogribs embarrassed accompanying officials of the government of the Northwest Territories by accusing them of permitting houses built by the Federal Department of Indian Affairs for status Indians to be occupied by non-Status Indians and Métis, of allowing these houses to fall into a state of disrepair, and of charging excessive rent. A nettled Territorial official riposted that "Most of the people haven't paid any rent," and his superior added, "They were allotted to the Housing Association: they were the people who said who should get the houses." This exchange ensued:

> **Sub-chief:** We didn't really have very much authority over who lived in these houses. People didn't move out when we told them.
>
> **Territorial official:** They were the only people who had the authority actually to move someone out. Unfortunately they often didn't tell us when someone moved out and someone else moved in. They'd call us when there was something wrong, to fix it: that was it.
>
> **Sub-chief:** We didn't really know if the people paid rent or not.
>
> **Territorial official:** We used to send the Housing Association a copy of the housing accounts every month: that showed who paid what. The last meeting of the Housing Association was in January and then some people quit and then there wasn't anyone to send the housing report to. We wrote various letters to them but they didn't answer telephone calls.

Tsigonde (1972:Issue 6), the local paper with an Indian and Métis readership, ended its account of the affair, to the indignation of Territorial personnel, with the assertion that people "were told by the head of the Treaty party that the Government would be paying for everything."

When confronted with such endemic retaliatory passivity, civil servants, whose career advancement may depend on the growth of a compliant clientele (in that they need local support to demonstrate to their superiors the success of their programmes) attempt to cope either by disengaging (an administrator advocated giving the Indian Affairs houses to Indians so that there would be no rent to be collected and no services to be given: "They would still get the services, but they would come out of Welfare and not out of my budget," he explained) or by fostering the growth of "Indian" administrative bodies with whom officials might correspond and reach binding agreements.

Fostering the growth of such administrative bodies is presented as a way of encouraging independence but, whatever the intent, the effect is to co-opt Indians into the Euro-Canadian bureaucratic structure. The Department of Local Government of the Northwest Territories declares itself anxious to end paternalism and "to encourage participation and independence for northern residents through the development of strong Local Government" (Northwest Territories, Government of, 1971). Its young community workers are ideologically, committed to furthering "independence" manifested in the form of efficient fully-elected Settlement Councils. Once efficient administration has been demonstrated, a community is rewarded by being upgraded to hamlet status and being given an enlarged budget and enhanced powers. Such hamlet councils owe more to Western notions of government than they do to anything indigenously Athabaskan: witness the labyrynthine bureaucratic procedures laid out in the Department's *Secretary-Manager's Manual* (Northwest Territories Government of, 1971). The Indian Brotherhood protests that "...our people do not want to be under this kind of pressures from outside methods of doing things," (Indian Brotherhood of the Northwest Territories, 23 April 1971) but a senior Yellowknife administrator observed that "they get more money faster [than the band councils they replace] because the Commissioner has made no bones about doing away with all this Indian rigmarole."

THE CASE OF THE IBNWT

Of singular importance among the Indian administrative structures which government has nurtured is the Indian Brotherhood of the Northwest Territories. Indian Affairs funds the Brotherhood because "it would be practically impossible to carry out initial policy-making discussions with 550 Band chiefs individually, hence, the assistance in establishing a sound organizational structure to help us obtain the views of as many Indians as possible" (personal communication, Acting Chief of Indian-Eskimo Bureau, 1970). Government's need for a "sound organizational structure" is apparent in the Report of the commission appointed to investigate the unfulfilled provisions of Treaties 8 and 11 as they apply to the Indians of the Mackenzie District (the Nelson Commission of 1959) in which it is noted that

> A meeting of all the Chiefs had been convened at Forth Smith in 1957 for the purpose of acquainting them with the problem and the possible solution to it, and they had been advised to discuss the matter with their fellow Band members with a view

to expressing a firm opinion when called upon to do so at a later date. On at least two occasions subsequently all bands were reminded of the necessity of reaching some opinion and on the last occasion were informed that the Commission would be visiting them and would expect some definite answers. However, as mentioned above, the Commission's meetings with the bands disclosed a lack of understanding of the problem, a lack of preparedness, and few definite opinions.

In 1970 the Department of Indian Affairs and Northern Development funded a summer meeting in Yellowknife of the board and executive of the fledgling Indian Brotherhood of the Northwest Territories to discuss the distribution of lands not yet allocated under Treaties 8 and 11.[9] The young executive officers of the Brotherhood were severely constrained by the fact that the department had given sufficient money to furnish the chiefs with hotel accommodation for three nights only. When it seemed that business would not be completed on schedule they were beside themselves with anxiety, and therefore forced the pace. Of necessity they abandoned all notions of "Indian time," and began commanding their elders in a manner more commonly associated with Whites. When chiefs of the upper Mackenzie did not arrive at the opening session a plane was dispatched to summon them; proxies were appointed for those who could not be reached at camp. Chiefs who were dilatory in attending gatherings were publicly scolded from the chair. And, according to one insider, "They [the then Executive officers] withhold the expenses they give you: thirty-five dollars a day. Out of that you pay your hotel room, your food bill, and you've got a little spending money over. They hold this for three days because they don't want the people to spend it all on the bar."

The chiefs, who constituted the Board of the Brotherhood and were nominally in charge, appeared to have no more control over the executive than they had over White government officials. Members of the executive, young and confident products of the Euro-Canadian school system, were fluent in English and dominated their bewildered elders, who sat rigidly, hands shading eyes from unaccustomed fluorescent light. When called to order the chiefs repeatedly cried out their chairman's first name, but to no effect.

The behaviour of the then members of the executive, like the behaviour of many an Indian-White intermediary on White-sponsored "Indian" administrative structures in the north, gave rise to the observation, popular among both Indians and Whites of the political left and of the right — but heatedly contested — that it was not "truly Indian" and that it was, rather, the behaviour of "red apples" who had "lost touch with the grass roots."

Such name-calling must be interpreted in the light of work by ethnomethodologists. Wieder (1974b:108, 134) demonstrates that the meaning of a social label is indexical, that is, that it is relative to the place in which it is spoken, what the hearer knows about the speaker, the time at which it is spoken, and an indefinitely extendable collection of other contextual matters; and that since contexts vary, "no definite set of criteria for using labels could be stated in any case"[10] (see also Leiter, 1980:204). Bloch (1971:80, 85), similarly, recognizes that Merina kinship terms are prodigiously elastic in use, that "as value judgements, kinship terms contain elements of great significance which have nothing to do with what we normally think of as kinship and need to be defined in a much wider framework," and concludes that we should regard all categorical terms as value judgements and view their use as strategies.

THE POLITICS OF ETHNIC LABELLING

The context in which the name-calling occurred was a competitive struggle for the control of the Indian Brotherhood of the Northwest Territories. To dismiss a leader, or potential leader, of that organization as a "red apple" is to say, not that the person referred to has a particular objective ethnic or racial makeup but, rather, to say that, in the opinion of the speaker, such a person is not fit to hold office. A local rival of the then president attempted to undermine him in the press (News of the North, 10 September 1970) by characterizing him as not a true northerner. A cleric, disquieted by the fact that someone close to the leadership of the organization had advocated the extermination of priests, dismissed the then current executive as having "nothing Indian about them except their Treaty number." His favoured church-going candidate was in turn assailed by a conservative chief who pointedly observed, "I know your parents are Indian, but I don't know whether you are an Indian or a White man."

Labels include and exclude — ethnicity is, as Ronald Cohen (1978: 387) puts it, "a series of nesting dichotomizations of inclusiveness and exclusiveness" — and thus labelling is a political act. To label someone as essentially like oneself is to activate a latent solidarity, to recruit someone as a potential ally, and simultaneously to rebuff others. The objective likeness may be commanding or it may be trivial, and even illusory. As ethnicity subsumes such a multiplicity of interacting factors it is always feasible, given sufficient motivation, to "discover" what in fact we create, i.e., significant degrees of likeness or unlikeness.

As might be expected in time of tumultuous change, contemporaries of the Brotherhood Executive regarded their conservative elders with ambivalence. "We feel strange talking to the old people," remarked a candidate for the presidency. "They should talk to us. They say we are not good Indians. They mean we can't chop wood quick and things like that." Another youngster wrote to *Tsigonde* (1973:6) "By watching the Chief treat the young people, I feel that the fact they are educated means nothing to him. If it means nothing to him, when he goes to a meeting why doesn't he stand up and say what he has to say in English. How come when he receives letters from the Government he doesn't open it and read it himself and then answer it by himself. The young people's education means nothing to him, but he needs their education to do his job as Chief."

Nevertheless, members of the executive exerted themselves in cultivating a conservative image. One took Dogrib lessons from his mother, concurrently with the writer, and secured funds to enable his father to instruct Indian teenagers in hunting and trapping techniques; another participated with evident trepidation in the arduous and traditional fall caribou hunt;[11] another pointedly travelled to Yellowknife's "Indian village" Treaty parlay by canoe rather than by popular motor transport.[12] Not that they were cynical dissemblers: rather, they belong to the class of what Isajiw (1974:121) calls "'ethnic rediscoverers' *i.e.* persons from any consecutive ethnic generation who have been socialized into the culture of the general society but who develop a symbolic relation to the culture of their ancestors."

Ethnic labelling in the north has consequences which go far beyond whoever controls the brotherhood. He who attributes an ethnic label to another or to himself performs two interrelated operations: he assigns a person to a category, and he attaches certain prerogatives or liabilities to that person by virtue of the prerogatives or liabilities that attach to the category. That is why labelling is of such moment. Whites and Indians in the Northwest Territories diligently attempt to manage the meaning of ethnicity, so to detach old obligations from, and attach new privileges to, their own ethnic categories (Watson, 1979). That is what Dogribs attempt when they argue that while they are entitled to abundant welfare in return for ancestral lands, they cannot be expected to work regular office hours. That is what Euro-Canadians attempt when they argue that while the Northwest Territories is theirs "because we made it," they cannot be expected to mollycoddle Indian "welfare bums." As the *News of the North* (1 August 1968) opines:

> The Canadian people cannot expect to go on forever support-
> ing a special section of the government to wet-nurse this small
> minority of the population with its special privileges and special
> handicaps. As long as we maintain this anomaly, special status
> will be the excuse of many of these people for not facing up to

the fact of having to work for a living and actually go to work regularly.

Labelling has implications for the control of the north itself. When the Commissioner of the Northwest Territories declared "We are all Northerners," the President of the Indian Brotherhood countered, "We are all not Northerners; we are the Indian people" (IBNWT *Minutes*, 1 July 1971). When an alliance of Indians and Métis was essayed under the rubric *Dene*, the President of the Métis Association of the Northwest Territories declared that the Indian Brotherhood and the Métis Association could not work together unless the Indian Brotherhood were to recognize "the distinct Metis culture and identity." The context in which such remarks are to be understood is that of a contest for political control of the north. It is only superficially about who is an "Indian" or a "Northerner" etc. Ethnicity is merely the idiom in which the contest is fought out.

Social actors construct the ethnicity they think they discover. The President of the Métis Association asserted before the Berger Commission that "the Métis people for one, believe that they, as a distinct group of people with both Indian and white origin, are entitled to compensation from the Federal Government as a result of our "Indian title" or whatever rights have accrued to us because of our origin and association with the Indian people." He also staked a claim for Aboriginal rights *(Native Press,* 26 November 1976). The president of the brotherhood accused him of "speaking only for a small minority of the Métis businessmen who were afraid the Dene nation concept would threaten their investment." Contrariwise, sub-chief Liske had earlier demanded rhetorically "where were the métis in 1921?" when Treaty No II was ratified *(Native Press,* 18 March 1971). Clearly objective cultural or racial similarities and dissimilarities between and among the people of the north are not the point, and, if we want to know if somebody "is" or "is not" an Indian, a Métis, a Dene, or a northerner, there is little to be gained by examining the person *per se.* What is at issue is control of the north: ethnic labelling is a means to that control.

NOTES

1. I gratefully acknowledge the assistance of the Canada Council in funding two field trips to Yellowknife, one of six months' duration in 1970 and one of one month in 1972. Thanks also to hospitable informants in Yellowknife, and to colleagues who made helpful comments on an earlier draft of this paper: A. Brannigan, J.S. Frideres, J. Hymovitch, D.L. Mills, K. Nielsen, V. Serl.

2. Indians, Métis and Whites are pegs on which to hang an argument. I could as well have written about tribes of anthropologists, and one day I shall. The paper is to be entitled "Anthropological Savagery."

3. Information supplied in 1970 by a paid Métis informant. He identified a total of 77 Métis and 88 Indians resident in Yellowknife at the time of survey and was able to furnish information about 67 of the Métis and 63 of the Indians.

4. From a tape recording in the possession of the Indian Brotherhood of the Northwest Territories.

5. This belief assumes the status of what Pollner (1974a) has called an "incorrigible proposition."

6. See Becker (1960) on side bets.

7. The phrase is from Garfinkel (1967:22).

8. Such hostile stereotypes as are to be discerned in Yellowknife seem to me, after having lived twenty years in South Africa, remarkably lacking in economy and integrity. Further, the Whites most apt to give expression to them (construction workers, miners, bush pilots) are the very ones who consort most freely with Indians. White-collar workers are more likely to complain that "it's well known that the Dogrib are the hardest of all to get to know," which complaint is echoed by Cohen (1962:60) and by Honigmann (1946:4).

9. Glazer and Moynihan's (1975:10) observation that "the strategic efficacy of ethnicity as a basis for asserting claims against government has its counterpart in the seeming ease whereby government employs ethnic categories as a basis for distributing its rewards," seems pertinent.

10. Wieder's (1974a) study of the "convict code," which the inmates and staff of a half-way house for drug addicts employ in interpreting inmate behaviour, is highly, suggestive of how laymen and anthropologists alike accomplish a formulation of "Indian culture," and of how they employ this formulation in interpreting the behaviour of "Indians" to themselves and to each other.

11. Control of even the highly conservative fall hunt appears to have slipped from the hands of Dogribs. A senior chief missed the beginning of a caribou hunt because the seaplane intended for his conveyance was dispatched before his appearance by a game warden who explained, "He got all tanked up the night before, then turned up half an hour late I told them to leave because there is no point in holding up a plane at $250 an hour for somebody to sober up."

12. Many Whites collude with Indians in this romantic presentation, especially for the benefit of White audiences. Vide René Fumoleau's film, *I was Born Here.*

PART III _____

Canada: The Reclamation of Aboriginal Identity

INTRODUCTION

Traditional Aboriginal political organization has undergone much change in the last century in Canada as well as elsewhere in the world. It has been particularly affected by the growth of national and regional political organizations which have been a prominent part of the Canadian political scene for the last several decades. This development of new political structures, which has been influenced by acculturative pressures, contact and negotiation with the dominant non-Native society, has had several effects on Native self-awareness and concepts of identity. Regional and provincial organizations have contributed to new concepts of ethnic and cultural boundaries, and national organizations have contributed much to concepts of Native versus non-Native as opposed to other (but still important) ethnic or national feelings such as "Cree" or "Ojibwa." One of the most dramatic examples is how various provincial and regional Métis and non-Status Indian organizations revitalized the concept, meaning and ethnic boundaries of "Métis" in the early 1960s in Canada (Sawchuk, 1978). The papers in this section examine the ways contemporary Aboriginal peoples in Canada have been reclaiming their own identity, through the use of political organizations, and by other means.

In a paper specially revised and updated for this volume, Sawchuk discusses the effects of the constitutional definition of Aboriginal peoples on the Métis and non-Status Indians of Canada. Section 35(2) of the *Constitution Act, 1982* defines the Aboriginal peoples of Canada as comprising the Indian, Inuit and Métis peoples of Canada, but non-Status Indians are not mentioned. While the legal repercussions of this omission are by no means clear (non-Status Indians may yet be defined as falling under either the definition of "Métis" or "Indian"), it has driven a wedge between the long-standing political alliances of the non-Status Indians and the Métis in the prairie provinces. Several organizations that previously represented both the Métis and non-Status have been restructured to represent Métis constituents exclusively, and many new organizations, some on the provincial level representing non-Status Indians, some on the urban level representing "C-31s" (non-Status Indians who have regained their Status under Bill C-31, but do not necessarily have a reserve community they can go to) are now being developed.

Armitage and Kennedy give a detailed example of how manipulation of ethnicity or Aboriginality can be a powerful political tool in opposing state structures. The Innu of eastern Quebec and Labrador have been engaged in a long struggle to end low-level military flight training over their traditional territory. They have done this, in part, by using ethnic symbols to present an image of themselves as peaceful, non-violent Aboriginal peoples besieged by an uncaring and powerful war machine which is destroying the wildlife and the Innu culture that is dependent upon it. Not surprisingly, the state's response is to deny that the Innu practice "traditional" hunting practices to any extent, in effect questioning the very existence of these people as a distinct society.

The final paper in this section by Boisvert and Turnbull examines some of the problems of defining Métis today (an issue already considered by Watson in the previous section). Among other things, they look at the extent of self-identity of Métis respondents to the 1981 Canada census. What they find surprising is that so many people from all over Canada identified as Métis. This is unexpected because the traditional geographical location of the Métis is located in the prairie provinces and Northwest Territories. While they correctly point out that mixed Indian and European ancestry is not, by itself, a sufficient condition for identifying as Métis, either for purposes of the Canadian constitution or in other situations, there is some evidence that this is how the term is considered in other parts of Canada. Their reiteration of the difficulties, and in some cases irrelevance, of the distinction between non-status and Métis once again brings home the point that the ethnic boundaries between Canada's Aboriginal peoples are still dynamic and subject to change.

THE MÉTIS, NON-STATUS INDIANS AND THE NEW ABORIGINALITY: GOVERNMENT INFLUENCE ON NATIVE POLITICAL ALLIANCES AND IDENTITY[1]

Joe Sawchuk

INTRODUCTION

A measure of an ethnic group's powerlessness and the relative extent of its domination by the larger society surrounding it is the ease with which a foreign or inappropriate identity (according to the group's own standards) can be imposed on it for political expediency or other reasons. Thus, immigrants entering Canada have often been forced to accept definitions of identity imposed on them by immigration officials or the government, as Ukrainians were once defined as "Galicians," or "Ruthenians." This insensitivity to a group's own concept of self-identity may induce members of the group to fight for a recognition of their ethnicity on their own terms (even though in doing so they often end up radically restructuring or reformulating their identity themselves). Another possibility however, is that the imposed identity may become accepted and institutionalized, and even vigorously defended by the people in question. To a certain extent, this has happened with the Native people of Canada, who have long had definitions of "nativeness" imposed on them by the larger society, and who have often accepted these definitions as their own. This is best exemplified by the definition of "Status Indian" under the *Indian Act*, but a more recent example is the definition of "Aboriginal peoples" as provided by the Canadian Constitution.

An imposed identity rarely provides as effective or spontaneous a means of political organization as a self-proclaimed or self-developed identity does. While a number of Canadian Native political organizations have appeared, based on these imposed identities, Status Indian organizations such as the Assembly of First Nations (AFN) and several organizations representing the "residual" categories of non-Status Indian and Métis such as the Native Council of Canada (NCC), have often been more an expression of dissension in the Native community of Canada than an expression of solidarity, as is perhaps inevitable in any situation in which identity is imposed "from above."

Canadian history would seem to demonstrate that few Native people have made a concerted attack on government-imposed definitions of nativeness. Rather, those favourably affected by such definitions have tended to accept them, while only the dispossessed have rejected them. Thus, Status Indians have rarely expressed concern over the problems of the non-Status (Dyck, 1980:37); and Status organizations, apparently concerned over the possibility of already-scarce resources being redistributed over an even larger population, have often opposed recognition of non-Status Indians.

Native organizations continue to be susceptible to further manipulations of their members' identities. For example, much of the political activity of both the Métis and non-Status Indians in the last two decades can be seen as a reaction to the inclusion or exclusion of people under the arbitrary government definitions expressed in the *Indian Act*.[2] The once-strong alliance between the Métis and the non-Status Indians has been subverted by the constitutional entrenchment of Aboriginal rights in 1982. The new political realities being faced by these groups have had some significant effects on the perceptions of ethnicity and group membership.

THE CONSTITUTION ACT, 1982

Section 35(2) of the *Constitution Act* reads as follows:

> In this Act, "Aboriginal peoples of Canada" includes the Indian, Inuit and Metis peoples of Canada.

Conspicuous by its absence from this definition is any explicit mention of the non-Status Indians of Canada. This does not mean that the non-Status Indians are definitionally excluded from the Constitution; neither Indian, Inuit nor Métis is defined in the Act, and it could be argued that the term Métis was intended to include the category of non-Status Indians (Lysyk,

1982:470). Alternatively, non-Status Indians might eventually be subsumed under the constitutional definition of Indian (Sanders, 1981:420). However, these are questions which have never been satisfactorily determined, either at constitutional conferences or in discussions on the inherent right of Aboriginal self-government. Bill C-31, an amendment to the *Indian Act* (Canada, House of Commons, 1985) also has had a profound effect on this issue, since many non-Status Indians have been able to gain Indian status by its enactment,[3] while others have been denied.

However non-Status Indians become categorized, their exclusion from any direct mention in the Constitution has already affected their political organizations. Many Métis and non-Status Indians perceive the Constitution as having driven a wedge between them, and there has been a drastic drop in the ability of the two groups to continue an effective political alliance. This ability has always been weak on the national level, as the Native Council of Canada (NCC), the ostensible national voice of the Métis and non-Status Indians, has demonstrated. Several important Métis provincial organizations were conspicuously absent during the years NCC tried to bridge the vast regional differences and interests between Métis and non-Status Indians across Canada (the 1970s and 1980s). But it was a different story regionally, especially in the prairie provinces, where the two groups had been working together in a united political front for the last fifteen years, even to the extent that some non-Status Indians began to identify themselves as Métis (Sawchuk, 1978). This long-standing alliance has now been broken, and Métis and non-Status Indians have already formed two distinct political organizations in Saskatchewan and are likely to do so in other provinces.

This may not be a totally negative development. The original alliance of Métis and non-Status Indians was a marriage of convenience, at least in part. The two groups formed a residual category of Native peoples "left over" from the definition of Status Indian under the *Indian Act.* It was only natural that they should join together to form a single political unit. They shared a similar heritage and faced similar problems: poverty, a lack of government recognition, and exclusion from many of the considerations to which they felt their Aboriginal status entitled them.

With the apparent exclusion of non-Status Indians from section 35(2) of the *Constitution Act, 1982,* and the arbitrary working of Bill C-31, a new residual category has been created, this time occupied by the non-Status Indians alone. Save for those who will be affected by Bill C-31, non-Status Indians now face rejection both by the *Indian Act* and the Constitution. In practical terms, this translates into a rejection by both Status Indians and Métis.

At first glance, it appears that these two residual categories are on different planes. An observer unfamiliar with Canadian practise might view the *Indian Act* merely as peculiar legislation which excludes certain Native peoples (*i.e.* non-Status Indians and Métis) from some government services, while on the other hand exclusion from the Constitution would imply a total denial of identity. Such a view, however, would fail to take into account the extent to which the term "Indian" as defined under the *Indian Act* has been internalized and accepted among Canadian Indians. Today, many Status Indians (as well as many non-Status Indians) regard status *as a confirmation of their identity as Native peoples,* often the only, or official, confirmation. Whatever the differences between these two imposed definitions (one by the *Indian Act,* the other by the Constitution), the addition of a new source of exclusion for non-Status Indians has been enough to tear apart the union between them and the Métis.

Evidence of this was provided by the formation of the Métis National Council (MNC), a breakaway organization from the Native Council of Canada and a federation of the three prairie Métis political organizations, the Métis Association of Alberta (MAA), the Association of Métis and Non-Status Indians of Saskatchewan (AMNSIS), and the Manitoba Métis Federation (MMF). For years the Native Council of Canada had been plagued with problems associated with the attempt to represent both the Métis and non-Status Indians, two constituencies which had little in common in most parts of Canada. It was originally conceived as a federation of all the provincial Métis and/or non-Status Indian organizations. This proved to be an unwieldy structure, as each province had a slightly different organizational framework, which made the selection of delegates on an equitable basis difficult. For example, Alberta had one vice-president, while Manitoba had six. More importantly, differences over regional policies and particular interests kept the organization badly split. For a time during the 1970s and 1980s, Alberta's was the only prairie Métis organization which remained in the NCC.

The NCC's greatest problem was in reconciling differences between western Métis and eastern non-Status Indians. This difficulty was exacerbated in 1982 when non-Métis were elected to both the offices of president and vice president. The fact that the vice-president was not even non-Status, but was a Status Indian, particularly angered the Métis delegates. Western Métis and non-Status leaders, who had never been enamoured of the NCC before, now simply dismissed it as irrelevant, claiming "it was in the hands of Indians."

The issue came to a head in February 1983, at a preparatory meeting for the upcoming March 1983 First Ministers' Meeting on the Constitution.

When the constitutional accord had been reached several months previously, Section 37 of the *Constitution Act* had called for a conference to be held within a year on matters directly affecting the Aboriginal peoples of Canada. Two seats each were to be provided for the three national organizations representing Status Indian, Inuit and Métis/non-Status Indians. At the preparatory meeting, it was proposed that NCC fill its two seats with the president and vice-president, which meant that neither of the official representatives at the conference would be Métis. Until that time the understanding had been, at least on the part of the prairie organizations, that NCC's seats were to be filled by one Métis and one non-Status Indian representative. In the face of this exclusion, the three prairie Métis organizations formed their own association, the Métis National Council (MNC) as an alternative to the NCC. The leaders of the MNC immediately sought their own seat at the constitutional conference, pointing out that 75% to 80% of Canadian Métis lived in the west, and that they were not being represented at the conference to their satisfaction.

Justice Minister Mark MacGuigan at first refused the request, but the Métis threatened to boycott the meeting unless given a seat. They also asked the Ontario Supreme Court for an injunction blocking the constitutional conference unless the MNC was represented *(Globe and Mail*, 2 March 1983). After further negotiations, the Justice Minister agreed to give the new organization a seat at the meeting, and MNC withdrew its application for an injunction. MNC was also granted credentials for fourteen delegates and five observers *(Globe and Mail,* 9 March 1983). This was the first overt move by the Métis to disassociate themselves from non-Status Indians on the national level.

EFFECTS ON ETHNICITY

Much has changed since I first started research among the Métis in the summer of 1969. At that time, as today, there was much public concern and discussion in the Métis communities over "who," "what," and "when" was a Métis. This concern was also visible at provincial-level meetings of the Manitoba Métis Federation. Similar concerns were evident in Saskatchewan and Alberta. Unlike the current trend, however, these earlier public discussions of the criteria of identity led to a fairly broad definition of Métis. Generally, the members of the community agreed that anyone of mixed White-Indian ancestry was a Métis and eligible to join the Métis associations. Little attention was paid to time-depth or generation; a "first generation" Métis (or non-Status Indian) was as welcome to join as someone who could trace his/her ancestry back to the early days of the Red River Settlement.

In Alberta, which has in one area of the province a history of Black-Indian as well as White-Indian mixed populations, the term became, for a time, even more broadly defined and open with the dropping of the criterion of "White." This occurred at an annual assembly of the Métis Association of Alberta in which a person of mixed Black-Indian ancestry stood up and demanded recognition as a Métis by virtue of his Indian ancestry. As the result of a lengthy debate, it was agreed that:

> ...any person of mixed Indian and *Non-Indian blood,* or any non-Status Indian or their spouse...sixteen years of age or over, residing in the province of Alberta is eligible for membership in the Association (MAA: 1977; italics added).

This was a statement of eligibility for membership in the Métis Association of Alberta rather than a definition of Métis *per se,* but the term, with its emphasis on non-Indian rather than White, became accepted as a general definition of ethnicity as well. As late as 1982, the Alberta Federation of Métis Settlements defined Métis as "any person of mixed Indian and non-Indian ancestry who identifies as a Métis" (FMS 1982:31). Save for the qualification of self-identity, the definition is the same as that derived for the MAA almost ten years previously. This definition was deemed acceptable by the majority of MAA members for many years, and there was little conflict between Métis and non-Status members. For example, in the three years I spent working for the Métis Association of Alberta (1978-1980), I did not witness one serious — or even jocular — expression of antagonism between a Métis and non-Status Indian, nor any suggestion that there were problems or differences between the two. However, this state of affairs changed drastically after the explicit constitutional recognition of Aboriginality in 1982 included the Métis but ignored non-Status Indians.

Soon after its inception, the Métis National Council developed a definition of Métis which eliminated the reference to mixed ancestry, and provincial organizations were not long in following suit. At the 1984 Annual Assembly of the Métis Association of Alberta, an important new bylaw regarding the definition of Métis was passed:

> A Metis is an Aboriginal person who declares himself/ herself to be a Metis person, and can produce satisfactory historical or acceptable legal proof that he/ she is a Metis, or has traditionally held himself/ herself to be a Métis, and is accepted by the Metis people as a Metis *(AMMSA:* 1984).

As can be seen, the emphasis has shifted significantly from a concern with mixed ancestry to a concern for identification as a Métis, acceptance by the

Métis community and/or legal proof of ancestry.[4] The implications regarding non-Status Indians are quite significant.

When the revised definition was adopted, the vice-president of the Métis Association of Alberta publicly stated that this did *not* mean that all non-Status Indians would have to leave the association. Perhaps acknowledging the strong commitment to the Métis cause and culture that non-Status Indians had made in the last fifteen to twenty years, she said that "if they identify themselves as Métis and are accepted by the Métis community, then they have absolutely no problem" *(AMMSA,* 1984). Thus it would appear that there is still an opportunity for some non-Status Indians to take on the identity of Métis. But at least one group of non-Status Indians are unlikely to maintain their positions in the associations: professional politicians. Their public position makes them extremely vulnerable to attack from political opponents who can accuse them of being "Indian" rather than Métis, and therefore unqualified to speak for the Métis.

POLITICAL RAMIFICATIONS

It has been apparent for many years that the most likely result of the recent definition of Aboriginality would be the emergence of Native political organizations dedicated exclusively to the interests of non-Status Indians, which would significantly alter the structure of the Native political arena in Canada. Previously, there has been only one organization dedicated to the exclusive interests of non-Status Indians: Indian Rights for Indian Women (IRIW). This organization was formed to assist non-Status Indian women to lobby for changes to Section 12(1)(b) of the *Indian Act,* the section which rescinded the Indian status of those Indian women who marry non-Status Indians or non-Indians. Since funding regulations from the Secretary of State required IRIW to represent *both* Status and non-Status women, the purpose of the organization was effectively subverted from the beginning. Status women were generally unsympathetic to the cause of non-Status Indian women, and the organization eventually collapsed (Weaver, 1983:60).[5]

The fate of IRIW is not an unusual occurrence with government-financed Native organizations in Canada; government funding often determines the constituency of an organization as well as its operations. This is one of the trade-offs which must be faced by Native people in Canada if they wish to form government-financed political organizations or lobbying groups. For example, core funding was originally granted to NCC on condition that it represent both Métis and non-Status Indians (Weaver, 1983:70). The departure of all the western Métis organizations for a time placed NCC's operating budget in jeopardy, although NCC now has been restructured to represent non-Status Indians exclusively.

The history of the Métis Association of Alberta provides another example. In the early 1960s, the organization, which was originally founded in 1932, underwent a revitalization and reformulation (Sawchuk, 1983:67-78). At that time it received no government funding, and the president saw it as a vehicle to represent exclusively those Métis living on the eight Métis colonies in Alberta. When government funding finally became available a few years later, it was given on the understanding that the association would have to change its venue and represent all the Métis and non-Status Indians in all parts of the province. This resulted not only in a restructuring of the organization, but the replacement of the old leadership as well. Thus the very structure and purpose of the Aboriginal political apparatus in this country depends upon the conditions that the federal government may choose to place on funding. This circumstance is the fundamental weakness of almost all Native political organizations in Canada. Government subsidies may make the movements possible in the first place, but at the same time these subsidies make the Native people even more dependent upon the government.

This influence on the political activity of Aboriginal organizations is particularly evident among the Métis and non-Status Indians of the prairies. As in many Native organizations, the Métis associations of the prairies are witness to ruthless political in-fighting among leadership rivals. Until recently, the most frequent expressions of this infighting were internal struggles for control of government funding and programmes (Sawchuk, 1983). But the legal distinction between Métis and non-Status Indian has provided a new tool for politicians who are able to identify themselves as Métis and, at the same time, identify their most serious rivals as non-Status Indians.

This is best illustrated by the dissolution of the Association of Métis and Non-Status Indians of Saskatchewan (AMNSIS) in Saskatchewan. In the summer of 1987, at the Annual Assembly of AMNSIS at Batoche, a commission was set up to look at the possibility of forming two separate political organizations; one for the Métis and one for the non-status Indians, and to consider how the social, educational and development programs AMNSIS was running could be broken up to serve both constituencies should it be decided to split. But a pro-Métis faction took control of the commission, and at an inaugural meeting in February 1988 adopted a new constitution, revived the name of the Métis Society of Saskatchewan (the predecessor of AMNSIS) and declared that the MSS was now the official Métis organization of the province and that AMNSIS was disbanded. The president of AMNSIS, Jim Sinclair, filed for an injunction to halt the proceedings on the grounds that the membership had not voted to disband AMNSIS. However, the Queen's Bench ruled that the new MSS was a legal corporation. Sinclair appealed and the appeal court decided that a province-wide referendum should be held to determine the wishes of AMNSIS members. On August 20, 1988 the referendum was held. There was a very low turnout, which may indicate that the issue was of more interest to the various leadership factions than the rank and file. Nevertheless, the referendum was held, and the MSS contingent won, albeit by a fairly low majority (53%).

The dissolution of AMNSIS had been presaged for several years by the development of a political rhetoric which mirrored, emphasized and exacerbated the growing split between Métis and non-Status Indian. From the "we are all Métis" sentiment of the mid-1960s there was a move to a new phraseology: "Métis" versus "Indian." The bitterness which is revealed in this rhetorical pattern was particularly surprising to those of us who only a decade and a half earlier had observed the "coming together" of Métis and non-Status Indians, perhaps even to the extent of beginning to forge a common identity (Sawchuk, 1978). Such is not the case today in Saskatchewan. Rather, one sees extremely pointed and emotional criticism directed at non-Status Indians by Métis, and vice versa.

This first became evident at the 1984 annual assembly of the Association of Métis and Non-Status Indians of Saskatchewan, a few years before the actual dissolution. Jim Sinclair, the man who led the organization for many years, found himself being challenged on the basis that he was a non-Status Indian and not a Métis *(New Breed,* August 1984d:20). In the course of these attacks, he was constantly referred to as an "Indian," *not* a non-Status Indian. When a man who has been a leader of a Métis and non-Status Indian organization is suddenly labelled an "Indian," *not* Métis; *not* non-Status, very definite attitudes towards particular identities are being expressed. The message is clear: he is different from, and has different interests than, a sizable portion of the association. Thus the debate became reduced to the polar extremes of Métis and non-Status. In using the terms this way, some Métis were indicating that non-Status Indians no longer constituted a legitimate group, and that they should look to the Status Indians for their support. The irony is that while "non-Status" might be considered "Indian" by some Métis, they were still "non-Status" (or even "Métis") to Status Indians.

The split between the Métis and the non-Status had been coming for years. The first crack appeared when the Constitution recognized the Aboriginal rights of the Métis, Inuit and Indian, but not non-Status Indians. (Ironically, Sinclair was one of those who had worked for many years towards having Métis mentioned in the Constitution in the first place.) The

Constitutional exclusion of non-Status may not have been intended to exclude the non-Status Indians from recognition of their Aboriginal status. It was known, or at least anticipated, that the federal government would eventually pass legislation like Bill C-31 which would prevent people from losing status through marriage, and that some, anyway, would be able to regain status. So the easy assumption was that a great proportion of non-Status Indians would simply apply to get their status back through Bill C-31; and the rest, those who identified primarily as Métis, would join with that community. Thus, the category of non-Status Indian would gradually disappear.

It appears that this is an over-optimistic assessment, although it is one often put forth by Métis when asked to justify the exclusion of the non-Status from their organizations. But there is a large group of non-Status Indians who *are not* eligible to regain their status under Bill C-31. And many of these people either won't identify as Métis, or won't be accepted as Métis by the rest of the Métis population.

In many cases, they won't identify as Métis because they are stung by what they see as the racist reactions of those Métis who have been saying: "We don't want Indians in our organization." The Métis call these people "Indians" rather than non-Status Indians; while Status Indians, who for the most part were antagonistic to non-Status Indians regaining Status, call them "Métis." So the Métis are calling them "Indian," and the Indians are calling them "Métis." It has been a painful experience for these people no matter how they wish to identify themselves.

One individual discussed the effect that the break-up of AMNSIS had on him. He saw the Métis' rejection of Sinclair in particular, and non-Status in general, as a racist reaction against people who should (in his opinion) after all be working together, and it has caused him to reject his Métis identity:

> You know, I could go either way — my parents were Métis, and I used to think of myself as a Métis, but I can also get my status through C-31. I used to identify as a Métis, and was proud of being Métis.[6]

With that, he pointed to some pictures he had mounted on his recreation room wall. They were some posters from a Glenbow Museum exhibit of Métis artifacts that had been shown a few years ago. He had these beautifully framed.

> See, I used to be proud of being Métis; I had those pictures mounted. But now, after what happened, I don't care any more. I'm not going to call myself Métis any more. I'm going to apply for my status under C-31.[7]

Much of the name-calling can be attributed to simple political rhetoric. The annual assembly is precisely the kind of arena where rivals attempt to discredit each other and simultaneously inflate their own virtues. This sort of debate is usually for the public arena (Bailey, 1981:34-35). However, the emotional and racist comments that have surfaced over the course of this issue are not merely the product of the public forum. They are directly attributable to the uncertainty regarding the position of non-Status Indians in this country today. While grandiloquence, name-calling and rhetoric is often a function of uncertainty (Bailey, 1981:37), so is the emotionalism and bitterness that became observable in the relations between Métis and non-Status Indians in the late 1980s. Once this bitterness carried over into the behind-the-scenes arena, it became permanently disruptive.

This new pattern of rhetoric was much in evidence in the early power struggles in AMNSIS between the president, Jim Sinclair, and the vice-president, Clem Chartier. Chartier explicitly portrayed his challenge in terms of the disparity of interests between Métis and Indian (he dropped the term non-Status from his public statements almost completely), identifying himself as a Métis and his rival as an Indian. He also publicly supported the idea of splitting AMNSIS into two organizations — one for the Métis, one for non-Status Indians:

> (AMNSIS) is an association of two people, the Métis and the Indian. Some of us feel, and I am one of them, that in order for us to put forward a strong, vigorous argument, we have to be clearly identifiable as a distinct people...as long as we continue to have some obscurity between Métis issues and Indian issues, and we don't make a strong stand in a specific direction, we are going to be viewed as, perhaps not weak, but certainly vacillating (New *Breed*, August 1984b).

Stressing the Métis/non-Status dichotomy in this manner probably appealed to many leaders, non-Status Indians as well as Métis, as an effective political strategy. It would enable them to carve out a special niche for themselves while relegating many of their opponents to a separate political sphere. The AMNSIS case provides an excellent example of this. The president was an extremely astute and powerful politician, and his identification as a non-Status Indian was the only significant chink in his armour, albeit a negligible or irrelevant one before the constitutional definition of Aboriginality. One of the few effective strategies available to use against him (at least by a Métis) was the reification of the distinction between Métis and non-Status Indian. This is the tactic the vice-president appeared to choose. Thus he could point out (with some justification) that most of the programmes and activities of the provincial association, for example the

Gabriel Dumont Institute, were geared to recognition of the Métis heritage. He also used that fact to suggest that the non-Status Indians might be better served by their own organization. The other side of the argument is that the non-Status Indians would leave the association with nothing, other than perhaps a share of the core funding. To many, this is hardly a fair arrangement, considering the extent to which the non-Status Indians have contributed to the association's development.

The Métis National Council also became involved in this power struggle. Although originally MNC may have been set up as a *regional* association, representing Métis and non-Status Indians from the three prairie provinces, it soon developed the characteristics of an *ethnic,* or as they would have it, a *national* association, representing mainly Métis issues. This precipitated a struggle between Sinclair and Chartier over who should properly represent AMNSIS for MNC *(New Breed,* 1984b, 1984c, 1984d, 1985).

MNC was not the only organization to reflect the drive for exclusively Métis organizations. Several smaller breakaway Métis organizations emerged, albeit often briefly, over the past several years. These also mirrored the growing split between Métis and non-Status Indians. One such organization was the National Métis Alliance of Saskatchewan. This organization garnered some media coverage in 1983 by claiming support from the provincial Conservative government and by criticizing the Association of Métis and Non-Status Indians of Saskatchewan for permitting "non-Status Indians and Dene" to belong to it *(New Breed,* 1983). The president of this new organization questioned the official definition of Métis as used by AMNSIS, which defined a Métis as someone who identifies as a Métis, is accepted by the Native community as a Métis, and who has lived in a Métis community for a reasonable length of time. According to the president of the Métis Alliance of Saskatchewan:

> These standards are too loose. Having a membership card doesn't necessarily make you a Métis. A Métis is a Métis by virtue of his birth *(New Breed,* 1983).

This latter definition was certainly vague, but it did reflect the growing concern that many Métis had over the necessity of distinguishing "Métis" from non-Status Indian or Indian.

After the referendum that dissolved AMNSIS, the non-status Indian population of Saskatchewan was left without an effective political organization, and had no way of repudiating their exclusion from recognition as Aboriginal peoples. It was obvious that a new organization representing non-Status Indians had to be formed, and Sinclair was the obvious choice for leader. There *was* an organization in Saskatchewan already purporting to represent non-Status Indians and C-31s; the Native Council of Canada

(Saskatchewan) or NCC(S). Since the constitutional exclusion of non-Status Indians (and the prairie Métis forming their own inter-provincial organization), NCC tried to reformulate itself by representing non-Status Indians only, and attempted to set up provincial sub-groups (such as NCC[Alberta]; NCC[Saskatchewan]; etc.) It did not have much success in Saskatchewan, and folded soon after the referendum.

But in September of 1988, a new organization, the Assembly of Aboriginal Peoples of Saskatchewan (AAPS) was incorporated. The objective of AAPS was to protect the rights of "excluded Indians" in Saskatchewan. The terms of reference in its constitution indicate the rage that many Native people felt at having their identities imposed upon them (or more accurately, having Indian identity denied them). To quote from their submission to the Secretary of State:

> Our concept of freedom and liberation is to be politically recognized as *Indian people in the fullest sense of the word* and know that we are full partners in the Canadian Constitution...(our) mission is to protect...Indians that have been excluded from their rights as defined in the constitution (emphasis added)(AAPS 1989:1).

They launched a successful appeal to the Secretary of State for core funding for the fiscal year of April 1, 1989 to March 31, 1990 to get the new organization under way. Their first priorities were aimed at identifying the excluded Indians of Saskatchewan (in some 115 communities in Saskatchewan) and setting up local organizations and community based representatives of the provincial organization.

Such an organization will face many problems, however. First of all, there are several *kinds* of non-Status Indian, all with specific problems of their own, and it is not clear that one organization can cover all of them. For example, there are many non-Status Indians who are not eligible to regain Status through Bill C-31. There are still others who are eligible to regain Status through Bill C-31, but have not yet done so. Added to them are those non-Status Indians who *have* regained their Status, but who don't really have an Indian identity or a reserve community to go to (these are beginning to be referred to as "C-31s" in the prairies.) There is some talk of setting up special bands for such people (eg: the C-31s of Regina), and in some cases, special reserves. Other people need help in regaining Band membership in an existing Indian Band, plus getting land or houses within the Reserves, etc. Which groups AAPS could represent and which it could not is still unclear. But it may not survive in its present form for long, as there now seems to be a move to creating Native urban organizations which might prove a better alternative to address these questions. Some of the AAPS leadership has already moved towards working with such organizations.

IDENTITY AND GOVERNMENT CONTROL

The split of AMNSIS, and the creation of MSS and AAPS indicate that government-defined concepts of identity (in this case the Constitution and Bill C-31) are still capable of affecting Native people today. This is only the most recent of many such examples. History shows us that once these concepts have been internalized and institutionalized, it is often impossible to separate them from the Native culture or even to recognize them for what they are. A long-standing example of this phenomenon is the way band governments of reserves have been introduced and subsequently accepted by Status Indians as genuine expressions of Native culture. Band structure, with its concomitant "chief" is largely a White construct. Many Indian groups, for example those in the sub-arctic, had no formal or permanent leadership patterns; and while others in different parts of Canada may have had traditional patterns of appointing leaders and delineating their authority, these bear little resemblance to the patterns seen today on most Reserves. In an attempt to standardize the local governments of the various Indian communities across Canada, the central government began to impose a uniform structure of band management (consisting of a Chief and a certain number of Councillors, depending upon the size of the community) on all Indian communities.

This imposition of government structures was first provided for in the 1869 *Act for the Gradual Enfranchisement of Indians and the Better Management of Indian Affairs*. With little subsequent modification, this Act became the format for determining all governments of Native groups as they subsequently came under the control of the central government. Although there were many cases of prolonged resistance to the imposition of these regulations, this government imposed and designed structure often became accepted as a "traditional" and "Indian" leadership pattern, even among Indian groups which previously had no traditionally appointed "chief." This government-designed local structure has now been given a further legitimacy by Native peoples. The Assembly of First Nations (AFN) has based the principles of its organization on this format (its membership is composed of the Chiefs of most of the bands in Canada).[8]

In a similar manner, it is likely that the constitutional definition of Aboriginality will become institutionalized among the Métis, and they will no longer identify with the non-Status Indians. It is surprising how sensitive the identity of Canadian Native people is to outside political manipulation and expediency. Perhaps this is the inevitable result of the long-term, thorough subjugation Native people have experienced in this country.

It would be heartening if one could suggest that these imposed identities have been able to support an effective political resistance to Western subjugation. We can certainly see the definitions of Nativeness imposed by government reflected in the various organizations that constitute contemporary Native political activity today. There are Status organizations, non-Status organizations, Métis organizations, C-31 organizations, and Native Women organizations. But although many of these organizations have attained worthwhile goals, the various identities continue to subdivide the Native community, subverting much effective political action.

I am not suggesting that the political activities of the Native organizations have been in vain. They have had, and will undoubtedly continue to have, a profound and salutary effect on the Canadian scene and the welfare of their constituents. By designing their own education programmes and economic development projects, and by their recent work towards Aboriginal self-government, Status, Inuit and Métis/non-Status organizations have done much to offset the unrelenting pressure towards total assimilation directed against Native people in this country. The Métis organizations have been particularly successful in legitimizing their ethnic and Aboriginal identity. A few years ago, they were fighting to convince the Canadian government and public that they existed as a separate group or even that they were entitled to be regarded as an Aboriginal people. Today, that recognition is assured by the Canadian Constitution. This would never have come about had it not been for the persistent political activities of the Métis and non-Status Indian associations over the last several years.

However, these successes do not alter the fact that the constitutional definition of Aboriginality and other imposed classifications have subverted a significant political alliance between the Métis and non-Status Indians at the very least, and among all Aboriginal peoples at the most. Together, the Métis and non-Status Indians make up the largest bloc of Native peoples in the country. It is unlikely that they will be as politically effective if they form two opposing groups. The constitutional categories also ignore the Aboriginal rights of a significant proportion of the Native population. The non-Status Indians of the prairie Métis and non-Status Indian organizations have contributed at least as much to the success of these organizations as have the Métis, yet they have failed to achieve any equivalent, appreciable results for themselves.

The fact that Aboriginal peoples of Canada have been actively involved in the national Constitutional discussions and have broken ground in the recognition of their inherent right to self-government may indicate that outside imposition of identity may be coming to an end. A crucial part of any self-government package is determination of membership and by extension, identity. Of course, that does not guarantee that the categories Native people create for themselves will be any less divisive than those that have been imposed from above, or that the divisions between Métis, non-Status and Status that now exist can ever be healed. There remains a danger that even in the future, Canada's Native people may be co-opted into furthering their own political dispersal and impotence through the mechanism of self-government. However, it is extremely unlikely they could create any structure more divisive than that which the Canadian state has already imposed on them from above.

NOTES

1. This is a revision of a paper originally published in *Canadian Ethnic Studies* XVII, 2, 1985. The research for this version of the paper was supported by a grant from the Social Science and Humanities Research Council of Canada, which I gratefully acknowledge. I also wish to thank the many officials and members of AMNSIS, MSS, and AAPS for their generous assistance with this topic. All errors and misinterpretations in this paper are entirely mine.

2. Section 2(1) of the *Indian Act* simply states: "'Indian' means a person who, pursuant to this Act, is registered as an Indian..."

3. Bill C-31, *An Act to Amend the Indian Act*, House of Commons of Canada, 1st Session, 33rd Parliament, 33-34 Elizabeth II, 1984-85. Section 6(c) reinstates the status of those women deleted from the Indian Register as a result of Section 12(1)(b) of the *Indian Act* (*i.e.* those women who lost their status as a result of marriage to a non-Status Indian or non-Indian).

4. It is not clear what would constitute "satisfactory historical or acceptable legal proof." If historical proof is taken to mean that an individual must be able to demonstrate his or her descent from the Métis populations of the pre-1870 West, it must be remembered that the mixed populations of the time did not form a homogeneous or easily defined ethnic category. Besides the French-speaking, Roman Catholic mixed blood population (who were the only group that could properly be referred to as "Métis") there were also the English-speaking Protestant "half-breeds," sometimes referred to as "English Métis." There were also the Scots "half-breeds" or *Métis ecossais*, and several other terminologies such as "country-born," and "Rupert'slanders" (Foster, 1978:79-80). Presumably descent from any or all of these groups would entitle an individual to claim Métis status today, but this

has not yet been made clear by the MAA. This is only one of the problems that might be expected from a strict demand for historical proof.

"Legal proof" also raises some questions. While the Province of Alberta's *Métis Betterment Act* (R.S.A. 1970, c. 233, s. 1) defines Métis as "a person of mixed white and Indian blood having not less than one-quarter Indian blood" [sec. 2(a)], this is for the limited purpose of defining who is or who is not eligible for membership in one of the province's Métis Settlements. There are no federal government regulations determining "Métisness" through treaty numbers of ancestry. Sanders suggests that if there is a legal definition of Métis, it means the people who took Half-Breed grants under the Manitoba Act or the Dominion Lands Act and their descendants (Sanders, 1981:419-420).

5. That was not the end of Native women's voices at the national level, however. An organization which is very active today is the Native Women's Association of Canada, which is heavily involved in the Constitutional negotiations, attempting to protect women's and children's rights in any agreement on Native self-government.

6. Personal interview; Regina, 22 August 1988.

7. Personal interview; Regina, 22 August 1988.

8. However, with the contemporary push to self-government, several First Nations such as Gitksan Wet'suwet'sen and others have been developing structures for self-government based on genuinely traditional forms of Aboriginal government.

We shall explain how racism and redbaiting are part of a strategy employed by military expansionists in their efforts to destroy the moral claims of the Innu and to refute the Innu's definition of a 'public problem,' namely, the negative impact of military expansion. We shall first define three key concepts used in our discussion: racism, redbaiting, and ethnic boundary maintenance. The term racism, as used in this paper, refers to actions, attitudes, or policies determined by beliefs about racial or ethnic characteristics (Abercrombie *et al*, 1984:173). Racism may be (1) overt and individual; involving individual acts of oppression against subordinate racial groups or individuals, and (2) covert and institutional, involving structural relations of subordination and oppression between social groups' (Abercrombie *et al.*, 1984:173).

Redbaiting is a form of conspiratorial myth-making that accuses a category of people of having communist sympathies. It becomes a rhetorical theme when a threatened elite believes that the public will respond favourably to an anti-radical crusade (Levin, 1971:178).

Finally, ethnic boundary maintenance is a process of communicating ethnic symbols between different ethnic groups. This may occur on two different levels, local and regional/national (Paine, 1977:258). At the local level, symbols selected to communicate ethnic differences need only be relevant to the neighbouring ethnic group (Eidheim, 1971:68; Kennedy, 1982:9-10). In the context of contemporary 'Fourth World' ethnopolitics, however, ethnic boundary maintenance has increasingly involved the selection of specific cultural symbols readily identifiable by a broader regional, national or even international audience, using the mass media as the primary vehicle of communication (Dyck, 1986:32-33). It is this latter aspect of ethnic boundary maintenance that is our concern in this paper.

Our study makes use of texts and other relevant data obtained at political demonstrations, press conferences and public meetings organized by both the Innu and military expansionists. In addition, we examined texts from the electronic and print media for rhetorical statements representing each side of the debate. The texts were categorized according to the specific issues addressed (e.g., contemporary Innu land use), and an analysis was made of the contrasting rhetorical strategies evident in them.

One conclusion is clear from the outset: the military debate has seriously aggravated existing tensions in the Lake Melville area in which Happy Valley/Goose Bay is located, or put differently, it has accentuated existing (though latent) conflicting interests in the land and contrasting development goals for the region.[3] Thus, while a review of the military expansion is being conducted by a government appointed Environmental Review Panel (ERP) to determine potential environmental and socio-economic impacts, the military debate has already widened the cleavage between Innu and other residents (Canadian Public Health Association, 1987:59).

BACKGROUND

Impacts on the Innu Hunting Way of Life

During the historic period, Quebec and Labrador Innu practised a nomadic hunting and gathering way of life, dependent largely on the exploitation of migratory caribou and other animal species such as beaver, waterfowl, and fish. During the 1800s the Innu were increasingly integrated into the fur trade, but the most serious impacts on their hunting way of life did not occur until the 20th century.

During the last 40 years, the Quebec-Labrador peninsula has assumed increasing importance as a resource frontier. A number of resource developments, for example, the Churchill Falls and Manicouagan hydro-electricity projects, have interfered with Innu harvesting practices and have permanently eliminated large areas of land that would otherwise be available to the Innu for resource exploitation and management. The commencement of full-time schooling has also greatly affected the Innu hunting way of life. In the late 1950s, Innu were coerced into settling more or less permanently in communities where they could be more rapidly assimilated into the mainstream of Newfoundland or Quebec society. Innu parents were told that if they did not send their children to school on a full-time basis, they would have their welfare and family allowance cheques cut off (McGee, 1961:31, 147).

Alcohol abuse, family violence, a high attempted suicide rate, and cultural assimilation are some of the serious consequences that resulted from sedentariness. In the mid-1970s, some Innu communities decided that they wanted to stem the tide of imminent cultural collapse and sought funding to transport entire families out to the country. The Innu were inspired by the belief that if they do not actively use the land, their children will grow up ignorant of valued country skills, enabling the Canadian state to expropriate their land more easily.

Currently, the Innu number 9,600 people, approximately 1,000 of whom live in Labrador and the remainder in Quebec. During the fall, there are approximately 1,200 Innu who participate in harvesting activities in the two low-level flying zones located in Quebec and Labrador. These Innu come from the communities of Davis Inlet (total population 350), Sheshatshit (650), St. Augustin (145), La Romaine (640), Natashquan (470), Mingan (350), Matimekush (Schefferville Montagnais, 470), and Kawawachikamach (Schefferville Naskapi, 400).

Happy Valley/Goose Bay

In 1941, the Canadian and American governments built a large air force base near Goose Bay, Labrador. The base was used by the Canadians, British and Americans to ferry men and materials between North America and Europe, and after the war as an important operational base for the U.S. Strategic Air Command (SAC).

Since the 1960s, the original military and civilian population of Happy Valley/Goose Bay has differentiated into a complex social mosaic. This mosaic consists of different ethnic and class categories and is probably best presented historically. Most of the first civilians were Labrador Settlers (persons of mixed Inuit-European ancestry) who emigrated to Goose Bay to work.[4] Military regulations required them to reside in a new civilian dormitory town, Happy Valley (Zimmerly, 1975:241). In the 1950s, 1960s, and 1970s, this original civilian population was swelled by people from various parts of the world including Newfoundland, England, and the U.S. During this same period, the economic and political fortunes of some of this newly arrived civilian population improved dramatically, largely because of new entrepreneurial possibilities created by Goose Bay's role as a SAC base and service centre for coastal Labrador.

Simply stated, today's hierarchical class structure in Happy Valley/Goose Bay includes an elite and its clientele. The elite consists primarily of economically and/or politically 'successful' business people, health professionals, military personnel, and senior government employees who are predominantly non-Native born Labradorians (plus a few Settlers). The elite's clientele consists primarily of wage-labouring tradespeople, service sector and white collar workers, and unemployed people who are of both Settler and non-Settler origin. Most of the elite support military expansion, but it should be noted that the few opponents to military expansion in Happy Valley/Goose Bay are also elite outsiders. Whether for or against military expansion, the outspoken character of the members of the elite category is a reflection of their class position, that is, their educational, occupational or economic attributes allow them greater mobility than their clientele. Thus, businessperson 'X' or Doctor 'Y' can afford to speak for or against military expansion because he or she can, in principle, leave and find work elsewhere.

The position of the clientele group is more tenuous. Most people within the client category are relatively silent on the military debate and those opposing military expansion fear the social and economic consequences of making their opposition public. Others within this group await the economic benefits promised by the elite.

In 1976, the Americans abandoned their SAC operation in Goose Bay, and the closure of the Labrador Linerboard Mill the same year resulted in the loss of 600 jobs. There were other economic development projects that failed, but of more interest here is the contemporary political use of the rhetoric of failed development to justify the current military expansion at Goose Bay. Military expansionist and local politician, John Hickey, writes for example, "virtually every lumber-based or pulp-based operation that was tried in Labrador has gone broke, usually after massive injections of funds from both the public and the private sector" *(Evening Telegram,* 31 May 1986:6).

Military Training and Plans for Expansion

Low-level military flying did not commence over the interior of the Quebec-Labrador peninsula until 1957 when the Royal Air Force began sporadic flight training with lumbering Vulcan bombers. The West German air force commenced low-level training in 1980 and has expanded the scale of its operations ever since. Two massive low-level training zones, totalling 100,000 square kilometers, were designated in 1981 in which NATO aircraft are allowed to fly at altitudes as low as 30 metres.[5]

According to Innu reports, the aircraft fly so low that their exhausts make waves on the surface of lakes and rivers, ripple the canvas on tents, and sway trees. The Innu say that the loud and unexpected noise generated by low-flying aircraft is extremely traumatic especially for the young and the elderly.

On June 29, 1985, the Canadian government announced its intention to increase the scale of military flight training in the Quebec-Labrador peninsula either through bilateral agreements with individual NATO partners, or as a result of the construction of a $634 million NATO Tactical Fighter and Weapons Training Centre. With a NATO base, over 200 aircraft would be stationed at Goose Bay on an ongoing basis. There would be expanded low-level flying, air-to-air intercepts and large-scale air combat manoeuvres involving large numbers of aircraft. Much of this training would take place at supersonic speeds and produce frequent sonic booms.

INNU PROTESTS AGAINST THE MILITARY TRAINING

The first Innu protests against the military flight training activities date back to 1980 when the West Germans arrived. These protests were made exclusively by the Sheshatshit Innu represented by the Naskapi-Montagnais Innu Association. In the beginning, Innu protests took the form primarily of written correspondence with the federal ministers of Indian Affairs,

Environment, and National Defence. Innu concerns about the impact of the training activities on the environment and their health were met with perfunctory statements to the effect that government and the military were monitoring the training programme on an ongoing basis and had already implemented mitigative measures to avoid negative impacts on human health and wildlife (e.g., reconnaissance flights to determine concentrations of caribou, flight corridors, etc.).

The first stirrings of a more widespread and better organized campaign against the military expansion emerged in the fall of 1983 when a delegation of Innu from Sheshatshit and Sept-Iles/Maliotenam toured West Germany. The delegation received extensive media coverage and obtained the support of a number of organizations including the West German Green Party and Survival International.

Innu opposition to the military expansion in the region escalated further after low-level flights commenced over the hunting territories of Quebec Innu based in the four lower North Shore communities of La Romaine, St. Augustin, Natashquan and Mingan. During the fall of 1983, Innu from La Romaine and Natashquan had been overflown at their bush camps north of their communities and had not been notified in advance by DND that such overflights would occur.

Later that fall, the La Romaine Band Council reacted swiftly to the widespread complaints by members of the community who experienced the noisy, low-flying jets by immediately contacting the Department of Indian Affairs in Sept-Iles as well as the regional Innu political association, the Conseil Attikamek-Montagnais (CAM). Frustrated by the government's apparent unwillingness to stop the expanding low-level flying in their territory, the Innu Band Councils from La Romaine, St.Augustin, and Mingan decided to join with the Sheshatshit Innu in a national protest campaign. Two Innu from Sheshatshit and two from La Romaine conducted a ten-day tour to Ottawa, Toronto, Montreal, and St. John's sponsored by Project North (a national church-funded Native support group), the Ligue des droits et Libertés in Quebec, and the Native Peoples Support Group of Newfoundland and Labrador. The CBC television news programme, 'The National,' aired a special report on the problem just as the tour commenced and gave a relatively sympathetic view of the Innu concerns.

The Innu tour motivated the Newfoundland government to hold a news conference at the end of October to respond to Innu statements about the impact of the military flights on their health and wildlife. Joe Goudie, then Minister of Rural Agricultural and Northern Development, stated in a news release that "absolutely no evidence now exists to support the claims of some natives that low-level flying is having an adverse effect on their traditional activities, caribou migration and on the health of local residents" (26 October 1984). Goudie added that, while the Newfoundland government was firmly committed to the military expansion, "to help revitalize the economy of Happy Valley-Goose Bay," it would conduct a $350,000, two-year study of the impacts of low-flying jets on caribou.

In May 1985, the Sheshatshit Innu organized an "Assembly" of Innu leaders at North West Point, about four miles from Sheshatshit. The gathering was held in an enormous Innu tent on a carpet of fir boughs that surrounded two centrally placed sheet metal wood-burning stoves. Innu families set up tents in the immediate vicinity of the main meeting tent and cooked bannock and caribou meat on outdoor fires. A "traditional" *makushan* or ritual feast of caribou meat and bone marrow was held at the end of the meeting. Innu leaders from two Labrador and four Quebec communities signed a declaration prepared by the La Romaine Band Council demanding a complete cessation of the military training activities in their territory.

While the Assembly was being held, a North American Aerospace Defence (NORAD) exercise called "Amalgam Brave," was being staged out of Goose Bay. It involved a large number of aircraft from the Canadian Armed Forces and U.S. Air Force. Military aircraft occasionally flew over the gathering site at a height of 600 metres, disturbing the relative tranquillity of the Assembly.

While intended primarily as a vehicle to facilitate discussion among Innu leaders about the military expansion, the Assembly proved to be a media event of no small significance. The setting for the Assembly was perfect from a media point of view. The contrast between the 'traditional' tents and cooking activities of the Innu, and the military jets flying by overhead, provided the media with numerous high quality 'visuals' for their stories. The image emerged of a beleaguered indigenous people making their last stand in the face of insurmountable odds. The CBC 'National' did another story on low-level flying, and this time was joined by other media such as the CBC French network and 'Le Point' in Quebec, the *Montreal Gazette*, and Canadian Press.

In October 1985, Innu leaders from La Romaine and Sheshatshit met with a member of Greenpeace Canada at a location in the bush near the Lac Minipi bombing range, where they requested active assistance from the Greenpeace organization. News of Greenpeace participation in the 'Innu Campaign Against the Militarization of Nitassinan' did not become public until the New Year, and was met by Newfoundland and Labrador politicians with outrage and vehement denunciations. Due to its opposition to the Newfoundland seal hunt, Greenpeace enjoys little public support in Newfoundland and Labrador.

In May 1986, Penote Michel, an Innu leader from Sheshatshit, accompanied an Innu family from La Romaine on a more extensive European tour that included Great Britain, Italy, France, Belgium, the Netherlands, and West Germany. The Innu received extensive media coverage and met with a number of senior government officials (e.g., Juliano Amato, deputy Prime Minister of Italy).

Other events in the Innu protest campaign have included the following:

- Innu leaders from Sheshatshit held a news conference in St. John's in November 1985 with George Erasmus, National Chief of the Assembly of First Nations (AFN), to pubilicize AFN support for the Innu in their fight against the military;

- an 'International Joint Action Against Low-level and Supersonic Flight Training' was organized for April 1, 1986, involving rural peoples and Native groups from the U.S., Europe, and other parts of Canada, where military flight training is considered an environmental and health hazard by local residents;

- Quebec and Labrador Innu complained to the International Human Rights Federation which sent a five-person 'Field Mission' to Goose Bay, Sheshatshit, and La Romaine in May, 1986;

- at the end of May, 1986, Innu leaders from Sheshatshit and an Innu family from La Romaine participated in peace demonstrations and a news conference in Halifax at a time when NATO foreign ministers were meeting to discuss general matters concerning the state of the alliance;

- at the beginning of June, 1986, an Innu leader from Sheshatshit and a member of Greenpeace locked themselves in a van in front of the parliament buildings in Ottawa and bombarded Members of Parliament with loud tape-recorded jet noise;

- Innu leaders and community members from Quebec and Labrador made energetic and impassioned interventions before the federal Environmental Review Panel (ERP) when it held meetings in September and October, 1986, in La Romaine, Sheshatshit, Schefferville, Davis Inlet, Happy Valley/Goose Bay, Montreal, and Hull;

- in November, 1986, a six-person delegation from the Conseil Attikamek-Montagnais (CAM) visited France and NATO headquarters in Belgium. The delegation met with a number of peace, union, and environmental groups, two members of the European Parliament, as well as Canada's ambassador to NATO;

- in April, 1987, Innu from Sheshatshit set up five tents at the end of the Goose Bay runway to protest the resumption of low-level flying.

MILITARY EXPANSIONISTS FIGHT BACK

The military expansionists consolidated their strategy during the summer of 1985. Businesswoman Claris Rudkowski's Jamaican holiday was interrupted and she was called back to Goose Bay to become President of the Chamber of Commerce. Rudkowski is of Settler origin and was raised in Sheshatshit/North West River. In her inaugural speech, she referred to the recent North West Point Assembly as a "media event" reminiscent of the anti-sealing movement's tactics, and warned her audience that if pro-military expansion forces did not act quickly and decisively, they would become the "endangered species" (*The Labradorian*, 12 June 1985:18).

By August, 1985, the Happy Valley/Goose Bay elite had formed the 'Concerned Citizens for a Positive Future' (CCFAPF), with Claris Rudkowski as its chairperson. The group included members of the Labrador North Chamber of Commerce, Happy Valley/Goose Bay Town Council, and Mokami Regional Development Association. The CCFAPF's aim was to counter groups opposed to military expansion; it identified and published a list of nine 'anti-military' groups (including Innu), and proposed several strategies to deal with them. One of these strategies was to ask the local ministerial association, comprised of the clergy of most of the local Lake Melville Christian denominations, to host a series of public talks and to explain the nature of its relationship with Project North (*Northern Reporter*, 13 September 1985:7).

The second Innu tour of Europe attracted considerable media attention, and military expansionists in Happy Valley/Goose Bay complained of insufficient funds to publicize their views properly. Their complaints were soon answered. During the May 31, 1986 visit of NATO ambassadors to Goose Bay, then federal justice minister, John Crosbie, announced a federal/provincial grant of $140,000 to the town of Happy Valley/Goose Bay, Labrador North Chamber of Commerce, and Mokami Regional Development Association to establish a new organization, the 'Mokami Project Group,' to promote military expansion in Labrador. Two months later, Steve Michelin, an Iron Ore Company engineering technician, Labrador City councillor and President of the Combined Councils of Labrador, was hired as Project Officer for the group. Michelin's background made him ideal for the job. A Settler by origin, he was once president of the 'Height of Land' branch of the Labrador Heritage Society, and had helped organize a group lobbying for a separate Labrador electoral seat.

Members of the Mokami Project Group, including Claris Rudkowski and Happy Valley/Goose Bay mayor, Hank Shouse, made vigorous interventions at the Environmental Review Panel (ERP) meetings in Happy Valley/Goose Bay, Montreal, Hull and St. John's. They claimed their purpose was to counter the arguments presented by the Innu, their supporters, and various environmental and peace groups.

Military expansionists also sought support from elected municipal governments throughout the province. However, their efforts appear to have been unsuccessful on the north coast of Labrador. As the transcripts from the ERP meetings on the coast suggest, the majority of Inuit and Settlers in northern Labrador oppose low-level flight training. The Labrador Inuit Association, which represents both of these ethnic groups, stated its official opposition to military expansion at the ERP meetings, but pointed out that it "has deliberately not entered into the public forum of debate on these issues because the issues are so polarized, so full of emotion and hidden agendas that rational debate at that level is hopeless" (Andersen, 1986:1645).

THE RHETORIC AND STRATEGY OF CONFLICT

During their campaign against military expansion, the Innu identified several destructive impacts caused by military flight training. These related to health, culture, wildlife, and Aboriginal or national rights. The Innu argued that:

- their children are being traumatized by the unexpected jet noise, elderly Innu are in danger of having heart attacks, and Innu in general risk hearing loss. At one point, Innu leaders from La Romaine stated that one of the children in the community suffered a ruptured eardrum as a result of exposure to the jet noise. According to La Romaine band councillor, Camille Mestenapeo:

  > The noise of the planes...causes temporary deafness. One's ears ring for one to two hours after a jet has flown over...The effects on the health of the...[Innut] in the region are very serious (quoted in Bradbury, 1985:9-11).

- various animal species are becoming ill and dying, beaver are losing weight, water is being contaminated by exhaust fumes, fish are dying, and caribou migration patterns are being altered. Declining game populations are eroding the Innu hunting way of life. Etienne Lalo of La Romaine claimed that:

  > All the animals are scared of the jets, from all the noise made by them. The caribou, the caribou that roams around in heavily

wooded areas, it also gets scared. The beaver just stays put in his lodge; he can't go out and fix his lodge, he just stays put and eventually loses weight. All the animals lose weight – they don't eat (*Native Issues,* 1984, 4(1):19).

- the Innu were the first people to occupy Quebec-Labrador. The state has no right to intrude without permission on Innu territory so as to rent the land out for war games. This viewpoint is expressed by Peter Penashue in an interview with the *The Globe and Mail.*

    Why is the military here without our consent? The Canadian Government has opened the door of our house and let in foreign military to have a cup of tea. You don't do that in your house, do you? If Innu people feel we don't want the military, so be it. We have our rights. Our land claims haven't been settled (*The Globe and Mail,* 22 September 1986).

- military expansion is occurring in spite of Innu land claims, and environmental and health concerns which is evidence of the state's lack of any real commitment to support Native cultures. An April, 1986, news release by the Innu National Council made this point:

    We have in practice been treated as if we were sub-human, expendable life to be destroyed or altered to serve the interests of the military and the alien government who, without right or legitimate title, expropriate our land (*The Evening Telegram,* 29 April 1986).

In presenting these arguments to the public, the Innu engage in what Eidheim refers to as "ethnic dichotomization," the mobilization of specific ethnic symbols from the total cultural repertoire of such symbols and themes at an ethnic boundary in order to create symbolic oppositions (Eidheim, 1971:68-82). Paine (1985:190-235) illustrates how this process operates in his discussion of a Norwegian hydro-electricity project controversy in 1979 that pitted the Saami against the Norwegian state. The power of metaphor, and the creation of moral and symbolic oppositions by way of "ethnodrama" are shown as important ingredients in the creation of ethnic dichotomies and the mobilization of public support for the Saami cause.

Like the Saami, the Innu must employ powerful "David and Goliath" metaphors for what the Canadian state is doing to their health and "traditional" way of life. The raw materials used to construct these oppositions and metaphors consist of a variety of symbols taken from the total repertoire of Innu cultural practices and beliefs. Images of Innu hunting, trapping and fishing, dressed in "traditional" clothing, eating "traditional foods," as well as statements about respect for the land and the elderly are used to convey the message that the Innu are a people who love nature, peace and tradition. When juxtaposed with images of military aircraft and the base at Goose Bay (with the assistance of the electronic media), the image emerges of a peaceful people being crushed by a huge and impersonal war machine.[6] An example of metaphor here is the Innu Assembly at North West Point in May 1985, where Innu tents were juxtaposed to the intense military flying activity associated with the NORAD exercise, "Amalgam Brave". The military aircraft are a metonym for powerful industrial society and the fearful arms race, while the tents are a metonym for "traditional" Innu culture and powerlessness (Paine, 1985:203).

The Innu are thus engaged in the creation of a "public problem" which they hope will be accepted as valid and serious enough by the public to warrant opposition to the military expansion in Quebec-Labrador. However, in order for the Innu to succeed in mobilizing such opposition, the public must make two kinds of judgment about the cause of the problem they face: cognitive and moral judgments (Dyck, 1986:32). In Gusfield's view,

> The cognitive side [of a public problem] consists in beliefs about the facticity of the situation and events comprising the problem – our theories and empirical beliefs...The moral side is that which enables the situation to be viewed as painful, ignoble, immoral. It is what makes alteration or eradication desirable (Gusfield, 1981:1).

The Innu have identified the threat to their hunting, trapping, fishing and gathering activities and wildlife resulting from military flight training as the public problem they want addressed by Canadians and Europeans. The public has been asked to make cognitive and moral judgments regarding what is happening to the Innu people, but these judgments are to be made as a result of a sober consideration of the factual basis of claims of injustice by the Innu.

Our primary concern here is with more specific rhetorical claims made by the Innu in the context of this dispute. Our focus is, on the one hand, on the rhetoric Innu use in bringing a "public problem" to the attention of the public outside Quebec-Labrador, and, on the other hand, the techniques used by military expansionists to erode the factual and moral basis of this problem, as defined by the Innu. What is particularly notable in the conflict between the Innu and military expansionists is the way in which the latter have responded to the Innu arguments. For example, the following counterrguments have been advanced in response to the Innu:

- Innu claims that their children are traumatized by low-level jet noise and other concerns about health impacts are exaggerated. John Crosbie, federal Minister of Transportation, summed up this point of view in the following way:

There's more noise, by the way, from a snowmobile. There's more danger to you, there's more danger could be caused to you by going around all winter on your posterior on a snowmobile than is likely to be caused to your ears. And look at all the children running through this country with plugs in their ears and the volume turned up listening to the modern music. My God, that does more damage than a hundred low-level flights could do, poor little blighters, to have those things in their ears (CBC TV, speech to NATO ambassadors in Goose Bay, 31 May 1986).

- the claims of the Innu about environmental impacts have no basis in reality; there is no evidence of negative impacts on wildlife. John Crosbie's address to the Newfoundland Conservative Party's annual meeting in October, 1986 is typical of many challenges to Innu statements about the impact of military jets on the wildlife:

    To the amusement of his fellow Conservatives, Mr. Crosbie jokingly referred to the controversial issue of low-level military flights in Labrador as a 'great environmental menace.' Referring to an increase in the caribou herds in those parts of Labrador where the military conducts training flights, Mr. Crosbie said, 'The stags have been made downright macho by low-level flying' (*The Sunday Express*, 12 October 1986:1).

- Innu claims of ownership to the territory are extremely restricted in nature and certainly do not include veto powers over any kind of development. The Settlers have legitimate claims to the land as well and they are generally supportive of the military expansion. Mayor Hank Shouse has the following comment to make about Innu title to the land:

    We've heard all the arguments, all the innuendos, all the lies. They talk, they brag that it's their land, that they were here first…I'd like to think if I were here for thousands of years at least I could be self-supporting (*The Globe and Mail*, 22 September 1986).

- the Innu no longer pursue a traditional way of life. They use aircraft to travel out to the bush and depend extensively on store-bought provisions. Welfare cheques and unemployment insurance payments sustain this way of life in the country. The Innu no longer harvest extensively and are living "high on the hog". The traditional values emphasizing the proper treatment of the elderly have disappeared. This point of view is expressed by Hank Shouse and Claris Rudkowski. Shouse says:

> They're living the rich sportsman's idea of a vacation at some-
> one else's expense. White people's tax dollars are supporting
> the Indians (*The Globe and Mail*, 22 September 1986).

Rudkowski adds:

> The 'prestige given to the elderly' was unhappily demonstrated
> in the recent forest fire evacuation when elders were ignored
> and swept aside in the rush for safety (*The Labradorian*, 27
> November 1985).

- the Innu are lazy and "sponge" off the government. Their reasons
  for going into the country, are not to preserve an age-old way of life,
  but to avoid having to work. This point of view is expressed in an
  editorial by Iris Brett, editor of *The Northern Reporter*, and wife of
  Herb Brett, a member of the Mokami Project Group. Brett entitles
  her editorial 'The Jig's up Gentlemen,' as though she has finally
  caught errant schoolboys with their hands in the cookie jar. She
  writes:

  > Who is foolish enough to think that, if low flying were to cease
  > tomorrow, [Innu leaders] Bart Jack, Ben Michel and Greg
  > Penashue would go back to living off the land? There is a
  > difference between 'living off the land' and 'living off the fat of
  > the land' but these gentlemen have yet to learn the distinction
  > (*Northern Reporter*, 11 June 1986).

- the Innu are not ecologically aware. They leave garbage all over the
  place in their communities and in the country and wreck their
  houses. This point of view is expressed by Claris Rudkowski in a
  letter to the editor of *The Labradorian*. She writes:

  > The present Innu 'sensitivity and concern for the land' is seen
  > in the abandoned encampment mess after the Northwest Point
  > Innu Assembly—the mounds of garbage in the villages and trail
  > of litter left at the camp sites in the country (*The Labradorian*,
  > 27 November 1985).

- all cultures change. Innu must realize that they cannot forever
  continue their hunting way of life. They should 'get with it' and take
  up salaried occupations. If they were not so 'pigheaded' they would
  recognize the employment opportunities that will result from military
  expansion.

The ethnopolitical strategies and rhetoric employed by military expansionists have two primary goals: (1) to destroy the factual basis of the
"public problem" as defined by the Innu as well as the raw materials they
use to create ethnic dichotomies and moral/symbolic oppositions;[7] and (2)
to pollute these moral/symbolic oppositions by introducing third parties into

the equation whose motivations for being involved in the conflict can be shown to be illegitimate. Let us start by dealing with the first goal.

Military expansionists attempt to subvert Innu efforts to employ powerful metaphors and create moral/symbolic oppositions. This is done by attacking the raw materials used to create these metaphors and oppositions. Statements are made to the effect that the Innu way of life is not traditional, they are like us. They are not ecologically aware, they leave garbage all over the place. They are not being abused by us, we provide them with all kinds of financial programmes and services for which they are not grateful.[8] In challenging the Innu in this way, military expansionists actually attempt to undermine the moral claim made by the Innu against the Canadian state, as well as Innu strategies to employ what Paine calls the "politics of embarrassment" (1985:214; Watson, 1979). They attack the validity of the first and second premises in the following syllogism upon which Innu moral claims against the Canadian state are based: (1) moral states do not allow indigenous cultures to be threatened by military jet noise; (2) the Canadian state allows the Innu culture to be threatened by military jet noise; therefore, (3) the Canadian state is not moral. Military expansionists argue that these premises are fallacious because: (1) military jet noise does not undermine indigenous cultures; and (2) in any event, the Innu no longer possess an indigenous culture.[9]

Racism enters into this equation when military expansionists make statements about Innu behavior and motivation which denigrate them as a people and deny the validity and continuing vitality of their culture. Until recently, most of this racism did not spread into the broader political arena (*i.e.*, outside Labrador) where it could quickly erode their own moral claims in support of military expansion.[10]

Regarding the second goal of military expansionists, efforts are made to portray the Innu as being manipulated by outsiders; not ordinary outsiders, but ones with special "hidden agendas". "Hidden agenda" is, in fact, a powerful *banner word*, a truncated enthymeme that suggests some kind of potentially sinister threat, but leaves the specific character of the threat unstated.[11] The inference is that some devious and dark force is at work behind the scenes that seeks to undermine all legitimate authority and morality. In Labrador, the military itself, as well as its advocates, attempt to argue that peace groups and "professional agitators" are behind the scenes, encouraging the Innu to oppose the military flight training. In effect, military expansionists are saying, "If it was not for these agitators, there would be no problem with our Innu neighbours with whom we normally get along so well".

Some military expansionists have taken the 'hidden agenda' and 'outsider' theme a step further by suggesting that communist agents are behind the scenes attempting to destroy NATO, democracy and, for that matter, Christianity. The archetypal threat to western democracy, Christianity, individualism and free enterprise is advanced in the form of the "communist conspiracy" as the true dark hand guiding the actions of the Innu and their supporters. Despite its facetiousness, Iris Brett's letter to God in a *Northern Reporter* editorial forcefully expresses this viewpoint.

> Of course, communist and communist sympathizers are quick to pounce on the unrest among your Innu people. They infiltrate their encampments under the guise of humanitarians, advisors and the like. They are skilled in manipulating the international media and convey the message at home and abroad that the white settlers of Labrador are crucifying the Innu and 'stealing their land' (*Northern Reporter*, 6 August 1986).

Mokami Project Group member, John Hickey, is perhaps the most vocal advocate of the communist conspiracy theory. According to Hickey:

> We've heard that beavers have left their houses; that ducks are dying within the egg; that we're all going to be sterile because of the radiation of these low-level aircraft. All false, false, false, false information. This is propaganda which is fed to the Innu people by Marxists, Leninists, socialists, communists (*The Sunday Express*, 19 April 1987:3).

The communist conspiracy theory is of course an age-old strategy used to destroy the moral claims made by protest groups against a government. The so-called "Red Scare" which occurred in the U.S. in 1919-20 was provoked by fears of a Bolshevik Revolution in the U.S. and by numerous labour strikes at the time. Similar outbreaks of redbaiting occurred during the McCarthy era and the Vietnam war. In 1974, for example, the Central Intelligence Agency conducted a massive and illegal domestic intelligence operation against the anti-Vietnam movement, a movement already accustomed to surveillance by the Federal Bureau of Investigation "Red Squads" (Zaroulis and Sullivan, 1984:415). More recently, peace groups have come under fire because of questions about their political agendas and national loyalties. For example, on July 4, 1983, the "Women's Encampment for Peace and Justice" began a Greenham Common-style protest near the Seneca (New York) Army Depot. The women's refusal to carry American flags led to a rash of flag waving by local residents and to accusations that the women must be 'crazy communists' and should be "maced" or "nuked" (Jones, 1983:16).

As far as the conflict over military flight training in Quebec-Labrador is concerned, the communist threat is advanced as a particularly powerful synonym for outside interference. Its purpose is to shift the axis of opposition away from *Innu versus military* to *outsiders (communists) versus military.* Because of its role in the anti-sealing controversy, Greenpeace serves quite adequately as a substitute for communists in the context of Newfoundland and Labrador politics. The communist/Greenpeace threat is mobilized as a challenge to the actual means by which the Innu oppose the state. Here, we take note of Paine's mention of the Ghandian dictum that a "worthy end must be seen to be using worthy means...in the practice of moral opposition" (Paine, 1985:215). In Newfoundland and Labrador it is not difficult to argue that support from Greenpeace and "communist-inspired advisors" is certainly an illegitimate means to accomplish an end, no matter how just that end may be. Any group resorting to such means must have the moral basis of its protests questioned.

CONCLUSION

The rhetoric concerning military expansion reported above resembles other debates over resource development between groups along a frontier.[12] As in Labrador, these debates normally feature "frontiersmen," that is, those favouring the "rational" development of the hinterland, and an opposing group which may include indigenous people, environmentalists, or some coalition of the two. Maybury-Lewis describes the position of frontiersmen toward indigenous people.

> Settler societies are everywhere unscrupulous about the rights of the autochtonous peoples whom they dispossess. The frontiersmen and their supporters in the metropolis can always be relied upon to be resolutely anti-Indian or anti any other native people (Maybury-Lewis, 1985:146).

Maybury-Lewis' frontier is the hinterland of Brazil and is structurally similar to the Labrador case. But are all frontiers and the factions they generate structurally similar? We think not and propose two types of what we will call "frontier situations".

The first is relatively stable insofar as no major resource developments polarize existing groups. Indeed, intergroup social relations are characterized by accommodation and mutual avoidance rather than by overt conflict. Sentiments ranging from resentment to racism may exist but are not elevated to the level of publicized rhetoric. Braroe's (1975) description of the Whites and Plains Cree of Sweet Grass illustrates the stable frontier situation. Here, the "conquered" Indians appear to accept their "inferior" status while secretly practising their real culture. The stability of relations is maintained by mutual ignorance and, we suggest, by the absence of some major development project. Interactions between Eidheim's (1971) coast Saami and Norwegians, and Tonkinson's (1974) Aborigines and White Australians, also occur in stable frontier settings.

The second or dynamic frontier situation occurs when a major development is proposed. Intergroup conflicts intensify. Derogatory or racist stereotypes enter the public arena as vitriolic denunciations of the Aboriginal population. In the controversies between Nishga and loggers in British Columbia (Raunet, 1984), and Indians and mining companies on the Colorado plateau (Churchill, 1986), development advocates accused Natives of having a dubious claim to land" (Maybury-Lewis, 1985:139), of being assimilated and no longer relying on the land for subsistence (Asch, 1983:204) or, in any event, of not using contested lands as 'rationally' as Whites would (Raunet, 1984). All these accusations have been hurled at the Innu.

Ultimately, the military expansion debate in Labrador is about power and domination. The Innu and their supporters face formidable odds and it is hardly surprising that the international campaign against military expansion has so far 'failed'. State support of military expansion is justified in the name of national interests (*i.e.*, Canada's contribution to NATO) and by provincial concerns about high unemployment. For both politicians and the public, the rhetoric of the promise of jobs overpowers Innu attempts to convince Canadians that military expansion is a 'public problem'.

NOTES

1. This paper is a revised version of a paper presented at the Annual Meeting of the Canadian Ethnology Society in Quebec City, 14 May 1987. We thank Raoul Andersen, James MacLean, Robert Paine and the anonymous CRSA reviewers for their helpful comments and suggestions, but assume responsibility for the interpretations presented here. This manuscript was submitted in August 1987 and accepted in May 1988.

2. Military expansionists in the Happy Valley/Goose Bay region have been supported financially by the federal and provincial governments. Since its formation in the spring of 1986, the most important non-governmental group advocating military expansion, the Mokami Project Group, has received at least $654,000 from the federal and provincial governments to lobby and conduct media relations in support of low-level flying and the proposed NATO base. To our knowledge, this is the first time in Canadian history that government has provided a

substantial amount of funding to a frontier group (see note 12 below) for the express purpose of challenging the political activities of Native people. Such financial support is explained by Brass who argues that "the state is not simply an arena for group conflict nor an instrument for class domination but a relatively autonomous entity that tends, however, both to favour some classes and ethnic groups at particular points in time and also to develop relationships with elites within particular communities to serve its own interests. Those interests include local control, administrative convenience, and the gathering of popular support" (Brass, 1985:9).

3. Another land use controversy between Innu and non-Innu occurred earlier in this century. Repeated conflicts arose between the Innu and Labrador Settlers when the latter established traplines along the Churchill River on lands the Innu considered to be their hunting and trapping territory (Zimmerly, 1975:202-204).

4. The use of the term "Settler" is problematic in the context of contemporary ethnic relations in Labrador. Residents of northern and central Labrador, who are of mixed Inuit-European ancestry, refer to themselves as Settlers or Labradorians. The Labrador Inuit Association accepts the Settlers as full members, and refers to them as Kablunangajuit. Since the commencement of the debate over military expansion in Goose Bay, a rival organization has emerged which claims some of the same membership as that of the LIA. This organization, the Labrador Métis Association, refers to the Settlers of central Labrador as 'Métis' (Kennedy, 1987).

5. NATO air forces currently training out of Goose Bay include Canada, the United States, West Germany, Britain, and the Netherlands.

6. The role of the media, electronic and print, is extremely important in the development of metaphor and moral/symbolic oppositions. The extent to which the media conveys the juxtaposition of metonyms to create "David and Goliath" metaphors, as defined by the Innu, depends on whether or not the individual journalists, producers, and editors endorse (svmpathize with) the ethnodramas staged by the Innu, and accept the Innu definition of the "public problem". We should note here that a statement was made in October 1984, by La Romaine Innu to the effect that "an Innu child had his eardrum broken as a result of exposure to low-level jet noise". This claim was "refuted" by CBC journalists in Newfoundland after consultation with a number of doctors. As a result, a large measure of scepticism developed among certain journalists working within the province. The claim jeopardized the credibility of Innu statements about the negative health effects of jet noise, and, as a result, eroded the factual basis of their "public

problem". The "burst eardrum" statement laid the foundation for the claim heard so frequently in government circles that the Innu are exaggerating the health and environmental effects of low-level jet noise.

7.   The Newfoundland government's philosophy and practice *vis-à-vis* Aboriginal groups is explicitly assimilationist; no category of "citizen" shall receive special rights (e.g., hunting rights) within the province. When a state actively denies the distinctive identity and any special rights claimed by a Native group, the group must go to great lengths to emphasize its ethnic uniqueness within the population at large. Innu ethnic dichotomization, therefore, is an ongoing, dynamic process of identity negotiation with the non-Innu population in Labrador and provincial government in St. John's, and predates by many years the current conflict over military expansion in the region.

8.   In his study of Dene-White ethnic interactions in the Northwest Territories, Watson argues that "Belief in Indians' indebtedness and boundless ingratitude is an ideological weapon in the hands of Whites in their competition with Indians" (Watson, 1979:105; 1981).

9.   The first premise is based on the following syllogism: (1) indigenous cultures are threatened when human health and wildlife are harmed; (2) military jet noise harms human health and wildlife; therefore, (3) military jet noise threatens indigenous culture. The second premise is based in part on the following syllogism: (1) military jet noise threatens indigenous peoples' culture; (2) the Innu culture constitutes an indigenous culture, therefore, (3) military jet noise threatens Innu culture.

10.   In November 1986, *L'actualité* published an article on the topic by Guy Deshaies that was widely denounced in Quebec because of its racist content. To our knowledge this is the only example of racist polemic on the military issue that has been disseminated to the public outside of Newfoundland and Labrador.

11.   An enthymeme is a syllogism in which either a premise or the conclusion is suppressed. Banner words are words or phrases that 'ignite' the prejudices of an audience, that "contain no proposition but are such that they are likely to induce a proposition by inference" (Paine, 1981:14-15, 23). "It is not at all unusual for an argument to be *rhetorically* more powerful and persuasive when stated enthymematically than when enunciated in complete detail" (Copi, 1961:216).

12.   We define frontier as a geographic, political and cultural concept designating the point of contact between an immigrant population or expanding nation-state and an indigenous population. In North America, the frontier has generally appeared whenever the lands of indige-

nous people become valued because of their strategic military or agricultural importance, the presence of mineral or hydro-electric potential, or because they are considered wastelands suitable for military testing or the dumping of industrial wastes. Frederick J. Turner's frontier thesis (Hofstadter and Lipset, 1968; Mattson and Marion, 1985) and John L. O'Sullivan's concept of manifest destiny (Brown, 1980:16) are particularly relevant here. Turner's historiography sought the roots of American culture on the western frontier rather than in Europe (Mattson and Marion, 1985). In his view, the frontier was both "free," that is open for development, and the "meeting point between Savagery and Civilization" (Turner as quoted in Drinnon, 1980:461). The "Indian-hating" manifest on the frontier at Goose Bay illustrates Drinnon's observation that each time "proper Americans" and Native Americans met, a "perennial rebirth" of Indian-hating and subjugation was a necessary counterpart of nation-building (Drinnon, 1980:463). Manifest destiny, on the other hand, justified United States territorial expansion and subjugation of Indian populations (Drinnon, 1980; Hietala, 1985; Horsman, 1981). Versions of both ideologies are used today in the rhetoric of military expansionists.

WHO ARE THE MÉTIS?

David Boisvert and Keith Turnbull

The Métis are an Aboriginal people with a long and important history in Canada – a people that has had its Aboriginal rights denied for too long. We will describe in this paper how the Métis emerged and developed in the various parts of Canada, particularly the Northwest. We will also show how, in the Northwest, they were cheated out of their Aboriginal rights, and elsewhere denied them entirely.

The new Canadian Constitution may or may not do very much to rectify this situation, but it provides a glimmer of hope. Section 35 of the *Constitution Act, 1982* declares that the "existing aboriginal and treaty rights of the aboriginal peoples of Canada are hereby recognized and affirmed." It then goes on to define the Aboriginal peoples of Canada as including the Indian, Inuit, and Métis peoples.[1] It remains to be seen whether this will suffice as the basis of recognition for the Aboriginal rights of the Métis. The injustices done to the Métis as a people cry not only for writing, but for *righting.*

Some people disagree with the view that the Métis are an Aboriginal people – their chief spokesperson today being Thomas Flanagan (1983a:321-322), who has sought recently to prove that the Riel Rebellion of 1885 was unjustified (Flanagan, 1983b). We disagree with Flanagan on many points, but in this paper we take particular issue with his claim that the Métis are not an Aboriginal people, and we do so within Flanagan's own definition of Aboriginality. In our view, to continue to deny Aboriginal rights to Aboriginal peoples goes against both the spirit and intent of the new Constitution.

But the new Constitution in its turn raises many thorny questions about the Métis. The fact that the Métis are included in the Constitution's enumeration of Aboriginal peoples means that we must now start defining and identifying these Métis people. This is not a simple matter. Unlike the Indians, the Métis have not been the subject of a special registration procedure. Rarely have they been identified through the census, and every time they have been, the census data have been rendered problematic owing to the difficulty of coming to grips with the Métis as a demographic concept. The difficulties are real enough. Depending on the definition used, there may be as many as 3,000,000 or as few as 80,000 Métis in Canada today.

This issue of Métis identification has emerged as the most important question confronting the political development of the Métis. It gave rise to a major split in Aboriginal organizations when in March 1983 the Métis National Council established itself as a separate group from the Native Council of Canada, largely over differences regarding who should be considered Métis. In this paper, we will analyze the problem of Métis identification in Canada today. At issue is the future constitutional guarantees of the Métis people as well as the fate of the non-Status Indian population. We will argue for an expansive definition of Métis for constitutional purposes — one that, while rooted in history, recognizes that Métis exist everywhere in Canada and that new cohorts of Métis after 1876 tended to be identified as non-Status Indians. We conclude that many non-Status Indians can legitimately be considered Métis.

PROBLEMS WITH DEFINING MÉTIS TODAY

As is well known, "Métis" is a French word used to describe a person of mixed Indian and European ancestry. In the nineteenth century, in Western Canada, Métis was the name given to the mixed-blood population of French descent, and "half-breed" designated those of British, mainly Scottish, ancestry. The Ojibway called the Métis *wissakodewinni,* which means "half-burnt woodmen," or "bois-brule" in French, and Bois-Brules was the name the early French-speaking Métis of the Northwest used to describe themselves (Sealey, 1978a:7). However, today the term Métis has supplanted all these other terms and has come into general use to describe every person of mixed Indian and European ancestry.

The first problem with identifying the Métis is that this notion of mixed ancestry is not in itself sufficient to identify the Métis. The person involved must also positively identify himself or herself as Métis. There are many persons of mixed blood today who, identifying with either their Indian or

European forebears, would not choose to call themselves Métis. Despite their mixed Indian and European ancestries, for example, neither Premier Peter Lougheed of Alberta nor Johnny Calihoo (who helped to establish the Indian Association of Alberta) would, on the basis of self-identification, be considered Métis. But self-identification may tell us more about who to exclude than who to include as Métis. Is it necessarily the case that anyone of mixed ancestry who identifies himself or herself as a Métis is a Métis? In the absence of any more precise formulation of a Métis identity, we conclude that there is no reason to exclude anyone who self-identifies as a Métis from being considered Métis.

The 1981 census reports that 98,260 individuals self-identify as Métis. Unfortunately, the census is severely limited due to the ambiguity of the question asked: "To which ethnic or cultural group did you or your ancestors belong *on first coming to this continent?*" Intended to be an "improvement" on the question in earlier censuses which referred explicitly to paternal heritage alone, this formulation hardly solved the problem: the question still directed people of mixed ancestry to think of their European ancestor, almost always male. Perhaps the surprising thing is that, in spite of a well-founded, historical mistrust of government, in spite of their social and economic status, and in spite of the wording of the census question, so many people identified themselves as Métis.

The figure of 100,000 self-identifying Métis is well below the estimates made by the Aboriginal organizations themselves. The Native Council of Canada has estimated that there are between 750,000 to 1,000,000 Métis and non-Status Indians in Canada (Daniels, 1979:1), while the 1981 census identifies only 170,000. As we shall see later in this paper, the non-Status Indians form an important element of Canada's mixed-blood population after 1876, and they are in every province associated politically with Métis. They are often considered together in social statistics. The 1981 census shows that the number of non-Status Indians is larger than that for Métis in all provinces and territories other than the three Prairie provinces and the Northwest Territories. However, one of the interesting things brought out by the 1981 census is that people identify as Métis in every part of Canada. Sixty-six per cent of Métis live in the Prairie provinces, but there are sizeable Métis populations in the Northwest Territories, Ontario, British Columbia and Québec. This indicates that a definition of Métis for constitutional purposes that is based on self-identification would lead to the identification of Métis on a small but significant scale in every part of Canada.

The fact that there are Métis in every part of Canada may not appear very surprising, but it does clash with the one alternative definition of Métis offered to date which tries to provide a more precise definition of Métis

Table 1: Native People by Type: Canada and Provinces/Territories

Area	Total Population	Total Native People	Inuit	Status Indian	Non-Status Indian	Métis
Canada	24,083,496	491,460	25,390	292,700	75,110	98,260
Newfoundland	563,747	4,430	1,850	1,010	1,185	385
Prince Edward Island	121,223	625	30	400	140	50
Nova Scotia	839,801	7,795	130	5,905	1,155	605
New Brunswick	689,373	5,515	5	4,235	865	415
Québec	6,369,068	52,395	4,875	34,400	5,810	7,310
Ontario	8,534,263	110,060	1,095	70,190	26,090	12,680
Manitoba	1,013,703	66,280	230	39,710	5,855	20,485
Saskatchewan	956,441	59,200	145	37,470	4,135	17,455
Alberta	2,213,651	72,050	510	35,810	8,595	27,135
British Columbia	2,713,615	82,645	515	54,085	19,085	8,955
Yukon	23,074	4,045	95	2,770	990	190
Northwest Territories	45,537	26,430	15,910	6,720	1,205	2,595

Source: Canada, Statistics Canada, Census (Ottawa, 1981).

identity. This is something that cannot be done simply on "ethnological" grounds. Linguistically, most Métis today speak English, some speak French, while many speak at least one Indian language as well. In the nineteenth century, a distinctive Métis speech known as *Michif* began to develop in Western Canada (Crawford, 1981; 1983; Préfontaine, 1978).[2] It is a mixture of French and Cree, but while it is still spoken here and there, it is not the language most commonly used. Culturally, the Métis appear to have borrowed elements from both Indian and European cultures and united them in what might be called a creative synthesis. But there has always been quite a variation in how these cultural influences have been mixed, with some Métis drawing more from the European and others more from the Indian cultural sphere. Perhaps the most that can be said is that Métis culture is a synthesis of Indian and European cultures, but it is very difficult to define this synthesis in any formal way.

It is possible, however, to derive a more specific definition of Métis identity if we examine the Métis in historical terms. The creation of Métis identity is an historical process. History shows that a distinct Métis identity did emerge in the Northwest — a vast territory stretching up from the tip of Lake Superior to the Rocky Mountains and from the American border to the treeline — in the nineteenth century. It is only in the West that the Métis consciously evolved into a distinct people — a "new nation" as they called themselves. These people are known as the *historic Métis* and they can provide the foundation for a more precise definition of Métis identity — namely that the Métis people today are the descendants of the historic Métis people of the Northwest. This is the claim being advanced by the Métis National Council. It is a strong claim that deserves careful evaluation. But it cannot easily be reconciled with the notion that there are Métis people elsewhere than in the Northwest.

ORIGINS OF THE MÉTIS

Historically, a Métis population developed wherever Europeans and Indians met for any long period of time. Mexico today, with its large *mestizo* population, is a case in point. In North America, the fur trade was especially conducive to contact between European men and Indian women — so much so that the Métis are often regarded as the children of the fur trade. But in Acadia there is evidence of considerable inter-mixing between French settlers and the Micmac and Abenaki Indians prior to 1755, which shows that under certain circumstances even agricultural settlements can produce a mixed-blood population (Dickason, 1981).

However, the fact remains that in the North American context the Métis were a product of the activities of fur traders, and one sees a Métis population developed in each of the great fur trade hinterlands: first, the St. Lawrence drainage basin, then the Great Lakes Region of what is today the United States, followed by the Hudson Bay area, and finally the Northwest. These areas were exploited variously by the English and the French, but there were significant differences in the way these European powers exploited the fur trade. The English, who could usually count on better quality goods with which to trade than could the French, established a limited number of forts close to supply lines with Europe and expected the Indians to come to these forts to trade. English fur trade companies relied heavily on Indian middlemen – the Iroquois in the St. Lawrence and a variety of tribes in the Hudson Bay area – to collect furs in the hinterland and transport them to the forts for shipment to Europe in the proper season. This meant that any mixing with the Indian peoples occurred only around the forts, and hence the English-speaking Métis population developed only at those points. The French, on the other hand, had the habit of sending men out to trade with the Indians. This they did both because of the more competitive nature of the French fur trade and in order to compete with superior English goods. The result was that throughout the seventeenth and eighteenth centuries there were, in almost any given year, hundreds of Frenchmen in Indian country, often living with the Indians themselves, staying as briefly as a season or as long as a lifetime. It is not surprising, therefore, to find that the largest Métis population to develop was of French origin.

There were also important differences in official policy and cultural attitudes towards the Indians. Although the English had an important presence in the St. Lawrence fur trade, centred on Albany, New York, it is principally from their activities in the Hudson Bay area that we get a glimpse of English policies and attitudes. Officially, the Hudson's Bay Company, which was granted a trading monopoly in the area called Rupert's Land in 1670, prohibited its employees (actually indentured labour) from having relations with Indian women. But, in the face of the inevitable, the Company relaxed its prohibitions by the end of the eighteenth century (Judd, 1983:25-27). The children of the resulting unions – at least those involving the most important company men – were treated with consideration, which meant that the Company endeavoured to ensure that males received a "civilized" education, sometimes sending them to Europe for this purpose. But as they were "country-born," the Company was under no obligation, as it was with its European workers and agents, to return them to Britain at the end of their terms with the Company. These country-born "half-breeds" came to provide the Company with an important indigenous workforce, but owing to what can only be termed racist attitudes prevalent among the English, these "half-breeds" were denied access to the higher ranks of the Company management at the forts. This tended to establish the English half-breeds of the Hudson Bay area as a separate caste. Too European to integrate with the Indians, and too Indian to integrate with the Europeans, the English half-breeds came to form a conspicuous element within the population around Hudson Bay (Giraud, 1945).

The French had quite different policies. France did not encourage emigration to its colonies and therefore sought wherever possible to assimilate the local population as French citizens. Officially, an Indian could become a full citizen of the colony of New France the moment he converted to Christianity, meaning of course, Catholicism (Dickason, 1981; Peterson, 1978:46-47). [3] This policy met with only limited success, although the Huron settlement around Québec City, the Iroquois at Caughnawaga, and the Micmac today are proof that the work of the missionaries was not completely without results. From the start there were no barriers preventing Frenchmen from having Indian wives. For the French the controversy was how, rather than whether, this should take place. Officially, only Christian marriages were approved. The missionaries went to great lengths to ensure that Indian wives were baptized, and in the process given French names, and that marriages were properly solemnized – a fact that makes it difficult today to trace the extent of intermarriages between Indians and Frenchmen in early Québec. However, in the fur trade hinterlands, the custom was to take wives *à la façon du pays*, that is, according to Indian customs – a practice that the missionaries decried and that the government of the colony attempted to suppress from time to time (with little success). There is little doubt that the early French and Indian peoples intermingled a great deal. It has been estimated that no less than forty per cent of French Canadian families could trace at least one Indian ancestor in their family trees (Smith, 1974:88). [4]

The Indians, for their part, seemed to place few restraints on having their women accept "White men." Marriage customs among the Indians were less formalized than in Christian Europe. Customs varied from people to people, but on the whole seemed to have involved little more than the consent of a young woman or her parents to propositions made by a man. Divorce, too, procedurally at least, was a relatively simple matter of taking your bags and leaving. "Wife-sharing" – in which one man lent his wife to another for a duration that could last years – was a common practice. Polygamy, while not especially prevalent, was virtually expected of chief men. In this environment, "les coureurs de bois" did not find it particularly difficult to form relations with Indian women. The relationship was advantageous for more than one reason. Indian women provided the basic know-how needed to survive in the bush, and were a source of auxiliary labour. To the Indian community it often provided a kinship link to the White traders, whose goods had become necessary for survival.[5]

What happened to the children of such unions is very difficult to document. We know of only a few French and even English men who returned with their Indian wives to New France or Britain. Some "freedmen" stayed permanently in the country of their Métis families. Most men could eventually leave, abandoning their Indian wives and Métis children. It can be assumed that many Indian women would then return to their families and their tribes, where by all accounts their Métis children were viewed as real assets by the communities. Obviously much would depend on the age of the child — a very young child would assimilate entirely with the Indians, but an older child might keep enough of the father's way of life to remain distinct from the rest of the group. In the Hudson Bay area, the practices of the Hudson's Bay Company and English attitudes served to block ready assimilation with either of the parental cultures, but in the hinterland controlled from New France, the tendency was for Métis children to assimilate with either one or the other of their parents' peoples (Dickason, 1981:29). In the Great Lakes Region, history records the presence of a distinct French-speaking Métis community after the fall of New France in 1763 — a remnant of the French presence in the area. It did not have the numbers or the collective consciousness that the Métis of the Northwest would later develop. It was swamped by American immigration following the War of 1812, and disappeared by 1840, except for a small element which found its way to places like Sault Ste. Marie (Peterson, 1978; 1981).

The Métis developed quite differently in the Northwest. Although the French had penetrated this region with La Vérendrye in the late 1730s, all French outposts in the area were abandoned with the outbreak of the Seven Years' War. The French never did return. The Métis population of the Northwest developed mainly after the fall of New France. In 1765, new and predominantly Scottish fur trading interests took over the old French fur trading empire in Montréal and advanced into the Northwest. In 1783, these interests merged into a stable monopoly to carry out the Northwest trade, and formed the Northwest Company (examined in detail by Innis, 1956:166-280). Throughout the course of its activities, the Northwest Company relied on French Canadian canoemen and guides to man the brigades of canoes needed to maintain its long supply lines, which stretched from Montréal to the Athabasca country. These men pursued the fur trade much as they had in the past. Competition drove the Hudson's Bay Company to alter its practices and to establish forts and outposts in the interior as well. By the early 1800s, it is estimated that there were from 1,000 to 1,500 men working for these companies in the Northwest (Innis, 1956:237-238), a country then occupied principally by bands of Cree, Saulteaux (Ojibway), and Assiniboine Indians.

The Métis population of this area grew rather rapidly. Giraud informs us that Métis grouped at Pembina as early as 1812 and Morton tells us that by 1821 there were already 500 of them there (Giraud, 1945:513, 648; Morton, 1967a:61). Pembina was a Métis settlement on the Red River just south of the present Manitoba border; from here the Métis organized their buffalo hunts to the hunting ranges of the Sioux. The buffalo hunt is all-important in Métis history and probably accounts for the early organization of the Métis into a distinct community. We shall deal with this later. But 500 Métis at Pembina suggests that there were at least that number again elsewhere in the Northwest, working around the various forts and outposts of the fur trade. Thus, between 1765 and 1820 a distinct Métis population had already been created in what are now the Prairie provinces.

The year 1811 is important in Métis history because that is the year in which the first settlers set out to Lord Selkirk's colony for dispossessed Scotsmen at Red River. The establishment of a settlement at the confluence of the Red and Assiniboine rivers appears to have been very much in the interests of the Hudson's Bay Company, but it threatened the supply lines of the Northwest Company. A conflict issued in which both settlers and Métis were ultimately pawns, but which led them to violence at the Battle of Seven Oaks (1816). Cuthbert Grant, son of a wintering partner in the fur trade and the most elevated Métis in the territory, led the supply brigade that massacred a group of armed settlers at Seven Oaks. The political history of the Métis dates from that battle – a battle that inspired Pierre Falcon, the national poet of the historic Métis, to compose "La Grenouillère," a song giving the Métis account of the battle (MacEwan, 1981:28-29).[6] From that time on, the Métis were a political force in the Northwest.

Conflict between the rival companies ended in 1821 when they merged into the Hudson's Bay Company. The merger led to the rationalization of the fur trade and a very significant reduction in the labour force it required. Giraud estimates that the population of the Red River Colony grew by more than 700 individuals between 1822 and 1824, largely as a result of Hudson's Bay Company layoffs and retirements (Giraud, 1945:688). After 1826, the Colony received no fresh immigration from Europe, actually losing some of the earlier colonists, and depended entirely on the Northwest for its population growth. In 1824, Catholic missionaries attracted about 200 Métis from Pembina to settle in the Colony, some staying around St. Boniface and some going on to form the settlement of Grantown just west of the Colony

Table 2: Population of Red River 1821-1870

Year	European	French Métis	English Métis	All Métis	Indians	Total
1821	419	(500)*	--	--	--	500
1822						1,280
1824						2,000
1838	1,600	--	--	3,400	--	5,000
1844	2,000	2,500	1,500	4,000	--	6,000
1857	1,000	4,000	2,000	6,000	--	7,000
1870	1,600	5,720	4,080	9,800	560	11,960

Source: W.L. Morton, *Manitoba: A History* (Toronto, 1957), p. 61 for 1821; M. Giraud, *Le Métis canadien* (Paris, 1945), p. 688 for 1822 and 1824; Gilles Martel, "Quand une majorité devient une minorité: le Métis francophones de l'Ouest Canadien," in Dean Louder and Eric Waddell, *Du continent perdu à l'archipel retrouvé* (Québec, 1983), p. 59 for 1838 to 1870 inclusive.

*French Métis at Pembina in 1821.

(Giraud, 1945:650-655; 714-715). After that it is the Métis who account for most of the Colony's population increase, as table 2 shows.

There appears to have been significant differences at this time between the English- and French-speaking Métis, with the English Métis more tied to direct employment with the Hudson's Bay Company. The French Métis were, however, the most dynamic element in the population. Their chief activity was the buffalo hunt.

At the time, the buffalo wandered the Plains in their millions and provided the main source of food for all the Plains Indian tribes year-round. When the fur trade penetrated the West, buffalo meat in the form of *pemmican* became the staple diet of the canoemen and other workers of the fur trade, playing the same role as corn did in the earlier eastern fur trade. The fur trading companies encouraged the Indians to trade pemmican, but this was never a very secure source of supply as the chief buffalo hunting Indians did not hunt furs much and, with the buffalo fulfilling virtually all their needs, were less dependent on company goods. To secure supplies on the scale needed by the fur trade, the companies would at first hire "freedmen" to stock forts and outposts and later came to rely almost entirely on Métis hunters. By 1820, the summer buffalo hunt had become a regular organized affair for the Red River Métis (Giraud, 1945:650-651). From 540 carts in 1820, the annual Red River buffalo hunts grew to about 2,000 carts by 1850 and to over 3,500 in 1870. It is estimated that during these Red River hunts alone, the Métis killed over 11,000,000 buffalo (McLean, n.d.:224-226). The "surplus" of this hunt was traded to the Hudson's Bay Company and sold to the other colonists of Red River, who through most of the nineteenth century relied almost as much on the buffalo for sustenance as on the meagre products of their fields (Spenger, 1978).

The Métis themselves seem to have relied on the buffalo as much as the Plains Indians did. In addition to the summer hunt, the Red River Métis organized a smaller fall hunt to get what was known as "viande verte" for the early winter months. Moreover, the practice of *hivernement* was widespread. That is, Métis families would leave the settlement in small groups during the winter to locate in areas where game was more plentiful, such as the Qu'Appelle Valley, the Touchwood Hills, Turtle Mountain, and Cypress Hills and areas in the parkland where buffalo could usually be found when the snows got too deep on the Prairie. Others spent the winter fishing and trapping near forts. Giraud gives us convincing evidence that the Métis at Red River, and certainly those elsewhere in the Northwest, for the most part lived a *nomadic* existence (Giraud, 1945:801-824).

The issue of whether or not the Métis were nomadic is an important one. Thomas Flanagan writes that "aboriginal title makes no sense unless the imperial power makes a distinction between agricultural and nomadic existence," asserting that only the latter can qualify as Aboriginal (Flanagan, 1983a:321-322). He then goes on to argue that the Métis are not an Aboriginal people by this definition. Whatever the validity of Flanagan's definition (an issue which is beyond the scope of this paper), his conclusion about the Métis is not warranted by the historical evidence. A group of Métis, however, did stay the winter in Red River. Here the Métis had river lots where they practised a little farming and gardening to supplement their food supply, but there is no evidence that the Métis ever practised farming on a major scale (Clark, 1983).

The 1840s were an eventful time for Red River and the Northwest in general, for this decade saw the development of Minnesota and the emergence of American fur traders in the Northwest. These American traders not only traded furs, but buffalo robes and hides as well. The Hudson's Bay Company attempted to protect its trading monopoly in the Northwest, but the Métis could not be stopped from trading with the Americans. In 1849, at the trial of Guillaume Sayer, who had been charged with trading in furs with the Americans, Louis Riel Sr. led a band of 300 Métis who surrounded the court house and secured the release of the accused after he had been convicted. From then on, free trade prevailed in the Northwest.[7] This was later to have disastrous consequences for the Plains Indians when, after the Civil War, American traders entered the West selling "firewater" to the buffalo-hunting Indians in exchange for buffalo hides. But for the time being, it showed the political strength of the Métis and the powerlessness of the Hudson's Bay Company.

From 1840 on, freighting operations with St. Paul (Minnesota) became increasingly important. The Red River cart had been invented by 1814. It was made entirely of wood, was light, was well-suited to the Prairie, and could carry up to 1,000 pounds. The Métis used it to haul buffalo kills, much as the Indians used the travois. The cart also proved to be well-suited to carry goods between Red River and St. Paul and from Red River to the Prairie and parkland forts such as Edmonton. As Morton writes:

> The opening of free trade with St. Paul gave rise to a new occupation and a new kind of tripman, the occupation of cart-freighting and the men who contracted to carry freight by cart to St. Paul, or the Saskatchewan. It was an occupation much like that of boat tripping, seasonal, casual, and varied. After 1850 the carts were organized in brigades of indefinite and growing numbers, and wound, lurching and shrieking, by the Crow Wing and other trails over the height of land to St. Paul. When in 1858 the Hudson's Bay Company began to bring

in goods by St. Paul as well as by York, it opened a new supply route to the West overland by Fort Carlton on the Saskatchewan to Edmonton. The trail to Portage la Prairie was extended to Fort Ellice and on to Carlton, and goods moved by cart all the way from the upper Mississippi to the upper Saskatchewan (Morton, 1967a:83-84).

Most Métis owned at least one cart. Existence depended upon it. But there is little doubt that some Métis owned more and that some were heavily involved in the freighting business — the beginning, perhaps, of a Métis bourgeoisie.

Such were the people that Louis Riel, who was born in October 1844, grew up with. Buffalo hunters for the most part, they had a reputation as expert shots and knew the Northwest well. Although most had a river lot of some kind, the French Métis spent much of the year on the move, and this brought them into continual contact with the Indians. They had picked up the survival skills and languages of the Indians, but had also inherited much from their voyageur ancestors: the log cabin on the river lot, the *ceinture fléchée*, the Catholic faith, the French language, and even the Red River cart. They lived in distinct communities and had settlements all over the Northwest from Lac Ste. Anne to the Milk River, in present-day Alberta, and from St. Laurent in Central Saskatchewan to Turtle Mountain on the American border. They formed the dominant population of the Red River Colony. What the land could not provide, they secured through trade with the Hudson's Bay Company and American traders. They exchanged furs and products of the buffalo hunt for manufactured goods. Currency was still rare, but jobs and casual labour with the Hudson's Bay Company provided a source of income. Many Métis, particularly the English Métis, could read and write; some, such as Cuthbert Grant and Louis Riel, were educated, although most (not surprisingly in early nineteenth-century North America) remained illiterate. As trade expanded after 1840, some Métis became relatively prosperous as traders and freighters. On the eve of the takeover of the Northwest by Canada, the Métis were developing rapidly and were showing a vitality that was very promising for the future.

Within a generation of the takeover of the Northwest by Canada in 1870, the foundations of the political economy of the historic Métis would be gone. The buffalo disappeared from the Western Plains by 1879. The coming of the railroad shattered the Red River cart freighting commerce. And Confederation destroyed the political force of the Métis. All that remained was land, and they were cheated out of this as well.

CONFEDERATION AND DISPOSSESSION

In the 1860s, immediately prior to Confederation, policy over Native affairs was divided. The Colonial Office directly administered Indian affairs in the Atlantic provinces, but in Central Canada it had delegated this responsibility to the colonial legislature in 1860. It left the Hudson's Bay Company in charge of the Northwest (McNab, 1983). The Hudson's Bay Company treated the Métis as "country-born" for legal purposes, and tended to regard them very much as part of the Native population of the area. But since its main goal was only to extract furs, the Company never did attempt to extinguish Aboriginal title.

In Canada, a policy had been adopted early of extinguishing Indian title to land through the procedure set out in the *Royal Proclamation* of 1763 — through treaty between the Crown and the Indians. Even before Confederation, action had been taken to extinguish Aboriginal title in the lands of the Upper Great Lakes, a region which later became part of the Province of Ontario. At this time, the authorities first confronted the question of what to do with the Métis. William Robinson laid down a principle that was widely followed later on:

As the half-breeds of Sault Ste. Marie and other places may seek to be recognized by the Government in future payments, it may be well to state here the answer that I gave to their demands on the present occasion. I told them I came to treat with the chiefs who were present, that the money would be paid to them — and their receipt was sufficient for me — that when in their possession they might give as much or as little to that class of claimants as they pleased. To this no one, not even their advisers, could object, and I heard no more of the subject (cited in Taylor, 1983:153).

This suggested that Métis could be allowed into treaty if the Indians agreed. The Canadian government basically adopted this policy. It did not recognize a distinct Métis claim, but considered that the Métis were either Indians, in which case they could be admitted to treaty as Indians, or "Whites," in which case they could be treated like general citizens. The Métis had to be either one or the other.

In the Northwest the Canadian government encountered a distinct Métis people. Canadian authorities were rudely awakened to this fact when in 1869 Canada acquired Rupert's Land from the Hudson's Bay Company for $300,000 and the grant of one-twentieth of all the lands in the Fertile Belt (Stanley, 1936:41). In reaction, the Métis organized a provisional government that refused entry to the lieutenant-governor whom John A.

Macdonald had appointed to administer the newly acquired territory. Negotiations followed that led eventually to the *Manitoba Act of 1870*. It set the foundation for a new policy towards the Métis in the Northwest.

The Provisional Government of 1869-70 was led by Louis Riel and the French Métis. It had the support of most elements in Red River, including the English half-breeds, French Canadians and other original settlers, and, most importantly, the Catholic clergy. The clergy acted as mediator in the negotiations with the Canadian government. Only a party of recent Canadian immigrants from Ontario opposed the Provisional Government, and one of their hotheads by the name of Thomas Scott was executed by the new government.

At this time, the Métis did not advance their demands as an Aboriginal claim. They did not ask to be treated as Indians and admitted into treaty. Rather, a bill of rights was drafted by the Council of the Provisional Government which called for provincial status for the Red River Colony. The Métis, after all, made up eighty per cent of the population of the Colony and had, since the 1840s, urged the Colonial Office to establish Red River as a separate colony with responsible government (McNab, 1983:94). Basically, the Bill of Rights sought responsible government for Red River, protection of the political and property rights of the present inhabitants, separate schools for Protestants and Catholics, guarantees of both French and English as official languages, equitable fiscal arrangements with Ottawa, and all the powers of a province for the Colony. This explicitly included a provision that asked that "the local Legislature of this Province have full control over all the lands of the Northwest" (de Tremaudan, 1982:90-92).

The Canadian government accepted most of these demands, which are now part of the *Manitoba Act of 1870*. But John A. Macdonald and his government were adamant that public lands would have to be placed in the hands of the federal government. This was one of the most sticky points of the negotiations (the other was amnesty); it was here that the question of Métis Aboriginal rights first arose. Father Richot, sent by the Provisional Government to negotiate with Macdonald and Georges Etienne Cartier in Ottawa, records the position he took when these ministers informed him of their position on public lands:

> We could by no means let go control of the lands at least unless we had compensation on conditions which, for the population, actually would be the equivalent of control of their province (cited in Heinemann, 1984:167; Morton, 1967b:140).

Negotiations proceeded to find a compromise that might be acceptable to both the Métis and the federal government. The compromise finally involved setting aside a reserve of 1.4 million acres of public lands in

Manitoba for the "children of half-breed heads of families." This was incorporated in Section 31 of the *Manitoba Act*. That this land reserve was intended as compensation for the loss of control over public lands is made evident by James Wilkes-Taylor, an American representative of the U.S. Secretary of State and close friend of Joseph Howe, then Secretary of State for the Provinces, who wrote to the U.S. Secretary of State, Hamilton Fish:

> I proceed to an analysis of the *Manitoba Act*....The grant of 1,400,000 acres to the children of the halfbreed residents was regarded as an equivalent for the "control by the local legislature of the public lands" within a circumference of Fort Garry, of which the distance to the American line formed the radius (cited in Morton, 1967b:168).[8]

Riel was later to argue that, as 1,400,000 acres was then one-seventh the area of Manitoba, the Métis had been granted a right to inherit one-seventh of the lands of the entire Northwest (Martel, 1979:44). Certainly there is considerable controversy over the basis for this decision. The political explanation is that it was a grant in lieu of provincial control of public lands. But at one point Father Richot had sought to make clear that "in asking for control of the lands of the province, they (the settlers of the Northwest) have no intention of causing the loss of the rights that the Métis of the northwest have as descendants of the Indians" (cited in Heinemann, 1984:165). This may be the origin of the rationale in the *Manitoba Act of 1870*, to the effect that the grant was explicitly made "towards the extinguishment of the Indian Title to the lands in the Province." John A. Macdonald later defended Section 31 of the *Manitoba Act* on the grounds that it was designed to extinguish Métis claims to Indian title, but he also said that he had done this for reasons of political "expediency" (Flanagan, 1983a:318-319).

This expedient solution to the public lands issue created a Métis title of some kind to the lands of Manitoba and later to lands elsewhere in the Northwest. Unlike what had happened in the rest of Canada, in the Northwest the Métis were recognized as having a distinct Aboriginal claim to the land. The federal government's priority at that time was the settlement of the West, and for this it required clear title to all public lands. Extinguishment of Aboriginal title therefore became a priority. In the Northwest, this meant extinguishing both an Indian and a Métis claim to the land. In the decades that followed the *Manitoba Act*, the federal government devised a way of doing this that created a sharp distinction in the way that it dealt with the Indian and Métis titles. The Indians alienated their title as they had done in northern Ontario — through treaty. The Métis were offered *scrip* — certificates issued to individuals by the government to be redeemed in public land.

There was nothing in the negotiations over the *Manitoba Act* to indicate that scrip would be the means used to deal with the claims of the Métis. Father Richot seems to have believed that the 1.4 million acres would be promptly set aside for the Métis in continuous reserves around the major parishes and distributed to the Métis in accordance with procedures that they themselves would develop. He expressed his consternation with the final draft of the *Manitoba Act*, which stated simply that the land "shall be granted to the said children respectively, in such mode and on such conditions as to settlement and otherwise, as the Governor General in Council may from time to time determine." He writes:

> The Bill appeared very much modified. Several clauses displease me fundamentally. I saw Sir George and Sir John, we complained to them. They declared that in practice it amounted to the same thing...that for the present it would be impossible to get the Bill passed if one changed its form....The two Ministers, seeing that we were strongly opposed, promised us, among other things, to authorize by Order in Council, the persons we choose to name ourselves, as soon as might be after the Bill should be passed, to form a committee charged with choosing and dividing, as may seem good to them, the 1.4 million acres of land promised (cited in Heinemann, 1984:169, Morton, 1967b:99).

This was not, however, to be the procedure used. First, there were delays in making the land grant to the Métis. The government argued that Indian title to the lands of what was then the "postage stamp" province of Manitoba had first to be extinguished. This was largely completed by August 1871. Then a census had to be taken and the land survey completed. This delayed the allocation of the Métis land grant for a few more years. In April 1871, the federal government passed an Order-in-Council setting land regulations for Manitoba. These regulations initially provided that grants would be made not only to the children of half-breed heads of families, but to every half-breed head of family resident in the province before 15 July 1870. But the grant to half-breed heads of families was soon rescinded. In July 1872, the federal government instructed the Lieutenant-Governor to start selecting townships to make up the 1.4 million acres (Sanders, 1979:11). The idea was to reserve a broad area of land exclusively for Métis children. Distribution of land was actually started in 1873.

Then the government in Ottawa changed, and so did the rules. Distribution was halted. In May 1874, the Mackenzie government introduced legislation that set out its policy on Manitoba lands. This legislation first introduced scrip as a means of extinguishing Métis claims. The act provided that grants were to be made to all half-breed heads of families as well as to their children, but that grants to half-breed heads of families could be taken either in the form of 160 acres of land or for a scrip worth $160. The original 1.4 million acres reserved for Métis children was allocated to them on the basis of 240 acres for each child (Order-in-Council, 7 September 1876): it was distributed mainly from lands around Métis parishes in a series of draws in which the names of allottees were placed in a box and drawn. Draws were made in 1877, 1878, 1879, and 1880. By the time land distribution to Métis heads of families had taken place (30 October 1876 at the earliest), the federal Cabinet had already established that grants to them could *only* be made in the form of a scrip of $160 applicable to the purchase of Dominion Lands in Manitoba. The scrip was issued in denominations of $20 and was redeemable by the bearer (see Heinemann, 1984:195-196; Sealey, 1978b:1-30). It functioned very much like money. It was known as *money scrip* and was the only form of scrip issued in Manitoba

The delays in selecting the Métis lands were probably the most important factor in the dispossession of the Métis in Manitoba. While the Métis were waiting for their lands – including not only their "half-breed grant," but patents to their pre-1870 river lots as well – immigration from Ontario was altering the demographic and political balance of the Colony, now the Province of Manitoba. Between 1871 and 1881, Manitoba's population tripled, increasing from 18,995 in 1871 to 65,954 in 1881. In the first years, the new arrivals from Ontario consisted notably of General Wolseley's troops, who arrived in the Colony in August 1870 and promptly proceeded to instigate a reign of terror against the Métis. Members of the Provisional Government were harassed, Riel's mother was attacked, and some Métis were killed. Lepine, who had been a member of the Provisional Government, was arrested (de Tremaudan, 1982:103-106). Meanwhile, the federal government dragged its feet on the issue of amnesty, which had been left pending when the *Manitoba Act* was negotiated, and convinced Riel not to run in the federal election of 1872. Ontario had to take its vengeance for the execution of Thomas Scott. Arrivals from Ontario were slowed down by the Depression which hit in 1873, but there were still 11,970 new arrivals in 1875, and over 40,000 immigrants arrived in Manitoba between 1876 and 1881 (Morton, 1967a:176-177). While the Métis waited for their grants and patents, these settlers pre-empted many Métis lands – sometimes laying claim to river lots whose occupants had gone to hunt.

Meanwhile, the Métis were leaving the province in droves. Harassed by an unfriendly government, their leaders Riel and Lepine sent into exile for five years in 1875, their lands usurped or made the object of fast speculation, and with many going hungry, they sold out and moved further into the Northwest. They went mainly to their old points of *hivernement* in the parklands and the hill country of the Prairies (Giraud, 1954). There, the settlers had not yet penetrated. Some Métis tried to live, as the Indians were then trying to do, off the remnants of the buffalo herds. Others, such as those around Batoche, had seen the end coming for the buffalo and were trying to adjust to a more agricultural life.

Those around Batoche and other places such as the Qu'Appelle Lakes started to petition Ottawa for a recognition of their rights in the Northwest. In 1879, the federal government acknowledged these rights by passing an amendment to the *Dominion Lands Act* that stated:

> To satisfy claims existing in connection with the extinguishment of the Indian title, preferred by half-breeds resident in the Northwest Territories outside Manitoba, on the fifteenth day of July, one thousand eight hundred and seventy, by granting land to such persons, to such extent and on such terms and conditions, as may be deemed expedient (cited in Taylor, 1983:162).

But as in Manitoba, the government took no action to implement its promises.

The late 1870s and the 1880s were especially hard years for the original inhabitants of the Northwest. The buffalo herds were on the verge of disappearing and the Indians were starving. Agriculture was precarious, and depression generalized, after the land boom ended in Manitoba. During this time, the federal government was busy negotiating treaties with the Indians to alienate their Aboriginal title. Between 1873 and 1877, the federal government negotiated the numbered treaties with the Indians occupying the Prairies, and in the process encountered Métis. At first, the federal negotiators thought it advisable to allow Métis who were living with the Indians to be admitted to treaty.

Under Treaty No. 3, covering the region around the Lake of the Woods, a group of Métis was allowed to adhere to the treaty at the request of the Indians and was even established on separate reserves. Elsewhere, Métis were admitted as parts of Indian bands. But by 1876, the federal government had begun to adopt a more stringent stand on the admission of "half-breeds" into treaty. In that year it passed the *Indian Act*, Section 3(e) of which laid down the policy:

> Provided also that no half-breed in Manitoba who has shared in the distribution of half-breed lands shall be accounted an Indian; and that no half-breed head of a family (except the widow of an Indian, or a half-breed who has already been admitted into a treaty), shall, unless under very special circumstances, to be determined by the Superintendent General or

his agent, be accounted an Indian or entitled to be admitted into any Indian treaty (cited in Taylor, 1983:162).

By 1877, Métis requests for adhesions to treaty were beginning to be refused (Taylor, 1983:161).

By the late 1870s, the federal government's policy began to make a sharp distinction between Indian and Métis. But while Indian treaties had been negotiated on the Prairies, by 1880 nothing had yet been done to satisfy Métis claims, despite repeated representations. As had occurred earlier in Manitoba, surveyors appeared to divide the land into townships and sections before anything was done to secure the patents of the original settlers, most of whom were Métis. In the face of these hardships, the White settlers and the Métis around Batoche sent for Louis "David" Riel who was then living in exile in Montana. Riel returned in the spring of 1884 and succeeded by December in organizing the inhabitants of the Saskatchewan District to send a "petition of rights" to Ottawa. It set out the grievances of Indians, Métis and White settlers, who were then organized in a "settlers' union" (Morton, 1938:94-95), and asked for very much the same as the Provisional Government had done in Manitoba fifteen years before — provincial status, responsible government, just representation in Parliament and the Cabinet, and the control of public lands (*Saskatchewan History*, 1970).

The federal government never did reply to this petition. In January 1885 it did, however, appoint the Street Commission, the first of the Northwest scrip commissions, and instructed it to start an enumeration of the Métis born in the Northwest before 15 July 1870. But events overtook the Commission. In March 1885, on the basis of a rumour that the Canadian government was dispatching an armed force to Batoche, the Métis took up arms and, under the leadership of Louis Riel, formed a new provisional government (Stanley, 1936:316).

It appears that Riel believed that he could repeat what he had done earlier in Manitoba and force the Canadian government to negotiate with him. However, this time he did not have the support of the clergy, and the White settlers and the English Métis soon abandoned him. Moreover, unlike 1870, the Canadian government now had armed forces in the Northwest in the form of the Northwest Mounted Police. An engagement with a group of police and St. Albert volunteers at Duck Lake ended in a Métis victory under the command of Gabriel Dumont, which encouraged the Poundmaker and Big Bear Indian bands in the area to rise against the Canadian authorities. But in a matter of months, the Rebellion was put down by an expedition of the Canadian militia under General Middleton, which had been transported to the West over the as yet only partially completed lines of the Canadian

Pacific Railway (C.P.R.). A major result of the Rebellion was that it enabled the Macdonald government to rationalize the provision of desperately needed subsidies to the C.P.R. It also sent Louis Riel to the gallows, and the repercussions are still being felt today.

The Rebellion had one further result. On 31 March 1885, soon after the Rebellion had started, the federal Cabinet authorized the issue of scrip in the Northwest Territory. At first the government had in mind the issue of money scrip, as in Manitoba, but upon being informed that the Métis of the Qu'Appelle Valley were demanding grants of land, the Cabinet decided that scrip could be issued either in land or in cash (McLean, n.d.:335). This established the two forms of scrip—land scrip and money scrip—which became the instruments that the federal government used to extinguish Métis claims to the lands of the Northwest.

SCRIP AND SPECULATION

Scrip was a very peculiar way of dealing with what was supposed to be a Métis claim to Aboriginal title. It purported to deal with Aboriginal claims on an individual basis rather than collectively. Scrip had been used first in the United States, where it was given to original settlers in territories about to become states, and to military personnel to encourage settlement of the West. There is little evidence that it was used as a technique to extinguish Indian title. In Canada, scrip was first used in Manitoba, where it was issued not only to the Métis but also to original settlers and to the men in General Wolseley's expedition. Later it was given to personnel of the Northwest Mounted Police and to the volunteers in Middleton's army. But Métis scrip was not only the most important form of scrip issued; it also had special characteristics.

All scrip was ultimately redeemable *only* in public land. *Money scrip* was a certificate that could be exchanged for a value in land equivalent to the value of the certificate. A $240 scrip allowed the holder to purchase public land to the value of $240. The amount of land it could buy was therefore dependent on the price of land. Made out to the *bearer*, it could accordingly be easily transferred from person to person. Furthermore, the money scrip made out to Métis, unlike the money scrip issued to others, was considered personal property and therefore fell under personal property laws instead of real estate laws. Once money scrip fell into the hands of the speculator it was no longer treated as personal property but as real estate. These characteristics made money scrip the most popular form of scrip with speculators until land prices started to rise dramatically after 1900 (Heinemann, 1984:244-245).

Land scrip could be exchanged for the amount of land specified in the certificate. A 240-acre scrip entitled the allottee to claim 240 acres of unoccupied public land. This scrip was made out directly to the allottee, who alone could claim the land. Moreover, land scrip was considered real estate and was always treated as such in law. Consequently, it was more difficult to exchange and less popular with speculators. Those who obtained land scrip usually had to resort to fraud to claim the lands instead of the allottee. But as land prices rose in the West, particularly after 1900, land scrip became the more popular form of scrip with speculators since it gave the possessor a claim to a fixed amount of land whose monetary value was fast increasing. By this time, many of the earlier difficulties with exchanging land scrip had been done away with, and after 1893, the federal government recognized assignments of land scrip (Heinemann, 1984:245; Sanders, 1979:13).

In addition to the Manitoba distributions, scrip was distributed to the Métis of the Northwest between 1885 and 1910 in a series of thirteen scrip commissions, which were responsible for receiving and approving applications from Métis for scrip. These commissions would travel to different communities where Métis were expected to collect to meet with the commissioners. Naturally, not all Métis made it to the audiences of the scrip commissions, but it appears that most did. The Northwest Half-breed scrip commissions of 1885, 1886 and 1887 dealt with the Métis in those parts of the Northwest that had already come under treaty. When Treaty No. 8 was negotiated in 1899, an innovation was introduced which had the scrip commissioners meet with the Métis at the same time as Indians were negotiating treaty. In 1900, the federal government decided to extend scrip issues to children born in the Northwest Territories between 15 July 1870 and the end of 1885 — and later to any Métis born in the territory before 1885 but resident in the United States. This resulted in the appointment of another series of scrip commissions in the early 1900s. The number of Métis dealt with in scrip commissions is present in Tables 3 and 4.

It is impossible to discuss scrip without referring to its importance as an instrument of speculation. It was well understood in the 1870s and 1880s that the issuance of scrip to Métis would result in their selling the land. The federal government, whose primary interest was settlement, did not believe the Métis would make good agriculturalists and did not want to have to reserve large tracts of land for them as it had done with the Indians. Scrip enabled it to meet its commitments to the Métis without having to create Métis reserves and, in its view, take land out of production. This view is made clear by James Trow, member of Parliament and chairman of the

David Boisvert/Keith Turnbull

Table 3: Scrip Issue in Manitoba

	Claims	Land Grants (acres)	Money Scrip ($)
Children of Half-breed Heads of Families	6,034	1,448,160	nil
Children of Half-breed Heads of Families (Supplementary Benefits)	993	nil	238,300
Half-breed Heads of Families	3,186	nil	509,760
Total:	10,213	1,448,160	48,060

Source: Chester Martin, "*Dominion Lands*" *Policy*, Canadian Frontiers of Settlement Series, ed. W.A. Mackintosh and W.J.L. Long (Toronto, 1938), 239; D. McLean, *A Research Resource Book of Native History* (Paper prepared for the Gabriel Dumont Institute, Regina, 1981), 346-7; and Joe Sawchuk, Patricia Sawchuk, and Theresa Furguson, *Métis Land Rights in Alberta* (Edmonton: Métis Association of Alberta, 1981), 105.

Table 4: Scrip Issue in the Northwest Territories

Year of Scrip Commission	Claims	Land Scrip (acres)	Money Scrip ($)
1885	1,815	55,260	279,201
1886	1,414	2,640	61,689
1887	753	3,120	122,424
1888	881	nil	183,568
1889	1,190	110,520	286,800
1900	3,306	477,840	315,000
1901	1,190	117,680	344,267
1903	1,326	296,564	55,564
1904	136	32,640	nil
1906	498	54,480	65,040
1908	178	28,560	14,160
1909	31	7,440	nil
1910	86	18,480	2,160
1923	172	(a cash grant issue of 41,290 instead of scrip	
Total	12,976	1,205,224	1,729,873

Source: As for table 3.

parliamentary committee on colonization, who stated in 1877 with respect to reservations of land in Manitoba:

> Many of these reservations of land are not in the interest of the Province, and must and will retard legitimate colonization, unless thrown open for settlement. Bringing into the market the half-breed reserves is a step in the right direction (Morton, 1938:49).

There is evidence that speculation in Métis lands had started even before scrip was introduced. Speculation became so active in anticipation of the 1873 allocations that the Manitoba legislature, which at that time counted eleven Métis among its twenty-four members, felt obliged to pass the *Half-Breed Land Protection Act* (Ens, 1983; Sprague, 1980a; 1980b). This legislation sought to cancel all sales of Métis lands prior to the issue of patents and to ensure that the Métis who had already sold their lands could retrieve them. But the Métis did not keep their political influence in the province. By 1877, or shortly before land grants actually began, the act was amended to guarantee that any sale made or executed by deed after the amendment came into effect would be legal and effective. In 1878, the Manitoba legislature adopted an act that provided that Métis children could alienate their property at the age of eighteen, despite the fact that the age of majority was then twenty-one. In 1879, the Métis lost all political say in the affairs of Manitoba, and in the following years a series of acts was passed to facilitate speculation in Métis lands – a development that resulted in the rapid dispossession of the Métis. These acts culminated in *An Act Relating to the Titles of Half-Breed Lands*, assented to in May 1885, which declared that all sales of the lands of Métis children were legal, "notwithstanding any defect, irregularity, or omission in the carrying out of the sale" (Ens, 1983:10). The largest number of alienations of Métis children's claims occurred in 1880. As for the money scrip issued to "half-breed heads of families," it was alienated at the going rate of $0.30 to $1.00 of face value. By 1886, only twenty per cent of Métis lands still remained with the allottees.

Any doubts about the importance of speculation in these scrip issues can be quickly put to rest by examining who ultimately got their hands on the scrip. Table 5 shows who redeemed scrip.[9] Métis scrip ended up in the

Table 5: Distribution of Scrip Redemption

Distribution	Percentage of Notes	Number
Allottees	11	2,800
Dominion Land Agents	8	2,100
Small Speculators	12	3,100
Private Institutions and Large Speculators	17	4,500
Chartered Banks	52	13,500
Total	100	26,000

Source: L. Heinemann, *An Investigation into the Origins and Development of the Métis Nation, the Rights of the Métis as an Aboriginal People, and their Relationship and Dealings with the Government of Canada,* (Research report prepared for the Association of Métis and Non-Status Indians of Saskatchewan, Gabriel Dumont Institute, Regina, 1984), 247.

hands of others. It was used to claim agricultural land but also to claim timber rights, coal rights and pre-exemptions. Scrip could be accepted for rent and acted as collateral for debts. Most *money scrip* was sold by the Métis for cash at one-third of the face value of the certificate on average. Most *land scrip* was exchanged for goods—traded with local businessmen and farmers in exchange for farm animals, implements, seed, groceries or other supplies (Heinemann, 1984:234). For the Métis it acted as cash in a cash-starved economy; for others it acted as a source of profit.

An industry developed around scrip speculation with some financial institutions, such as the private bank of Osler, Hammond and Nanton, or the firm of McDougall and Secord, virtually specializing in it. However, much of the field was occupied by the small speculator. That most scrip fell into the hands of the chartered banks (52 per cent) is probably an indication of the success of scrip as an agent for the creation of money in the Northwest. Banks could lend and hence create money in exchange for scrip (McLean, n.d.:329-331). The fact that so much scrip fell into the hands of the banks is probably as much an indication of tough times in the West as it is of the banks' eagerness to acquire land.

It has always been difficult to understand why the Métis sold their scrip. Clearly, the Métis did not use scrip as the speculators or as the settlers did. Perhaps it was because they lacked the capital to become either speculators or settlers. Without the means to become active speculators, why should the Métis go through the time and expense of patenting a few acres of land just for the purpose of selling it to a settler at some point in the future? Any lands they were interested in lay around their communities, and the fact that these might already be occupied made the land offer of dubious value to them. And if they did take land, with what were they to buy the seed, the horses and the implements needed to start farming when they did not even have the equipment to work successfully the lands already in their possession? These are, however, secondary reasons which highlight the fact that the Métis did not have the same interest in scrip or in land as certain White men did. The chief reason the Métis sold their scrip lies in the *absolute impoverishment* that they, as a group, were experiencing at precisely the same time that scrip was being issued in the Northwest. The decades following the Northwest Rebellion were very hard times for the Métis. They were stigmatized for the Rebellion. With the buffalo gone, their main source of subsistence had disappeared. Many resorted to a subsistence economy based on hunting, fishing and trapping. Others tried to put the one possession they had left—their carts—to some productive use. For a while freighting continued to be an important source of employment, but this disappeared as the railroad pushed its way to all the major Prairie centres.

For a period between 1884 and 1897, peaking in the early 1890s, many Métis, once the great buffalo hunters of the Plains, found employment in picking up the buffalo bones that littered the Prairie landscape. These were sold to a few businessmen who shipped them by the train load to St. Louis and Chicago for use as fertilizer and as an agent in the production of white sugar (Barnett, 1979). Under these conditions, the most valuable aspect of scrip to the Métis might well have been the ready cash it could provide to feed and clothe families that had been reduced to destitution and starvation. They simply needed money and supplies more than a piece of land.

THE MÉTIS SINCE 1885

The history of the Métis since 1885 is a story of the disintegration of a once proud and independent people. The pauperization of the Métis in the 1890s certainly contributed immensely to this process, as the Métis were forced either to adopt a hunting, fishing and trapping way of life (indistinguishable from that of most Indians in the North), or to move to the cities where they started to form a distinct "Native" population in search of work and a roof over their heads. A few Métis practised subsistence agriculture in places such as Batoche, but even here the strongest linkages developed with nearby Indian reserves. The Métis population dispersed throughout the Northwest, and even into the United States, where some found a home with the Chippewa (Ojibway) Indians on the Turtle Mountain Reserve. But what contributed most to the disintegration of the Métis people was federal government policy.

The federal government's policy of treating Métis differently from Indians when it came to extinguishment of Aboriginal title had rather unexpected effects in the twentieth century. Treaties imposed certain continuing responsibilities on the federal government for the welfare and upkeep of Indians on reserves. They set aside certain lands for the exclusive use of the Indian peoples; these lands had to be administered; and treaties required Ottawa to make annual payments of money and supplies to the Indian peoples concerned. Treaty Indians were treated as wards of the federal government, towards whom the federal government had a continuing trust responsibility.

Scrip placed the Métis, of course, in a very different situation than the treaty Indian. The virtue of scrip in the federal government's eyes was not only that it served to extinguish Aboriginal title, but that it did so without creating Métis reserves, and without imposing any continuing obligations on Ottawa to look after the Métis. Once scrip was issued, the federal government felt that it had absolved itself of any further responsibility for the Métis. By and large, since at least the 1940s, it has denied responsibility to do anything for the Métis.

Initially, this created a clear distinction between Métis and Indians. Indians could benefit from treaty. Métis could not. Although in the negotiation of the numbered treaties in Western Canada federal commissioners had often allowed Métis to adhere to Indian treaties, starting in 1876 the federal government began to enforce a stricter segregation between Métis and Indians. In 1880, the federal government went a step further and amended the *Indian Act* to allow any Métis, defined as a person of mixed-blood, to withdraw from treaty upon refund of the annuities received. In 1884, the federal government went further still and permitted withdrawal without reimbursement of annuities (Taylor, 1983:159). Once withdrawn, a Métis could receive scrip. As a result, of the 3,446 claims approved by the scrip commissions of 1885, 1886 and 1887, 1,292 were to persons who had formerly been in treaty (Sanders, 1979:13). Thus even Métis living with the Indians were induced to remove themselves from band lists and to take themselves off the federal government's "wardship" roll. The federal government continued this strict policy of dealing with "half-breeds" through scrip, and Indians through treaty, during the negotiation of treaties eight (1899), ten (1906-1907) and eleven (1921). The advantage of doing this was that a significant part of the Aboriginal population was removed from the federal government's charge.

Throughout the late nineteenth century and the twentieth century, the federal government continued to seek ways to limit or diminish the number of Indians for whom it accepted "wardship" responsibilities. This was accomplished through provisions in the act for "enfranchisement," a term that refers to the fact that Status Indians did not until 1960 have the right to vote. An Indian might voluntarily enfranchise, but the act also contained several provisions that forced an Indian person to become enfranchised under certain conditions. The most infamous of these provisions is Section 12(1)(b), which states that any Status Indian woman who marries someone without status is automatically enfranchised. An enfranchised Indian had his/her name struck from the band lists and no longer had any right to live or to hold property on a reserve. Without being on the band list, it was virtually impossible for enfranchised Indians to continue to benefit from treaty rights. The effect of these provisions, since 1876, has been to create a new class of Native persons — persons who had, or whose ancestors had, lost their status under the *Indian Act* — a group called *non-Status Indians*.

Throughout the twentieth century, there was a great mixing of these non-Status Indians with the Métis in Western Canada, and many started to identify as Métis. This is not surprising if it is borne in mind that after 1885 the single most important circumstance structuring the identity of Native peoples was federal Indian policy and the distinction created by federal Indian policy between persons of Aboriginal descent who benefitted from treaty and had rights under the *Indian Act* and those who did not. The non-Status Indians were then brought to share precisely that circumstance which most distinguished the Métis from the Indians after 1885: the fact that they stood outside treaty. Like the Métis, Indians who lost status drifted to the cities or settled in rural communities where they practised the same kind of life as most Métis: hunting, fishing, trapping, occasional guiding, prospecting, farming. In the West, many non-Status Indians congregated in Métis rural communities.

The association of non-Status Indians with Métis can be understood in other ways as well. The majority of non-Status Indians lost their status because they married Europeans. In effect, non-Status Indians testify to the continuation of *métissage* after the *Indian Act* was passed in 1876. They represent new cohorts of Métis created since that time. But whereas persons of mixed-blood born prior to the 1880s were generally considered to be Métis, new cohorts of Métis created after that time were identified as non-Status Indians. Generally speaking, the same processes gave rise to both the Métis and the non-Status Indians, but legal distinctions between the two groups remain.

Federal policy had other pernicious effects as well. By 1923 the federal government had extinguished the Aboriginal title of all Métis who had lived in the West. The issue of scrip in Manitoba was limited to people who had resided in the province as of 15 July 1870 – the date of the takeover of the Northwest by the Government of Canada. In the Northwest outside Manitoba, the date fixed for eligibility to claim scrip was at first the same, but in 1900 was changed to include all children born prior to the end of 1885 – the year of the Riel Rebellion. When treaties eight, ten and eleven were negotiated, the Métis who were resident in the territory at the time treaty was made with the Indians were given scrip or money. After that, no more scrip was issued. The fact that scrip was issued only to certain persons created a distinct class of persons: the *scrip Métis*. These Métis can be identified and they have descendants. Based on a rough tabulation from the scrip count, which indicates that somewhere in the order of 26,000 Métis received scrip, the number of descendants of the scrip Métis must be about 80,000 today. This can lead to a very strict definition of Métis as *scrip Métis* – a person roughly identified with the historic Métis of the Northwest. Federal policy towards the Aboriginal peoples thus ended up creating three distinct classes of Aboriginal peoples in the West: Status Indians, non-Status Indians, and Métis. This created differences not only between treaty and non-treaty Indians but between non-Status Indians and scrip Métis as well. The fact that Métis and non-Status Indians shared the same social conditions and that both groups were excluded from treaty and from the *Indian Act* led them in most provinces to set up common associations to promote their interests. Most of these associations are of recent vintage, having been established since 1960, although some, like the Alberta Métis Association, have a longer history. In 1971, these provincial associations grouped into a national organization, the Native Council of Canada, which until recently represented all Métis and non-Status Indians. In 1983, the Western Métis established their own organization, the Métis National Council, and acquired separate representation in constitutional negotiations. Both organizations represent Métis and non-Status Indians, although the Métis National Council does so in regions where Métis predominate and the Native Council of Canada does so in regions where the non-Status population is generally more significant. The major difference between the two organizations is that the Métis National Council takes the position that the Métis referred to in Section 35 of the Constitution are the Métis people developed historically in the Northwest, while the Native Council of Canada argues that any person of mixed Indian and European ancestry who identifies as a Métis is a Métis for the purposes of Section 35. At issue in this controversy is the question of whether those people who identify as non-Status Indians today should, for the purposes of the new Constitution, be considered Indian or Métis, since there is no separate listing for them otherwise.

Another result of the federal government's policies was that they tended to force both Métis and non-Status Indians to look to the provinces for relief. The federal government denied that it had any continuing responsibility to look after the Métis or any Indian who had lost status, but this denial did not make the poverty and plight of the Métis and non-Status Indians any less real, or their needs any less urgent. Provincial governments for their part always hesitated to assume burdensome responsibilities such as the Métis promised to be. Only in Alberta can anything be said to have been done to try to relieve Métis poverty. As early as 1896, the federal government, which still had control of public lands in that province, was persuaded by Father Lacombe to grant the Jesuits some land for the purpose of establishing a Métis reserve. This project floundered on the rocks of financial troubles and Church paternalism, and the reserve that Father Lacombe had established — St.-Paul-des-Métis — was disbanded in 1910 and most of the land sold to French Canadian homesteaders from Québec (Sawchuk, Sawchuk and Ferguson, 1981:159-185; Stanley, 1978a).

During the Depression, the Métis in Alberta did succeed in having the provincial government set aside lands for them. Under the leadership of men like Jim Brady, Malcolm Norris and Peter Tomkins, the Métis established their first important organization in that province: "L'Association des Métis d'Alberta et des Territoires du Nord-Ouest," established on 28 December 1932 (Dobbin, 1981:63). This association succeeded in lobbying the Alberta government to appoint the Royal Commission on Rehabilitation of the Métis in February 1933. Known as the Ewing Commission, it recommended essentially that certain unoccupied Crown lands be reserved for Métis collectively. This was seen as the most cost-effective method of dealing with Métis problems (*Report of Royal Commission on Rehabilitation of the Métis*, 1936:9). The Aberhart government acted on this recommendation in 1938 by passing the *Métis Population Betterment Act*, which established a number of Métis colonies in the Cold Lake/Lesser Slave Lake and Peace River areas of Alberta. Today there are still eight Métis colonies in Alberta, representing an area of 1.24 million acres reserved for Métis, upon which 4,000 of the province's estimated 30,000 Métis live (Ghostkeeper, 1982:1). This act defined Métis as persons of mixed White and Indian blood who were neither Indians nor non-treaty Indians as defined in the *Indian Act*. This essentially excluded non-Status Indians from the benefits of the act. In 1940, the definition of Métis was amended to add the qualification that the person also had to have at least "one-quarter Indian blood."

Much less was done for the Métis in the other Prairie provinces, and virtually nothing at all was done for the Métis elsewhere in Canada. In the late 1930s, the Saskatchewan government followed Alberta's example and established a Métis colony of sorts at Green Lake, but without legislative status. In the 1960s, the Thatcher government set up a few experimental farm projects for Métis in the province. This is the closest that the Métis in that province ever came to getting a collective land base of their own. In Manitoba, no attempt seems to have been made to provide Métis with a land base after the fiasco of the *Manitoba Act*. None of these actions on the part of provincial governments were predicated on recognizing Métis Aboriginal rights, but were justified rather as social welfare measures (Sanders, 1979:22).

The Métis have been granted Aboriginal claims recently in a few areas. The James Bay Agreement of 1975 recognizes the land claims of "non-Status Cree," who in an earlier age would probably have been considered Métis. The Métis have been included in the renegotiation of Treaty No. 11 (Mackenzie Valley) and will probably also be included in the recently announced renegotiation of Treaty No. 8 (Northern Alberta). In the early

1970s an isolated group of Métis were discovered when Grande Cache, Alberta, was being opened up for a mining development, and the Alberta government may have granted these people a distinct land claim. Overall, the Métis have not, however, been granted a distinct Aboriginal claim anywhere but in the old Northwest, and these Métis may already have had their Aboriginal claims extinguished through scrip.

CONCLUSION

The definition of Métis in the new Constitution faces at least three kinds of problems. First are the "ethnological problems" — not to be confused with metaphysical problems associated with the fact that mixed Indian and European ancestry is not, by itself, a sufficient condition for identifying the Métis in section 35. To deal with this problem, the Métis in Section 35 must above all be identified through a process of self-identification, but it is not clear if this is sufficient by itself to identify the Métis for the purposes of Section 35. Second are the historical problems which have to do with the fact that only in the old Northwest did the Métis constitute themselves as a distinct people and the fact that only here were they recognized as having a distinct Aboriginal claim. Are these the *Métis people* referred to in Section 35? The Métis National Council uses the historic Métis as the basis for its definition of Métis:

- an aboriginal people distinct from Indians and Inuit;
- descendants of the historic Métis who evolved in what is now Western Canada as a people with a common political will;
- descendants of those Aboriginal peoples who have been absorbed by the historic Métis (Métis National Council, January 1984).

This definition is historically sound. However, if strictly applied it threatens to exclude many persons in other parts of Canada who identify themselves as Métis but who do not necessarily identify with the historic Métis of the old Northwest. The 1981 census shows that such people exist.

Finally, there are the policy problems associated with the fact that since 1876 Indians who have lost their status under the *Indian Act* — non-Status Indians — have come to share with the Métis that condition which distinguishes Métis most from Indians — being Aboriginal peoples without Aboriginal rights under treaty or the *Indian Act* — while remaining distinguishable from them for legal purposes. The federal government has recently given most non-Status Indians the opportunity to regain status as Indians under the *Indian Act*, and many may choose to do so. But not all will. It then becomes important to realize the arbitrary nature of the legal distinction between Métis and non-Status Indians. The processes that produced the Métis did not suddenly come to a stop in 1885. Not only were the Métis in the Northwest in 1885 growing as a result of self-generation (unions between Métis and Métis), but new cohorts of Métis were always being created as a result of unions between Indian and Métis, White and Métis, and White and Indian. Since 1885, the same processes have continued to operate and have probably accelerated. The non-Status population which has developed since 1876 is living proof that these processes have not stopped. A good portion of non-Status Indian women lost their status because they married Whites or Métis. In either case, the children of such unions are mixed-blood and have just as much right to call themselves Métis after 1885 as the children of such unions before 1885. Not all may choose to do so, but to use 1885 as the cut-off date for determining who can be a Métis is to dismiss new cohorts which have come into existence since then. If we fail to include these people in the definition of Aboriginal peoples found in Section 35, we threaten to perpetuate a system that denies Aboriginal rights to persons who clearly share all the conditions of Aboriginal people in Canada today.

NOTES

1. See the *Constitution Act, 1982*, Sections 35(1) and (2).

2. Michif uses French nouns in a Cree syntax and was a language quite widely used among Western Métis, to judge from the variety of places where it is still spoken today.

3. Article 17 of the *Charter of the Company of New France* read: "The Savages who will be led to the faith and to profess it will be considered natural Frenchmen, and like them, will be able to come and live in France when they wish to, and there acquire property, with rights of inheritance and bequest, just as if they had been born Frenchmen, without being required to make any declaration or to become naturalized" (quoted in Dickason, 1981:8).

4. This estimate was made by Jacques Rousseau, a Québec biologist, in 1970.

5. For a description of marriage customs among the Indians and the nature of the relationship between Indian women and fur traders see McLean (n.d.:43-60).

6. Probably the most accurate version of "La Grenouillère" can be found in MacEwan (1981:28-29).

7. For a description of the Métis role in the free trade struggle see Giraud (1945:888-944).

8. Taken from Wilkes-Taylor Papers, W.D. Smith, Manitoba Record Society (Editor), 1968:171.

9. Table 5 is based on research done by the Association of Métis and Non-Status Indians of Saskatchewan (AMNSIS), which has traced the history of roughly 15,000 individual scrip cases. The table extrapolates the data to include all of the approximately 26,000 notes that were delivered (Heinemann, 1984:247; McLean, n.d.:347).

Part IV _____

Canada: Individual Responses to State Definitions of Aboriginal Identity

INTRODUCTION

Most of the papers we have considered to this point have been concerned with the effects of legislation on group identity as opposed to individual identities. This section is particularly concerned with individual responses to imposed identity. To some extent this has been anticipated by the previous works in the other sections, as the ultimate concern of group analysis must be the individual. The three papers that follow are particularly focussed on the person rather than the group.

In a paper specially written for this volume by S.W. Corrigan, we come face to face with the most callous form of forced identity change, the systematic removal of Native peoples' children for socialization by the dominant society. Whether in the context of apprehension and foreign adoption of Native children, or removal for education, the record is a dismal and disheartening one. For years, the child welfare services in Manitoba and elsewhere in North America have been a steady source of forced assimilation, as Native children were routinely apprehended and sold for adoption ("sold" is *not* hyperbole; money routinely changed hands between agencies in the United States and Canada for Native children). One of the most distressing, yet illuminating examples of the effects of this policy in Corrigan's paper is the individual who has had not one, but five separate identities imposed upon him; complete with five separate birth certificates and five different birth dates! Corrigan contrasts this story with that of a successful adoption *within* the Native community, which illustrates that adoption need not be routinely accompanied by identity loss. The dismal effects of taking children out of the society to "educate" them, supposedly so they can become functioning members of the dominant society, then returning them to their own society where they are totally unprepared for day to day living is also explored.

The next two papers are concerned with the way in which status laws have affected Native women and group boundaries in the past and in the present. Weaver's account, which was written in 1974, concerns the famous case of Mrs. Bedard, originally of the Grand River Reserve in Ontario. Because of her marriage to a non-Native, Mrs. Bedard was removed from the band list, and lost permission to reside on the reserve. This in itself was nothing unusual, but Mrs. Bedard challenged these laws in court. She was one of several women who challenged Section 12(1)(b) of the *Indian Act* in the 1970s. She met with concerted resistance from the Native community itself, and Weaver's paper is an analysis of why that was so. It remains a good example of the effects of Section 12(1)(b) on women's status and the boundary maintenance of the reserve—a clash that was seen by the community as between "women's rights" and "Indian rights". It illustrates the way a once matrilineal and matrilocal society internalized the values and criteria of community boundary maintenance set for it by the dominant society through the *Indian Act.*

Green's article is the more recent, and it concerns the effects of Bill C-31, the amendment to the *Indian Act* which removed Section 12(1)(b). One of the basic aspects of self-government is the right of First Nations to determine their own criteria for citizenship. Green discusses the ways in which Bill C-31 may violate this right, by not allowing Band Councils total control over determining membership, at least in the case of women marrying non-Status males. She also considers what this means for women who may have been expelled from their reserves because of their choice of marriage partners, and what they face now that they are reinstated into the band. It is a contentious issue, and the rights of women who are reinstated are still not clear.

UNDERGROUND POLICY: AN ESSAY ON IDENTITY AND THE ABORIGINAL VICTIMS OF NON-ABORIGINAL STRUCTURES[1]

Samuel W. Corrigan

DANIEL

Daniel thinks he turned 21 in 1992. He's not certain, of course, although he does have a birth certificate. More properly he has birth certificates: five of them in all. None of these were issued in the province where he was born and where he now lives, though. That province cannot find any record of his birth under the four possible names and birth dates he used in seeking such a certificate. There is probably a record of his birth somewhere in the hospital where he was born, too. But again, the hospital is unable to find any reference to him from the time he might have been born. He knows that none of the five birth certificates issued to him in the past are correct. Each of the five, issued legally if not properly, shows a different birth name,[2] a different set of birth parents, a different birthplace and — indignity upon indignity — a different birth date.

Daniel is a victim. He is a young man, a Status Indian, a member of a Band in western Manitoba. He is confined to a wheelchair, the result of a childhood car accident. His history is a familiar one. Apprehended by an organization almost euphemistically named "Children's Aid Society", he became a ward, a pawn in the hands of non-Aboriginal bureaucrats. Placed in a foster home, he was very happy for three years. Then he was sold. An American social service agency wanted children, and Daniel was available.

Money changed hands, and Daniel was exported to the United States against his will. Then began a series of adoption placements, some of which seemed to work, and a smaller series of formal adoptions. In between these placements, Daniel spent time in hospitals and in juvenile detention facilities.

Over the course of his career as a player in the musical chair syndrome of the child welfare system, Daniel was issued the five birth certificates, each one attesting to his legitimate status as the son of particular parents. While one might question the ethics of this, one can generally understand an agency arranging for, perhaps, one birth certificate. Agencies and child welfare workers often believe that it is necessary to create a new history for each adopted child, apparently so that the child will *belong,* will have a status, a place within a family. The side effect of this, intended or not, is to bury any true history of the child, a history which might in some ways be unpleasant, but which invariably incorporates many other people.

We know today that many adults, adopted as children, are able to discover their "real" histories, the actual events which led to their adoptions, and the original or "birth" families of which they are or were a part. Mechanisms now exist in most jurisdictions to assist those parents and children, separated by the system, to contact each other. The process is normally cumbersome and always very lengthy. Serious restrictions are placed upon searches although often some minimal information is released to individuals directly involved in those separations.

Daniel, remember, is a Status Indian, a member of a Band, and a beneficiary under one of the numbered Treaties. He was born in an accredited hospital in rural Manitoba, treated in a major teaching hospital in an urban area, and then apprehended by a large child welfare agency. He was sold to a very large agency in the United States, and lived in at least four different states with numerous families. He was shipped around from family to home to treatment centre, loved occasionally, helped at times in his attempts to cope with strange environments, and at other times abused in imaginative ways. He was invited back to Manitoba by an Indian child welfare agency and members of his birth family, and after painful reunions and further separations, settled in Manitoba. One would think it would be simple to recover or reconstruct the early history of this youth, whose birth took place only a generation ago. Nothing would be further from the truth. Various agencies and wings of government, and many individuals, have both conspired and acted individually either to bury or to erase and eliminate the history of Daniel, even managing to prevent him ever from learning his true birth date.

IDENTITY: INDIVIDUALS AND GROUPS

The identity of any person begins in a family, in the small network of individuals which surrounds the young, growing child. It is forged gradually as the child encounters people outside that family unit, as the developing individual begins to differentiate herself or himself from others. Typically Aboriginal youngsters begin to identify themselves as Aboriginal, for example, only as contact develops with non-Aboriginal people. The identity of individuals grows and focusses then within a like group, the kinsmen, and in distinction to unlike people, the non-kin, who may also be socially or culturally different. Further aspects of an individual's identity grow and become apparent in the turmoil of adolescence, to form the fully developed adult, the whole person, that complex of statuses which allows people to function with a certain degree of security in a wide variety of social circumstances.

Identity is also founded within a group, a collection of individuals who are viewed as similar by outside observers, and who are likely to value a group identity which both binds them together and distinguishes them from others. Sometimes the impetus for this group identity comes from within; such things as marriage regulations may reinforce that group exclusivity. Sometimes it comes from without, as in the recognition of linguistic or national groups by others. And, in a few cases, that group identity is imposed, with or without the consent of the members, by external bodies as a matter of law. The status of Indian in Canada, a definition developed and required by non-Aboriginal people for some Aboriginal people, is a classic case in point.

ELIMINATING ABORIGINAL IDENTITY

Tobias (1976) has characterized Canadian Indian policy in terms of three general stages, protection, civilization and assimilation. The concept of protection, stemming in part from the *Royal Proclamation* of 1763, and relating primarily to land and trade, essentially meant non-interference in Indian social and cultural practices. By the early part of the 19th century, however, a policy was developed which allowed the British to attempt the "civilization" of Indians through a combination of religious proselytization and the development of specific Indian reserved land settlements where groups of Indians could be located, converted, and "educated" (Tobias, 1976:14-15). By the time of the first *Indian Act*, nine years after Confederation in 1876, the goal had expanded from general "civilization" to outright "assimilation". The goal was expressed most cogently through the provisions of that 1876 *Indian Act,* notably through measures for education, administration and enfranchisement which continued through to 1985. (It is significant, I think, that many of the provisions of the current *Indian Act* in 1992 mirror much of the 1876 version, especially in terms of Band adminstration.)

As part of the long term process of assimilation, the Canadian government and a great many Canadian individuals and agencies practiced cultural genocide over a long period of time. That phrase was never used, of course. Indeed one suspects that these practitioners of destruction rarely knew the consequences of their policies and their actions. They genuinely believed, at least in most cases, that what they were doing was for the long term benefit of Aboriginal people, even if it did involve short term pain. We know now that the scale of cultural havoc was very great, and that these policies and actions involved very long term pain indeed. That this swath of ultimate bigotry did not eliminate Aboriginal cultures is due more to the survival instincts and anger of Aboriginal people, and the general ineptitude of non-Aboriginal agents of change, than to any design on the part of either government or private agencies.

I will focus on three areas in which non-Aboriginal society, through a variety of agencies, attempted to erase and supplant Aboriginal identity. The first of these involved direct federal government action, the notorious "potlatch laws" which sought to eliminate Aboriginal ceremonial activity. It must be remembered that although these are among the best known provisions of the *Indian Act*, much other legislation in Canada was also devoted to the repression of Aboriginal cultural expression. The potlatch law is one illustration of this, but the same principles applied in areas such as governmental systems, marriage and inheritance, and social control systems.

Second, I will examine education using only a single example, the effect of a residential school upon a hunting people in the 1950s and 1960s. These church-operated agencies of change brought a single-minded — some would say a bloody minded — determination to the conversion of Aboriginal people and identity to non-Aboriginal standards. Theirs was an unabashed, unapologetic mission, still largely defended for its overall goal, even if the methods involved brutality and abuse. Again, this one example must be seen as just that: many dozens of residential schools thrived across Canada in the 19th and 20th centuries, even in the prairie provinces where treaties generally called for schools on reserves.

Third, the recent abuse of child welfare legislation from the 1950s through the 1980s will provide a further example. Although I will take a broader approach in this section, it is again only a set of statistical and anecdotal vignettes of what is probably the most terrifying genocide in Canada since the placing of bounties upon the heads of the Beothuk Indians in Newfoundland in the 18th century. In this case, not only were the past policies and practices of literally dozens of agencies and hundreds of individuals culturally genocidal — often openly and admittedly so — but many of the same policies and practices apply today, in 1992, in urban Canada.

I have used the phrase "underground policy" in the title of this essay to refer to a particular phenomenon, the actual function or effect of a policy or set of policies. Policy, as it is enunciated at a ministerial or cabinet level, is generally both high-minded and general, even vague. As it is reduced to a series of guidelines and statements to fit various bureaucratic needs — such as finance, delivery, appeal and review — it tends to be refined and enlarged, and often becomes written in stone. It is, moreover, gradually re-interpreted as it filters down the hierarchy, first for convenient application in sometimes very large and scattered bureaucracies, and then by the unique perspectives and biases of the individuals who must apply it firsthand. The actual *practice* of any policy is often far removed from its noble intent. The *delivery* of a policy involves so much translation for convenience that it is likely to bear little resemblance to any prior plan. The final *effect* of any policy is frequently both different from its original goal and, at the individual level, harmful through its application.

"Underground policy" in this sense refers to the actual affects of this policy re-interpretation and delivery where the policy results in the widespread application of measures which universally effect people in ways not necessarily spelled out in the conception of a single policy. Thus the potlatch laws, designed to end particular ceremonies deemed dangerous or undesirable, had the final effect of damaging Aboriginal identity, whether they were applied in areas where there were potlatches, or elsewhere, where there were other ceremonies. The residential schools, designed to provide education for a non-Aboriginal world, also had the clear effect of destroying Aboriginal identity in many ways.

What is most disturbing about underground policy, as I will suggest later, is that it is indeed perceived by large numbers of individuals for what it is: in these cases, purely and simply a means of eliminating aspects of Aboriginal identity, or cultural genocide. That these policies continued so long — and in the case of child welfare continue today — with such widespread and unapologetic awareness by non-Aboriginal people, can only be considered astounding.

The simple fact is that many Canadians still feel Aboriginal people need to change culturally. Sometimes these persons are given the opportunity of interacting with Aboriginal people from positions of power and strength, as agencies such as correctional systems, schools and child care authorities. They may then attempt to eliminate elements of Aboriginal identity from their Aboriginal charges, while deliberately trying to implant their own cultural chauvinism. They genuinely believe they have the right to do this, even though many Canadians would rightly characterize their behaviour and attitudes as oppressive and destructive.

POTLATCH AND ABORIGINAL IDENTITY

Canada has an extensive record of seeking cultural change for Aboriginal people, often in subtle ways, but also through overtly brutal mechanisms. Some of the more blatant attempts at cultural change can be found in several particularly repressive pieces of legislation which outlawed specific cultural practices. As but one example, both LaViolette (1961) and Cole and Chaikin (1990) have detailed the so-called "potlatch laws" which were used to attempt to erase numerous elements of Aboriginal belief and practice. Although aimed specifically at the potlatch and other ceremonials of the Aboriginal peoples of the Northwest Coast, the laws spilled over to affect people on the prairies as well, many of whom had rituals, such as Sun Dances, prohibited. These laws began in 1883 and ended in 1951 when they were quietly left out of a new *Indian Act*. During their 68 years they were only spottily enforced, but were used to great effect to intimidate people. They were also used as a form of bribery/coercion, as in the 1920s when senior members of the federal bureaucracy "allowed" individuals to surrender treasured cultural items, such as masks, in return for suspended sentences rather than jail terms for participating in potlatch (Cole and Chaikin, 1990:120-121). Many participants, however, still received both time and humiliation in prison.

What were the potlatch laws and the ensuing jail terms for Aboriginal potlatch participants all about? Put simply, potlatch was a complex series of actions which involved the giving of material goods, often European in nature, and extremely valuable non-material goods, such as names and rights of various kinds, to other people within one's own society. It was a widely recognized and followed practice which signified important changes of social status, such as marriage and death. It provided an underpinning to social rank as well as, in some areas, to economic resources.

Obviously the specifics of the potlatch varied from society to society, indeed from village to village. Nonetheless, whether it underscored social rank, or validated changes of status, or facilitated the transmission of resource rights, the potlatch was considered by its participants to be an integral part of their societies. It did not appear to harm anybody, although certainly some Aboriginal people, notably those who were under the sway of missionaries, had opted out of any potlatch participation. What is very clear is that these ceremonies were uniquely Aboriginal; non-Aboriginal people did not participate and were not in any way a part of these events. Moreover, the potlatch as it functioned in the late 19th century normally involved the consumption of large quantities of non-Aboriginal goods, a factor which one would presume benefitted non-Aboriginal people.

The Canadian government however, responding to local non-Aboriginal people (and some Aboriginal people aligned with Christian mission efforts), decided to outlaw the practice. The first objection to the potlatch seemed to reflect more upon non-Aboriginal moral perspectives, rather than European religions. Although the two might very well be intertwined, in fact many of the objections in both the 19th and 20th centuries indicated that what non-Aboriginal people viewed as particularly repugnant were the economic involvements of potlatching: it was considered offensive for Aboriginal people to maintain well defined credit systems within their own societies. It was also considered somehow dangerous that Aboriginal people would accumulate large amounts of material goods and then distribute them in massive give-aways to other Aboriginal people. Those few Aboriginal people who objected to potlatching apparently considered the practice to be too "Aboriginal" in nature; at least some of their objections appear to have been written by non-Aboriginal missionaries.

The breadth of the legislation embodying the potlatch law allowed it to be applied to the ceremonies of Aboriginal people in other regions of the country as well. On the prairies, for example, the concept of individuals vowing to sacrifice themselves with skin piercing during Sun Dance for the ultimate good of the society as a whole was also considered to be somehow subversive. Many plains Indians ceremonies, especially the Sun Dance, were effectively banned, while others such as powwows were officially frowned upon. Interestingly, the painful tattooing rituals of so many Aboriginal people were considered reasonable, however, perhaps because they were also an acceptable practice for non-Aboriginal people, and thus were not considered to be "mutilation". It is significant that those practices which were banned in Canada were those which were exclusively Aboriginal. Practices shared by both Aboriginal and non-Aboriginal people were believed to be legitimate; they did not underline any separate or unique Aboriginal identity.

What this legislation meant then, for its 68 year reign of repression, was a willingness – indeed a zealousness – on the part of non-Aboriginal governments to eradicate practices which underscored both personal and group *Aboriginal* identity. Practices which were common both to Aboriginal and non-Aboriginal groups and which could not thus be directly related to Aboriginal identity as different from that of others, were tolerated.

EDUCATION AND ABORIGINAL IDENTITY

The residential school system which functioned through the 1970s has long been recognized as a major force in diminishing both the personal and cultural identities of Aboriginal children. Although the system was designed primarily for Status Indian children, the schools often cast their nets widely, thus including many other Aboriginal children too. This was particularly the case in the 19th and early 20th centuries, when the legal — external — definition of Indian was much broader than it is now. Many have written of their experiences in residential schools, with variations related to the particular school. Virtually all of these stories have some common elements, however, notably including hunger, physical brutality and, most dramatically, beatings for speaking an Aboriginal language. Some of these autobiographies reflect great humour (Johnston, 1989; Willis, 1973), but all refer to the dehumanizing process through which children of many cultures were forced into particular molds of belief and behaviour. What was not generally realized, of course, was that the mold into which children were forced was typically not representative of non-Aboriginal cultures; it was instead an artificial construct with rules and standards which would generally be considered strange by most Canadians. In fact, all too often the adults responsible for these schools fitted Dunning's (1959a) concept of "marginal men", people who did not fit well into non-Aboriginal life, who were not typical of non-Aboriginal people, and who, although serving as agents of change, were basically inept both in Aboriginal and non-Aboriginal cultures. In many cases the individual children seem to have been lost in the system, victims of personnel more concerned with the structure of their employment than with their charges. King, for example, notes an incident at a school in Yukon, where the staff was very much concerned about a pet cat: "No child at Mopass was the object of such deep concern as was that cat" (1967:68).

The pattern of cultural abuse through education continued until very recent times. It is necessary to understand that all parents have some sense of themselves and their lives, that is, a sense of "culture". Parents raise their children according to particular standards which are generally accepted within their society. Essentially parents want their children to be able to function as they themselves function in a given society and culture. To that end, particular perspectives on right and wrong, on propriety and impropriety, on good and bad, are brought to bear in raising children. There are particular ways of behaving which are considered proper, and manners which are considered not proper; moreover these are generally recognized standards with which children are raised to help them become fully functioning and acceptable adults in the society. The process takes a long time in humans: at a minimum fully 15 years, although in some cultures, such as the Beaver, it may take from 20 to 30 years before children are considered to be fully functioning, self-subsistent adults (Ridington, 1971).

It is obvious that any significant change in the standards of raising children – standards which determine adult behaviour – will have major effects upon both adult society over the long term and individual identity in the short term. The individual who is raised to function in a manner markedly different from others in his or her society will clearly suffer when his or her behaviour fails to meet the expectations of adults in the society. The damage to personal esteem, and to the individual's ability to succeed within a group, can be enormous. Sindell (1968) outlined some of the changes of socialization which residential schools imposed upon Mistassini Cree youngsters in the 1960s. The Cree had no choice in the matter, of course. Having defined them as Indians under the *Indian Act,* the state then required their children to attend school. The state also determined the school in which they would be educated to non-Aboriginal standards, and arranged for their transportation some 500 kilometres away from their homes. The differences for these children were enormous.

For the first five to seven years of their lives, Mistassini children grew up in a Cree world, with virtually no contact with non-Aboriginal people, except for the scary bogey-man creature who was defined as "White" (Sindell, 1968:83). Their behaviour developed to fit the particular expectations of their families. They were surrounded by kinsmen, including parents, grandparents, siblings, parents' siblings and so on. As children they could turn to anyone for assistance, whether child or adult, but they were expected to become self-reliant, to meet their own needs as much as possible rather than depending upon others. The child would eat when it was hungry and sleep when it was tired, answering those needs as it saw fit on its own. The child was also expected to explore the world in which it lived, to discover and learn by experience. Thus the Cree "walking out" ceremony, the feast held when a toddler first walked out of the tent or house to the outside world, was a major event. It marked the start of the individual's voyage of discovery in the world outside its immediate family, the start of a journey through the living part of its existence, the beginning of an adventure of learning and experience which would guide the individual into old age. Children had to learn to survive in the bush, the environment in which as hunters they would make their living and be co-dependent with others, both human and non-human. As in most hunting cultures, children were expected to explore and to learn, to experience and profit from their investigations of the whole world about them. Rarely was the child restrained in this process, and then only if it faced extreme danger through lack of experience. The child was believed to be a whole person after all, not a "baby" but an individual who would become an adult only through experience. In that process the individual would sometimes stumble and fall, but would learn to function as a big person through those experiences, and would become an independent, self-reliant adult able to contribute to the society as a whole.

In a child's early years the composition of the domestic group shifted considerably as the small group of kinsmen lived now in a town, now in a bush camp. The number of people with whom the child interacted changed regularly, as did the individuals, so that the child did not build up a dependence upon only a few persons. It was necessary too for the child to interact and cooperate with many others in a variety of tasks. There were many duties which had to be performed in the Mistassini household if the unit was to survive, especially in the bush where hunger was always a threat to some extent. Thus cooperation was necessary and children, as full individuals, though lacking in experience, were expected to pull their weight as much as possible, always with allowances for their size and strength. The child, after all, was Mistassini, a full member of a small group of interacting kinsmen; it had to grow and learn as Mistassini, not as something else. At the same time, virtually all of the childrens' play was imitative of adult tasks; that is, children learned adult roles by playing at them, by gradually gaining experience in those tasks. There was no separation of child and adult worlds except by experience and ability.

Because of the small size of Mistassini groups, and the precarious nature of survival in the bush, Mistassini must cooperate. This means that individuals must function for long periods of time in small, closely-knit groups, and it means a strong negative view of aggression and hostility. Children learned, through experience, example, and words, that one did not contradict or refuse others, that one did not strike others. Physical aggression was considered dreadful, but even overt hostility, through words or actions, was viewed in negative terms. Individuals needed to cooperate; they could turn to others for support, both emotional and material, but they were expected to be self-reliant and at the same time to assist others without being asked.

It almost goes without saying that physical punishment of children was exceptionally rare. A child might be redirected or even marginally corrected, as with a light slap, in its process of discovery and growth, but punishment as a concept was a foreign idea, negatively viewed.

After growing up in what many would view as an environment of discovery, support, cooperation and peace, with a mix of adults and children, all perceived as full individuals, the Mistassini child was sent to the residential school for extended periods of time. There the behaviour demanded, the role expectations for these small persons, and the standards for their socialization, were dramatically different.

The child entered significant contact with non-Aboriginal people for the first time in this school. And suddenly the mix and numbers of people were different. Now the child found itself in a children's world, with large numbers of children and very few adults. Moreover, the roles of adults and children were remarkably different: children were simply not allowed to perform normal adult tasks, while adults rarely did the same things as children. Not only did the relative numbers of adults and children change, but so too did the range of children with whom the Mistassini youth could interact. Now all children were segregated on the basis of age — older and younger — and gender — male and female — with relatively little contact allowed among them. For the Cree child there is no rational explanation for such an unnatural division of children who are, after all, people. This separation of the individual from siblings and other members of the society certainly serves no useful purpose in Mistassini culture; but then too it would be hard to think of any useful purpose such a separation might serve in non-Aboriginal culture either.

A series of much more serious changes are forced upon the behaviour of these children, however. First the staff of the school tend to lock up necessary supplies and tools, and then require that all tasks be done according to a formal schedule. This means that all activities, whether school, "play", or chores, are done by a strange time pattern, rather than as necessary. At the same time children must eat and sleep according to a strict schedule. This scheduling is not possible in the bush prior to coming to school, nor will it be possible later in life when the Cree adult must hunt to survive. Far more significant is what happens to the child's ability to function as a self-reliant individual. Now the child is no longer able to answer some important needs of its own on its own; now the child is taught dependence upon others, adults, and that dependence is keyed to the whims of the adult "leaders." Should the child need or want equipment or tools of some sort, whether classroom pencils or sporting equipment, it must ask an adult rather than take the initiative of acting independently.

Even more damaging to Cree standards, the imbalance of adults and children and the total control of the children by the adults forces the many children to compete against each other for the attention of the few adults. Thus not only is self-reliance effectively eliminated (although it is usually held to be a valuable non-Aboriginal characteristic!), but competition is encouraged among the Cree students, rather than cooperation. Indeed success in competition – through whining or noise – achieves material rewards for children in this system. Far from being encouraged to cooperate to assist each other unasked, to complete necessary tasks for the good of all, things which are necessary for Cree adults, Mistassini children are taught in school to seek personal gratification, to best others, to achieve rewards for themselves at the expense of others. In the process of effectively stamping out self-reliance and cooperation, and encouraging self-centredness and material rewards, the school does something else. In virtually all activities, but especially in recreation, the adults in the school support and reward aggression, indeed overt hostility. Children, for example, tend to be encouraged to form teams rather than to play as a whole, and to compete aggressively and openly against each other. Even more striking is the adult behaviour towards the children: corporal punishment occasionally, with much yelling and sternness. The children are also exposed to television, with its heavy stress upon individual achievement, good or bad, through aggression and hostility.

When children return home to their families in Mistassini, they are different. The difference is not simply of age or experience. For the latter, of course, the experience the children have gained is of little use in the Cree community, and they will have failed to experience much that is necessary to become a proper Cree adult. What is especially disturbing is that these children will have been resocialized to standards radically different, indeed diametrically opposed, to those of their parents. They will not be able to function in Mistassini society and culture as do those who do not suffer the residential school.

One of the reasons for the inability of these youth to function well at home is not just the curriculum of the school, which is generally irrelevant to a hunting life anyway, but the styles of teaching and expected learning. Children in hunting societies – indeed probably in all societies where people live with the land – learn more by observation and experience than by any formal instruction. Theirs is a form of visual learning, in which children gradually acquire skills necessary for their survival in the bush by observing and experiencing their environment. The process, which can take a full generation, does involve some formal instruction as elders pass to their young their knowledge of the bush and their life, but it is overwhelmingly a visual form of instruction. The residential school, on the other hand, specializes almost exclusively in oral and literary instruction, forms of teaching which typically serve urban populations very well, but which are simply unsuitable for the lives which the Mistassini children are expected to follow when they return home, or for the knowledge which they need to survive in the bush.

At the same time as the children fail at becoming adequate hunters when they return to Misstassini, so too these Cree youth are also frequently unable to function adequately in non-Aboriginal cultural milieus. As Wintrob has noted (1968), the children basically fail to meet the standards of knowledge, behaviour or ethics of Mistassini adults, and similarly fail to meet those same kinds of standards outside the culture. It is obvious that this must mean great disappointment for Cree adults, whose children are no longer properly behaved. But even more damaging is the effect this inadequacy of experience and understanding must have upon the self-esteem of these youth. Who are these persons now? Are they Cree? These children-becoming-adults can see very clearly that they do not have the same footing in the culture as others; at the same time those who try to succeed in non-Aboriginal urban areas too often fail to succeed because of their basically Cree standards. The result is what Wintrob has termed "psychic stress" encountered by "youth experiencing conditions of rapid social and cultural change" (Wintrob, 1968:93).

Was personal identity conflict, and the inability to function well in different circumstances the goal of education for Aboriginal people? Obviously it was not, unless the underlying goal was always to destabilize individuals to the point where whole societies and cultures could be somehow reworked to eliminate elements of Aboriginality. It is certainly hard to believe that such a system of brutality and indignity could last for a hundred years without the perpetrators being aware of its functions. I will return to this theme later.

ABORIGINAL PEOPLE AND THE CHILD WELFARE SYSTEM

Aboriginal societies in Canada long maintained their own child and family support systems, so that until the 1950s, most Aboriginal children in need of care from persons other than their natural parents were cared for within the society. In many regions of the country the pattern continued into the 1990s. Indeed, Inuit communities in Canada typically have among the highest adoption rates of any societies in the world, often with anywhere from 20 to 30 per cent of residents adopted by others (Guemple, 1979). This pattern accommodates not simply the needs of children for adult care-givers, but also a conscious recognition of the need to provide for all people within one's own culture. Up until the 1950s most Aboriginal communities in Canada found means to maintain their youth, generally among kinsmen. In many Aboriginal societies the family resided in several households linked by economic and social ties beyond simple kinship bonds, and children often moved easily among those households but within the same family. (This reflects, of course, the non-Aboriginal "extended family", a concept generally imperfectly understood by non-Aboriginal people, and even less perfectly applied, will-nilly, by them to Aboriginal cultures.)

By the early 1960s, Aboriginal populations began to grow dramatically, and alcohol became more readily available. This followed on the heels of declining economic opportunities for Aboriginal people. Trapping had begun to decline in northern areas, in some cases as early as the 1920s, while agriculture, with increasing mechanization, provided fewer and fewer jobs in the south. The result was significant social disruption. To a large extent Aboriginal communities found they were unable to maintain social order, a situation exacerbated by their legal position as essentially colonized people.

One of the manifestations of this disorder was seen in a greatly increased need for child welfare services. Unable to provide those services on their own, for legal and economic reasons, Aboriginal communities turned to non-Aboriginal authorities for help. In some cases this meant simply extra care given to rural and remote areas by provincial governments already considered responsible, while in other cases it meant new agreements allowing the provinces or their agent voluntary societies to provide services, if the latter word is correct. Thus began what has been termed the "sixties scoop" (Johnston, 1983:23).

The "sixties scoop" refers to a period which extended into the 1980s at least in some areas, during which enormous numbers of Aboriginal children were apprehended by non-Aboriginal authorities, some to be placed with foster and adoptive parents, often far away, many to be effectively sold to other countries. The numbers and proportions of children involved were incredible, so much so that a Family Court judge investigating Aboriginal child placements in one province termed the practice of placement with non-Aboriginal families as "cultural genocide" (Kimelman, 1984:51). In British Columbia, for example, by 1980, fully 1 in 3 of the children who were in the care of child welfare agencies was Aboriginal; in Manitoba, 3 out of 5; while in Saskatchewan, 2 out of every 3 children in care were Aboriginal (Johnston, 1983:27; 39; 40).

The result of this almost wholesale apprehension of Aboriginal children was outrage and the development of Aboriginal agencies and Aboriginal child welfare services across Canada. By the late 1980s, a significant proportion of Indian families were served by Indian agencies, although non-Indian Aboriginal communities and most urban areas still lacked culturally appropriate service. What then were the results? By 1989, fully 3 out of 5, or 60%, of all the children in care in Manitoba were *still* Aboriginal! The only difference was that between 65 to 75 per cent of the Indian children in care were the responsibiltiy of Indian agencies. The Manitoba government was no longer alienating large numbers of Aboriginal children from Aboriginal families by exporting then to other provinces or countries. Instead they continued to alienate these children from their cultures and their communities by adoptive placements within the Province: almost half (47.8%) of all Aboriginal children adopted in a 22 month period in 1988-1989 were placed with non-Aboriginal families, apparently without thought as to numbers or consequences (Barkwell, Longclaws and Chartrand, 1989:50).

By the early 1990s, the Aboriginal agencies were burdened both with the large numbers of children and adults who had suffered under the non-Aboriginal agencies, and the legacy of the significant social and family disruption which had begun in the 1950s and snowballed though the 1980s. Many of the problems faced by the Aboriginal family services were the same as those experienced by their non-Aboriginal predecessors; but they also had to play catch up, working with the many thousands of abuse victims of that earlier period and with their victims in turn. The difference, and it is almost certainly a significant one, is that much more of the treatment and virtually all of the placements are culturally appropriate. Instead of placing children in culturally alien homes where the expectations for children are very different from the societies into which the children were born, they are more likely to be placed in homes of cultural similarity. Although the parents may be different in their life skills and abilities, and in their functioning in both Aboriginal and non-Aboriginal societies, they will be fully cognizant of the cultural standards which the childrens' natural parents were unable to impart because of their own problems. This does not by any means guarantee perfect treatment for the abused, the neglected or the traumatized, but it does ensure that the caregivers will not represent a standard of belief or behaviour which virtually guarantees later identity conflicts.

ABORIGINAL IDENTITY AND THE CHILD WELFARE SYSTEM

For reasons which are not fully understood, the adoption or fosterage of Aboriginal children in Canada (or by export) is fraught with serious consequences. Logically, all cross-cultural adoption is risky in terms of later, especially adolescent, identity conflict. It is possible that some measures might reduce the risks inherent in such placements, including deliberate cultural awareness and cross-cultural contact, and placement at birth, although there is uncertainty even here. The singular fact, however, is that the adoption of Aboriginal children by non-Aboriginal parents can and often does have tragic results.

Although relatively little research has been done on the effects of the non-Aboriginal adoption of Aboriginal children, work which has been done recently is of high quality in design and control. Bagley (1991) compared five different groups of adolescents, controlling among other things for temporary adolescent distress. The five groups included White children adopted by White parents; non-adopted White children; non-White children from Asia and South America adopted in Canada by White parents; Aboriginal children adopted by White parents; and finally a group of non-adopted Aboriginal children. These latter are of particular interest. Although the children in the first four categories all resided in a large urban centre, the non-adopted Aboriginal children all lived on rural Indian reserves. Moreover, these children had been identified by their bands as being from families in need of support services. In every case at least one sibling had been apprehended and removed from the household for alleged neglect. None of the children in this sample had ever been removed, but at least half had lived with other kin at some time. This was not, in other words, a group of model youngsters from model families, but rather youth continuing to live in families already identified — by Aboriginal people — as troubled.

Various measures were applied to assess the identity and self-esteem of the children, and the success of the adoptions, with some surprising results. It is clear that the adoption of Aboriginal children by non-Aboriginal parents is unlikely to succeed: by the age of 17, nearly one-half of those adoptions had ended in the separation of the child from the home. Moreover, according to Bagley, the adopted Aboriginal children

> had significantly poorer self-esteem, and they were also more than three times as likely as any other group to have had problems of suicidal ideas (1991:67).

At the same time, the profiles of the non-adopted Aboriginal youth were comparable to those of non-adopted White children.

Four measures in particular are of some interest here, identity integration, suicidal behaviour, marked behaviour problems at the time of interviews (defined as "one or more of rebellion; running from school or home; drug or alcohol use; delinquency; sexual acting out") and the relative self-esteem of the children within the overall sample. These results are compared here in Table 1.

Table 1: Proportions of Adolescents Exhibiting
Particular Characteristics

Category of Children	#	Lack of Identity Integration	Suicidal Ideas or Self-Harm	Marked Behaviour Problems	Lowest Quartile of Self-Esteem
Aboriginal Adoptees	37	48.6%	40.5%	59.5%	64.9%
White Adoptees	42	14.3%	9.5%	11.9%	30.9%
Intercountry Adoptees	20	10.0%	10.0%	15.0%	25.0%
Non-Adopted Whites	40	7.5%	12.5%	15.0%	22.5%
Non-Adopted Aboriginals	23	13.0%	8.7%	17.4%	26.1%

Adapted from Bagley, 1991:66; 69; 70

It is obvious that Aboriginal children who are adopted by non-Aboriginal parents are at great risk; whether they would be at greater risk if they were not removed from their homes is questionable, of course, but the comparison of these children with the Aboriginal children in troubled families certainly makes the question moot. It would be instructive to have a similar survey of Aboriginal children placed in Aboriginal families, although it is worth remembering that half of the non-adopted Aboriginal children did have placements in related Aboriginal households, in the sense that they had lived in other households of their families.

The point of this research in this context is clear: many thousands of Aboriginal children are clearly at risk through non-Aboriginal placements each year. Consider the figure of 48.6% of Aboriginal adoptees who lack identity integration, and the 64.9% of Aboriginal adoptees with low self-esteem, as just two areas of concern, and then extrapolate from this study in southern Alberta to all of Canada. In Manitoba, for example, over 2350 Aboriginal children were in the care of child welfare agencies in the late 1980s. Add to that the number of children adopted each year, allow for the number of new children entering the system each year since the 1960s, and include children from other provinces, and the total reaches literally tens of thousands of Aboriginal children placed either for fosterage or adoption in non-Aboriginal homes. Lest one think this is an exaggeration, Johnston (1983:57) noted that between 1971 and 1981 over 3700 Status Indian children alone were adopted in Canada by non-Indians. This figure does not include the 1960s, most of the 1980s, other Aboriginal children, export children, or the large majority of placements, that is children in foster homes! Although Bagley's study has not yet been replicated, and little research information is available for foster placements, the clear implication is that at the very least a great many thousands of Aboriginal children have suffered a significant lack of identity integration and a dramatic loss of self-esteem while enmeshed in the child welfare system of Canada.

DEVALUATION, IDENTITY AND STATE STRUCTURES

Barkwell, Gray, Chartrand, Longclaws and Richard (1989) have outlined a process of personal and cultural devaluation, a syndrome which they feel contributed then – and now – to a significant problem between Aboriginal people and the criminal justice system. Individuals who are subject to this cultural and personal devaluation will experience four characteristics:

- *rejection,* leading to physical and relationship discontinuity and personal insecurity;
- *negative imaging,* in which individuals who are identifiably different are perceived negatively;
- *low personal autonomy,* leading to control and/or patronizing behaviour by others; and
- *involuntary poverty,* through the lack of trust accorded by others and the individual's consequent low self-esteem.

Where individuals in large numbers experience this devaluation, whole communities will suffer. Two features of the personal disarray to which this leads, of course, are likely to be difficulty in interpersonal relationships, and substance dependency. Those in turn may well manifest themselves in increased child welfare needs.

Devaluation, then, leads not only to increased involvement with the criminal justice system, but to increased involvement with the child welfare system. It is not surprising that the proportion of children in the custody of child welfare authorities in Manitoba who are Aboriginal – 60% – is the same as the proportion of children in custody of the youth correctional system in Manitoba who are Aboriginal!

Many individuals have suggested that these repressive and oppressive measures were at least well intentioned if not innocent; developed from legitimate concerns, if heavy handed in application. Cole and Chaikin, for example, speak of the potlatch provisions of the *Indian Act* as being almost legitimate in intent:

> What was evil, perhaps, was not so much the law itself as the massive, unreflective power and paternalism of which it was merely one exemplification (Cole and Chaikin, 1990:179).

I do not here suggest that there was any single grand scheme to eliminate or erase Aboriginal identity. That came instead out of a general perception held by non-Aboriginal people that their way of life and their philosophies were superior to those of others. Whether it was misguided altruism or massive group insecurity which led so many to try to impose their values upon Aboriginal people is almost beside the point now. What is important is the fact that this same perspective continues today, whether in the justice system (see for example, Corrigan and Barkwell, 1991), in the legal insistence upon bilateral inheritance and succession systems written into the *Indian Act,* or in the imposition of state definitions of personal identity upon Aboriginal people (Sawchuk, 1985). Even the protracted process of negotiation towards Aboriginal self-government is subject to this, with basic parameters for government systems set in the final analysis by non-Aboriginal governments.

What is at issue here is perception. Will non-Aboriginal people and non-Aboriginal governments continue to insist upon the elimination of Aboriginal identity through underground policy as the paradoxical price of full Aboriginal participation in Canadian society? Aboriginal societies have survived so far, but not without horrendous pain and vast numbers of individual victims. The fact that those societies continue to exist in spite of the countless victims of our state structures is testament to the strength of Aboriginal identity. Whether or not Aboriginal people, Aboriginal societies and Aboriginal cultures can survive further assaults by the underground policies of non-Aboriginal governments remains to be seen.

CORA

Cora is an Aboriginal woman in a small city in northern Manitoba who knows something about the reality of the informal child welfare system within an Aboriginal family. She was born into a dysfunctional family. Her mother and father, plagued by alcoholism, arranged to place her with an elderly childless couple for care on a trial basis. After the placement seemed to work, both couples sought a formal – that is, non-Aboriginal – guardianship arrangement though the government, so that the caregivers could receive financial assistance to raise her.

Unfortunately the foster family was dysfunctional also, again with serious alcohol problems; so that Cora sought refuge with relatives:

> I was in true actuality raised in a communal family. My foster parents' relatives looked after me when my foster parents were drinking. I went home to my foster family when it was safe to do so. I was cared for in my times of need by my Swampy Cree extended family.

At no time did the government child welfare authorities interact with Cora or her families following the initial guardianship arrangement. During most of this period Cora maintained welcome contact with her birth mother and, while at school one day, was delighted to meet her older brother and sister, children she did not previously know about. They had been apprehended by the child welfare authorities for neglect, and placed with a non-Aboriginal family in the same community. "From that day," noted Cora, "I didn't feel so alone."

Cora's birth mother died when she was eight; her foster parents when she was ten. She was then cared for by another relative, an individual so remarkable that he was universally liked and respected by Aboriginal and non-Aboriginal people equally. Indeed, the band of which he was a member later chose to name their new school after him following his death, a rare occurrence in Canada. Cora noted that

> He and his family gave me the stability and love that a child needs in order to develop into a productive and useful member of Cree society and Canadian society. Culture is something that is, a way of life. I am Cree first and foremost, but also a member of Canadian society. My foster family raised me to be proud of who I am, to be proud of my identity. I grew up valuing and respecting God, the Great Spirit, and all of God's creation.

Cora's brother and sister were not so fortunate. They were split up and shipped about the province to different non-Aboriginal families. Neither can communicate, either in words or values, with their Cree families.

There are both striking similarities and one massive difference between the stories of Cora and Daniel. Both suffered from dysfunctional family placements, Cora within an Aboriginal context, Daniel in a non-Aboriginal context in the United States. Both were ultimately placed with families which genuinely loved and cared for them. But Cora grew up as a proud functioning member of a Cree family in a Cree community. Nobody ever took away her Aboriginal identity. Daniel, on the other hand, lost virtually all Aboriginal identity, learning that he was Aboriginal only when his birth sisters finally located the teenager in the United States. He was stripped even of his birth date, the victim of one of Canada's most notorious and longest running scams: the elimination of Aboriginal identity whenever and wherever possible.

NOTES

1. I am indebted to Pat Sawchuk and Joe Sawchuk for helpful comments on an earlier version of this paper. I have also benefitted considerably from discussions with Arthur W. Blue on the nature of learning styles and concepts of identity and self-esteem.

2. Hourie (1991) relates a story of a van load of children being taken to market in the United States. As the van left Winnipeg for the border, one hour distant, a very young Aboriginal child was carefully taught his new name. Woe betide the accompanying workers if one of the children not learn his or her new name by the time they reached the U.S. immigration officials at the border!

JUDICIAL PRESERVATION OF ETHNIC GROUP BOUNDARIES: THE IROQUOIS CASE

Sally M. Weaver

Barth has recently argued that ethnic group boundaries are not solely generated by the ethnic group itself, but must be a product of interplay between the group and the host society (Barth, 1969). The boundaries, he claims can be crossed by people, ideas and material goods without necessitating the discontinuance of the group or the dissipation of the "cultural stuff" inside. He argues that the major determining factor distinguishing an ethnic group is that its members identify and are identified by externals as belonging to a category distinguishable from other categories. It is with the problem of boundary maintenance of these groups, or what Barth refers to as the social arrangements of cultural differences, that this paper is concerned.

Specifically the purpose is to present an encapsulated ethnography of a boundary maintenance struggle at a local level. The "scene" is the Grand River Reserve, with its resident population of nearly 5,000 Iroquois residing in the heart of Ontario's industrial belt. The issue is whether the criteria for boundary maintenance of the band should be changed. These criteria are of a social not a cultural nature, and unlike other ethnic groups in Canada, the criteria are enshrined in federal legislation. More exactly, the question is who shall be allowed the right to interact as permanent members of the band, rather than in what cultural terms they interact. Furthermore, the formal criteria for this group, as for all Indian bands in Canada, have historically been determined by the host society, not the ethnic group itself.

Consequently, because a band has little control over the promulgation of formal societal laws, it can face a situation in which the membership criteria are changed to a perceived detriment to the group's limited resources and continuance. Thus the "externals" can be seen to destroy the existence of the group. The ethnic group must then appeal to the host society in an attempt to convince it that the boundaries must remain unchanged, or altered in an acceptable fashion. The Six Nations did just that in appealing to the judiciary in order to retain the legal *status quo.* It asked the courts to retain the legal requirement that Indian women lose their legal status after marrying outside the band.

The judicial arena became the forum for the symbolic battle between "Indian rights" and "women's rights". This was no less true at the local level than at the national level. From the Six Nations' perspective the struggle before the courts testifies to the degree to which a once matrilineal and matrilocal society has internalized the boundary maintenance criteria set for it by the host society and has thereby become especially vulnerable to external control.

The paper is presented in three parts. The historical position of the band on the question of marriage of their women to Whites will precede a discussion of events of the court case and local attitudes on the issue. It will conclude by indicating that the Six Nations achieved a condition which Barth (1969:17) claims is necessary for the persistence of an ethnic group — the principle that different standards may be applied to ethnic groups than would otherwise be utilized or tolerated in the host society.

HISTORICAL BACKGROUND

Since the Grand River community was formally established in the 1840s it has had to fend off White encroachment on its lands. In 1847 when the chiefs of the Six Nations were allotting land on their newly created reserve to their band members, they indicated in a council resolution that they disapproved of their women marrying non-Indians, and that such women would face exclusion from the band and its assets:

> (Resolved) That any women of the Six Nations who may from this date cohabit or inter-mary with any white or black men shall also lose all the benefits of and to be derived from the presents and funds of the Six Nations Indians and be excluded from all their privileges (Six Nations Agency Archives, 1847).

Although locally applied with much partiality, the resolution had been prompted by the determination to retain Indian land in Indian occupancy, and to avoid the high cost of removing White squatters such as the band had just encountered. Their original land base in 1784 of some half-million acres had dwindled to 55,000 acres by the 1840s. Their band funds were at the same time being depleted by an ill-fated investment in a navigation scheme.

The legislation of 1857 was more generous in its criteria for band membership than was the council of chiefs. By this legislation persons of Indian blood and all those inter-married with them (and their off spring) who resided on Indian lands were eligible for band membership (Canada, Province of, 1857). But by 1869, having faced the problem of White males occupying Indian land (Weaver, 1971) the federal government restricted band membership to patrilineal descent criteria, thereby excluding women from band membership upon marriage outside the band (Canada, Government of, 1869). This provision has remained in the *Indian Act* to the present time. Theoretically married out women were to lose by law their rights of residence and band membership, but in practice at Six Nations many remained on the reserve permanently, and held land in their own name rather than in that of their husband's. Children from these marriages, although legally not entitled to band membership were at times placed on the band lists as were their husbands. Personal friendships and kinship ties provided positive avenues for access to band membership, and older people can still remember when "the last" Whitemen were added to the lists by the chiefs.

As the decades passed and Ottawa became more determined to keep accurate records of band membership, local partiality came to play a more minor role in admissions to the band lists. Despite the band council's persistent protests against the addition of illegitimate children to the lists, it rarely succeeded in securing the removal of these children because of the difficulty of obtaining information on the paternity of the child. Although the band council today seems to desire the removal of the illegitimate provisions of the *Indian Act*, it has not provided a solution for the status mother on the reserve.

Although the band council has come to play a decreasing role in both the determination and the application of criteria for band membership, it has assumed an increasing interest in the presence of non-band members residing on the reserve. It has assumed the power to grant or withhold permission of residence to outsiders. This second line of defence becomes the local action by which the corporate quality of the band is seen to be preserved, presumably by preventing those undesirables from living in the community.

The awareness of the limited resources in land and capital funds lies behind many of the council's actions. With the addition of any personnel to the official band list, comes the possibility that in the future these members may voluntarily enfranchise and claim their rightful share of the capital funds. Once the wealthiest band in Canada, with capital assets of almost one million dollars, the Six Nations have symbolically placed their pride of independence in these funds, among other resources. Today reduced to some $800,000 the band council and the community carefully guard these monies which are augmented only by small sums of revenue from the extraction of mineral resources. Without a tax base and dependent upon government grants for specific programs[1] the band council tries to keep additions to the membership list at a minimum, and residence of non-members on the reserve to those who are at least economically viable.

While it is known to the reserve public that unauthorized persons illegally reside permanently on the reserve, these residents are not interfered with unless complaints are made about them to the band council. In the last decade it has become local custom that non-band members should request permission from the band council to reside on the reserve, and this applies equally to anthropologists. The band council has been generous with these requests, most of which have been for temporary residence. Many requests come from Six Nations women who have married out and wish to resume residence for a variety of reasons. Missionaries and teachers face no problems in securing permission, and this applies to Six Nations women who teach on the reserve but have White husbands.

Problems arise when financially dependent families approach council with the likelihood that welfare services, housing or other support may be required to maintain the family. If controversy is generated when economically viable people approach the council, the reasons are usually of a political nature or because the applicants might pose economic competition for local residents. Requests that come from Six Nations' women who have married out and whose marriages have not proven stable pose the further possibility that the women may wish to assume permanent residence "at home". Although there is no norm among the Christians that marrying out is undesirable, there is little sympathy for those who do so and then want to return home permanently. Since many women do not officially record their marriages with the Indian administration they, in fact, do not claim their capital share of the band funds, but the knowledge that they can do so is a threat to the limited band funds. The further fact that intermarriage is frequent strengthens the concern about resource dissipation. In the past decade approximately half of the registered marriages have been to non-band members, and of these half have been of Indian women marrying non-Indian men. If the boundary of band membership is crossed by either money going out or men coming into the community (legally if the *Indian*

Act provisions were changed, or temporarily through band council permission) the accumulated effect over the years would be the undeniable presence of many Whitemen or the decrease of capital assets with its symbolic implications. Even the traditionalist Longhouse adherents, who comprise 20% of the population, and who prefer marriage to occur not only among band members but within the Longhouse community, share the desire to retain the assets of the band and to keep the reserve free of White male residents.

In 1970 the band council was faced with the problem of a woman requesting residence, and during the subsequent year giving certain indications by her actions that she wished to remain a permanent resident. Her request for residence became translated by certain events into a legal argument that she be allowed to regain her legal status, despite marriage outside the band. With such status she could retain uncontested right to permanent residence.

THE CASE AND LOCAL LEVEL EVENTS

Bedard vs. Isaac et al case materials (Ontario, Supreme Court, 1971) indicate that Mrs. Bedard, the plaintiff in the case, was born on the reserve but despite her marriage to a White man in 1964 her name still remained on the band lists in 1971 when the case was begun. She lived off the reserve from the time of her marriage until 1970, when having separated from her husband, she returned with her two pre-school age children to live in the house willed to her by her mother. As local custom required, she appeared before council asking permission for herself and her children to reside on the reserve. Council granted her six months residence during which time she was to dispose of her property as the *Indian Act* requires. When the six months expired, she reappeared asking council for a year's extension, indicating that she was in the process of transferring title of her property to her brother. Instead of a year, she was granted a six month extension, and informed that further residence requests might depend upon her compliance with the council's wishes that she not provide hydro electric services to a neighbour, as had been rumoured. The band required that the neighbour apply directly to the council for such services, because the band bonded Six Nations customers for Ontario Hydro through a longstanding agreement.

Six months later she again appeared in council, but this time was told that she would be given a final two month period in which to find accommodation off the reserve, and that further extensions would not be granted. When the expiry date had passed, the council by resolution requested the

Superintendent to serve quit notice on Mrs. Bedard. Fearing physical removal without having accommodation elsewhere, Mrs. Bedard sought legal counsel who then filed suit for a temporary injunction to prevent the band council from evicting her until the case could be heard in the courts. Two weeks later Mrs. Bedard's name was officially removed from the band list by the registrar in Ottawa.

By launching the case Mrs. Bedard brought the local level events at Six Nations directly in touch with the broader one of Indian women's rights which was proceeding through the courts at the same time. Mrs. Lavell, originally from a Manitoulin Island reserve, had married a White man and while living in Toronto became influenced by the women's rights movement. She had launched a suit against the Attorney General of Canada claiming that she had lost Indian status because of discriminatory provisions of the Act which deny women Indian status upon marrying out, but do not deny men retention of their legal status. Mrs. Lavell had lost her first hearing[2] but her appeal was to be heard a month after the band council served quit notices on Mrs. Bedard, and before the Bedard case was heard.

Aside from the broader issue of women's rights, Mrs. Bedard's case locally became associated with factional tensions which had reasserted themselves. Although Mrs. Bedard was not a political activist, the legal counsel she chose was simultaneously legal advisor to one of the Confederacy supporters who was a defendant in a case initiated by the band council. The case originated from the reassertion by the Confederacy of its right to govern the reserve. The hereditary chiefs had ruled the reserve until they were deposed in 1924 by the federal government and since that time they had challenged the legitimacy of the elected council. In the summer of 1970 its supporters had padlocked the council house doors in Ohsweken, thereby preventing the band council from holding its meetings there, and its employees from performing their duties. Council laid suit against certain Confederacy supporters, and the case was pending during the Bedard hearings. The legal argument which was to be put forward for Mrs. Bedard (and one of the Confederacy supporters in the "pad-locking" case) involved the assertion that the *Indian Act* was in itself based on racial discrimination, and therefore that it should be abrogated with the exception of a few sections. This argument is seen by most Six Nations people, including most Confederacy supporters, as the ultimate threat to Indian rights. Although not a Confederacy supporter, nor a women's rights advocate, Mrs. Bedard became a symbol to the reserve public of a major threat to the continuance of the ethnic group — its territorial integrity and "closed" community.

Behind the public issues of women's rights which attracted much local and national press coverage, lay the deeper dilemma facing the community — the problem of denying one's female relatives permanent community residence and involvement, in order to "save" the corporate interests of the band, which, it is argued, would be destroyed if their White husbands were given Indian status or allowed to reside permanently on the reserve. While Mrs. Bedard was not asking for residence for her husband, it was feared that this kind of request would be the next "step" in an evolution of events which would lead to the dissipation of the Indian community. As one Six Nations newspaper editor wrote: "For a fact we would all wish to see our sisters back but would willingly sacrifice selfish family interests to preserve the security of the Reserve as a whole" (*Tekawennake*, 13 October 1971:5-6). One Confederacy supporter was less sympathetic, claiming "You have made your bed — now lie in it" (*Brantford Expositor*, 1971a). Another Confederacy supporter suggested that the matrilineal line was the only true criteria, and upon appealing to the hereditary chiefs, Mrs. Bedard would find that she still held membership despite the band council's ruling (*Brantford Expositor*, 1971b). Even young women supported the no sympathy line. In a letter to the editor of the local reserve newspaper a 16 year-old high school girl wrote:

> Now today we are proud of being Indian, but if we lose our Reserve where will we be able to express our pride and about what?
>
> So let's band together and keep our Reserve. The whites have taken enough of our reserve as it is (*Tekawennake*, 27 October 1971:3).
>
> **Note:** *(editor's note) It is very pleasing to see a young student interested in the welfare of the Reserve. This generation is responsible for the handing down of the Reserve intact to the next generation, and so on. Editor.*

After the Bedard hearing there was even less public support for women retaining their status after marriage outside the band. The monetary gain such women could claim at the expense of the band became a subject for public comment in the reserve press:

> We understand that when an Indian woman marries a non-Indian her name is removed from the registered Indian Band list and immediately she is sent a cheque — an equity of her share of Indian Band Funds, much as a person is 'pair off' from the family estate. Strange that no mention has been made of this equity by either of the two women in question (Lavell and Bedard). Did they accept the equity or not? Should the case stand every cent should be returned to the band funds with interest for band funds are used for Reserve upkeep. The

decision of the Supreme Court of Canada will be a momentous one on Rights Ruling for the entire Indian race in Canada. Editor (*Tekawennake*, 8 December 1971:7).

The local White press, however, was sympathetic to both women's rights and to Mrs. Bedard. One newspaper claimed that the council operated with a high degree of partiality in treating these cases, for the band council while evicting Mrs. Bedard gave permission to a few other Indian women who had married out to reside on the reserve with their White husbands

> Almost as disturbing as the discriminatory nature of the law is the selective manner in which it is being enforced by the Six Nations council. Chief Councillor Richard Isaac admits that several other families in the same legal position as the Bedards are living on the reserve. But he says that no action will be taken to remove these families unless their members formally request council's permission to remain (as did Mrs. Bedard) or a complaint is lodged against them. This means that Mrs. Bedard is, in effect, being penalized for her honesty (*Brantford Expositor,* 1971c).

The claim of being penalized for complying with local norms had been made by many reserve residents who blamed Mrs. Bedard for council's response, arguing that if she had not gone to council, she would still have been on the reserve without creating all the problem and publicity she had caused. As one woman said "It serves her right, she shouldn't have gone to council in the first place."

Council, in granting permission to the other women to reside on the reserve with their White husbands, however, was treating economically viable families. Mrs. Bedard had been forced to rely on welfare assistance for a short period during her residence, and the council tries to keep these types of demands on its budget to a minimum if possible. Consequently the earlier charges in the local press that the Bedard case was being treated in a discriminatory fashion were directed at the selective approach taken by the council, not at the sexist discrimination in the *Indian Act* provisions.

Whether or not the council was felt to be partial in its decisions, concensus on the reserve is very strong against married-out women returning home. It is argued that the husband is morally and legally responsible for the maintenance of his family, and that the council's limited budget should not be further strained by his negligence. The fact that many women have suffered similar misfortunes and have accepted them without returning to the reserve sustains the opinion that recent appeals should not receive special treatment.

Adding support to the council's position, was the official position paper of the Association of Iroquois and Allied Indians which was produced in response to Chrétien's white paper of 1969. The Association, comprised of band council representatives from most Iroquoian reserves in Ontario, and a few non-Iroquois ones, argued for the retention of the provision which caused married-out women to lose their status.

> The latest Court decision, (Lavell) that an Indian woman, by marrying a non-member of the Band, does not lose her Indian status, poses more problems for her children than it solves. It is the legal and moral duty of the husband to support his wife. Consequently, by the Indian Act, the Indian woman lost her Indian status and took the status of her husband. This section in the Indian Act, was *merely a legislative embodiment of what had become Indian custom.*
>
> When an Indian ceases to be a member of the Band by reason of enfranchisement, a payment of shares out of the capital fund of the Band should be abolished. The right to be paid out of the capital funds has been abused. Often times the children have been made to suffer by parents becoming enfranchised.
>
> All the sections in the Indian Act dealing with "Definition and Registration of Indians" must be revised. Guidelines must be set within the Indian Act but the application for membership, and perhaps membership itself must be the decision of the Band council concerned [emphasis mine] (Association of Iroquois and Allied Indians, 1971:63-64.

Although Confederacy supporters publicly argued that the AIAI represented only the elected band councils of the reserves, and not the "true" governing bodies, the hereditary chiefs, it is significant to note that on this rare occasion the "hereditary supporters" did not take a public stand opposing council's ruling on the Bedard eviction, or opposing the provisions against women in the *Indian Act*.

When the Bedard case came to court in November of 1971 the Lavell ruling had already gone in favour of Mrs. Lavell retaining her Indian status (Canada, Federal Court of Appeal, 1971). Mrs. Bedard's case was won to the extent that she was regranted her legal status, but the judge avoided the larger issue of whether the entire *Indian Act*, as her lawyer had argued, should be abrogated because of its racist basis. Legal counsel for the band council argued that there were historic reasons for the section relieving Indian women from band status upon marriage to Whites, and he argued against the application of the Bill of Rights to the *Indian Act*. While the greater threat of Indian rights being destroyed by the abrogation of the

Indian Act was lessened, the council was solidly opposed to Indian women regaining status and appealed the case. The case was jointly heard with the Attorney General's appeal of the Lavell decision in the Supreme Court of Canada in February of 1973 (Sanders, 1972). The final judgement brought down in August of 1973 was met with mixed reactions (Canada, Supreme Court, 1973). The component associations of the National Indian Brotherhood of Canada had intervened in the case to argue against Lavell and Bedard, and against the threat that the application of the *Bill of Rights* to the *Indian Act* would entail. For women's rights groups the judgement was seen as a travesty of justice. The first test of the protection that the *Bill of Rights* could have afforded to equal treatment of men and women had proven a failure. At Six Nations the judgement was seen as a victory for the protection of Indian rights and the continuance of the band boundaries free of threatening change. Having won the larger victory, the council had not seen fit to remove Mrs. Bedard from the reserve.

CONCLUSION

The question arises here – for what category are the boundaries to be maintained? A distinction naturally has to be made between the band and the community. The band is a legal unit (not a legal corporation in the strict sense) not a social unit. It is manifested in the band list, which is a list of the corporate members who by patrilineal descent (legally imposed) gain ascribed status upon birth or by marriage in a certain category – legal Canadian Indian, and Six Nations band member. As a band member each has a right to reside on the reserve, and each shares a collective interest in capital assets and resources. These properties are held in perpetuity for the members by the Crown and members do not have freedom to dispose of them without prior consent of the Crown. They also have certain rights in relation to their properties, such as the freedom from land and estate taxes. Although all band members have the right to live on reserve lands, only about two-thirds of them chose to do so. Thus by living on the reserve and interacting through kinship, friendship and institutional arrangements they create the community. It is the community with its band council *and* Confederacy system which takes the responsibility upon itself for protecting the "corporate" assets and rights of the band. The community is the societal base from which the defensive posture toward the "externals" eminates, and it is the locus of action to defend criteria for membership recruitment.

The community acts to defend, then, two types of boundaries; those of the band and those of the community. Community residence for temporary purposes is seen as the immediate purview of the band council. It acts to keep out those whom it deems undesirable, and it does so without formal official criteria. The rationale is that undue influence of White residents in the community can interfere in the Six Nations people's independence in running their internal affairs, and making their own decisions. But the band council and community have little control in the application of the criteria for official band membership. These criteria are set by parliament, and applied impersonally from Ottawa and consequently are not sensitive to local attitudes. Although the band council does not approve of Ottawa having sole control on band membership, it perceives any change in the criteria which would admit an additional category of persons to the band list a threat to the limited resources of the band. Therefore it will defend the *status quo* on issues such as the Bedard case. This case was seen as "the first step" to the possible admission of the children and the husband of married-out women, to reserve residence, and band status. But by attempting to remove Mrs. Bedard from residence the council initiated a legal challenge to the criteria for band membership. Once involved in the case, it confronted a changing external societal milieu which supported the equality of women. The band council's legal argument in effect asked the courts to sustain discrimination against Indian women, and by judicial decision to do so, the host society set forth one of the conditions clearly necessary for ethnic group persistence — the application of a "double standard".

NOTES

1. The annually accruing interest on the capital funds is insufficient to meet the fiscal operating costs of community services on the reserve.

2. Judgement in County Court of the Judicial District of York by Judge B.W. Grossberg, 21 June 1971.

SEXUAL EQUALITY AND INDIAN GOVERNMENT: AN ANALYSIS OF BILL C-31 AMENDMENTS TO THE INDIAN ACT

Joyce Green

INTRODUCTION

The recently passed Bill C-31, *An Act to Amend the Indian Act*, alters several sections of the *Indian Act*. The most significant of these amendments is removal of Section 12(1)(b), which stripped Indian status from Indian women who married non-Status Indians or non-Indians. As well as removing Section 12(1)(b)'s application to future marriages, Bill C-31 makes it possible for women who have lost status via Section 12(1)(b), and for their children, to apply for status and band membership.

While some Bill C-31 amendments address issues other than reinstatement of persons affected by Section 12(1)(b), it is beyond the scope of this paper to examine all sections of the new Act. Only the status provisions relative to Section 12(1)(b) will be considered, together with implications for Indian government.

It has become apparent over the past two decades that the federal government has been increasingly uncomfortable with a number of *Indian Act* provisions, Section 12(1)(b) in particular. With the condemnation of this section by the Royal Commission on the Status of Women in Canada (Canada, Government of, 1970), the unsuccessful *Lavell* and *Bedard* challenges to the *Indian Act*,[1] and the successful *Lovelace* case,[2] public and international opinion has grown more critical of the *Indian Act*'s discriminatory provisions. The adoption of the *Canadian Charter of Rights and Freedoms* has made it impossible for the government to continue to tolerate this anomaly under any guise. With the coming into force of Charter equality guarantees on 17 April 1985, the government faced the unhappy prospect of being taken to court, and of losing. The *Indian Act* would be found inoperative insofar as themselves coincidentally deciding questions of First Nations[3] citizenship.

To date political consensus on resolution of this matter has evaded all parties. The longer a political solution is delayed, the more likely it is that a legal resolution will occur. The latter has fewer chances of securing an outcome satisfactory to all.

HISTORICAL OVERVIEW

The seemingly irresolvable issues deriving from Section 12(1)(b) and Bill C-31 are best appreciated in an historical and political context. The current *Indian Act* is one of the most recent of a series of legislative measures addressing the government-Indian relationship. The first such legislation, passed prior to Confederation, made no mention of Indian status. The first enactment dealing with Indian membership entitlement was in 1850 (Canada, Province of, 1850). Since this date other Acts dealing with membership entitlement, Indian Acts (Canada, Government of, 1879),[4] and revisions thereto have followed.

The policy objective of the various Indian Acts and of the reserve system has been assimilation. It was envisioned, first by colonial and then by Canadian governments, that Indians would assimilate as quickly as they were raised to Euro-Canadian standards, as determined by the minions of Indian Affairs. "Status" was a temporary designation. With assimilation, it was expected that both status and reserves would become redundant and disappear.

It was in 1857 that restrictive definitions were attached to the concept of status. For example, male Indians who met certain criteria could be involuntarily enfranchised (Canada, Province of, 1857). Enfranchisement of the males automatically caused the enfranchisement of their wives and minor children. By 1869, Indian women marrying "any other than an Indian" lost their status and rights (Canada, Government of, 1869).

The *Indian Act* of 1876 further emphasized patrilineal descent and legitimate birth as criteria for Indian status. These criteria were integral to European notions of the male-female relationship and the role of women in society. European societies were patrilineal and patriarchal. Women were legally the property of their husbands, as were their children. Consistent with this view, Section 11(1)(f) of the *Indian Act* decreed that non-Indian and non-Status women marrying Status Indian males took the status designation of their spouse.

That the *Indian Act* is discriminatory is incontestable.[5] Many sections other than Section 12(1)(b) single out classes of Indians for special treatment. For example, there are different inheritance provisions for legitimate and illegitimate children. The Act decrees involuntary enfranchisement for wives and minor children of males who voluntarily enfranchise. Formerly, enfranchisement was required if, for instance, an Indian wished to pursue higher education, become a member of some profession, or join the armed forces.[6] Until 1956 Indians had to renounce their status to exercise the rights of Canadian citizenship.

For some years those sections of the Act discriminating on different bases had been targetted for revision by the affected groups and by equal rights advocates. The most successful attack on the Act was the *Drybones*[7] challenge to Section 94 (now Section 95) of the *Indian Act* which differentiated between Indians drinking on and off the reserve. In upholding the *Canadian Bill of Rights,* the *Drybones* decision held that Section 94 of the Act was inoperative as offensive to the Bill of Rights.

Encouraged by this victory, activists and Indian women's lobbies supported the *Lavell* and *Bedard* challenge to Section 12(1)(b),[8] arguing that the section was pernicious in its repercussions consequent to a choice of spouse and discriminatory in that its effects are not extended to Indian men (Jamieson, 1978:3).[9] Lavell and Bedard sought a ruling that Section 12(1)(b) was inoperative as offensive to the Bill of Rights. Their challenge failed in a Supreme Court of Canada decision which stripped the Bill of Rights of its potential protection of *de facto* equality. Equality of the law was held to be equal application of the law. Uniform discrimination against Indian women was in law "equality." The implications for all challenges to Canadian legislation based on Bill of Rights' guarantees were obvious.

It seemed there was no recourse from the discriminatory provisions of the Act, short of political pressure for legislative revision or repeal. That was not forthcoming, as status Indian organizations used the Act as a lever to gain governmental concessions on other important Indian issues (Cardinal, 1977:110).[10] The rights of Indian women were to be held hostage for the political goals of Indian organizations.

With the Canadian judicial appeal process having been exhausted and with the conviction that Section 12(1)(b) represented a fundamental injustice that had to be corrected, opponents to it turned their attention to the remedies offered by international law. Canada had ratified the International Covenants on Civil and Political Rights, and Economic, Social and Cultural

Rights, attached to the International Bill of Human Rights. As well, Canada had signed the optional Protocol, by which this nation agreed that a Canadian dissatisfied with the decision of the court of last resort could appeal to the United Nations Human Rights Commission.

In 1975 Sandra Lovelace, a Maliseet Indian who lost her Indian status via Section 12(1)(b), took the issue to the United Nations Human Rights Commission, contending that Canada was in violation of several sections of the Covenants named above. Because her marriage had taken place before Canada had ratified the Covenants, the Commission could not find Canada guilty of sexual discrimination.[11] Retroactivity is not contemplated in international law. However, the court did find Canada in violation of Section 27 of the Covenant of Civil and Political Rights. That section guarantees the right of all persons to enjoy their culture in their community. Lovelace's exclusion from her reserve violated this right. This decision resulted in some international censure of Canada for the Section 12(1)(b) provision.

After the Lovelace case, affected individuals, women's advocacy groups and equal rights proponents continued to pressure the federal government for removal of Section 12(1)(b) and reinstatement of Section 12(1)(b) women. At the same time, some status Indian organizations opposed removal of Section 12(1)(b) and reinstatement. The political pressure, unfavourable international opinion and the equality guarantee in the Charter combined to force the federal government to deal with legislative discrimination in the *Indian Act*. The former Liberal Government's proposed remedy was Bill C-47, *An Act to Amend the Indian Act*, which died in the Senate just before the Liberals were defeated in the September 1984 election. The issue awaited the Conservative Government, which responded with Bill C-31.

While addressing the discriminatory provisions of the *Indian Act*, the present federal government is trying to avoid the appearance of violating the authority of Indian government. Indian participants in the constitutional conferences have made it clear that Indian government is an Aboriginal right, and that citizenship falls within its parameters. Bill C-31 tries to please both sides, and predictably fully pleases neither.

BILL C-31 AND INDIAN GOVERNMENT

One right which Native people have consistently claimed is self-government and its concomitant responsibilities. Determination of First Nations citizenship is considered fundamental to this. Some Indian politicians argue that reinstatement of Indian women violates this right, and that the government is arbitrarily imposing its own lately-realized equality provisions on Indian nations. Others accept federal rectification of federally imposed discrimination, but fear the financial consequences of reinstatement of large numbers of women and first-generation children.

Band control of band citizenship is recognized in Bill C-31 providing bands have a membership code conforming to the equality provisions of the *Charter of Rights and Freedoms*. This will not satisfy bands claiming an inherent right to determine citizenship regardless of Canadian legislative criteria. The Bill creates two registers: one maintained by the Department of Indian and Northern Affairs Canada (INAC) (formerly the Department of Indian Affairs and Northern Development) and the other by the bands. Indian status held by virtue of the INAC list will not in some cases automatically confer band membership. This is a concession to bands demanding the right to control citizenship, while attempting to appease Section 12(1)(b) women and first-generation children demanding their Indian rights. The stipulation that INAC will go by its status register amounts to the INAC's insistence on ratification of band citizenship lists. The federal government reserves control of "status under the Indian Act." *Indian Act* status continues to limit federal fiscal responsibility under Bill C-31.

While there is no guarantee that all band members will be found on the federal register, neither is there a requirement that bands reflect the federal register. Of some solace to Indian governments opposed to reinstatement, this may still find itself subject to *Charter of Rights and Freedoms* challenge on the basis of separate treatment. Reinstated women will want the political rights attached to status, formerly synonymous with band membership, and will not be amenable to having their bands reject this indefinitely.

The onus is on those eligible for reinstatement (or, in the case of first-generation children, for instatement) to apply for both INAC and band status. Restoration of band membership logically includes reserve residency rights, though the Bill tacitly acknowledges that it may initially be impossible to realize these rights. There is a grace period for bands to assume control of membership pursuant to an approved code, and for reinstated women and their children to request enrolment. Bill C-31 makes it possible to limit the annual number of reinstatements to band lists. This limit is set at ten per cent of current band membership, spread over a time period until 1992.

It seems the Bill tries to respond to band government concerns that their reserves cannot physically, financially or socially contend with mass reinstatement. However, this measure does not address the issue of additional lands needed to accommodate those returning to the reserve; it says nothing about where these lands will come from and who will provide them.

It merely provides some time for bands to adjust, while delaying realization of rights supposedly guaranteed by the *Charter of Rights and Freedoms*. These measures, which extend beyond the three years Canada was given to fall into line with the Charter equality section, Section 15, delays rights of a segment of the population further and violates the intent of Section 15. Further, Bill C-31 does not provide any guarantees of the funds required to service the needs of the reinstated women and their children. While there is mention of funds for capital expenditures for community requirements precipitated by reinstatement, the Bill makes it clear that only community facilities are contemplated. There is a fainthearted guarantee of funds sufficient to service all eligible persons with specified services. It must be noted that the services in question, in many cases treaty rights, are grudgingly given by INAC to a limited number of status Indians at present. Health, education and social service funding are bandied about between federal and provincial governments, based on various guidelines such as residence of the applicant. This often leaves hapless Indians befuddled by bureaucracy and without their so-called rights. Further, the recent revelation of "Buffalo Jump of the 1980s," as the Neilson cabinet memorandum is colloquially known,[12] fans fears of the government's hidden agenda on Indian policy. This document advocates wholesale cuts of federal funding for Indian health, education, housing and other services, and transference of responsibility to the provinces.

In short, given restrictive federal funding of Indian rights and services at present and the lack of specific funding guarantees in Bill C-31, bands should not expect significant funding increases. Existing criteria would prevent all reinstatees from receiving their "rights" unless they resided on a reserve. *Indian Act* status will no longer confer band status and vice versa. Reserve residency rights will attach to band status. Reinstated women may well find themselves without any substantive rights if they are not guaranteed band membership, and if bands are not guaranteed the means to support their membership.

Under Bill C-31, the Minister of INAC must report to Parliament two years after the date of assent of Bill C-31 on the numbers of reinstatees, the "names and numbers" of bands controlling membership, and most significantly the "impact of the amendments" on Indian nations. There is no requirement for Indian participation in this report, nor for participation by potential and realized reinstatees. Without substantial participation by both these groups, any INAC report will be a superficial pronouncement of available statistics. A more useful tool would be a special all-party committee reporting directly to Parliament, with members of status Indian organizations, Native women's organizations, and other interested groups.

One hundred years of the *Indian Act*'s discrimination has created its own problems now. If the emotional resistance to reinstatement were to vanish overnight, problems would still remain. Reserve governments have insufficient resources to service the existing population. Natural population increase is not accounted for in government commitments to provide land bases. Bill C-31, with all its promise of making it possible for reinstatement to occur, makes it quite clear that additional reserve land is not contemplated. While limited federal funds exist to purchase additional Indian lands "as needed," there is no commitment to securing such lands. In most cases land would have to be purchased from the provincial government, with constitutional and jurisdictional disputes as the provinces balk at surrendering control and resources. One need only look to the Lubicon Indian Nation's experience to see an example of this.[13]

Nor does the Bill make a commitment that the federal government will deal with recalcitrant provinces to ensure land needs are met. The present and projected housing shortage is not addressed. While Bill C-31 will make monies available for community needs such as health centres, increased educational requirements and the like (if all funds are not cut off by the budget-minded Tories) there is no commitment to provide the means for supplying private residences. Perhaps greater than the need for community services is the need for lands for residential and economic development.

THE REINSTATEMENT DEBATE

Proponents of the Section 12(1)(b) amendment point to the inequality arising from the differential treatment between Indian men and women; to the injustice of having to choose between status and one's choice of spouse; to the immorality of such a choice being imposed on them. Opponents point to the right of First Nations to determine their own citizenship without federal interference, citing Section 12(1)(b) as past interference. Frequently, opponents point to the inability of reserves and Indian governments to meet current population demands, and to the intolerable stress a population influx would precipitate in the community. The Blood Tribe's position, for example, encapsulates this widespread feeling, in terming reinstatement *via* Bill C-31 a "ham-fisted" response to a complex issue.[14]

Objections to reinstatement of Section 12(1)(b) women and to granting status to first-generation Indian children are grounded in three bases. The first is political: the federal government is once again dabbling in internal Indian government matters, and Indian governments are unhappy about it.

Bands protest that enforced reinstatement violates the right of First Nations to determine their membership, and that this is part of Aboriginal and treaty rights. Still, bands have rarely protested the systematic loss of their women citizens who fell within the ambit of Section 12(1)(b), and the discrepancy of logic is apparent.[15] If it is all right to separate Indian women from the reserve but not all right to return them, the issue seems to be the women rather than control of citizenship. If such is the case, at least some First Nations are guilty of discrimination on the basis of sex and of a woman's choice of spouse.

The second base of opposition to reinstatement is economic. The vast majority of Indian governments are very poor. Indian land bases are static. For most bands, the band capital and land bases are inadequate to service the existing population, and the government has made no guarantee that it will fill the gap. Bands find themselves unable to provide for their existing populations. Employment opportunities are limited. Housing needs cannot be met. There is insufficient land for current residential, recreational and economic requirements. For example, the Blood Tribe has stated to the Standing Committee on Indian Affairs that it suffers an unemployment rate of eighty-five per cent; and a high incidence of alcoholism and other forms of social maladjustment common to impoverished, unemployed and colonized people; and that a large number of people are landless and cannot be housed.[16] The Bloods point out that enforced reinstatement of people with claims on inadequate reserve resources will result in community tensions. The returning women and their children stand to be scapegoated by people who presently cannot be provided with minimum necessities.

The Minister of Indian Affairs, David Crombie, has said that he anticipates reinstatees will take their turn at the housing and services queue. Nevertheless, apprehension flourishes on the reserve that reinstatees will somehow benefit at the expense of the present population.

The third base of opposition is emotional. Having had Section 12(1)(b) imposed for over a century, some Indian people have internalized what is an assimilative colonial instrument. There are those who defend the *Indian Act* as the last bastion of Indian rights, who see tampering with the Act as tantamount to tampering with the treaties; who assert that removal of women in the Section 12(1)(b) predicament is Indian custom. The colonial experience has created its own exponents on the reserve, and these factions are perhaps the worst that returning women must deal with. For these people, the reaction to Section 12(1)(b) reinstatement is purely emotional, without reference to logic, justice, political expediency or cultural imperatives. The rhetoric used is violent and emotional: Section 12(1)(b) women are accused of watering down Indian genes and destroying Indian culture. This same argument is not usually extended to Indian men who marry non-Indian women, these women became "Indians" by virtue of Section 11(1)(f) of the *Indian Act*.[17]

Other concerns articulated by at least one Alberta chief include the fear that reinstated women will gang together to force sale of reserve land *via* referendum. However, there is no indication that the women who have lobbied so long for their status will now deliberately destroy the land base their status entitles them to. Further, bands are free to set tribal constitutions in place stipulating residency clauses for purposes of political participation. Finally, in the most unlikely scenario that all reinstated women were in fact dedicated to destruction of the reserve, they do not constitute the population percentage necessary for such action.

CONCLUSION

Indian political arguments against reinstatement are substantive, and must be dealt with. Economic arguments are also substantive and deserve unqualified fiscal guarantees by the federal government. The emotional arguments must be laid to rest in the interests of the health of the Indian community in general, and the returnees in particular. If the emotional issue is not dealt with, reinstated women stand a chance of ostracization; their children run the risks of rampant racism. At worst, violence can be contemplated (Margetts, 1985:2).[18] It is dangerous to underestimate the degree of opposition to reinstatement. If reinstatement is dealt with on its bases, many people will likely change their views. A few hard-liners, not much impressed with history or logic, will continue their opposition. But the community will be better prepared to accept returning women and their first-generation children.

Bill C-31 provides no assurance of fulfilling land and residential requirements for returning reinstatees. And, while there is passing mention of funds set aside to allow bands to purchase land, there is no guarantee that such land would receive reserve status. Obviously land would most likely be purchased directly or indirectly from the provincial governments. The question of jurisdiction over resources and persons will be raised. The provinces traditionally have been reluctant to return jurisdiction to Indian governments. At the Constitutional Conferences held pursuant to Section 37 of the *Charter of Rights and Freedoms*, Alberta, British Columbia and Saskatchewan have made their views opposing substantive Indian government well known, and they are not disposed to compromise.

If serious about easing reinstated populations back into the reserve, the federal government must guarantee that land will be made available and that it will be given reserve status. Indian governments can then exercise full jurisdiction over it. Anything less welcomes provincial intrusion into Indian jurisdiction and undercuts Indian government.

Indian Nations have long invoked international legal precepts, covenants and declarations supportive of Aboriginal rights such as self-determination and cultural integrity. International standards are also quite specific on the matter of legal and political equality of treatment of all people. Indian nations will have to submit their governments to the requirements of international law if they intend to claim its benefits.

First Nations, if they are to act as such, need constitutions which articulate the goals of their nations and the relationship between nation, its citizens and other governments. Somewhere in this heady stuff there will have to be provisions defining who is a citizen; processes, if any, of naturalization; and the rights and duties of non-Indian reserve residents. A full catalogue of political, social, and economic rights and responsibilities must be constitutionalized by First Nations. Should any First Nation enact discriminatory provisions, Charter remedies and international law exist to defend individuals.

If Section 15 of the *Charter of Rights and Freedoms* is not to be another empty promise, Indian women must have the same rights and opportunities as Indian men. In addition, substantive self-government must be recognized as the right of Indian First Nations. This right will include control of citizenship, its processes and practices.

The means by which Section 12(1)(b) women lost their status supports federally-legislated reinstatement. The creation and implementation of the Act was premised on European concepts of how both female persons and non-White races were to be dealt with. Females, as property, did not possess individual rights separate from their male parent or spouse. Indians were to be raised to the colonial level of civilization and then assimilated into the colonial population, without special rights or legal status. The *Indian Act* was the instrument by which this would be achieved. Section 12(1)(b) was a minor section, completely consistent with the sexist tenor of the day. That the government recognizes its past sins is to be applauded. Now, it must also ensure that First Nations do not have to pay the costs of government expiation of those sins. Lands and funds, fulfillment of treaty obligations, and constitutional guarantees must accompany reinstatement. Finally, the federal government must recognize its future non-role in Indian citizenship matters, and the integrity of Indian self-government.

NOTES

1. *Attorney-General v. Lavell* and *Isaac v. Bedard*, SCC (1974) S.C.R. 1349; 1978 38 D.L.R. (3d) 481; 23 C.N.R.S. 197; II R.F.L. 333. Lavell and Bedard challenged Section 12(1)(b) of the *Indian Act* R.S.C. 1960, as offensive to the *Canadian Bill of Rights*, S.C. 1960. In a split decision upholding the *Indian Act*, the court held that equality under the law meant equal application of law. Since all Indian women marrying non-Status persons were dealt with *via* 12(1)(b), the section was not discriminatory.

2. *Re Sandra Lovelace*, United Nations Human Rights Commission 6-50 M 215-51 CANA. Lovelace charged that Canada was in violation of sections of the Covenants of Civil and Political Rights, and Economic, Social and Cultural Rights, insofar as Section 12(1)(b) discriminated against her as an Indian woman. The Commission held that Canada had violated Section 27 of the Covenant on Civil and Political Rights, in that she was denied the right, in community with other members of her ethnic and religious group, to enjoy her culture, profess and practice her religion, and use her language. Because Lovelace's marriage had preceded Canada's ratification of the Covenant, and because international law is not deemed to be retroactive, the Commission could not consider whether Section 12(1)(b) discriminated against her on the basis of her marriage. However, it is entirely possible for a status woman who marries subsequent to ratification to take the case to the United Nations Human Rights Commission, and to succeed on those grounds.

3. The term "First Nations" is used by Indian Nations to indicate their primacy as original self-governing nations on the Canadian political scene. It became popular parlance with publication of *Indian Self-Government in Canada:. Report of the Special Committee* (Canada, House of Commons, 1983a), also known as the "Penner Report" after Committee Chairman Keith Penner.

4. The first time that Canadian legislation dealing with Indians became known as the *Indian Act* was in 1876 (Canada, Government of, 1876).

5. References are to the *Indian Act* prior to the Bill C-31 amendments. These amendments have ameliorated many discriminatory provisions.

6. Many Indian volunteers returning from combat during World Wars I and II found they had been stripped of status in their absence. Proportionately more Indians volunteered for service than did any other ethnic group in Canada.

7. *R. v. Drybones*, S.C.R. 1970.

8. *Attorney General v. Lavell* and *Isaac v. Bedard* (see note 1).

9. Kathleen Jamieson says that the effects of Section 12(1)(b) extend "from marriage to the grave...and even beyond that. The woman, on marriage, must leave her parents' home and her reserve. She may not own property on the reserve and must dispose of any property she does hold. She may be prevented from inheriting property left to her by her parents. She cannot take any further part in band business. Her children are not recognized as Indian and are therefore denied access to cultural and social amenities of the Indian community. And, most punitive of all, she may be prevented from returning to live with her family on the reserve, even if she is in dire need, very ill, a widow, divorced or separated. Finally, her body may not be buried on the reserve with those of her forebears" (1978:3).

10. Harold Cardinal stated that: "Our alarm, which led to our decision to oppose the two women, was based on our belief that if the Bill of Rights knocked out the legal basis for the *Indian Act*, it would at the same time knock out all legal basis [sic] for the special status of Indians" (1977:110).

11. It is still possible for Canada to be found guilty of sexual discrimination contrary to the International Covenants. See note 2.

12. Memorandum to Cabinet, *Report of the Ministerial Task Force on Native Programs*, 12 April 1985.

13. The Lubicon Indians, recognized as a band by the federal government, have been trying for 40 years to obtain a reserve from Alberta. *The Natural Resources Transfer Agreement* of 1930 makes it incumbent upon the provinces to make reserve land available to cases such as the Lubicon's. Alberta remains intransigent.

14. Blood Tribe Presentation to the Standing Committee on Indian Affairs and Northern Development, on the matter of Bill C-31, 21 March 1985.

15. While the option has been available for some time, as of January 1985 only 111 bands had chosen to suspend operation of Section 12(1)(b).

16. Blood Tribe Presentation to the Standing Committee on Indian Affairs and Northern Development, 21 March 1985. Subject of Bill C-31.

17. Section 11(1)(f) was removed by Bill C-31.

18. Jenny Margetts, President of Indian Rights for Indian Women, has stated: "But even members of my own band, Saddle Lake, said they would shoot us if we moved back, and many women are afraid to move back" (1985:2).

Part V ─────────────────────

Canada: Sovereignty, Nationhood and Identity

INTRODUCTION

This section is concerned with the way 500 years of European ideas of nationhood, politics, and history have affected Native concepts of political organization and identity. Both of the articles in this section are concerned with the contemporary situation of Native people in Canada, yet remain informed by European concepts of "democracy" and "nation." The first selection, by Boldt and Long, attempts to delineate how European-Western concepts of sovereignty have affected the aspirations and political strategies of contemporary Native leaders. This is an important article, but the very fact that it is necessary to explain how sovereignty jibes with traditional "tribal" customs, values and institutions demonstrates the pervasiveness of the Eurocentric bias regarding Native identity and political structure in our social and academic writing.

This bias is made particularly clear in a response to Boldt and Long written by Flanagan (1985). Unfortunately, we were unable to obtain permission to print Flanagan's response in this volume. Flanagan objects to the current use of the term "nation" to describe Native social groups, as it strays from the meaning it has developed in European polity. It does not appear possible to him for "nation" to encompass Aboriginal political structures. He insists on interpreting nation in the context of national self-determination and international law, and states that "nation" and "state" are inextricably bound, (therefore making it impossible for individual nations to be located within a state). He makes much of the fact that the use of the term nation in "First Nations" is incompatible with the usage of 17th century publicists, who first began to call sovereign states nations, because Indian "nations" are (or were) closed societies based upon birth and marriage, defined by myths of common ancestry. He implies that it would be inappropriate for governing bodies to become part of the Canadian state based upon these criteria, at least for anything more than local autonomy on a municipal-type basis.

The ramifications of the concept of nation for the presentation of self (and other) for Canada's Aboriginal peoples is explored in the final paper in this section, by J.R. Ponting. There has been an increasing participation on the international stage for many of Canada's Aboriginal groups. A good example is afforded by the crises at Oka, Quebec. The Mohawks were able to generate enough interest on the international scene for the European Parliament to send a delegation to Canada on a fact-finding mission in January of 1991. Ponting analyzes the discourse between the federal government, the Mohawks and other Aboriginal peoples before this delegation.

As might be expected, the federal government emphasized the atypicality or deviance of the Mohawk as compared to other Aboriginal peoples. The Mohawk were classified as "lawless" in contrast to the rest of the Aboriginal groups who were "law-abiding." Most tellingly for the purposes of this volume, the federal government *challenged the Mohawk's own assertions of what was traditional in Mohawk culture...* as blatant an example of outside definition of "Nativeness" as one could expect to find anywhere.

Ponting also discusses the Mohawk's conceptions of "other" (in this case the federal government, and the Québécois.) The Mohawks' characterizations of the government as aggressive, uncivilized and concerned with imposing its own values on others are contrasted with their own conceptions of self (which they explicitly stated as shared with other Native peoples) as spiritual, linked with nature. They also drew a self-flattering contrast between themselves and the French Québécois. This conception of self and other is very similar to that put forth by the Innu as described by Armitage and Kennedy in Section III. In a sense, both the Mohawk and the Innu are buying into the distinction originally crafted in the colonial period, of a clear-cut difference between western society and Native. The major difference is that now the supposed moral superiority lies with the Native, not the European, and this time, some non-Indians seem to be accepting the idea.

TRIBAL TRADITIONS AND EUROPEAN-WESTERN POLITICAL IDEOLOGIES: THE DILEMMA OF CANADA'S NATIVE INDIANS

Menno Boldt and J. Anthony Long

In their quest for political and cultural self-determination, Indian leaders in Canada have adopted the European-Western concept of sovereignty as the cornerstone of their aspirations. They advance claims to inherent sovereignty in order to establish the legal, moral and political authority that will allow them to nurture and develop their traditional tribal customs, values, institutions and social organization. Thus, the concept of sovereignty represents for the current generation of Indian leaders a means to an end, rather than an end in itself.[1]

Recently, Indian leaders have taken their claim to inherent sovereignty into the international arena in an attempt to bring external political pressure to bear on the Canadian government. They feel that the more "enlightened norms" of international law and the United Nations' covenants on political and cultural self-determination will bolster their case for sovereignty, and will serve to counteract the negative treatment their claims have received at the hands of Canadian judges and policy-makers.

This study addresses the question: How does the European-Western idea of "sovereignty" complement traditional tribal Indian customs, values, institutions and social organizations? This question implies more than a linguistic or semantic analysis. It goes to the very heart of Indian culture. We approach this question by examining the implications and pitfalls of sovereignty for traditional Indian customs, values and institutions. We then proceed to explore alternative ideas for achieving political and cultural self-determination.

Before proceeding, however, three important points need to be made. First, our statements about traditional Indian society refer to the period prior to European-influenced change. The analysis, of course, has relevance for contemporary Indian society since many traditional values have persisted even in the face of systematic and coercive measures taken by European colonizers and their successors to eliminate these values. But, more significantly, there is a strong cultural nationalist movement among Indians aimed at reinstituting many traditional values and customs.

Second, we use the term "tribe" to refer to a type of social organization rather than a level of political jurisdiction. Historically, Indian tribes were autonomous and self-sufficient social groupings. The *Indian Act* organized Indians into legal entities called bands. But Indian people today still recognize the concept of tribe, just as they still recognize the concept of Indian nation. In our usage both "bands" and "nations" qualify as tribal societies.

Finally, although we use the term "Indian" we do not intend to imply that Canada's indigenous tribes constitute a single people in any sociocultural or political sense. Great diversity exists among tribes with respect to language, political styles, cultural heritage, and so on. However, there is now emerging a national cultural-political unity movement among Canada's Indians (Boldt, 1981a; 1982), and there exist today, as there have always existed, cultural traits and values which traditionally have been shared by most Indian tribes. These include reaching decisions by consensus, institutionalized sharing, respect for personal autonomy and a preference for impersonal controls over behaviour (Lurie, 1971).

TRIBAL TRADITIONS AND THE CONCEPT OF SOVEREIGNTY

Youngblood-Henderson has noted that, for Indians, sovereignty is "a matter of the heart" — an emotional, not an intellectual concept (Youngblood-Henderson, 1979:71-72). This probably helps to explain why their conceptions of how sovereignty would function in a tribal context are still embryonic and inchoate. In fact, much of the emotional appeal that sovereignty holds for Indians stems from its vagueness. It allows them to project onto it a promise of most of their political, sociocultural and economic aspirations without a rigorous consideration of the adequacy of their resources and instrumentalities for achieving it. Also, the ambiguity of the concept averts factionalism within Indian society, as each group is free to infer its preferred meanings and objective.

Indian leaders, in their discussion of sovereignty, focus attention almost exclusively on its instrumentality for checking the intrusion of *external* authority and power into their social and political structures and territory. That is, sovereignty is very narrowly conceived of as a strategy to free themselves from external intrusions into their society. In their preoccupation with the goal of self-determination they overlook almost entirely the signif-icance that the doctrine of sovereignty potentially has for ordering *internal* tribal authority and power relationships. Thus, Indian leaders have ignored the latent peril that the idea of sovereignty may hold for their traditional tribal customs, values, institutions and social organization. But, if they are going to advocate sovereignty as the foundation of their contemporary and future goals Indian leaders need to consider its implications for the central values of their tribal traditions – the very values they seek to protect. These values will not be preserved if the concept of sovereignty is inconsistent with their cultural legacy.

The potential consequences of sovereignty for Indian tribal traditions must be evaluated in the context of some key ideas contained in European-Western doctrines of sovereignty, namely, the concepts of authority, hier-archy and a ruling entity; and the notions of statehood and territoritality.

AUTHORITY, HIERARCHY AND A RULING ENTITY

The concept of *authority* is critical to any analysis of how the European-Western doctrine of sovereignty can function in the context of indigenous North American forms of the "band," "tribe," or "nation." Bodin and Hobbes wrote of sovereignty as it if were equivalent to absolute and perpetual authority derived either from God or the people. For Locke and Rousseau sovereignty arose from absolute authority derived from the voluntary agree-ment of independent wills (contract of association) delegating their authority to the government, the fiduciary sovereign (Merriam, 1968:83; Barker, 1960:100). Common to both of these conceptions of sovereignty, and generally implied in all European-Western concepts of sovereignty, is a principle of authority defined as the supreme, if not absolute and inalienable, power by the ruling entity to make decisions and to enforce them, if necessary, through sanctions or coercion.

Invariably linked with this principle of authority is the idea of a *hierarchy* of power relationships. This association between hierarchy and authority is exemplified in Haller's theory that authority is the base of sovereignty, and that sovereignty arises from the natural superiority of one over another (Merriam, 1968:65). Haller reasons that equals will not obey equals, hence sovereignty can only be exercised in a state of inequality where the stronger rules. For Haller this represented a universal law of nature—even among the birds of the air and the beasts of the forest the stronger always rules. This assumption of a hierarchy of authority relationships is general not only in traditional European doctrines of sovereignty but is also evident in contemporary conceptions of "popular sovereignty."

The European-Western assumption of hierarchical authority relationships implies a *ruling entity*, that is, a particular locus for sovereign authority. In European society this precept found expression in the authority of rulers. In fact, much of the philosophical debate about sovereignty has focussed on the appropriate locus for sovereign authority (Stankewicz, 1966:142). Even in the ideal sense of popular sovereignty, that is where authority is derived from the people, this authority, once it is delegated by the people, must be lodged somewhere. Thus, terms like "political rulers," "decision-makers," "government," and so on, are used to distinguish those who exercise authority from the rest of the members of society. These terms imply that an identifiable subset of the members of the total society have the power of authority in their hands (Easton, 1958:184).

How do these three key ideas—authority, hierarchy and a ruling entity—contained in European-Western concepts of sovereignty fit into traditional Indian society? In examining the question we want to stress that our discussion of authority, hierarchy and government in traditional Indian society has reference to the basic political culture of most tribes. We are not suggesting that everywhere, without exceptions, North American Indians adopt the same model.

Taking the idea of authority first, we note that the history and experience of North American tribal societies were very different from those of European societies. The European-Western notion of a sovereign authority had its origins in the system of feudalism and the associated belief in the inherent inequality of men. The indigenous peoples of North America, however, never experienced feudalism and most believed in the equality of men. In the Hobbesian doctrine of sovereignty, authority was deemed necessary to protect society against rampant individual self-interest. But in Indian tribal society individual self-interest was inextricably intertwined with tribal interests; that is, the general good and the individual good were taken to be virtually identical (Akwesasne Notes, 1977; Ortiz, 1979). Laslett's "onion skin" analogy aptly illustrates the mythical quality of individuality in traditional Indian society. To apprehend the individual in tribal Indian society, he says, we would have to peel off a succession of group-oriented and derived attitudes as layers of onion skin. The individual turns out to be a succession of metaphorical layers of group attributes which ends up with nothing remaining (Laslett, 1963:167).

Indians traditionally defined themselves communally (Svennson, 1980) in terms of a "spiritual compact" rather than a social contract (Youngblood-Henderson, 1979:77). The "tribal will" constituted a vital spiritual principle which for most tribes gained expression in sharing and cooperation rather than private property and competition. This obviated the need for sovereign authority to sustain the integrity of the society against the centrifugal forces of individual self-interest. Thus, the political and social experiences that would allow Indians to conceive of authority in European-Western terms simply did not exist, nor can it be reconciled with the traditional beliefs and values that they want to retain.

The idea of hierarchical power relationships contained in European-Western concepts of sovereignty is, likewise, irreconcilable with Indian history and experiences. In European thought the Enlightenment concept of egalitarianism emerged as a reaction and response to excesses resulting from the hierarchical doctrine of sovereignty. Egalitarianism was imposed on, and interacted with, the hierarchical concept of sovereign authority to produce more humane political structures. In traditional Indian society, however, the idea of egalitarianism did not emerge as a reaction to excesses of hierarchical authority. Equality was derived from the Creator's founding prescription. The creation myth held that, from the *beginning*, all members of the tribe shared and participated *equally* in all privileges and responsibilities. In their dealings with the British Crown, Indian representatives always used images of equality such as "links in a chain" or "going down the road together" (Youngblood-Henderson, 1979:58). Neither the members of the tribe nor outsiders who studied them found images of hierarchical political authority. The exercise of hierarchical authority would have been viewed as a device to deprive the people of equality.[2]

Traditional Indian beliefs and values also clash with the concept of a ruling entity—that is, a dichotomy of ruler(s) and the ruled (Miller, 1955). In Europe, even after the Enlightenment, it was not authority *per se* that came under question but rather who should exercise authority. New arrangements for exercising authority were devised including election and delegation. Most Indian tribes, however, did not accept that any man or agency had by virtue of any qualities, inherent or by transfer, the right to govern others, even in the service of the tribal good. The people ruled collectively, as a tribe, exercising authority as one body with undivided power, performing all functions of government. The tribe was not held to be the result of a contract among individuals, or between ruler(s) and ruled, but of a divine creation by the Creator. No human being was deemed to have control over the life of another. Therefore, the authority to rule could not be delegated to any one man or subset of members of the tribal group. This denial of personal authority extended even to the notion of transferring the right to govern within specified fixed limits. *Any* arrangement that would separate the people from their fundamental, natural and inalienable right to govern themselves directly was deemed illegitimate.

In place of personal authority, hierarchical power relationships, and a ruling entity, the organizing and regulating force for group order and endeavour in traditional Indian society was *custom* and *tradition* (Miller, 1955). Put another way, Indians invested their customs and traditions with the authority and power to govern their behaviour.[3] Customs were derived from the Creator. They had withstood the test of time and represented the Creator's sacred blueprint for survival of the tribe. By implication, therefore, everyone must be subject to custom; everyone, equally, came under the same impersonal authority. By unreservedly accepting custom as their legitimate guide in living and working together they alleviated the need for personal authority, a hierarchical power structure and a separate ruling entity to maintain order. Customary authority protected individuals from self-serving, capricious, and coercive exercise of power by contemporaries. Since customs are not readily changed, or new ones quickly created, authority was not easily or expediently expanded.

In the traditional myths, custom had a source and sanction outside the individual and the tribe. It was the handiwork of the Creator. Conformity to custom was a matter of religious obedience that accorded with the generally accepted moral standards of the tribe and it was not deemed necessary to appoint agents with authority to enforce custom. Custom carried authority of the type that Rees calls of a "moral kind," (Rees, 1963:58) that is, it obliges individuals, by conscience, to obey. This is quite different from law which is a dictum accompanied by an effective sanction (Merriam, 1968:138). Rule by custom, without a separate agency of enforcement, was possible in traditional Indian society because a face-to-face society can maintain order with few but broad general rules known to everyone. When large gatherings of diverse bands occurred (for the Sun Dance, for example) it was customary to temporarily make one of the Indian "societies" a peace-keeper (Lowie, 1943).

Rituals confirmed custom by investing it with a spiritual quality whose authority was rooted in a sacred beginning, a founding in the past. Through consecrated rituals the testimony of the ancestors, who first had witnessed the sacred founding, was passed from one generation to the next. Arendt (1958:102-104) has identified a similar concept of order in the Roman image of the pyramid which did not reach up hierarchically, but into the past—a past that was sanctified.

The absence of personal authority, hierarchical relationships, and a separate ruling entity carried profound implications for the exercise of leadership in Indian society. For example, elders played an essential and highly valued function by transmitting the Creator's founding prescriptions, customs and traditions. Yet they had no formal authority. The elders merely gave information and advice, never in the form of a command. The elders were revered not because of their power or authority, but because of their knowledge of the customs, traditions and rituals, and because of their ancestral links with the sacred beginning. Chiefs, like elders, also led without authority. Their personality or skills as warrior, hunter, and so on, would gain them a following, but the Chief was on the same level as the followers — personal domination over others did not exist. In fact, most tribes had a multiplicity of chiefs at any one time, each without sanctioning powers beyond personal charisma and proven ability. Even in the heat of battle a warrior had the option of participating or not, without prejudice. Self-direction (autonomy), an aristocratic prerogative in European society, was everyone's right in Indian society (Dorris, 1979:71).

An interesting model of nonauthoritarian leadership is contained in Paul-Louis Carrier's "coach-driver" analogy (Simon, 1969:244). In his analogy Carrier proposes that in a liberal state of affairs the government is like a coach-driver, hired and paid by those whom he drives. The coach-driver conveys his patrons, but merely to the destination and by the route they choose. To an uninformed observer the coach-driver may appear to be the real master, but this is an illusion. Carrier's model of non-authoritarian leadership only approximates the traditional Indian conception of leadership. In tribal Indian society leadership was more aptly symbolized by the relationship of a military drummer to his company. The drummer can establish a cadence but he has no authority to require individuals in the company to march to it. That authority comes from an "external source." For Indians this external source was always to be found in their sacred customs. Significantly, unlike Carrier's "coach-driver" who is subordinate to his patrons, the Indian leader, like the drummer, is not subordinate to the dictates of those who march to his beat. He is responsible only to the "external authority," that is the sacred tribal customs and traditions.

Government without rulers requires special procedures. The mechanism used in traditional Indian society was direct participatory democracy and rule by consensus. This implies an adequate level of agreement amongst all who share in the exercise of authority. Custom provided the mechanism to ensure that order did not break down through failure to achieve consensus.[4]

STATEHOOD AND TERRITORIALITY

In addition to the concepts of authority, hierarchy and a separate ruling entity, the European-Western doctrine of sovereignty subsumes two more ideas with special implications for Indian tribal traditions: the notions of statehood and territoriality. Merriam points out that, while an unresolved debate exists amongst scholars as to whether sovereignty is an essential characteristic of the state, all theorists of sovereignty implicitly, if not explicitly, assume that statehood is an essential and indispensable requirement for sovereignty to exist (Merriam, 1968:202-203). F. F. Hinsley has asserted that the emergence of the state as a form of rule is, by definition, a necessary condition for the exercise of sovereignty (Hinsley, 1966:16).

Indian tribes, prior to colonization, held an independent self-governing status which is best defined as "nationhood," not "statehood." In place of the "myth of a state" they had a "myth of the nation." As *nations* of people they regulated their internal and external relations. But, essentially unlike *states,* their foundation of social order was not based on hierarchical authority wielded by a distinct central political entity. Whereas the state represents a structure of hierarchical political authority imposed upon the community, the tribes, while they were highly organized, had not undergone the separation of the state from the community. They lacked separate state forms and government institutions. But it is a mistake to view traditional Indian nations as though they were at some primitive stage of development undergoing a transition to statehood. As noted earlier, authority and order in tribal Indian society rested on custom and the directly spoken will of the community. Indian nations had no need for statehood and the condition of hierarchical authority that statehood implies. Their community performed all of the necessary political functions: it kept the peace, preserved individual life, and protected its members from injustice, abuse and arbitrary actions by any of their number.

The concept of *territoriality* is also fundamental to European-Western doctrines of sovereignty and statehood. Brierly expresses this as follows:

> At the basis of international law lies the notion that a state occupies a definite part of the surface of the earth, within which it normally exercises...jurisdiction over persons and things to the exclusion of other states. When a state exercises an authority of this kind...it is popularly said to have sovereignty over the territory (quoted in Werhan, 1978).

Although Indian leaders today place great emphasis on land claims and their irrevocable rights to reservation lands, this represents a concession to European-Western political-legal influence. Traditionally, Indian notions of territoriality were not conceived of in terms of precisely fixed territorial boundaries. Tribes existed as spiritual associations that transcended narrow issues of territory (Melody, 1980). The basis for nationhood was their community, not a fixed territory or geographically defined citizenship.[5] Most tribes had no concept of private or collective land ownership. They believed all land belonged to the Creator who had made the land for *all* life forms to use in harmony. This belief imposed certain restraints on tribes in their territorial claims and in their relationship to each other.

The lack of precisely delineated and recognized territorial borders between tribes occasionally produced conflicts over hunting privileges, but tribes fought mainly over access to game in the territories not the territories themselves. Even when they were at war with each other Indian tribes displayed an abiding respect for each other's autonomy and community. As Ahenakew points out, "it was unknown among the First Nations that one nation could by force deprive another nation of its right to self-determination and to sufficient lands and resources to maintain the lives of its people" (Ahenakew, 1984). Because the notion of territoriality did not have primacy for them, victorious tribes did not colonize vanquished tribes in the way European states did. In short, whereas the European-Western concept of sovereignty was based on authority by the state over a piece of territory, clearly demarcated by boundaries, Indians traditionally based their concept of nationhood on their social community.

IMPLICATION OF ASPIRATIONS TO SOVEREIGNTY FOR INDIAN CULTURE

Indians in Canada are opting for sovereignty because they view it as the most promising doctrine for protecting their ancestral heritage from encroachment by external influences and powers. They want sovereignty not to justify indigenous coercive authority within their communities but, rather, to exclude the sovereign authority of the Canadian government.

As part of their political-legal justification for sovereignty, and to convince the Canadian government and the international community that their claim to sovereignty is legitimate, contemporary Indian leaders are reconstructing and reinterpreting their tribal history and traditional culture to conform to the essential political and legal paradigms and symbols contained in the European-Western concept of sovereign statehood. They are raising the fiction that Indian societies, prior to European contact, had hierarchically structured governments that exercised authority through a ruling entity as do states, and were in possession of territories clearly defined by political boundaries (Akwesasne Notes, 1977). To rationalize heir claim to sovereignty, Indian leaders are resorting to highly selective assumptions about the traditional exercise of authority by tribal groups; assumptions that contradict the images Indians hold of their traditional Aboriginal reality when they are not specifically making a political-legal case for tribal sovereignty. As we have argued, sovereignty was not relevant to their internal or external relationships. Furthermore, all claims to inherent tribal sovereignty, as distinct from claims to nationhood, are necessarily hypothetical ones since, historically, the European conception of sovereignty was not in the linguistic apparatus of Indians. It should be emphasized that this does not represent a cynical manipulation of political concepts so much as a misguided reinterpretation of traditional aboriginality.

By resorting to the expedient claim of inherent sovereign statehood, Indian leaders are legitimizing European-Western philosophies and structures of authority and decision-making within contemporary Indian communities. Most Indian communities initially opposed the imposition of European-Western models of elected "democratic government" and the associated bureaucratic administrative structures. They protested the hierarchical structures that relegated most tribal members to the periphery of decision-making. Yet, by adopting the European-Western ideology of sovereignty, the current generation of Indian leaders is buttressing the imposed alien authority structures within its communities, and is legitimizing the associated hierarchy comprised of indigenous political and bureaucratic elites. This endorsement of hierarchical authority and a ruling entity constitutes a complete rupture with traditional indigenous principles. It undermines fundamental and substantial distinctions between traditional Indian and European political and cultural values. The legal-political struggle for sovereignty could prove to be a Trojan Horse for traditional Indian culture by playing into the hands of the Canadian government's long-standing policy of assimilation.[6]

AN EXPLORATION OF ALTERNATIVE MODELS OF SELF-DETERMINATION

The Canadian government and Native Indians must find a way of coexisting that will allow each to preserve that which it deems essential to its survival and identity. The Canadian government has made clear that it will not accept full independence or absolute sovereignty for Canada's Indians (Canada, Government of, 1983:16). For most Indians, on the other hand, assimilation into Canadian culture and politics is repugnant and unacceptable. Thus, the acceptable model for a relationship between the federal government and Canada's Indians lies somewhere between assimilation and sovereignty.

Most Indian peoples are committed to a separate social system with corresponding networks of social institutions that are congruent with their historical tribal arrangements, and that are based on their traditional identity, language, religion, philosophy and customs. The Canadian government, while it is rigidly opposed to any concept of sovereignty and separate statehood for Indians, is ready to accept Indian self-government. The challenge for Indian leaders is to develop a model of self-government that is acceptable to the Canadian government, yet will give them internal self-determination without compromising fundamental traditional values. The option of pluralism suggests itself.

In his analysis of pluralism Kenneth McRae (1979:677-678) identifies three uses of the term: first, that of the British political pluralists (J.N. Figgis, Harold Laski and G.D.H. Cole) who viewed pluralism primarily in terms of alternative foci of citizen loyalties with respect to the sovereign state; second, that put forward by the American writers (A.F. Bentley, David Truman, Robert Dahl and others) which contains the central idea of countervailing but overlapping interest groups competing in policy formation; and, third, that expressed in the literature on colonial and post-colonial societies (J.S. Furnival, M.G. Smith, Leo Kuper and Pierre van den Berghe) which posits two or more social systems and associated constitutional networks within one political system. This latter use of pluralism, which allows for the presence of several nations within one sovereign state, is evident in the "consociational school" (notably Arend Lijphart, Gerard Lehmbruch, Hans Doalder, Jurg Steiner, and Val Lorwin).[7] A consociational arrangement is a significant step short of separation and sovereignty. Theoretically, it could accommodate the essential political requisites of both Indians and the Canadian government, but it compromises traditional Indian values because of its emphasis on rule by elites.

For Indians the issue is not one of choosing between different forms of sovereignty. All forms of sovereignty, whether monistic or pluralistic, involve the hierarchical exercise of authority by a ruling entity and are therefore incompatible with the cultural heritage they seek to preserve. A more promising political model can be found in the works of Vernon Van Dyke (1974; 1975; 1977; 1982). Briefly stated, Van Dyke challenges the "two-level theory of rights" (Van Dyke, 1974). He proposes that rights are not simply a question of the individual and the state but that ethnic communities meeting certain criteria should be considered as unities (corporate bodies) with moral rights and legal status accorded them as *groups* rather than as *individuals*. He proposes that ethnic communities, not only states, are entitled to be regarded as right-and-duty bearing entities. Traditional European-Western concepts of sovereignty provide no place for groups in the state. European philosophers such as Hobbes and Locke emphasized the role of the *individual* in his relationship to the sovereign state. Western liberal political theorists have continued this emphasis on the relationship between individual and state. Robert Nisbet identifies this as the most influential philosophy of freedom in modern Western society (Nisbet, 1962:224).

Van Dyke advocates a more complex paradigm, one that would permit both group and individual rights, legal and moral, to exist side by side. The objective is not to downplay equal treatment for individuals but to extend to groups equal rights to preserve their integrity. This model implies the principle that a *nation of people* have an intrinsic and inalienable collective right to self-determination. This principle, as Van Dyke points out, had legitimate status in the League of Nations Charter and now enjoys the same status in the United Nations Charter, where the moral, if not legal right to self-determination by *nations of people* is upheld.[8] While one possible outcome of the exercise of the right of nations to self-determination is sovereign statehood, it is clear that other arrangements are possible (Bell, 1964; 1967; 1975; 1980). Van Dyke cites Puerto Rico, which has chosen commonwealth status.

How does Van Dyke's model fit the historical and contemporary status of Indian tribes? Prior to colonization, Indian tribes operated as independent stateless nations, in their own right; not a derived, delegated or transferred right, but one that came into existence with the group itself. Under the *Indian Act* and by historical convention Indian tribes in Canada have retained their special group-based status and rights.[9]

Indians also constitute nations of peoples according to social science criteria. Walker Connor (1970; 1972; 1978) defines the essence of a nation "as a psychological bond that joins a people and differentiates it, in the subconscious conviction of its members, from all other people in a most vital way" (Connor, 1978:379). He adds, in another context, that "national consciousness is therefore accompanied by a growing aversion to being ruled by those deemed aliens" (Connor, 1970:93). Other social scientists have defined a nation as "a social group which shares a common ideology, common institutions and customs and a sense of homogeneity" (Plano and Olton, 1969). The very high level of cultural uniqueness and homogeneity of Indian tribal groups not only strengthens their political integration as nations, but also acts as a barrier to political integration into Canadian society. The fact that Indian cultural uniqueness has become politicized has created an additional serious obstacle to integration into the larger society.

Clearly, Indian tribes meet the criteria of nationhood. Indians' first loyalty is to their own group. They believe themselves to be nations.

Van Dyke's paradigm provides a framework within which the Canadian government and Indians may be able to negotiate internal self-determination that will provide Indians the opportunity to retain their group differences without sovereignty. The component unit representing Native people would be the "nation," based on traditional cultural and linguistic communities. The Indian nations would function in a constitutionally defined and guaranteed relationship with the provincial and central governments. Both the Canadian state and the Indian nations would be subject to domestic arrangements specified by general rules or particular treaty agreements regulating the relationship between them.

Indian peoples would be subject to Canadian sovereignty and control over their external affairs but there would be constitutionally defined limits to Canadian control over Indian internal affairs. Although the Canadian government, pursuant to agreements, would continue to exercise some indirect control over individual Indians (for example, in the area of criminal law), in those matters not covered by agreement or treaty, Indian nations would be paramount in setting policies over their own territories and people within their territories. They would exercise jurisdiction over their legal, political, social and economic institutions.

The Canadian federal system provides an institutional framework for accommodating Van Dyke's paradigm. It could be acceptable to the Canadian government because Indian nationhood does not require sovereignty, statehood or separation. It does not threaten the territorial integrity or impair the sovereignty of the Canadian state. The Indian minority would not be seen in competitive terms because it would not have equal weight to the majority. Negotiated limits would place Indians in a position where they could not significantly change the existing distribution of power. In fact, most Indians would shy away from exercising reciprocal authority over the broader, non-Indian political community. Their basic desire is for self-government over their own affairs, not participation in the governing of the rest of Canada through representation in Canada's Parliament or provincial legislatures.

Resolution of common problems or conflicts between the Canadian government and Indian nations could occur through political and administrative mechanisms involving consultative negotiations. Such a model, imbedded as a constitutionally guaranteed principle, would allow Indians the freedom they need to build the sort of communities they desire. Furthermore, by avoiding the issue of sovereign statehood this model conforms approximately to the United Nations' ambiguous strictures on self-determination of peoples (Emerson, 1971). This gives it greater legal, political and moral validity.[10]

CONCLUSION

The most critical political and legal objections of the Canadian government are directed at Indian claims to European-Western-style sovereigr statehood, not at the principle of self-determination. In a struggle to achieve sovereign statehood Indian people could very well provoke a full-scale power struggle with the Canadian government. Such a struggle would consume their limited human, political and economic resources in a futile exercise and could create a backlash in which the "nationhood" option might be eliminated. Furthermore, whereas the Indian condition of economic dependence is a serious constraint on aspirations to sovereign statehood, there is no necessary incompatibility between the current economic dependent status of Canadian Indians and a claim to nationhood. Perhaps more important for Indians than the political-economic *feasibility* of autonomous nationhood is its *compatibility* with their traditional beliefs. Autonomous nationhood, unlike sovereign statehood, would allow Indians to preserve traditional beliefs, values, customs and institutions, and to integrate these with emergent contemporary group interests.

For its part the Canadian government is confronted with two alternatives. It can continue its thinly disguised, much-despised policy of assimilation or, alternatively, it can adopt a policy of meaningful self-determination for Indian tribes. The Canadian government has a moral if not a legal obligation to deal justly and humanely with the Indian people. Should it deny their historical and legitimate claim to nationhood through political or legal stratagems, Indian feelings of injustice will persist. These feelings will inhibit improvement in their economic, social and political condition. If this situation is allowed to fester it could erupt in extra-legal actions culminating in violence (Boldt, 1981b). If, however, Indians are accorded "nation" status within the Canadian federation, and are dealt with fairly and honourably, such an arrangement could foster a sense of mutual trust, it could depoliticize cultural divergency and, in the long term, ease cultural cooperation with Canadian society. Thus, Native Indian loyalties might, over time, be voluntarily transferred to Canadian society.

NOTES

1. The claim to tribal sovereignty is regularly asserted by Indian leaders in Canada and is virtually always explicit in the written representations that provincial and national Indian organizations have made to the Canadian government. For example, see Assembly of First Nations (1982); Federation of Saskatchewan Indians (1977); National Indian Brotherhood (1979); Union of British Columbia Indian Chiefs (1980); and Assembly of First Nations (1983). The consensus among Indian leaders at the band level regarding inherent sovereignty was also strongly evidenced in the testimony of 567 witnesses, representing Indian bands from every province, before the Special Committee on Indian Self-Government of the House of Commons. The Committee has stated that witnesses unanimously rejected the federal government's proposed band-government bill principally because that proposal involved a delegation of power rather than a recognition of the sovereignty of Indian First Nations' governments. See Canada, House of Commons, 1983a:24.

2. It is worth noting that many of the values termed "enlightenment" values have been found by various students of Native Indian society to be indigenous, in approximate form and in varying degrees, to the cultures of many Native tribes in North America. See for example, Hamilton (1950); MacKenzie (1896:35); Forbes (1964); Catlin (1959); Smith (1949:13); and Josephy (1968:119). See also, in this connection, Boldt (1981c). It is a matter of historical record that philosophers from Montaigne to Rousseau were influenced by what they understood to be the enlightened state of North American Indians. Egalitarianism was the most prevalent, though not the universal, model. See, for exceptions, Drucker (1963:chapter 4). For such exceptional tribes sovereignty does not hold all of the cultural contradictions that we identify in this article.

3. In European-Western society we have something akin to this notion of authority in what Friedrich has called "procedural authority." Somewhat along this same line, the Americans substituted the impersonal authority of the Constitution for the personal of George III (Friedrich, 1958:54).

4. This is possible only in face-to-face societies such as the Indian tribes were. See Laslett (1963:158) for a discussion of the characteristics of such societies.

5. Laslett characterizes this de-emphasis of territoriality as one of the defining characteristics of the political form of a face-to-face society, because geographically defined borders are not suited for nor capable of giving a sense of political consciousness or identity to the members

of such groups. That is why Indians retained their sense of nationhood even during the forced mass-migrations. They carried their concept of "nationhood" on their backs (Laslett, 1963).

6. We are not here advocating the reconstructionist anthropologists' position that Indians should change into what they once were. But, neither should they be forced to adopt alien political ideas that distort what they value most in their cultural heritage. They should be free to adopt a model of government that will preserve what they value in their cultural traditions.

7. For a discussion of consociationalism in Canada see Bakvis (1981:62-189) and McRae (1974:253-299).

8. Additionally, a major treaty has been in force for Canada since August 1979. Article of the Covenant on Civil and Political Rights provides that:

    1. All peoples have the right of self-determination. By virtue of that right they freely determine their political status and freely pursue their economic, social and cultural development.

    2. All peoples may, for their own ends, freely dispose of their natural wealth and resources without prejudice to any obligations arising out of international economic cooperation, based upon the principle of mutual benefit, and international law. In no case may a people be deprived of its own means of subsistence.

    3. The States Parties to the present Covenant...shall promote the realization of the right of self-determination and shall respect that right, in conformity with the provisions of the Charter of the United Nations.

    As a party to this covenant, Canada is obliged to report on the "measures...adopted which give effect to the rights recognized" (Article 40[1]) to a body set up under the treaty called the Human Rights Committee.

9. The European colonizer's position on Indian sovereignty has been inconsistent and opportunistic; see Jennings (1979) and Werhan (1978). Initially, to avoid conflict amongst themselves, European powers introduced the doctrine of "discovery" to regulate competition for colonial territory. Subsequently, this doctrine was used as justification for declaring sovereignty over Indians on grounds that they were savages, they did not work the land, and had no civil government; see Keller, Lissitzyn and Mann (1958). At the same time, in order to avoid war and risk defeat, the British ostensibly recognized Indian tribes as sovereign nations and negotiated treaties with them. It is important to note that British claims to sovereignty over Indians were never based

on "consent of the people." Even today, although they live in a "representative democracy," so far as Indians in Canada are concerned, the Canadian government does not derive its powers to govern Indians from the consent of the Indian people.

10. Barker asserts that on moral and practical grounds sovereignty cannot exist for a "nation" which is a minority within a state. Because, if every national group in the world were assumed to be entitled to sovereign statehood it would create chaos and threaten the authority of existing sovereign states. See Barker (1951:139). Furthermore, the claim that Indian tribes existed as "sovereign states" is vulnerable to the argument that if ever they had such a status, they have now suffered a total loss of sovereignty because their paramount legislative authority has been effectively usurped by another state. The claim that they existed, and continue to exist, as "nations" is not as vulnerable to such an argument.

INTERNATIONALIZATION: PERSPECTIVES ON AN EMERGING DIRECTION IN ABORIGINAL AFFAIRS[1]

J. Rick Ponting

INTRODUCTION

As Marshall McLuhan's "global village" of telecommunications has become a reality and as the trend toward global interdependence has been accentuated through transnational patterns of trade and investment, various fields of domestic public policy have become subject to foreign influences to an unprecedented degree. Agriculture, forestry, the environment, and culture are but a few areas in which this is becoming true for Canada; Aboriginal affairs is another such field.

The main focus of this article is on the discourse used by Indians and the Government of Canada in explaining to an international audience the state of Aboriginal affairs in Canada,[2] particularly the events of the summer of 1990 at Oka/Kanehsatake and Kahnawake, Québec. The discourse examined took place during a January 1991 visit to Canada by a delegation from the European Parliament pursuant to a resolution passed by the European Parliament on September 13, 1990. This event is chosen because of its potential historical significance; that is, the visit by the European delegation has the potential to become influential in increasing the political will of the Government of Canada to significantly reform its relations with Aboriginal people.

The article begins with a cursory overview of some of the antecedents to the current internationalization of Canadian Aboriginal affairs. Next, the circumstances giving rise to the European delegation's visit will be identified and the interpretive themes characterizing the discourse through which Indians and the Government of Canada engage in the strategic presentation of self (and other) to the European audience will be described. How that discourse can strike a resonant chord in the European constituents represented by the delegation will be suggested. The article concludes with some reflections on the probable future intensification of relations between Canada and Europe on Aboriginal matters and suggests ways in which Europeans can be of assistance in the future as Canadians deal with the need for re-structuring the relationship between Aboriginal people and the larger Canadian society.

BACKGROUND

The term 'internationalization' is used to denote the establishment of relationships between foreign organizations and individuals, on the one hand, and actors in the Aboriginal affairs policy arena in Canada, on the other hand. Those relationships may be political, diplomatic, economic, or cultural, and they may be direct or indirect. An example of indirect internationalization would be the encroachment upon Indian lands by foreign owned corporations or by domestic corporations producing for a foreign market.

Indians would be quick to assert that the internationalization of Aboriginal affairs in Canada is nothing new. Various Indian nations, such as the Five Nations Confederacy, engaged in relations with the Europeans on a nation-to-nation basis during the early contact stage and later, including in their military alliances (Miller, 1989:63-79). Similarly, in the nineteenth century the Indian peoples of the prairies, such as the Blackfoot Confederacy, entered into treaties on a nation-to-nation basis with the descendants of the Europeans. More recently, Indian delegations have been sent to meet the British monarch to press Indian grievances, much like the delegations sent in 1906 and 1909 by British Columbia Indians in conjunction with their claim to Aboriginal title over lands (Campbell and Pal, 1991). However, in the last third of the twentieth century action on the international front has broadened and intensified in such a manner as to impart a whole new character to this aspect of Aboriginal affairs.

For the internationalization trend, perhaps the most significant development of the 1970s was the emergence of the concept of "The Fourth World" (Manuel and Posluns, 1974). Aboriginal people in Canada, operating now from a position of subordination, reached out to similarly afflicted indigenous people around the world in an attempt to build solidarity and to share strategic insights in the struggle against colonialism. One form which this outreach took was the creation in 1975 of The World Council of Indigenous People, under the leadership of then-President of the National Indian Brotherhood,[3] George Manuel and his colleague Marie Smallface Marule (Ponting and Gibbins, 1980:203). This era also witnessed the formation of the Inuit Circumpolar Conference and the beginning of the cultivation of United Nations' bodies as allies. The catalyst for the latter was Manuel's trip to the United Nations Conference on Human Environment in 1972 in Sweden, which was also the occasion for him to tour various Sami (Lapp) communities. This United Nations' involvement was eventually converted into Non-Governmental Organization status for the National Indian Brotherhood at the United Nations (Ponting and Gibbins, 1980:204).[4] Now eleven organizations of indigenous peoples—including the Grand Council of the Crees, the World Council of Indigenous Peoples, the Inuit Circumpolar Conference, and others—have consultative status with the United Nations' Economic and Social Council.

The United Nations in Geneva is a forum in which Canadian Indians became quite active in the late 1980s. That involvement was encouraged by the United Nations' earlier adoption of certain covenants and conventions[5] which are binding on signatories, the United Nations convening of two international conferences of non-governmental organizations ("NGOs") on the topic of Indigenous People and The Land (1977 and 1981) (Centre for Human Rights, 1990), and its establishment in 1982 of the Working Group on Indigenous Populations.[6] However, perhaps the pivotal development was a 1970 recommendation by the Sub-Commission on the Prevention of Discrimination and Protection of Minorities that a comprehensive study be conducted on the problem of discrimination against indigenous peoples. The final report of this study was released in 1986 (see Martinez Cobo, 1986/87) and provides important background for the work that the Working Group on Indigenous Peoples has been doing, with Canadian Indian involvement, on preparing a Declaration of the Rights of Indigenous Peoples.[7] In 1989 the Sub-Commission appointed a member of the Working Group on Indigenous Peoples to prepare a study "on the potential utility of treaties, agreements, and other constructive arrangements between indigenous people and States...[with] particular attention to universal human rights standards..." (Centre for Human Rights, 1990:11).[8] Further examples of the increasing salience of the United Nations for Canadian Aboriginal affairs is the involvement of Cree Chief Ted Moses as Rapporteur for a 1989 seminar in Geneva on the effects of racism and racial discrimination on the social and economic relations between indigenous peoples and states, and a United Nations-sponsored meeting of experts on indigenous self-government scheduled for 1991.

After four years of preparatory work in which Canadian Indians were closely involved as monitors and lobbyists, in 1989 the United Nations' International Labour Organization adopted the important Convention Concerning Indigenous and Tribal Peoples in Independent Countries (Centre for Human Rights, 1990:16).[9] This convention is legally binding on signatory States, of which Canada is not yet one. Article 7 raises the prospects for greater self-determination for indigenous peoples:

> 7.1 The peoples concerned shall have the right to decide their own priorities for the process of development as it affects their lives, beliefs, institutions and spiritual well-being and the lands they occupy or otherwise use, and to exercise control, to the extent possible, over their own economic, social and cultural development...

As Canadian efforts at constitutional patriation and reform were coming to a head in the late 1970s and early 1980s, Indians struck out in yet another new direction. This strategy, which built on the earlier tactic of appeals to the monarch, consisted of attempts to involve not only the Queen, but also the British Parliament and the British courts directly in the internal affairs of Canada. For instance, in October 1980 the National Indian Brotherhood opened an office in London in an unsuccessful effort to lobby British MPs to block patriation of the Canadian constitution until Aboriginal rights had been satisfactorily addressed (Campbell and Pal, 1991). Then, in December 1981, Lord Denning heard a British court case brought by Canadian Indians against unilateral patriation of the constitution without Indian consent. Such other tactics as a visit to London by a delegation of approximately three hundred Indian chiefs, some in traditional ceremonial attire, attracted media attention and stimulated European curiosity.

Internationalization has proceeded on many other fronts. In the 1970s and 1980s, government politicians and bureaucrats, Indian politicians, and academics undertook various fact-finding trips or research projects to inquire into lessons that might be learned from relations between indigenous people and the state in the U.S.A., Australia, New Zealand, Scandinavia and Africa. Academically, some important research and publications emerged from this period, such as the works of Weaver (1985), Dyck (1985), Morse (1984), and the research by Rudnicki and Dyck (Policy Development Group, 1983) for the Penner Committee on Indian Self-Government, to name just a few. The decade of the 1980s was also the period in which Indian leaders succeeded in drawing international figures to Canada to experience Indian conditions first-hand. One such early visit was by Britain's Lord Michael Morris, as arranged by Indian leaders Joe Miskokomon and Billy Diamond (MacGregor, 1989:190-192). Another was the special visit to

Fort Simpson, N.W.T. by the Pope in September 1987, which attracted enormous attention in Canada and abroad. A third was the controversial March 1987 visit to the Peguis reserve of Chief Louis Stevenson by Glenn Babb, South Africa's ambassador to Canada, while the visit to the Osna-burgh reserve in northern Ontario by South African Archbishop Desmond Tutu in 1990 was a later instance. These visits, and audiences which the Pope granted at the Vatican to various visiting delegations of Canadian Aboriginals (e.g., MacGregor, 1989:193-195) served to bolster perceptions of the moral legitimacy of their cause, or in the case of the Babb visit, to embarass the Canadian government into action.[10]

The struggles of various local Aboriginal peoples, such as the Lubicons of northern Alberta, the James Bay Cree, and the Innu of Labrador, have an international dimension to them. In the case of the Innu, the international dimension is military (low-level training flights by NATO training forces), while for the Cree and Lubicons the international dimension is economic. The Cree are threatened by a new phase of the James Bay project, which will produce power partly for export to the United States, while the Lubicons face the devastation of their forests and depletion of their oil reserves by multinational paper and oil companies acting in concert with the provincial government. International arenas such as the 1988 Winter Olympics and trips to Europe have provided a forum for protest by the Lubicons, while the James Bay Cree have enlisted the support of environmentalists in the United States and warned international investors of the risks to their investments if the James Bay II project proceeds without taking Cree interests into account (*Globe and Mail* staff, 1990).[11]

The European Parliament has emerged as another forum for action, some offensive and some defensive, by Canadian Aboriginal organizations. For instance, a European Parliament resolution of April 14, 1989 (European Parliament, 1989)[12] on the position of the world's Indians, includes refer-ence to "the violation of the territory of the Innu indians by low-altitude flights."[13] Also fought before the European Parliament has been the fur issue – an issue on which the European Parliament came under immense cross pressures. On one side was the vociferous animal rights lobby, while on the other were aligned such actors as the Government of Canada and Aboriginal organizations like Indigenous Survival International (founded 1984). A delegation from the European Parliament visited Canada in February 1990 on a fact-finding mission led by Irish parliamentarian Mary Banotti.[14] Responsible for ushering the issue through the European Parlia-ment, Banotti emerged as a political friend of Canadian Aboriginals who stood to lose much if a fur boycott or a fur-labelling plan were implemented in the important European market. Her skillful political leadership in the

European Parliament is credited with minimizing the damage to Canada's fur industry. It is significant that she was also a key member of the January 1991 delegation to Canada. Ms. Birgit Bjørnvic, Member of the European Parliament, also was a member of both delegations.

In response to these and other events, various European groups in support of Canadian Aboriginal organizations have formed in at least nine countries. Examples are The Working Group on Indigenous Peoples in The Netherlands, and Gesellschaft für bedrohte Völker in Germany.[15] German and Swiss support organizations are credited by a Mohawk spokesperson with being active in lobbying the European Parliament to pass the resolution of September 13, 1990.

1990: A SUMMER OF DISCONTENT, AN AUTUMN OF DIPLOMACY

During the Oka/Kahnawake crisis the Mohawks sought to involve the international community in several ways, only some of which came to fruition.[16] Four days into the crisis the Mohawks and Quebec Minister John Ciaccia reached agreement to refer all civil and criminal prosecutions to the World Court at The Hague (*Globe and Mail*, 17 July 1990:A1), but this agreement quickly fell apart. On July 20 a meeting of about 150 Chiefs from across Canada appealed to the international community and the United Nations to impose on Canada sanctions similar to those brought against South Africa (*Globe and Mail*, 21 July 1990:A1). The federal government dispatched an envoy to Geneva to intervene on its behalf before the United Nations Working Group on Indigenous Peoples (*Globe and Mail*, 27 July 1990:A2) and that body asked Canada to explain its treatment of the Mohawks (Campbell and Pal, 1991). On August 12 the Mohawks, the Quebec government and the federal government signed an agreement which called for the monitoring of events by the Paris-based International Federation of Human Rights. Although a large delegation from the Federation arrived, their ability to carry out their work was so constrained by security forces that they eventually gave up in frustration.

The crises at Oka/Kanehsatake, Kahnawake, and elsewhere in Canada during the summer of 1990 attracted media attention in Europe and resulted in other lobbying efforts there by Mohawks during and after the crises. To the anger of the Governments of Canada and Quebec, which argued that the European Parliament was acting on the basis of factual inaccuracies, the Mohawk lobbying efforts succeeded in convincing the European Parliament to pass the resolution of September 13 reproduced in the appendix to this article. Quebec responded the next day with a four-page letter to the President of the European Parliament.[17] After Canada snubbed[18] attempts to get the Canadian Ambassador to The European Communities (Ambassador Daniel Molgat) to meet on October 24 with members of the European Parliament on the Mohawk issue, the Subcommittee on Human Rights of the EP's Political Affairs Committee hosted an October 1990 visit to Europe by a delegation of prominent Canadian Aboriginal people.[19] They visited and made presentations to the European Parliament in Strasbourg, the European Parliament's civil service offices in Luxembourg, the World Court in The Hague, a conference on Canadian Aboriginal issues at the Institute for Social Studies in The Hague, and the inaugural All-European Canadian Studies Conference being held in The Hague at the same time. By the end of October a decision was taken by the Mohawks to establish the Mohawk Nation Permanent Delegation in Europe. Its staff consisted of Richard C. LaFrance (Okwaoraken), a Mohawk who was already living in The Hague. He was to become heavily involved in a liaison and lobbying capacity.

The Government of Canada responded to the extremely negative publicity that Canada was receiving in Europe by dispatching two envoys to brief Canadian officials in twelve cities in eleven European countries (Canadian Press, 1991). Canada also responded with a three-page letter from the Honourable Tom Siddon, Minister of Indian Affairs and Northern Development to Ken Coates, Chairman of the European Parliament's Human Rights Subcommittee. It was circulated in European Parliamentary circles and among European support groups, and prompted an angry three-and-one-half page rebuttal from the Mohawk Chargé d'Affaires in Europe, Richard LaFrance.[20] That rebuttal was sent to "over 50 european parliamentarians, some european support groups and of course many of our friends."[21]

In his October 5 letter declining to attend the October 24 meeting, Canadian Ambassador Daniel Molgat extended an invitation from Quebec and Canada for the European Parliament's Delegation for Relations with Canada to visit Canada to gather facts on Aboriginal matters. It appears that the proposed October 24 meeting was rejected because the Aboriginal delegation would be present or readily available to offer a rebuttal to the governments' positions. The federal government's attempt to structure the situation in an entirely different manner is revealed in the following passage in the Molgat letter: "The federal Government would agree to provide its position *as the last intervenor* in the European parliamentary procedure after the delegation visit [to Canada]" (emphasis not in original).

THE DRAMATIS PERSONAE

The visit to Canada by the European Parliament's delegation occurred in mid-January 1991. It was a unique combination of theatre, diplomacy, education, research, religion and lobbying. Half of it was orchestrated by the Mohawk Nation (the faction supported by the Warriors) of Kahnawake and the Longhouse members of Kanehsatake, while most of the other half was orchestrated by the Canadian federal government's Department of External Affairs. A three hour session at The Assembly of First Nations was organized by The Assembly of First Nations.

The European delegation was led by Mr. Gijs de Vries (Liberal, Democratic and Reformist Group, Holland). The delegation also included Ms. Mary Banotti (European People's Party, Ireland), Mr. Dieter Rogalla (Socialist Party, Germany), Ms. Birgit Bjørnvic (Rainbow Party, Denmark) and Ms. Cliodhna Dempsey (executive assistant). Not all were present for each presentation or briefing.

The list of presentations made to the European delegation is lengthy. Included among the persons from the Six Nations Iroquois Confederacy were: Kahnawake elected Chief Joe Norton and former elected Chief Andrew Delisle Sr.; Kanehsatake Longhouse members Walter David Sr. and Ellen Gabriel; a warrior from Kahnawake and another from Akwasasne; a clan mother and a Kahnawake male elder; four youths from the Kahnawake Survival School; and others. Other Natives making presentations at Kahnawake came from: the Dakota Ojibway Tribal Council in Manitoba; the Ontario Aboriginal Association; the Lubicons of Alberta (Chief Bernard Ominayak); the Algonquin Nation of Barrier Lake, Québec; the Peigan Nation Lonefighters Society (activist leader Milton Born-With-A-Tooth); the Grand Council of the Cree; the Lil'wet Nation; the Native Council of Canada; the Wendat Hurons (Grand Chief Max Gros-Louis); and the Squamish Nation.

At Kanehsatake the European delegation toured The Pines and the cemetary adjacent to the infamous golf course. The delegation heard informally from various Longhouse people such as Linda Cree, her father Walter David Sr., faithkeeper John Cree (Linda's husband), Ellen Gabriel, and Linda Gabriel. Various other members of the nearby community were heard in a separate brief meeting. Rather than advocating action or cataloguing grievances, the latter described the hurt and division which had become so acute within the community as a result of the events of the summer. Two other representatives from another sector of the Kanehsatake community were also heard the next day in Ottawa.

At the Assembly of First Nations the European delegation heard from Grand Chief George Erasmus; AFN Regional Chiefs Lawrence Courtoreille (Alberta) and Konrad Sioui (Quebec); Inuit Tapirisat of Canada Executive Director Ruby Arngna'naaq; Native Council of Canada President Viola Robinson; Akwasasne Chief Tom Porter (Mohawk Nation Council of Chiefs); Dene Nation President Bill Erasmus; and national spokesperson Gail Stacey-Moore from the Native Women's Association of Canada.

Academics, lawyers, and others also made presentations which are not considered here due to the fact that our focus is on the presentation of self by Indians and the federal government. It must be noted, though, that the academic and legal presenters were carefully selected by the Mohawks. In essence, they were a part of the Aboriginal discourse, for their presence contributed additional legitimacy to the Indian grievances, notwithstanding the fact that they did not always agree with each other or with the Aboriginal presenters.

Federal government intervenors included: the Canadian Human Rights Commission; the Department of Indian Affairs and Northern Development (Minister Tom Siddon and various senior officials involved in self-government, comprehensive claims, economic development, and Indian services); the Federal-Provincial Relations Office of the Privy Council Office; the RCMP (Assistant Commissioners responsible for Operations and for Aboriginal Policing); and a senior officer from the Canadian Forces.

METHODOLOGY

Parts of this article are written from the perspective of a participant observer. My involvement resulted from an invitation from the Mohawks to participate "as a neutral observer" and to make a presentation as part of the panel of academics. I was present during all of the Kahnawake sessions attended by the European delegation and during its visit to Oka and Kanehsatake. I was also allowed to accompany the delegation into its various Ottawa meetings with federal government officials, Minister Siddon, and Aboriginal organizations invited by The Assembly of First Nations.[22] In Ottawa I served the European delegation as a resource person who suggested questions and provided background contextual information. After the completion of the visit I provided the delegation with further observations, commentary, and analysis.[23]

None of the sessions were tape-recorded. Quotations included in this article are from my detailed written notes. The remarks of speakers are usually shown verbatim. On rare occasions they are paraphrased.

THE SETTINGS

The settings for the discourse described below were themselves a study in contrasts. They ranged from the solemnity of the Longhouse at Kahnawake, to the tranquility of The Pines at Kanehsatake, to a twenty-first floor meeting room at the Department of Indian Affairs' headquarters with its panoramic view of the Chaudière Falls on the Ottawa River. Other venues included the cavernous former bingo hall at Kahnawake (with its huge 'flea market,' frolicking children, curious townspeople, and ubiquitous white-sweatshirted Warrior security staff), the small United Church hall at Kanehsatake, the somewhat more 'high-tech' press centre at the Assembly of First Nations, the luxurious Muses Restaurant at the National Museum of Civilization, and the tightly secured External Affairs headquarters on Sussex Drive in Ottawa.

In some cases these settings conveyed a nontextual message which, intentionally or not, became part of the competitive discourse. For instance, the choice of the restaurant at the National Museum of Civilization, adjacent to the magnificent Great Hall with its Haida Village, conveyed an unspoken message of government respect for Indian culture. For the welcoming ceremonies the Mohawks' choice of the Kahnawake Longhouse, into which all men and women had to enter through separate doors, from the outset established the tone of spirituality and cultural distinctness of the Mohawk people which Mohawk political leaders would later convey verbally. Similarly, the choice of The Pines, in all its splendour and with all its bullet holes, as a meeting place in Kanehsatake was an obvious attempt to influence the Europeans by demonstrating that Mohawk discourse, such as their message as to the aggressiveness of the government, is anchored in reality.

INDIAN DISCOURSE

A 'frame' is an interpretation scheme that enables individuals to perceive, identify, and label occurrences which they observe. It is a set of categories through which individuals perceive and give meaning to events in the real world, either for themselves or, when used in discourse, for others. These categories organize experience and provide guides for action (Goffman, 1974).

A striking feature of the Indian discourse was its redundancy. That is, certain 'frames' or themes ran like a refrain through the presentations made to the European delegation by numerous Indian groups. Foremost among these themes was what might be called the *"untrustworthiness of government."* The federal government (ministers and bureaucrats), in particular, was repeatedly portrayed as betraying trust, being deceitful, lying, not dealing in good faith, and being insincere or hypocritical. A lightning rod for many comments of this genre was the remark in Minister Siddon's October 31 letter, as follows: "The method to deal with legitimate grievances is through dialogue and not at the point of a gun." Various Indian leaders pointed out that their people had always been peaceful and yet had not been able to get the Minister to meet with them. In a similar vein, Andrew Delisle Sr., a veteran Mohawk politician who described himself as having met with the Pope, the Queen, and all the Prime Ministers since Lester Pearson, accused Minister Siddon of having agreed at a late-night meeting early in the crisis to have Delisle arrange a meeting to help resolve the crisis and then the next day flatly denying the existence of such an agreement. Delisle charged that Siddon invoked the other federal government officials present as witnesses to the 'fact' that there was no such agreement. Perhaps Chief Tom Porter of the Mohawk Nation Council of Chiefs at Akwasasne captured the theme of deception most colourfully when he suggested that Canada should receive an award for 'lip-synching' peace and justice and human rights.

A second frame used by Aboriginal speakers and reinforced with sociological analytic skill by the Mohawks' non-Indian lawyer (Owen Young), was the theme of *the oppression of the dominant society's legal system*. A quotation from Andrew Delisle Sr. again captures the essence of this theme, especially as it is used as a counterpoint to government attempts to define the issue as one of "law and order." Said Delisle:

> The law that they want us to follow is the law that oppresses us.

Barrier Lake Chief Matchewan added:

> Our trustee [the Department of Indian Affairs] has not lifted a finger to help us …This land grab has been legitimated by the courts, who have refused to recognize our aboriginal rights to the land because we were 'infidels.' I call this racist.

Frequent reference was made also to governments' attempted evasion or circumvention or circumscribing of even those decisions rendered by the Supreme Court of Canada.

A third theme was that of *'government interference and imposition.'* For instance, Ellen Gabriel and others emphasized that the federal government interferes by telling Indians who their leaders shall be – that is, with whom the government is willing to deal. Kahnawake elected Grand Chief Joe Norton offered the following:

Unity is very important for a small people like us, but governments impose institutions that tend to divide us. My job is to do
away with my job.[24]

Said Larry House, of the Grand Council of the Cree:

Those sworn to protect us have been our worst enemies.
[Furthermore] requirements in the James Bay Agreement for
Cree involvement have been subverted by secret deals be-
tween government and corporations.

A fourth theme could be described as 'status exaltation.' This is a
common phenomenon among groups which are low or intermediate in
social status in the large society (e.g., Simpson and Yinger, 1972:199, 219).
Mohawks, in particular, repeatedly took the opportunity to draw contrasts
conceptions between Mohawks and French Québécois or to make jokes
about the Québécois; in each case, the Québécois were denigrated in
comparison to the Mohawks. For instance, one Akwasasne Mohawk commented as follows:

How can Quebec, with no economic base and no land base,
ask to become sovereign? How can Quebec be a nation when
they have no constitution? We have had a constitution since
before the American revolution.[25]

A Kahnawake leader added:

When they developed the James Bay and the Olympics, they
brought in foreign expertise, but we Mohawks use our own
expertise. We've never gone outside for expertise for our
accomplishments, like skis, toboggans, clothing...

Similarly, a representative from the Native Council of Canada said:

The only people who have lost a war in Quebec are the French.
We have not sold, ceded, nor surrendered our lands; nor have
we been conquered.

Aboriginal *nationalism* was a prominent theme interwoven throughout
the remarks of most speakers, as typified by Huron Chief Max Gros-Louis'
following statement which, like others' disavowals of Canadian identity,
evoked applause from the audience:

We do not use the vote because we are not Canadian and are
not Quebecers, and will never be!

Related to this was the repeated demand for sovereignty "and nothing
less." Assembly of First Nations Grand Chief George Erasmus put a less
threatening 'twist' on the message when he asserted:

The issues are not going to go away. Canada must come to realize that we are not a threat and do not wish to dismantle Canada. Rather, Native sovereignty strengthens Canadian sovereignty.

Solidarity with the Mohawks was a message which Aboriginal speakers were assiduous in conveying to the European delegation. This was well captured in the remarks of Frank Rivers from the Squamish Nation in British Columbia:

> If the Canadian government is going to walk over the Mohawks, they're going to have to walk over all of us...The Mohawks are setting standards for all the other First Nations.

Added his compatriot, Sam George,

> The Mohawks have given us the courage and strength to continue.

Terri John, from the Lil'wet Nation in British Columbia, emphasized the extent of the support for the Mohawks in the following remark:

> On July 12 we were one of one hundred and fifty communities across Canada which stood up to support the Mohawks...We are ready to take any action that is necessary if the Mohawks need our support.

Yves Assiniwi, of the Native Council of Canada, expressed NCC's "full support for the Mohawks" and went on to say:

> We are supporting the Mohawks because they are in the forefront of the issues we are all fighting.

Spirituality and Indians' links with nature were an ubiquitous theme. While Chief Tom Porter of the Mohawk Nation Council of Chiefs at Akwasasne expressed this theme eloquently, Peigan Lonefighter Milton Born-With-A-Tooth expressed it with directness and simplicity in the following remarks:

> Nature is our constitution. Nature is everything. It tells us who we are and how to think. Water is fundamental to growth, to cleansing, to food...In 1922 the real diversion [of the Old Man River] occurred. We merely opened the water to its original course. We healed the water...Nature is in us, just as we are part of Nature...The dam is a form of mental genocide...I end by giving respect to this land that we are on.

Kahnawake elder Frank Natawe spoke volumes on this topic with the following simple statement:

We are a people who do not supplicate. Instead, we give thanks for everything.

He then proceeded to explain Mohawk religious ceremonies. The sanctity of the Mohawks' Great Law of Peace and the two-row wampum treaty with the Europeans were underscored by numerous speakers.

Closely related to the themes of spirituality and closeness to nature were the themes of *peace and environmental protection.* Inuit Tapirisat of Canada Executive Director Ruby Arngna'naaq pointed out that Europeans unbalanced nature and that Inuit are negotiating "because we want to protect our environment from further raping." At one point Konrad Sioui suggested that Indians' problems with Quebec and other authorities are "mainly problems of the environment." He likened the James Bay II project to the destruction of the Amazon and added:

> The eyes of the world should be on James Bay II...The time will come when the Indians will be recognized as masters of balancing development and the environment.

Rowena General, a Warrior from Akwasasne, also described James Bay II as an ecological disaster, while Algonquin Chief Matchewan pointed out that the flooding of his people's territory, the construction of a highway through the heart of Algonquin hunting grounds, the use of clear-cut logging and chemical spraying, and the allowance of public moose hunting and sport fishing threaten his people's ability to put food on the table.

On the related peace dimension, Mohawk Grand Chief Joe Norton asserted:

> The government mentality is 'might is right' and that is put forward as the only answer...We are faced with a confronta-tional style of politics that is not conducive to peace...We've yet to see anybody come forward, federal or provincial, with an olive branch or even to set up the forums that will lead to solutions.

Ellen Gabriel's forceful remarks at Kahnawake concluded with the following remarks integrating the peace and environmental themes:

> We hope to work together for peace, because we're all respon-sible for peace, just as we're all responsible for our Mother [Earth].

The aggressive, uncivilized behaviour of government was an undercur-rent to many of the remarks of the Aboriginal presenters. This message, which calls to mind former Parti Québécois leader René Lévesque's fre-quent reference to his party's adherence to civilized ways in its quest for "sovereignty-association," was the thrust of the concluding remarks in the presentation by Milton Born-With-A-Tooth:

> The battle has just begun. The only thing that will stop us is when they start treating us like human beings — nothing more, nothing less. (Loud applause from audience.)

This is clearly a call for Aboriginal people to be treated with respect and dignity — two qualities which most Aboriginal presenters found to be wanting among Canadian governments.

The aggressiveness of Canadian governments was underscored through comparisons with international current events. For instance, Walter David Sr. compared the 'invasion' of Kanehsatake with the Iraqi invasion of Kuwait, while Assembly of First Nations Grand Chief George Erasmus used the same analogy for Canada's overall encroachment on Indian lands. Ellen Gabriel of Kanehsatake further developed the parallels to events on the broader world stage:

> They have low level flights that shake our houses. The army is still there. They try to localize it, but it is an international affair...They keep inflicting their police on us...We have to deal constantly with male chauvinistic attitudes from federal and Quebec negotiators...Our men were tortured with cigarette burns...On July 11 the SQ shot at unarmed women, children, and men. Canada has a history of using unnecessary force against Natives, such as at Restigouche...Your descendants [sic: forebears] who have come over here are a Mafia.

She went on to discuss the psychological scars borne by Mohawk children as a result of the summer events, and to draw parallels to South African apartheid, the Palestinian situation, and the Irish situation. Rowena General described his community of Akwasasne as having experienced "eight separate paramilitary invasions" beginning in 1988, and as still being 'occupied' today, since May 1990.

The aggressiveness and imposition of the federal government was frequently described as oppression. The Europeans expressed particular interest in the views of Indian youths. One Kahnawake student read a poem which described government oppression as "crushing us [Indians]" and "taking our breath away," yet as making Indian youth stronger. Reference by others to the ultimate imposition — namely, to government policies as "termination policies" — was also common and the word "genocide" was used by at least three presenters.

To summarize, the Indian rhetoric characterizes the federal government as an oppressive, untrustworthy, interfering, aggressive, and uncivilized opponent. Conversely, Indian rhetoric depicts Indians as being sovereign, spiritual and peace-loving people who are at one with nature and with each other, while simultaneously under siege from the state and its police.

THE FEDERAL GOVERNMENT'S DISCOURSE

Some of the patterns of discourse used by the federal government are very similar to those identified in the sociological literature as having characterized the mass media's coverage of the new left movement in the United States in the mid-1960s. For instance, Gitlin (1980:24-31) has identified delegitimization and marginalization (showing demonstrators to be deviant or unrepresentative), disparagement, emphasis on violence, and emphasis on internal dissention as prominent themes in mass media coverage of the new left.

Consistent with Gitlin's findings, the primary technique used by the Government of Canada was to cast the Mohawk issue as one of *"law and order"* or *"one law for all Canadians."*[26] Certainly, this is to be expected from the police (RCMP) and military, not only because of their training and world view, but because their organizations' personnel were or are on the front lines of the Mohawks' conflict with the larger society. Their behaviour conformed to expectations, as illustrated in the following remark by an Assistant Commissioner of the RCMP:

> This whole thing is about trying to make the laws of the land apply equally to all citizens.[27]

Like the Department of Indian Affairs, the RCMP also stressed the violation of Canadian and American law (gambling and the trans-border shipment and sale of cigarettes) by the Mohawks, particularly those of Akwasasne and Kahnawake.

Closely related was an emphasis on *Mohawk violence,* especially that of May 1990 at Akwasasne (2 fatalities) and an incident reported to have occurred on March 30, 1990. In that latter incident a Vermont National Guard helicopter was hit by groundfire alleged to have come from the Mohawk "commune" of Ganienkeh, a community which the federal government described as a training ground for Mohawk warriors. The RCMP also cited an incident in which an RCMP aircraft was said to have come under fire from Kahnawake. Significantly, the RCMP's closing remarks to the delegation, delivered at the final session of the delegation's visit, were also dominated by a focus on violence. Specifically, speakers cited an incident in which Mohawks using a 'payloader' were said to have attempted to overturn a manned RCMP cruiser at Kahnawake, and another in which a female member of the Sûreté du Québec was said to have been hit in the head by a steel crow bar wielded by Indians. "We have evidence[28] that this was a set up" the speaker added. Of course, the statement which Indian Affairs Minister Siddon made to the media and repeated to the European delegation, to the effect that the January 8, 1991 skirmish between the Sûreté du Québec and Kahnawake Mohawks was an "ambush" by the Mohawks, is another example of government efforts to portray the Mohawks as violent. Such a definition of the situation has, as its logical consequence, the corollary that the Mohawks cannot be left to police themselves.

The theme of Mohawk violence is highlighted by two other themes which contrast with it. These are the *restraint shown by the government* and the *atypicality or deviance of the Mohawks* in comparison with other Indians. In an opening address which gave the appearance of having been crafted by public relations experts, the representative of the Canadian Forces quoted as follows from the introduction to Maclaine's and Baxendale's (1990) book subtitled *The Mohawk Revolt at Oka:*

> This is a book about a tiny band of Indians who said 'Enough'...At the same time it is the story of a well-disciplined army that did the job it was sent to do...

In discussing the use of the minimum amount of force necessary as one of the principles governing the army's involvement, he built on the restraint theme with the following remarks:

> This requires we be able to justify all of our actions in a court of law. All our actions were rehearsed...We had to be prepared to accept the first casualty...All our actions were done in the public eye.

The theme of the atypicality of the Mohawks serves to localize what most analysts outside the federal government view as actually being a national and international issue. The atypicality theme was projected in Indian Affairs Minister Siddon's response when a member of the European delegation drew parallels with the radicalization of the youth in Northern Ireland and said "I think your history is going to come up and choke you." Said Siddon:

> I can see how you'd draw those parallels, having visited Mohawks. Elsewhere around the country, especially the North, there is a strong sense of discipline and respect and respect for the law.

A variant of the theme of the atypicality of the Mohawks was a theme which might be described, uncharitably, as *"look how our Indians love us."* This is reflected in the remarks of RCMP Assistant Commissioner Head, who is responsible for the RCMP's Aboriginal policing directorate. Dressed in a suit and wearing Aboriginal-style jewellery (ring and lapel pin) which reinforced the theme of a bond between Aboriginal people and the RCMP, he cited the RCMP's "long and cherished relationship" with Aboriginal people.

Another theme of the government's presentations can be described as *progress, generosity, and moral rectitude.* Indian Affairs Minister Siddon provided the classic statement of this theme when he told the delegation:

> Our country has an outstanding record of human rights.

Significantly, the Chairman of the European delegation would not allow the small amount of time available[29] to be consumed with such platitudes and interrupted the Minister before he could finish the statement. Nevertheless, the Minister returned to this theme moments later with reference to:

> our unblemished record of standing up for the underprivileged and oppressed anywhere in the world.

and again later when he added:

> We're a pluralistic society...[extending] hospitality to all races and colours.

Earlier, he had said:

> ...we have not been ungenerous, even to the point of robbing them of their self-respect.

Near the end of the meeting he added:

> Let me summarize with one statistic. In 1960 three percent of Indian students graduated from high school, but in 1986 the figure was 40%...We spend four times more per capita on aboriginals than does any other nation, over and above what we spend on everyone else...

Similarly, the RCMP presentation dealt at length with the various programs and mechanisms which the RCMP has instituted to respond to Aboriginals' needs.[30] Officials at the Department of Indian Affairs also discussed the numerous programmes offered by that department. In contrast to Indians' lawyers' statements about the federal government not adhering to Supreme Court of Canada rulings, Assistant Deputy Minister Richard Van Loon asserted:

> Since Sparrow [the May 1990 decision of the Supreme Court on the Sparrow case] we are more lenient on this. In the last three to four years we've tried to lean over backwards to help claimants meet this criterion.

Finally, *discreditation* of the Mohawks, especially the Warriors, was another theme promoted by the Government of Canada.[31] In addition to associating Mohawks with violence, intimidation of other Mohawks, and smuggling, discreditation took the form of challenging Mohawks' contentions of what is traditional in Mohawk culture. For instance, RCMP Assistant Commissioner Head told the Europeans:

> One clan mother told me that there is no such thing as a Warrior Society.

Discreditation also took the form of accusing Mohawks of not abiding by their customs. This can be interpreted as a counter, in kind, to the Indian theme of government hypocrisy. A further example of discreditation can be found in the remarks of Assistant Deputy Minister Roger Gagnon at the Department of Indian Affairs. Reporting on DIAND's December 1990 meeting with the Iroquois Confederacy, he said:

> They did not regard land as the central issue at Oka. Rather, they listed four other things.

Significantly, he listed only one of the four central issues raised by the Confederacy — the linkage of the Warriors to criminal elements in White society.

In summary, in the federal government's rhetoric the government is depicted as restrained, committed to the rule of law, generously responsive, and liberal. In contrast, the Mohawks are portrayed as atypical, factionally divided, and violent and criminally deviant. These latter depictions of Mohawks are reminiscent of those identified in the social movements literature (e.g., Marx, 1982) on liberal-democratic states' efforts to discredit social movements.

One can observe that for almost every theme projected by the Indians, an opposing theme could be found in the federal government's discourse. For instance, Indians' emphasis on peace was countered in government rhetoric by the emphasis on the Warriors' violence. Indians' emphasis on government aggressiveness is juxtaposed with government's emphasis on its restraint and on Mohawks' "ambush" behaviour. Indians' characterization of government as dishonourable faces government's claims to moral rectitude and its characterization of Mohawks as criminal. Indians' professed solidarity with the Mohawks is implicitly contested by the government's claim of the atypicality of the Mohawks. Indians' complaints that the federal government fails to heed the rulings of its own Supreme Court can be contrasted with government's definition of the events of summer 1990 as revolving around the upholding of the rule of law. Indians' indictment of government oppression stands in contrast to the government's documentation of its generosity, its claims that government is "leaning over backwards" to accommodate Indians, and its self-professed moral rectitude.

Indian emphasis on traditional spirituality is both juxtaposed with government actors' bureaucratic detachment and implicitly challenged when
government challenges the historical veracity of Indians' definition of what
constitutes "traditional." Indians decry government interference, while government decries Indian factionalism. Indians' demands for sovereignty meet
categorical rejection from government. Clearly, in the propaganda battle for
the hearts and minds of the Europeans there is much evidence that the
communications chasm or "two solitudes" identified by Ponting (1986:179-
180) has not disappeared in the intervening decade, for the two sets of
actors are barely within the same universe of discourse.

EUROPEAN RESPONSIVENESS

The discourses of both the Indians and the federal government have
the potential to strike some highly responsive chords in the diverse political
cultures which are found in western Europe and represented in the European Parliament. In some cases the impact upon Europeans is due to the
similarity with Europeans' own experience, while in others the impact is due
to the striking contrast between the European norm and the Canadian norm.
Only a few instances will be discussed here, and attention will be confined
to the Indian discourse.

Despite the abysmal showing of the Green Party in recent European
elections, the environmental theme advanced by the Indian intervenors can
be expected to capture Europeans'attention. Hints of this come from the
European delegation's reactions to the environment during the January
visit. The members of the European delegation were moved by the impressive beauty of the snowclad Pines at Kanehsatake/Oka and seemed incred-
ulous that the destruction of such beauty could be contemplated. That visit
was arranged by the Mohawks, who came equipped with 'props' (a cassette
recorder playing the tape of the Sûreté du Québec's strike on July 11). It
stretches the term "discourse" only slightly to portray the European
delegation's visit to The Pines as a form of discourse; in effect, The Pines
spoke through their majesty and silence. In another instance, when an
Indian speaker at Kahnawake mentioned the damage done to the land by
clear-cut logging, one of the delegates asked for an explanation of the term
'clear-cut.' Upon hearing the explanation she recoiled in dismay. These are
just two instances which are understandable in terms of European images
of Canada as a land containing much unspoiled wilderness. In the context
of existing European anger over perceived cruelty to animals in fur hunting
in Canada, it is probably not a difficult task to arouse European public
opinion against Canada through appeals which couple the theme of despo-

liation of environmental treasures with the theme of victimization of Aboriginal peoples perceived to be living in romantic harmony with that environment.

A second message in Aboriginal discourse which could evoke a strong reaction in Europe is the lack of respect accorded to Aboriginal people by the governments of Canada. As Europeans have related to other Europeans for many generations, they have come to appreciate the need to respect the identity and culture of the other and the need to preserve the honour of one's own side. Furthermore, as Europeans have gone through the surrender of parts of their sovereignty in the stages leading to the restructuring of 1992, they have been called upon to exhibit a certain bold trust and to act in good faith, lest the entire undertaking come unravelled. I submit that the Aboriginal refrain that the governments of Canada have not dealt honourably with Aboriginal peoples, that they cannot be trusted to act in good faith, is a message which will yield significant gains in sympathy among the European mass public. The President of the January delegation to Canada expressed this succinctly when he said at Kahnawake:

> Respect for the dignity of each other and for the identity of each other is essential. This we have learned through centuries of warfare in Europe. If there is no good will, no political arrangements can be successful.

Another example of how contrasting norms can arouse Europeans is to be found in the treatment of Aboriginal females sentenced by the courts to two years or longer in prison. Upon learning that such persons in western Canada are separated from their families by being sent all the way to Kingston, Ontario for incarceration, an Irish member of the European delegation pointed out that in her country there would be an outcry if a person were imprisoned only as far away as the next county.

Finally, educated Europeans recognize colonialism when they see it. Historically, various European countries, such as The Netherlands, France, Spain, and The United Kingdom, are implicated in colonialism at home and/or abroad. Indeed, some of the colonial policies about which Canadian Indians complain in their discourse probably had their origins in the same colonial affairs office as was generating policy to be applied in Ireland and elsewhere in the British Empire. The striking parallels are hard for Europeans to ignore if they know their own country's history. Furthermore, Europeans are acutely conscious of the potential for strife to become prolonged through the actions of security forces in colonial situations. Residents of the United Kingdom have the Northern Ireland case as a constant reminder of this. The Irish situation also sensitizes them to the radicalization of youth which occurs when an essentially political issue is militarized or criminalized.

THE FUTURE

The internationalization of Aboriginal affairs has progressed a great distance since 1970. For several reasons we should expect international involvement in this area to accelerate through at least the remainder of the 1990s. Aboriginal leaders' lobbying expertise is only one such reason. Another is the momentum of Aboriginal successes in this area. A demonstration that the momentum continues, seemingly unabated, at the United Nations is the decision by the United Nations Sub-Commission on the Prevention of Discrimination and Protection of Minorities, at its August 1990 session, to have a special rapporteur prepare a working paper on the question of the ownership and control of the cultural property of indigenous peoples (Anonymous, 1990).

At a more profound level is the possibility that Canada could take a place beside (or in lieu of) South Africa as the object of the world's moral indignation. As we have observed in the discourse projected at the European Parliamentary delegation, Aboriginal leaders are adept at portraying Canadian governments in terms of moral turpitude. As recent resolutions of the European Parliament and the United Nations have demonstrated, there is a growing interest in the international community in Canadian governments' handling of Aboriginal affairs. We should expect, also, that Aboriginal leaders' appeals to the world to engage in an economic boycott of Canada will become the focus of a much more concerted campaign as the stakes are raised in Aboriginal affairs.

Those stakes may be raised in one *or more* of several ways. One way is the radicalization of Indian protest tactics, such as in the James Bay II or B.C. logging disputes, with an attendant militarized response by Canadian governments. Another way is the very great possibility that the seething tensions between the Mohawks of Quebec, on the one hand, and the RCMP and Sûreté du Québec, on the other hand, will experience a major eruption which involves multiple Mohawk deaths. That would most certainly unleash massive confrontation across the country and could catapult Canada to the front of the world stage. The accompanying international pressures for action could result in the adoption of quite ill-considered and drastic policies, which would be reminiscent of the infamous 1969 White Paper fiasco.

A third way in which the stakes may be raised involves the restructuring of Canada in response to the challenge of Québec's sovereignty aspirations. With the collapse of the Meech Lake Accord and the effort by the

Québec Liberal Party and the Parti Québécois to outflank each other in their quest for the majority nationalist vote in Quebec,[32] Canada is destined for a profound restructuring of revolutionary proportions. It is my view that when the new constitution is written, Aboriginal rights in the present constitution are in grave danger of being jettisoned by the larger society and its political elite. For instance, that is the clear position of the increasingly popular Reform Party of Canada, a party which could hold a large number of seats in the next Parliament of Canada.

Jurisprudence since the adoption of the *Constitution Act, 1982* has clearly proceeded far in a direction opposite to what the formulators of that constitution intended.[33] Thus, the abolition, or drastic curtailment, of Aboriginal rights in a new constitution could be seen by some as a 'rectification' of that exercise of judicial independence. Abolition or curtailment is also consistent with the dominant ethos of *individual* rights which prevails in Canadian political culture, for Aboriginal rights are inherently *collective*. Furthermore, abolition or curtailment of Aboriginal rights is perhaps to be expected if one assumes that the negotiation of a new Québec-Canada arrangement will consume most of the store of good will and 'tolerance' which Canadian politicians and the mass public in Canada possess.

The thesis here is that this probable emasculation of Aboriginal rights in the new constitution of the new Canada will provoke an outraged response by Aboriginal people – a response in which they turn to international bodies and the court of world public opinion in a desperate attempt to cut their losses and preserve their dignity. Although the possible parallel should not be overdrawn, we have seen in the Iraqi case that the combination of desperation and assaulted collective dignity can produce highly unorthodox strategic and tactical responses.

In Canada, we might well be standing on the threshold of a paradigmatic shift in Indian policy. The question is whether that shift will proceed in a direction which meets Indians' fundamental grievances, or conversely, whether that shift will be a provocative one which changes the rules of the game and leads Indians to respond in kind by drawing in external allies from the international community. If the latter, then the Government of Canada will quickly lose the initiative and find itself fighting a defensive battle on other actors' terms.

European countries and the European Parliament can make a constructive, albeit modest, contribution to Canada's efforts to address the Aboriginal situation. We conclude with illustrations of such contributions. The illustrations chosen are predicated on the assumption that Europe is not yet ready for coercive measures against Canada, such as comprehensive or even sectoral economic sanctions.

On the economic front one of the most significant contributions would be the offering of trade privileges by European countries for manufactured goods involving a specified percentage of Aboriginal labour. In addition, European countries could offer domestic tax concessions to Europeans who invest in joint ventures with Aboriginal organizations abroad. These measures would address the dire need for economic development in most Aboriginal communities in Canada.

On the political front, the European Parliament could urge its member states to take an interest in Canadian Aboriginal affairs and in Canadian human rights abuses, such as by providing seed money for the educational programs of European groups supporting Canadian Aboriginals. Also, the European Parliament could urge Canadian legislators to establish targets and target dates for the attainment of improved Aboriginal conditions, such as in housing. This takes us into a realm of discourse which has not been addressed in this paper — namely, the prescriptive discourse directed back to Canadians by European legislators.

At the diplomatic and collegial level there is much that the European Parliament can do. For instance, in their future meetings with Canadian parliamentarians, European parliamentarians could discuss the constructive potential of re-structuring sovereignty — that is, of power-sharing, such as is to be done on a large scale in the European confederation in 1992. In informal interaction they could draw the many parallels between the European and the Canadian experience and try to convince Canadian legislators of the need for bold initiatives rather than mere incremental tinkering with the *status quo*. As part of that discourse they could address the issue of mustering the personal and political courage to go forward with such bold experiments. They could also draw from their experience to discuss how trust can be developed where suspicion and rivalry have prevailed in the past.

Finally, European parliamentarians could, by their example, provide Canadians with a lesson in genuinely respecting the dignity, culture, and identity of other actors involved in the political arena. Of course, the time has passed when mere symbolic politics might placate Aboriginal leaders. Yet, the adoption of a more respectful discourse on both sides could serve to facilitate the emergence of political and working relationships with which to better cope with some of the threats identified above.

APPENDIX

Resolution of The European Parliament on Indigenous Peoples
The European Parliament,

A. having regard to its earlier resolutions on indigenous peoples, in particular its resolution of 14 April 1989 on the position of the world's Indians,

B. concerned about the unjustified seizure of land by the Canadian authorities in order to make an extension for a golf course,

C. concerned with the position of the Canadian indigenous people and, in particular, with recent developments regarding relations between the Mohawk Nation and the Canadian and Quebec Governments,

D. having regard to the agreements signed on 12 and 14 August 1990 between the Mohawk Nation and the Governments of Quebec and Canada and the violation of these agreements by the latter:

1. Urges the parties concerned to cease hostilities and commit themselves to the use of judicious and prudent measures to secure a peaceful and just resolution to the current situation;

2. Acknowledges the Mohawk Nation's demands, as expressed in numerous treaties and agreements;

3. Urges the development and implementation of an agreement between Canada/Quebec and the Six Nations Confederacy about the fundamental freedoms and human rights of the Mohawk Nation;

4. Asks the Council to express to the Canadian Government its concern about recent developments with regard to indigenous peoples;

5. Calls on its delegation for relations with Canada to send observers to Quebec and to enter the Mohawk question on the agenda for the next interparliamentary meeting;

6. Instructs its President to forward this resolution to the Council, the Canadian and Quebec Governments and the authorities of the Six Nations.

NOTES

1. The author expresses his appreciation to the members of the European Parliament's Delegation for Relations With Canada (Mr. B. de Vries, Chairman), organizers from the Mohawk Nation at Kahnawake, Kanehsatake, and The Hague, to the Dean and Associate Dean (Research) of the Faculty of Social Sciences, and to the Vice President

(Research) and Associate Vice-President (Research) of The University of Calgary, all of whom made the present paper possible. Special thanks are extended to Ms. Cliodhna Dempsey for her invaluable assistance in fact-checking and in procuring documents from the European Parliament, and to Drs. Tom Langford and Les Pal for their comments on an earlier draft.

2. For a recent analysis of state discourse on Aboriginal affairs in an entirely different setting, see Mannette (1990).

3. The National Indian Brotherhood was the forerunner to the Assembly of First Nations.

4. In 1978 this chair was turned over to the World Council of Indigenous People.

5. These are: The International Covenant on Civil and Political Rights, The International Covenant on Economic, Social, and Cultural Rights, and the International Convention on the Elimination of All Forms of Racial Discrimination.

6. The WGIP, renamed the Working Group on Indigenous Peoples in 1988, reports to the Sub-Commission on the Prevention of Discrimination and the Protection of Minorities. The Sub-Commission, in turn, reports to the Commission on Human Rights, which reports to the Economic and Social Council, which, in turn, reports to the United Nations General Assembly.

7. Before it becomes binding, that draft will have to be approved by the bodies cited in the previous footnote, and then ratified by member states of the United Nations.

8. As a point of departure that study is examining thousands of treaties and agreements already in existence. The final report is due to the Sub-Commission in 1992 or 1993.

9. Also known as ILO Convention #169.

10. Personal conversation of the author with Chief Louis Stevenson, August 1988.

11. Cree Chief Billy Diamond is reported as having told The International Conference of the Nordic Association for Canadian Studies that Natives in Northern Quebec will block the James Bay II project and that European "investors invest at your own risk."

12. The preamble to this resolution refers to various events threatening the world's Indians, such as "the threat of genocide in the Amazonian area of Ecuador."

13. This matter was brought before the European Parliament in Document B2-605/87 by Mr. Vandemeulebroucke and Mr. Kuijpers.

14. For a summary of that delegation's visit to Canada, see Banotti (1990).

15. I am grateful to Okwaoraken, Mohawk Nation Permanent Delegation in Europe, for providing a list of thirteen European support groups, some of which have a mandate which extends beyond Canada to include indigenous peoples in the United States and South America.

16. I am grateful to Dr. Leslie Pal, Department of Political Science, The University of Calgary, for sharing with me the chronology of events which he formulated from newspaper coverage. See Campbell and Pal (1991).

17. Letter of September 14, 1990 from John Ciaccia, Ministre des Affaires internationales et Ministre délégué aux Affaires autochtones, to Baron Enrique Crespo.

18. Letter of October 5, 1990 from Ambassador Daniel Molgat to Gijs de Vries, Chairman of the European Parliament's Delegation for Relations with Canada.

19. This delegation included Manitoba MLA Elijah Harper, Mohawk elected chief Joe Norton from Kahnawake, former Kahnawake elected chief Andrew Delisle Sr., warrior Kenneth Deere, Ontario Aboriginal Association lawyer Chris Reid (a Métis), Kahnesatake Longhouse members Ellen Gabriel and Walter David Sr., Native Council of Canada spokesperson Christopher McCormick, Inuit Tapirisat of Canada Executive Director Ruby Arngna'naaq, Assembly of First Nations Vice-President Lawrence Courtoreille, and Iroquois Confederacy Chief Terry Doxtator.

20. Letter of November 20, 1990 from Richard LaFrance to Ken Coates.

21. Fax of November 21 from LaFrance to J.R. Ponting.

22. I did not accompany the European delegation on its Montreal visit with La Ligue des Droits et Libertés du Québec and Quebec cabinet Ministers Christos Sirros and John Ciaccia or its Ottawa meetings with the Canadian Human Rights Commission, the House of Commons Standing Committee on Aboriginal Affairs, and the University of Ottawa Human Rights Centre.

23. Although the European delegation used most of my questions, they posed many questions of their own, most of which were rather trenchant. Also, the background information which I provided was merely a small fraction of the voluminous amount provided by the numerous intervenors and briefers.

24. Chief Norton's reference is to the division created among the Mohawks by the introduction of the *Indian Act*'s system of an elected chief and council.

25. The Iroquois constitution, of which the Mohawks are a part, is The Great Law of Peace. It is far more than a mere proverb extolling the virtue of peace. It comprises 117 precepts which establish government structures and norms like other constitutions more familiar to western political systems. One of the more readily available reprints of it is in the appendix to Maclaine and Baxendale (1990:99-121).

26. Subsequent to the Europeans' visit federal Justice Minister Kim Campbell employed this same theme, but with a twist (Curran, 1991).

27. This assertion was made on January 17. During the January 14 panel presentations the European delegation received a lengthy exposition of the mythical nature of the notion of "one law for all Canadians."

28. This evidence was neither volunteered by the RCMP nor requested by the European delegation. Readers who have expectations to the contrary should remember that these meetings were constrained by norms of diplomacy and that they therefore did not bear much resemblance to the cross-examination that one might expect in a court of law.

29. This session took place within a few minutes of the outbreak of war in the Persian Gulf and the Minister had to leave for a Cabinet meeting after about forty-five minutes with the European Parliament delegation.

30. Reference here is to the recruitment of "400 to 600" Aboriginal members and on-going efforts to attract more, the Special Constable Program, the Aboriginal Constable Development Program, the National Advisory Committee, and the Local (detachment level) Liaison Committees.

31. It is not a large leap from the discreditation of the Mohawks to the discreditation of the legitimacy of the European delegation itself. On various occasions the European delegation was chastized by federal government speakers for "getting your facts wrong" (e.g., the resolution of September 13, 1990 referred to the "unjust seizure of land" from the Mohawks), for the low proportion of European parliamentarians who were present for the vote on the resolution, or for being too reliant upon television's portrayal of events.

32. To wit, the Liberal Party's January 1991 Allaire Report entitled *A Quebec Free to Choose.*

33. Section 35 states: "The existing aboriginal and treaty rights of the aboriginal peoples of Canada are hereby recognized and affirmed." The adjective "existing" was intended to circumscribe Aboriginal rights, but the Supreme Court of Canada has taken an expansive interpretation instead.

PART VI _____

Some Comparisons: The United States

INTRODUCTION

A comparison with Aboriginal identity policies in the United States is useful for two reasons. One, it demonstrates that the imposition of state-defined concepts of Aboriginal identity is pervasive in other jurisdictions besides Canada. Secondly, the striking similarities between the two countries underscores important aspects of the Canadian scene, such as a reminder that there are many different First Nations, and not simply a single entity of "Indian". Churchill refuses to characterize the Indigenous populations of the United States as a racial or an ethnic minority, because there is no single "ethnicity" which could accurately cover the 400 Aboriginal nationalities found there. This is equally true for Canada which has over 50 languages and/or Native societies represented.

Churchill also feels that the Indigenous peoples of North America make up sovereign nations in the strictest sense of the term; taking issue with the long-standing legal definition of them by Chief Justice Marshall as "domestic dependent nations." Many American Indian groups see themselves as coherent and viable nations unto themselves before they consider themselves part of any Aboriginal conglomeration, or even part of the United States. A point that Churchill does not make, however, is that there is a wide range of individual beliefs among the members of the various Indian nations. This can range from individuals who see the United States as their country first, pointing with pride to their service in the armed forces, etc., to those who deny that they are citizens of the U.S.A at all, and travel with passports issued by their own nation (as many people of the Six Nations do).

M. Annette Jaimes takes a similar tack in characterizing American Indian peoples as fully sovereign nations. But she narrows in on an issue of particular interest for this volume; the issue of citizenry or membership of these nations. In particular, she describes the federal U.S. policy of Indian identification, which centres on notions of "blood quantum" adopted by Congress in 1887 as part of the *General Allotment Act*, and which interferes with the rights of Native groups to determine their own membership policies. Like the definition of "Indian" in the Canadian *Indian Act*, it has had the effects of denying a significant proportion of Native people any official recognition of their Aboriginal heritage or rights. In Jaimes' view, federal blood quantum policies can be seen as nothing less than genocidal in their implications; an attempt at eventually defining Indians out of existence. However, she is also able to document that many Indian nations are beginning to defy the federal standards of blood quantum and are adopting membership policies in line with their own interests and traditions.

THE SITUATION OF INDIGENOUS POPULATIONS IN THE UNITED STATES: A CONTEMPORARY PERSPECTIVE[1]

Ward Churchill

The contemporary situation of the indigenous peoples of the United States (American Indians, Native Americans, Amerindians, etc., in the popular vernacular) is generally misunderstood to be that of ethnic or racial minorities. This is a fundamental misconception in at least two primary ways.

First, there is no given ethnicity which might be correctly said to encompass those who are indigenous to what is now construed as U.S. territoriality. Rather, there are at least 400 distinctly identifiable ethnicities comprising what is lumped into the catch-all category of "Native American." Similarly, at least three noticeable different racial divisions prevail within the overall group; persons of the so-called "Athabascan stock" (such as Navajos and Apaches) are as physically different from Iroquoian peoples (Mohawks and Cherokees, for example) as Mongolians are from Arabs.

Second, notions of ethnic or racial minority status fail profoundly to convey the sense of national identity by which most or all North American indigenous populations define themselves. This characteristic, not the factor of ethnicity, is most important in understanding the reality of Native North America today. It is this sense of themselves as coherent and viable nations which lends substance and logic to the forms of struggle undertaken by these peoples over the past quarter-century.

When we speak of North American indigenous peoples as nationalities, it is essential to understand that the term is not being employed rhetorically, metaphorically or symbolically. To the contrary, it is intended that a precise meaning be imparted. We contend that the indigenous peoples of the North have constituted and continue to constitute nations in the strictest definition of this term, and we assert this on the basis of three major premises.

(1) There is a doctrine within modern international law known as "the right of inherent sovereignty." Basically, this principle holds that a people constitutes a nation simply because, "since time immemorial," it has always done so, for example: from the point of its earliest contact with other peoples or nations the people in question have been known to possess a given territoriality, a means of providing its own subsistence, a common language, a structure of self-governance, a form of legality, and means to determine its own membership and social composition.

Such is the case with the various "tribes" indigenous to the North American continent. To posit but one extremely clear example, the Iroquois Confederacy (composed of the Mohawk, Tuscarora, Seneca, Onondaga, Cayaga and Oneida nations) which held – and to some extent still hold – territory in the modern-day state of New York and adjacent areas of Canada, was possessed of a democratic representative governmental system so developed and refined at the point of historic contact with Europeans that Benjamin Franklin acknowledged having adapted it (with a number of corruptive alterations based in class, race and sex) as the model upon which he based the U.S. governmental structure.

The Iroquois "Longhouse" governance mechanism remains intact and functioning to this day. Similarly, the languages of the Confederacy are still commonly spoken, the tradition of legality established by Hiawatha through the "white roots of peace" remains in effect, and the Iroquois nations' means of defining their own membership (including the sovereign prerogative of naturalizing citizenry) has never been abandoned. A number of other indigenous nations exhibit very comparable contemporary characteristics.

(2) Conventional understandings of international law and custom restrict treaty-making and treaty relationships to the level in interaction prevailing between nations, in the most technically precise meaning of the latter term. This is reflected in U.S. domestic law at the highest level. Articles I and VI of the U.S. Constitution clearly restrict U.S. treaty-making prerogatives to the federal rather than state, local or individual levels, and assert that the federal government is itself enjoined from entering into treaty relationships other than with *fully* sovereign entities (for example, the U.S. federal government is not empowered to legally enter into treaty relations with provincial, state or local governments, or with individuals).

The fact that the United States government, roughly between the years 1790 and 1870, willingly entered into 371 treaty relationships with various indigenous peoples in North America goes far toward corroborating their claim to status as sovereign national entities under the right of inherent sovereignty. It also established beyond all reasonable doubt that these peoples enjoy valid legal claims to sovereign national status under both international and U.S. domestic law. It might be said – perversely under the circumstances in which the indigenous nations of North America now find themselves – that the United States, above all nations or even groups of nations, has gone to the greatest lengths to formally recognize the full legitimacy of their sovereign status. Of such paradoxes are modern international relations born.

(3) Of course, it can be argued – and it has been, by U.S. officials and others – that although North American indigenous nations present an impeccable case on moral grounds, and a technically valid legal case as well, pragmatic considerations of "the real world of the 20th Century" preclude actualization of their national autonomy and self-determination. Within this perspective, indigenous nations are too small, both in terms of landbase (and accompanying resources) and in size of population(s), to survive in the contemporary international context.

At first glance, such thinking seems plausible enough, even humane. At second glance, however, it can be seen to overlook the examples of tiny European nations such as Monaco and Lichtenstein who have survived for decades in the midst of the greediest and most warlike continental context in the history of the world. Further, it ignores the fact of even smaller national entities among the islands of the Pacific whose current sovereignty the U.S. not only is willing to acknowledge, but whose recent admission to the United Nations the U.S. willingly endorsed. The contradictions here are readily apparent; and the mode of thinking at issue is really a veneer, the rationalization "justifying" colonialism and "assimilation" (the contemporary U.S. euphemism for genocide, where indigenous North Americans are concerned).

Closer examination reveals even further inaccuracy within the posture of apologists for present-day U.S. "Indian policy." The Navajo Nation, for example, holds a landbase considerably larger than a number of Caribbean islands – such as Grenada – each of which hold an obvious and unquestionable right to sovereignty and self-determination. The Navajo population is also greater than that of Grenada and a number of other smaller Caribbean islands. In addition, the Navajo Nation possesses an estimated 50 billion tons of low-sulphur coal, approximately 40% of all known "U.S." reserves of uranium, substantial deposits of oil and natural gas, and assets in diamonds, gold, silver, copper, gypsum and bauxites.[2] This is aside from a limited, but real grazing and agricultural capability. By any standard of conventional economic definition, the Navajo people hold a relatively wealthy resource posture as compared to most 3rd and 4th World nations, and not a few capitalist ones. To say that Navajo lacks the ability to survive in the modern context while simultaneously postulating that Grenada has assumed proportions of being a threat to U.S. "national security" as lately as 1984 is to engage in the height of cynicism and absurdity (on both counts).

While Navajo is perhaps the clearest example of the potential for complete autonomy on the part of indigenous nations internal to the U.S., it is by no means the only one. The combined Lakota reservations possess an aggregate landbase exceeding that of the Navajo and, although they exhibit a somewhat less spectacular range of mineral assets, this seems largely offset by their greater agricultural/grazing potential in combination with a considerably smaller population size. Other, smaller indigenous nations possess landbases entirely adequate to their population sizes and many possess rich economic potentials which vary from mineral assets and agricultural grazing lands to timbering and fishing/aquaculture. Small manufacturing enterprises and even tourism are also viable options in a number of instances.

Overall indigenous holdings in what the U.S. terms its "energy resource reserves" include some 60% of uranium, 40% of readily strippable low-sulphur coal and perhaps 15% of known oil and natural gas.

Moreover, all this is true even without just resolution of many treaty-based claims lodged by various indigenous nations against the U.S. relative to vast tracts of land and resources which were simply expropriated by the latter (in direct contravention of both domestic and international law), or before indigenous nations begin to truly exercise sovereign prerogatives such as the naturalization of citizens. The Lakota Nation alone, were its 1868 treaty with the United States to be honoured by the latter, would find itself in possession of an area amounting to nearly 5% of the 48 contiguous states; naturalization of persons residing within the various treaty areas (and those wishing to place themselves or willing to relocate for purposes of coming under indigenous governance and jurisdiction) might well increase the citizenry of Native North America by several millions.

In combination, these three points explain why we hold that the indigenous peoples of North America retain every right not only by virtue of ethics and morality, but in terms of legality and current viability to conduct their affairs as sovereign nations. The liberation struggle we wage is thus not one extended against the discrimination and class exploitation visited by a dominant society and its bourgeoisie upon ethnic and racial minorities within the United States, although we staunchly oppose these conditions and fully support those who actively resist them. Rather, as colonized nations we are pursuing strategies and courses or action designed and intended to lead the decolonization *within* a colonizing "mother country." Hence, while we share a common oppressor with our brothers and sisters of African, Latin and Asian origins within the U.S., the goals, objectives and many of the means of our struggle must be understood in terms necessarily different from theirs. We, "The Indians" of the North and "Los Indios" of the South, of all the people of the Americas, struggle for the liberation of our homelands rather than for the liberation of land upon which to build our homes. We, of all the people of the Americas, engage in our struggles from the basis of our cultures, our freely collective societies born in and long since integral to this hemisphere, rather than struggling to create liberatory cultures allowing the expression of human freedom.

It is from this perspective that the recent history of North American indigenous struggle—the occupation of Alcatraz Island, the Bureau of Indian Affairs Building in Washington, D.C., and Wounded Knee, the battles over fishing rights fought by the Nisqually, Suquamish, Lummi and other Northwestern nations, the armed resistance demonstrated on the Pine Ridge Reservation and all the rest—must be viewed and thus correctly understood. It is this understanding by which the sacrifices of our warriors— brothers and sisters such as Buddy LaMont, Byron DeSersa, Pedro Bissonette, Anna Mae Aquash, Joe Stuntz, Tina Trudell, Richard Oaks (all fatalities of the Movement), Leonard Peltier, Dino and Gary Butler (political prisoners), and many others—takes on its true meaning. And it is from this meaning that one can appreciate the substance of the struggles in which we engage at this very moment: the unswerving resistance of some 10,000 traditional Navajo people in the Big Mountain area of Arizona (headed by the true tribal leadership composed of elder women) to U.S. plans to forcibly relocate them from their land in order to stripmine the coal underlying the area. Or, in the Black Hills area of South Dakota, the ongoing occupation of Yellow Thunder Camp, a part of an effort undertaken by traditional Lakata elders and the American Indian Movement to recover Lakota treaty territories. Or the ongoing efforts in the state of Washington by traditional indigenous people to retain their treaty-guaranteed livelihood based upon fishing. Or the struggles, including armed resistance, of the Mohawk people of New York to retain control of their communities and to implement alternative technologies leading to greater self-sufficiency (and corresponding independence from the United States). Many other examples, of course, might be cited to illustrate each of these points.

At a level broader than the specific and localized confrontations mentioned above, the American Indian Movement continues to wage its struggle against the various mechanisms by which the U.S. government asserts its doctrine of "plenary power" over all North American indigenous nations. This effort can only be understood correctly as a campaign to reinforce and protect the various indigenous sovereignties at issue from a range of U.S. juridical instruments and concomitant policies. Among these, although the illustrative list is hardly exhaustive, are two bits of legislation accruing from the 1880s: the *Severalty Act* (popularly termed "The Dawes Act") which served to forcibly privatize in 160 acre parcels Indian reservation land which had formerly been held and utilized as collective property, and the so-called "Seven Major Crimes Act" which extended U.S. jurisdiction over all indigenous territories within the U.S. for the first time. Also at issue is the Indian *Citizenship Act* of 1924, by which the United States unilaterally imposed its citizenship upon all indigenous persons within its borders (without, however, negating the Aboriginal citizenship status of these persons; indigenous people were made "dual citizens" of both the U.S. *and* their own original sovereignties). Again, the *Indian Reorganization Act* of 1934, by which the U.S. created a system of colonial puppet regimes on many reservations in an attempt to supplant traditional indigenous governmental forms, is a major focus of AIM resistance.

At another level still, the international diplomatic arm of the American Indian Movement—the International Indian Treaty Council, representing some 98 indigenous nations throughout the hemisphere—works continuously to acquaint other nations with the realities of Native American sovereignty. The role of the Treaty Council is not only educational/informative in the international community, but to establish alliances and other forms of working relationships with governments around the world. This goal of creating government-to-government relations is pursued with the utmost seriousness because, in the end, it is through recognition of themselves as fully sovereign entities within the international arena that indigenous people in the Americas perceive the sole possibilities of a just and permanent resolution of the difficulties they now confront.

At this juncture, it becomes both possible and appropriate to pose the question of what concerned persons, organizations and governments might do to assist the indigenous nations of North America in their liberation struggles. At the individual and organizational levels, it seems safe to observe that while the possibilities are myriad and often complex, substantial methods of rendering mutual support have been developed between the indigenous movement and the Black, Chicano, Puerto Rican and Asian communities within the United States and, in some instances, abroad.

These must, of course, continue to be strengthened, developed and perfected. However, the prognosis in this regard appears good in many ways.

At the level of governments the situation has been much less thoroughly explored and seems considerably more sensitive. We would certainly not contend that the forms of support and assistance extended by governments such as that of Cuba, or those of other friendly and progressive nations such as Nicaragua, Libya, Vietnam, etc. be military, in terms of trade or the like. Rather, we would suggest that perhaps the single most important — indeed, crucial — sort of direct support which might be provided at the intergovernmental level would be the formal recognition of the sovereign status of the various nations indigenous to U.S. territoriality, a welcoming of these nations into the modern international community as peers. There are a wide array of possible routes to such an end, and we are not positing any one of these as being inherently superior to another. Recognition need not be conveyed through summit conferences, meetings of heads of state or via official proclamations; it can be a matter as simple as honouring the passports of indigenous nations for purposes of entering and exiting supportive nations. This, to be sure constitutes a formal recognition of our national sovereignty, and it obviously frees us from an unwarranted dependence upon our colonizer in travelling abroad to pursue our agenda of decolonizing our various nations. This would be a small beginning, no doubt, but nonetheless an important one; it is from precisely such small beginnings that substantial changes in the course of nations can emerge.

It is important, vitally important, that we continue our common struggles and not lose hope of eventual, final victory over the forces which oppress us all. We must remember that Angola, Mozambique and Guineau Bisseau were colonized by the Portuguese for five hundred years. Five centuries of struggle, and all the pain which comes with such a history, but today the Portuguese have been ejected from each of these places. These countries are now free of colonial rule. Cuba was colonized for more than 400 years; today Cuba is free. The Irish have been colonized for full eight centuries and they are still not decolonized, but today their struggle for liberation continues and, in some ways, it is stronger than ever before. Eventually, the Irish too will be free. And so it is with Puerto Rico and the Caribbean, with Americans of African descent and those of Chicano and Asian ancestry, as well as those indigenous to the Americas. In the end, each group in its own way and according to its own vision, will be free.

Venceremos!

NOTES

1. This paper was presented at the Second Seminar on the Situation of the Black, Chicano, Cuban, Native American, Puerto Rican, Caribbean and Asian Communities in the United States; Havana, Cuba, December 4-6, 1984. Ward Churchill was a delegate at the seminar representing the International Indian Treaty Council.

2. *Note on Internal Colonialism*: The International Indian Treaty Council believes that one of the major problems which has confronted us in attempting to articulate the status of the indigenous nations of this hemisphere has to do with the specific form of colonialism imposed upon us, "internal colonialism." The idea of internal colonialism is undoubtedly somewhat unorthodox. The conventional spectrum of analysis of the phenomenon of colonization ranges from that adopted by the United Nations (which requires definitionally that an ocean separate the colonizer from the colonized in order for a "true" condition of colonization to exist) to that of conventional socialist thinking which, with certain exceptions, subscribes to a less specific though similar sort of interpretation. Internal colonialism does not occur, however, with the more typical forms of exploitation evident under imperialism. Rather, it is the result of a peculiarly virulent form of socio-economic penetration wherein the colonizing country literally exports a sufficient proportion of its population to supplant (rather than enslave) the indigenous population of the colony. Such a method has been termed elsewhere as "settler colonialism." Often under such conditions, the settler population itself revolts at a certain point against the mother country regime and establishes itself as an independent or quasi-independent sovereignty; the indigenous peoples/nations consequently become colonized entities within a given national territoriality rather than subject to the more classic form of colonization from abroad. Aside from the United States, the modern world witnesses several other leading examples of this state of affairs. Among these are Australia and New Zealand, South Africa and, of course, Israel. Also, until that nation was liberated by African revolutionary forces, Rhodesia was at least an aspirant example. Current indications are that the phenomenon of internal colonialism has been dramatically underestimated as a global condition. It requires serious study on the part of progressive intellectuals and governments, as well as the development/implementation of effective ways and means of supporting impacted nationalities as soon as possible.

FEDERAL INDIAN IDENTIFICATION POLICY: A USURPATION OF INDIGENOUS SOVEREIGNTY IN NORTH AMERICA

M. Annette Jaimes

By all accepted standards of international jurisprudence and human decency, American Indian peoples whose territory lies within the borders of the United States hold compelling legal and moral rights to be treated as fully sovereign nations. It is axiomatic that any such national entity is inherently entitled to exercise the prerogative of determining for itself the criteria by which its citizenry, or "membership," is to be recognized by other sovereign nations. This is a principle which applies equally to super-powers such as the U.S.S.R. and to non-powers such as Grenada and Monaco. In fact, it is a tenet so widely understood and imbedded in international law, custom, and convention, that it bears no particular elaboration here.

Contrary to virtually universal practice, the U.S. has opted to unilaterally preempt the rights of many North American indigenous nations to engage in this most fundamental level of internal decision-making. Instead, in pursuit of the interests of their own state rather than those of the nations which are thereby affected, federal policy-makers have increasingly imposed "Indian identification standards" of their own devise. Typically centering upon a notion of "blood quantum"—not especially different in its conception from the eugenics code once adopted by Nazi Germany in its effort to achieve "racial purity," or currently utilized by South Africa to segregate Blacks and "coloreds"—this aspect of U.S. policy has increasingly wrought havoc with the American Indian sense of nationhood (and often the individual sense of self) over the past century.

The present paper will offer a brief analysis of the motivations underlying this federal usurpation of the American Indian expression of sovereignty, and point out certain implications of it.

FEDERAL OBLIGATIONS

The 371 formally ratified treaties entered into by the U.S. with various Indian nations represent the basic real estate documents by which the federal government now claims legal title to most of its landbase. In exchange for the lands ceded by the Indians in perpetuity, the U.S. committed itself to the permanent provision of a range of services to Indian populations (*i.e.*, the citizens of the Indian nations with which the treaty agreements were reached), which would assist them in adjusting their economies and ways-of-life to their newly constricted territories. For example, in the 1794 *Treaty with the Oneida* (also affecting the Tuscarora and Stockbridge Indians), the U.S. guaranteed provision of instruction "in the arts of the miller and sawyer," as well as regular annuities paid in goods and cash, in exchange for a portion of what is now the State of New York (Kappler, 1973:3-5). Similarly, the 1804 *Treaty with the Delaware* extended assurances of technical instruction in agriculture and the mechanical arts, as well as annuities (Kappler, 1973:7-9). As E.C. Adams frames it:

> Treaties with the Indians varied widely, stipulating cash annuities to be paid over a specified period of time or perpetually; ration and clothing, farming implements and domestic animals, and instruction in agriculture along with other educational opportunities...[And eventually] the school supplemented the Federal program of practical teaching (Adams, 1946:30-31).

The reciprocal nature of such agreements received considerable reinforcement when it was determined, early in the 19th century, that "the enlightenment and civilization of the Indian" might yield—quite aside from any need on the part of the U.S. to honour its international obligations—a certain utility in terms of subordinating North America's indigenous peoples to Euroamerican domination. Secretary of War John C. Calhoun articulated this quite clearly in 1818:

> By a proper combination of force and persuasion, of punishment and rewards, they [the Indians] ought to be brought within the pales of law and civilization. Left to themselves, they will never reach that desirable condition. Before the slow operation of reason and experience can convince them of its superior

advantages, they must be overwhelmed by the mighty torrent of our population. Such small bodies, with savage customs and character, cannot, and ought not, to be allowed to exist in an independent society. Our laws and manners ought to supercede their present savage manners and customs...their [treaty] annuities would constitute an ample school fund; and education, comprehending as well as the common arts of life, reading, writing, and arithmetic, ought not to be left discretionary with the parents...When sufficiently advanced in civilization, they would be permitted to participate in such civil and political rights as the respective States.[1]

The utter cynicism involved in Calhoun's position—that of intentionally using the treaty instruments by which the U.S. conveyed recognition of Indian sovereignty as the vehicle upon which to destroy that same sovereignty—speaks for itself. The more important point (for purposes of this study), however, is that a confluence of U.S. strategic interests had congealed around the notion of extending federal obligations to Indians by 1820. The tactic was therefore continued throughout the entirety of the period of U.S. internal territorial conquest and consolidation.[2] By 1900, the federal obligations to Indian nations were therefore quite extensive.

FINANCIAL FACTORS

As Vine Deloria, Jr., has observed:

The original relationship between the United States government and the American Indian tribes was one of treaties. Beginning with the establishment of the federal policy toward Indians in the Northwest Ordinance of 1787, which pledged that the utmost good faith would be exercised toward the Indian tribes, and continuing through many treaties and statutes, the relationship has gradually evolved into a strange and stifling union in which the United States has become responsible for all of the programs and policies affecting Indian communities (Deloria, 1976:2).

What this meant in practice was that the government was being required to underwrite the cost of a proliferating bureaucratic apparatus overseeing "service delivery" to Indians, a process initiated on April 16, 1818, with the passage of an act *(U.S. Statutes at Large,* 13:461) requiring the placement of a federal agent with each Indian nation, to serve as liaison and to "administer the discharge of Governmental obligations thereto." As the number of Indian groups with which the U.S. held relations had increased, so too had the number of "civilizing" programs and services undertaken, ostensibly in their behalf. This was all well and good during the time-span when it was seen as a politico-military requirement, but by the turn of the century this need had passed. The situation was compounded by the fact that the era of Indian population decline engendered by war and disease had also come to an end; the population eligible for per capita benefits, which had been reduced to a quarter-million by the 1890s, could be expected to rebound steadily in the 20th century. With its land-base secured, the U.S. was casting about for a satisfactory mechanism to avoid paying the ongoing costs associated with its acquisition.

The most obvious route to this end, of course, lay in simply and overtly refusing to comply with the terms of the treaties, thus abrogating them.[3] The problems in this regard were, however, both two-fold and extreme. First, the deliberate invalidation of the U.S. treaties with the Indians would (obviously) tend to simultaneously invalidate the legitimacy which the country attributed to its occupancy of much of North America. Second, such a move would immediately negate the useful and carefully nurtured image the U.S. had cultivated of itself as a country of progressive laws rather than raw force. The federal government had to *appear* to continue to meet its commitments, while at the same time avoiding them, or at least containing them at some acceptable level. A devious approach to the issue was needed.

This was found in the so-called "blood quantum" or "degree of Indian blood" standard of American Indian identification which had been adopted by Congress in 1887, as part of the General Allotment Act (25 U.S.C.A. 331, popularly known as the "Dawes Act" after its sponsor, Massachusetts Senator Henry Dawes). The function of this piece of legislation was to expedite the process of Indian civilization by unilaterally dissolving their collectively (*i.e.*, nationally) held reservation land holdings. Reservation lands were reallocated in accordance with the "superior" (*i.e.*, Euroamerican) concept of property: *individually* deeded land parcels, usually of 160 acres each. Each Indian, identified as being those documentably of *one-half or more Indian blood,* was entitled to receive title in fee of such a parcel; all others were simply disenfranchised altogether. Reserved Indian land which remained unallotted after all "blooded" Indian had received their individual parcels was to be declared "surplus," and opened up for non-Indian use and occupancy.

Needless to say, there were nowhere near enough Indians meeting the act's genetic requirements to absorb by individual parcel the quantity of acreage involved in the formerly reserved land areas. Consequently, between 1887 and 1934, the aggregate Indian landbase within the U.S. was "legally" reduced from about 138 million acres to about 48 million (Collier,

1934:16-18). Moreover, the allotment process itself had been manipulated in such a way that the worst reservation acreage tended to be parceled out to Indians, while the best was opened to non-Indian homesteading and corporate use; nearly 20 million of the acres remaining in Indian hands by the latter year was arid or semi-arid, and thus marginal or useless for agricultural purposes (Deloria and Lytle, 1983:10).

By the early 1900s, then, the eugenics mechanism of blood quantum had already proven itself such a boon in the federal management of its Indian affairs that it was generally adapted as the "eligibility factor" triggering entitlement to *any* federal service from the issuance of commodity rations to health care, annuity payment and educational benefits. If the federal government could not repeal its obligations to Indians, it could at least act to limit their number, thereby diminishing the costs associated with underwriting their entitlements on a per capita basis. Concomitantly, it must have seemed logical that if the overall number of Indians could be kept small, the administrative expenses involved in their service programs might also be held to a minimum. Much of the original impetus towards the federal preemption of the sovereign Indian prerogative of defining "who's Indian," and the standardization of the racist degree-of-blood method of Indian identification, derived from the budgetary considerations of a federal government anxious to avoid paying its bills.

OTHER ECONOMIC FACTORS

As the example of the General Allotment Act, used above, clearly demonstrates, other economic determinants than the mere outflow of cash from the federal treasury figure into the federal utilization of blood quantum. The huge windfall of land expropriated by the U.S. as a result of the act was only the tip of the iceberg. For instance, in constricting the acknowledged size of Indian populations, the government could technically meet its obligations to reserve "first rights" to water usage for Indians while simultaneously siphoning off artificial "surpluses" to non-Indian agricultural, ranching, municipal and industrial use in the arid west (Hundley, 1979). The same principle pertains to the assignment of fishing quotas in the Pacific Northwest, a matter directly related to the development of a lucrative non-Indian fishing industry there (American Friends Service Committee, 1970; Cohen, 1986).

By the 1920s, it was also becoming increasingly apparent that much of the agriculturally worthless terrain left to Indians after allotment lay astride rich deposits of natural resources such as coal, copper, oil and natural gas; later in the century, it was revealed that some 60% of all "domestic" uranium reserves also lay beneath reservation lands. It was therefore becoming imperative, from the viewpoint of federal and corporate economic planners, to gain unhindered access to these assets. Given that it would have been just as problematic to simply seize the resources as it would have been to abrogate the treaties, another expedient was required. This assumed the form of legislation unilaterally extending the responsibilities of citizenship (though not all the rights; Indians are still regulated by about 5,000 more laws than other citizens) over all American Indians within the U.S.

> Approximately two-thirds of the Indian population had citizenship conferred upon them under the 1877 Allotment Act, as a condition of the allotment of their holdings... [In 1924] an act of Congress [8 U.S.C.A. 1401 (a)(2)] declared all Indians to be citizens of the U.S. and of the states in which they resided... (League of Women Voters, 1977:24).

The Indian Citizenship Act greatly confused the identification and loyalties even of many of the blooded and federally certified Indians insofar as it was held to hold legal force, and to carry legal obligations, *whether or not* any given Indian or group of Indians wished to be a U.S. citizen. As for the host of non-certified, mixed-blood people residing in the U.S., their status was finally "clarified"; they had been definitionally absorbed into the American mainstream at the stroke of the Congressional pen. And, despite the fact that the act technically left certified Indians occupying the status of citizenship in their own indigenous nation as well as in the U.S. (a "dual form" of citizenship, so awkward as to be sublime), the juridical door had been opened by which the weight of Indian obligations would begin to accrue more to the U.S. than to themselves. Resource negotiations would henceforth be conducted between "American citizens" rather than between representatives of separate nations, a context in which federal and corporate arguments "to the greater good" could be predicted to prevail.

In 1934, the effects of the citizenship act were augmented by the passage of the Indian Reorganization Act (25 U.S.C.A. § 461; also known as the "Wheeler-Howard Act," after its Senate and House sponsors). The expressed purpose of this law was to finally and completely usurp the traditional mechanisms of American Indian governance (e.g.: the traditional chiefs, council of elders, etc.), replacing them with a system of federally approved and regulated "tribal councils." These councils, in turn, were consciously structured more along the lines of corporate boards than of governmental entities. As Section 17 of the IRA, which spells out the council functions, puts the matter:

> [An IRA charter] may convey to the incorporated tribe the power to purchase, take by gift, or bequest, or otherwise, own, hold,

manage, operate, and dispose of property of every description, real and personal, including the power to purchase restricted Indian lands and to issue in exchange for corporate property, and such further powers as may be incidental to the conduct of corporate business, not inconsistent with the law.

Indeed, since the exercise of such typical governmental attributes as jurisdiction over criminal law had already been stripped away from the council by legislation such as the 1885 Major Crimes Act (18 U.S.C.A. § 153), there has been very little for the IRA form of Indian government to do but sign off on leasing and other business arrangements with external interests. The situation was/is compounded by the fact that grassroots Indian resistance to the Act's "acceptance" on many reservations was overcome by federal manipulation of local referenda.[4] This has left the IRA governments in the position of owing Washington rather than their supposed constituents for whatever legitimacy they may possess. All in all, it was and is a situation made to order for the rubber-stamping of plans integral to U.S. economic development, at the direct expense of Indian nations and individual Indian people.

This is readily born out by the fact that, as of 1984, American Indians received, on the average, less than 20% of the market royalty rates (*i.e.*, the rates paid to non-Indians) for the extraction of minerals from their land. As Winona LaDuke observes:

> By official census counts, there are only about 1 1/2 million Indians in the United States. By conservative estimates a quarter of all the low sulphur coal in the U.S. lies under our reservation land. About 15% of all the oil and natural gas lies there, as well as two-thirds of the uranium. 100% of all U.S. uranium production since 1955 has been on Indian land. And we have a lot of copper, timber, water rights and other resources, too. By any reasonable estimation, with this small number of people and vast amount of resources, we should be the richest group in the United States. But we are the poorest. Indians have the lowest per capita income of any population group in the U.S. We have the highest rate of unemployment and lowest level of educational attainment. We have the highest rates of malnutrition, plague disease, death by exposure and infant mortality. On the other hand, we have the shortest life-span. Now, I think this says it all. Indian wealth is going somewhere, and that somewhere is definitely not to Indians. I don't know your definition of colonialism, but this certainly fits into mine (LaDuke, 1984).

In sum, the financial advantages incurred by the U.S. in its appropriation of the definition of Indian identity have been neatly joined to even more powerful economic motivators during this century. The previously noted reluctance of the federal government to pay its bills cannot be uncoupled from its desire to profit from the resources of others.

CONTEMPORARY POLITICAL FACTORS

The utilization of treaties as instruments by which to begin the subordi-nation of American Indian nations to U.S. hegemony, as well as subsequent legislation such as the *Major Crime Act,* the *General Allotment Act,* the *Indian Citizenship Act,* the *Indian Reorganization Act,* and the *Termination Act* all carry remarkably clear political overtones. This, to be sure, is the language of the colonizer and the colonized, to borrow a phrase from Albert Memmi (1967) and in each case the federal manipulation of the question of American Indian identity has played its role. These examples, however, may rightly be perceived as being both historical and as parts of the "grand scheme" of U.S. internal colonialism (or "Manifest Destiny," as it was once called).

Today, the function of the Indian identity question appears to reside at the less rarified level of maintaining the status quo. In the first instance, it goes to the matter of keeping the aggregate Indian population at less than 1% of the overall U.S. population, and thus devoid of any potential electoral power. In the second instance, and perhaps of equal importance, it goes to the classic "divide and conquer" strategy of keeping Indians at odds with one another, even within their own communities. As Tim Giago, conserva-tive editor of the *Lakota Times,* asks:

> Don't we have enough problems trying to unite without... additional headaches? Why must people be categorized as full-bloods, mixed bloods, etc.? Many years ago, the Bureau of Indian Affairs decided to establish blood quanta for the purpose of [tribal] enrollment. At that time, blood quantum was set at one-fourth degree for enrollment. Unfortunately, through the years, this caused many people on the reservation to be categorized and labeled....[The] situation [is] created solely by the BIA, with the able assistance of the Department of Interior (Giago, 1984:337).

What has occurred is that the limitation of federal resources allocated to meeting U.S. obligations to American Indians has become so severe that Indians themselves have increasingly begun to enforce the race codes excluding the genetically marginalized from both identification as Indian citizens and consequent entitlements. In theory, such a posture leaves greater per capita shares for all remaining "bona fide" Indians. But, as American Indian Movement activist Russell Means has pointed out:

> The situation is absurd. Our treaties say nothing about your having to be such-and-such a degree of blood in order to be covered. No, when the federal government made its guarantees to our nations in exchange for our land, it committed to provide certain services to us as we defined ourselves. As nations, and as people. This seems to have been forgotten. Now we have Indian people who spend most of their time trying to prevent other Indian people from being recognized as such, just so that a few more crumbs — crumbs from the federal table — may be available to them, personally. I don't have to tell you that this isn't the Indian way of doing things. The Indian way would be to get together and demand what is coming to each and every one of us, instead of trying to cancel each other out. We are acting like colonized peoples, like subject peoples... (Means, 1985).

The nature of the dispute has followed the classic formulation of Frantz Fanon, wherein the colonizer contrives issues which pit the colonized against one another, fighting viciously for some presumed status within the colonial structure, never having time or audacity enough to confront their oppressors (Fanon, 1963). In the words of Stella Pretty Sounding Flute, a member of the Crow Creek band of Lakota, "My grandmother used to say that Indian blood was getting all mixed up, and some day there would be a terrible mess....[Now] no matter which way we turn, the white man has taken over" (Martz, 1986a).

The problem, of course, has been conscientiously exacerbated by the government, through its policies of leasing individual reservation land parcels to non-Indians, increasingly "checkerboarding" tribal holdings since 1900. Immediate economic consequences aside, this has virtually insured that a sufficient number of non-Indians would be resident to reservations that intermarriage would steadily result. During the 1950s, the federal relocation program — in which reservation-based Indians were subsidized to move to cities, where they might be anticipated as being subsumed within vastly larger non-Indian populations — accelerated the process of "biological hybridization." Taken in combination with the ongoing federal insistence that "Indian-ness" could be measured *only* by degree of blood, these policies tend to speak for themselves.

Even in 1972, when, through the *Indian Education Act* (86 *Stat.* 334), the government seemed finally to be abandoning blood quantum, there was

a hidden agenda. As Lorelei DeCora (Means), a former Indian education
program coordinator, puts it:

> The question was really one of control, whether Indians would
> ever be allowed to control the identification of their own group
> members or citizens. First there was this strict blood quantum
> thing, and it was enforced for a hundred years, over the strong
> objections of a lot of Indians. Then, when things were suffi-
> ciently screwed up because of that, the feds suddenly reverse
> themselves completely, saying its all a matter of *self*
> identification. Almost anybody who wants to can just walk in
> and announce that he or she is Indian — no familiarity with tribal
> history, or Indian affairs, community recognition, or anything
> else really required — and, under the law, there's not a lot that
> Indians can do about it. The whole thing is suddenly just *laissez
> faire,* really out of control. At that point, you really did have a
> lot of people showing up claiming that one of their ancestors
> seven steps removed, had been some sort of "Cherokee
> princess." And we were obliged to accept that, and provide
> services. Hell, if all of that was real, there are more Cherokees
> in the world than there are Chinese (DeCora [Means], 1986).

Predictably, Indians of all perspectives on the identity question reacted
strongly against such gratuitous dilution of themselves. The result was a
broad rejection of what was perceived as "the federal attempt to convert us
from being the citizens of our own sovereign nations, into benign members
of some sort of all-purpose U.S. minority group, without sovereign rights"
(Means, 1975). For its part, the government, without so much as a pause
to consider the connotations of the word "sovereign" in this connection
elected to view such statements as an *Indian* demand for resumption of the
universal application of the blood quantum standard. Consequently, the
Reagan administration has, during the 1980s, set out to gut the *Indian
Education Act* (Jones, 1984:3-4) and to enforce degree of blood requirements for federal services, such as those of the Indian Health Service
(Martz, 1986a).

At this juncture, things have become such a welter of confusion that:

> The Federal government, State governments and the Census
> Bureau all have different criteria for defining "Indians" for
> statistical purposes, and even Federal criteria are not consis-
> tent among Federal agencies. For example, a State desiring
> financial aid to assist Indian education receives the aid only for
> the number of people with one-quarter or more Indian blood.
> For preference in hiring, enrollment records from a Federally
> recognized tribe are required. Under regulations for law and

order, anyone of "Indian descent" is counted as an Indian. If the Federal criteria are inconsistent, State guidelines are [at this point] even more chaotic. In the course of preparing this report, the Commission contacted several States with large Indian populations to determine their criteria. Two States accept the individual's own determination. Four accept individuals as Indian if they were "recognized in the community" as Native Americans. Five use residence on a reservation as criteria. One requires one-quarter blood, and still another uses the Census Bureau definition that Indians are who they say they are (American Indian Policy Review Commission, 1977:89).

This, without doubt, is a situation made to order for conflict, among Indians more than anyone else. Somehow, it is exceedingly difficult to imagine that the government would wish to see things turn out any other way.

IMPLICATIONS

The eventual outcome of federal blood quantum policies can be described as little other than genocidal in their final implications. As American Studies scholar Patricia Nelson Limerick recently summarized the process:

Set the blood quantum at one-quarter, hold to it as a rigid definition of Indians, let intermarriage proceed as it had for centuries, and eventually Indians will be defined out of existence. When that happens, the federal government will be freed of its persistent "Indian problem" (Limerick, 1987:338).

Already, this conclusion receives considerable validation in the experience of the Indians of California, such as the Juaneño. Pursuant to the "Pit River Consolidated Land Settlement" of the 1970s, in which the government purported to "compensate" many of small California bands for lands expropriated during the course of non-Indian "settlement" in that state (at less than 50 cents per acre), the Juaneño and a number of other "Mission Indians" were simply declared to be "extinct." This policy was pursued despite the fact that substantial numbers of such Indians were known to exist, and that the government was at the time issuing settlement checks to them. The tribal rolls were simply ordered closed to any new additions, despite the fact that many of the people involved were still bearing children, and their population might well have been expanding. It was even suggested in some instances that children born after an arbitrary cut-off date should be identified as "Mispanic" or "Mexican" in order that they benefit from federal and state services to minority group.[5]

When attempting to come to grips with the issues raised by such federal policies, the recently "dissolved" California groups, as well as a number of previously unrecognized ones such as the Gay Head Wampanoags (long described as extinct), confronted a Catch-22 situation worthy of Joseph Heller. This rested in the federal criteria for recognition of Indian existence in the present day:

1. An Indian is a member of any federally recognized Indian Tribe. To be federally recognized, an Indian Tribe must be comprised of Indians.

2. To gain federal recognition, an Indian Tribe must have a land base. To secure a land base, an Indian Tribe must be federally recognized (Native American Consultants, 1980:2).

As a Shoshone activist, Josephine C. Mills, put it in 1964, "There is no longer any need to shoot down Indians in order to take away their rights and land [or to wipe them out]...legislation is sufficient to do the trick legally" (Armstrong, 1975:175). The notion of genocidal implications in all this receives firm reinforcement from the federal propensity, during the second half of this century, to utilize residual Indian landbases as dumping grounds for many of the more virulently toxic byproducts of its advanced technology and industry (Churchill and LaDuke, 1985:107). By the early '70s, this practice had become so pronounced that the Four Corners and Black Hills Regions, two of the more heavily populated locales (by Indians) in the country, had been semi-officially designated as prospective "National Sacrifice Areas" in the interests of projected U.S. energy development (Churchill, 1986:13). This, in turn, provoked Russell Means to observe that such a move would turn the Lakota, Navajo, Laguna and other Native nations into "national sacrifice peoples" (Means, 1983:25).

AMERICAN INDIAN RESPONSE

Of late, there have been encouraging signs that American Indians of many perspectives and political persuasions have begun to arrive at common conclusions regarding the use to which the federal government has been putting their identity, and the compelling need for Indians to finally reassert complete control over this vital aspect of their lives. For instance, Dr. Frank Ryan, a liberal and rather establishmentarian Indian who has served as the director of the federal Office of Indian Education, began, during the early 1980s, to reach some rather hard conclusions about the policies of his employers. Describing the federal blood quantum criteria for benefits eligibility in the educational arena as "a racist policy," Ryan went on to term it as nothing more than "a shorthand method for denying Indian children admission to federal schools [and other programs]" (Ryan, 1979:3). He went on to conclude that, "The power to determine tribal membership has always been an essential attribute of inherent tribal sovereignty," and called for abolition of federal guidelines on the question of Indian identity without *any* lessening of federal obligations to the individuals and group affected (Ryan, 1979:41-44). The question of the [re]adoption of blood quantum standards by the Indian Health Service, proposed during the '80s by the Reagan administration, has served as even more of a catalyst. The National Congress of American Indians, never a bastion of radicalism, took up the issue at its 43rd Annual Convention, in October of 1986.

The NCAI produced a sharply worded statement rejecting federal identification policy:

> [T]he federal government, in an effort to erode tribal sovereignty and reduce the number of Indians to the point where they are politically, economically and culturally insignificant, [is being censured by] many of the more than 500 Indian leaders [attending the convention] (Martz, 1986b).

The statement went on to condemn:

> ...a proposal by the Indian Health Service to establish blood quotas for Indians, thus allowing the federal government to determine who is Indian and who is not, for the purpose of health care. Tribal leaders argue that *only* the individual tribes, *not* the federal government, should have this right, and many are concerned that this debate will overlap [as it has, long since] into Indian education and its regulation as well [emphasis added] (Martz, 1986a).

Charles E. Dawes, Second Chief of the Ottawa Indian Tribe of Oklahoma, took the convention position much further at about the same time:

> What could not be completed over a three hundred year span [by force of arms] may now be completed in our life-span by administrative law...What I am referring to is the continued and expanded use of blood quantum to determine eligibility of Indian people for government entitlement programs...[in] such areas as education, health care, management and economic assistance...[obligations] that the United States government imposed upon itself in treaties with sovereign Indian nations...We as tribal leaders made a serious mistake in accept-

ing [genetic] limits in educational programs, and we must not make the same mistake again in health programs. On the contrary, we must fight any attempt to limit any program by blood quantum every time there is a mention of such a possibility...we simply cannot give up on this issue—ever...Our commitment as tribal leaders must be to eliminate any possibility of *genocide* for our people by administrative law. We must dedicate our efforts to insuring that our Native American people[s] will be clearly identified without reference to blood quantum...and that our sovereign Indian Nations will be recognized as promised [emphasis added] (Dawes, 1986:7-8).

On the Pine Ridge Reservation in South Dakota, the Oglala Lakota have become leaders in totally abandoning blood quantum as a criterion for tribal enrollment, opting instead to consider factors such as residency on the reservation, affinity to and knowledge of, as well as service to the Oglala people (Martz, 1986a). This follows the development of a recent "tradition" of Oglala militancy in which tribal members played a leading role in challenging federal conceptions of Indian identity during the 1972 Trail of Broken Treaties takeover of BIA headquarters in Washington, and seven non-Indian members of the Vietnam Veterans Against the War were naturalized as citizens of the "Independent Oglala Nation" during the 1973 siege of Wounded Knee.[6] In 1986, at a meeting of the United Sioux Tribes in Pierre, South Dakota, Oglala representatives lobbied the leaders of other Lakota reservations to broaden their own enrollment criteria beyond federal norms. This is so, despite recognition that, "in the past fifty years, since the Indian Reorganization Act of 1934, tribal leaders have been reluctant to recognize blood from individuals from other tribes [or any one else] (Martz, 1986b).

In Alaska, the Haida have produced a new draft constitution which offers a full expression of indigenous sovereignty, at least insofar as the identity of sovereignty and citizenry is concerned. The Haida draft begins with those who are not acknowledged as members of the Haida nation and posits that all those who marry Haidas will also be considered eligible for naturalized citizenship (just like in any other nation). The children of such unions would also be Haida citizens from birth, regardless of their degree of Indian blood, and children adopted by Haidas would also be considered citizens (*Haida Constitution*, 1982). On Pine Ridge, a similar "naturalization" plank had surfaced in the 1982 TREATY platform upon which Russell Means attempted to run for the Oglala Lakota tribal presidency before being disqualified at the insistence of the BIA (TREATY, 1982:3). An obvious problem which might be associated with this trend is that even though Indian nations begin to recognize their citizens by their own standards rather than those of the federal government, the government may well refuse to recognize the entitlement of unblooded tribal members to the same services and benefits as any other. In fact, there is every indication that this is the federal intent, and such a disparity of "status" stands to heighten tensions among Indians, destroying their fragile rebirth of unity and solidarity before it gets off the ground. Federal policy in this regard is, however, also being challenged.

Most immediately, this concerns the case of Dianne Zarr, an enrolled member of the Sherwood Valley Pomo Band of Indians, who is of less than one-quarter degree of Indian blood. On September 11, 1980, Ms. Zarr filed an application for higher educational grant benefits, and was shortly rejected as not meeting quantum requirements. Zarr went through all appropriate appeal procedures before filing, on July 15, 1983, a suit in federal court, seeking to compel award of her benefits. This was denied by the district court on April 2, 1985. Zarr appealed and, on September 26, 1985, the lower court was reversed on the basis of the "Snyder Act" (25 U.S.C. S297), which precludes discrimination based solely on racial criteria.[7] Zarr received her grant, setting a very useful precedent for the future.

Still, realizing that the utility offered by U.S. courts will necessarily be limited, a number of Indian organizations have recently begun to seek to bring international pressure to bear on the federal government. The Indian Law Resource Center, National Indian Youth Council and, for a time, the International Indian Treaty Council and World Council of Indigenous peoples have repeatedly taken Native American issues before the United Nations Working Group on Indigenous Populations (a component of the U.N. Commission on Human Rights) in Geneva, Switzerland, since 1977. Another forum which has been utilized for this purpose has been the Fourth Russell International Tribunal on the Rights of the Indians of the Americas, held in Rotterdam, Netherlands, in 1980. Additionally, delegations from various Indian nations and organizations have visited, often under auspices of the host governments, in more than 30 countries during the past decade.[8]

CONCLUSION

The history of the U.S. imposition of its standards of identification upon American Indians is particularly ugly. Its cost to Indians has involved millions of acres of land, the water by which to make much of this land agriculturally useful, control over vast mineral resources which might have afforded them a comfortable standard of living, and the ability to form themselves into viable and meaningful political blocks at any level. Worse, it has played a prominent role in bringing about their generalized psychic disempowerment; if one is not allowed even to determine for one's self, or within one's peer group, the answer to the all-important question "who am I?," what possible personal power can one feel he/she possesses? The negative impacts, both physically and psychologically, of this process upon succeeding generations of Native Americans in the U.S. are simply incalculable.

The blood quantum mechanism most typically used by the federal government to assign identification to individuals over the years is as racist in its form as any conceivable policy. It has brought about the systematic marginalization and eventual exclusion of many more Indians from their own cultural-national designation than it has retained. This is all the more apparent when one considers that, while one-quarter degree of blood has been the norm used in defining Indian-ness, the quantum has varied from time-to-time and place-to-place; one-half blood was the standard utilized in the case of the Mississippi Choctaws and adopted in the Wheeler-Howard Act, one-sixty-fourth was utilized in establishing the Santee rolls in Nebraska. It is hardly unnatural, under the circumstances, that federal policy has set off a ridiculous game of one-upsmanship in Indian Country: "I'm more Indian than you" and "You aren't Indian enough to say (or do, or think) that" have become common assertions during the second half of the 20th century.

The restriction of federal entitlement funds to cover only the relatively few Indians who meet quantum requirements, essentially a cost-cutting policy at its inception, has served to exacerbate tensions over the identity issue among Indians. It has established a scenario in which it has been perceived as profitable for one Indian to cancel the identity of his/her neighbor as a means of receiving his/her entitlement. Thus, a bitter divisiveness has been built into Indian communities and national policies, sufficient to preclude their achieving the internal unity necessary to offer any serious challenge to the status quo. At every turn, U.S. practice *vis-à-vis* American Indians is indicative of an advanced and extremely successful system of colonialism.

The outcome of the particular process examined in this paper can only be that Indians, both as peoples and as individuals, will eventually be defined out of existence. Arithmetically, it is calculable that by some point in the next century, the simple act of suddenly enforcing the quarter-blood standards across the board would result in the aggregate Indian population *appearing* to be near zero. This, in turn, would allow the federal government to "justifiably" close the books on Indians, write off all remaining obligations to such people, and declare them extinct (as has already been done with the Juaneño and other groups). In this sense, federal control and manipulation of the criteria of Indian identity carries obvious implications, not only of colonialism, but of genocide.

Fortunately, increasing numbers of Indians are waking up to the fact that this is the case. The recent analysis and positions assumed by such politically diverse Indian nations, organizations and individuals as Frank Ryan and Russell Means, the National Congress of American Indians and the Indian Law Resource Center, the Haida and the Oglala, are a very favourable sign. The willingness of the latter two nations to simply defy federal standards and adopt identification and enrollment policies in line with their own interests and traditions is particularly important. Recent U.S. court decisions, such as that in the Zarr case, and growing international attention and concern over the circumstances of Native Americans are also hopeful indicators that things may be at long last changing for the better.

We are currently at something of a crossroads. If American Indians are able to continue the positive trend in which they reassert their sovereign prerogative to control the criteria of their own membership, we may reasonably assume that they will be able to move onward, into a true process of decolonization and reestablishment of themselves as functioning national entities. The alternative, of course, is that they will fail, continue to be duped into bickering over the question of "who's Indian" in light of federal guidelines, and thus facilitate not only their own continued subordination, expropriation and colonization, but ultimately their own statistical extermination.

NOTES

1. Calhoun is quoted in *American State Papers: Indian Affairs* (Volume II), Wilmington, Delaware, 1972:183-184.

2. The bulk of the obligations in question were established prior to Congress' 1871 suspension of treaty-making with "the tribes" (Title 25, Section 71, U.S. Code). Additional obligations were undertaken by the federal government thereafter by "agreement," and as part of its ongoing agenda of completing the socio-political subordination of Indians, with an eye toward their eventual "assimilation" into the dominant culture and polity.

3. This stategy was actually tried in the wake of the passage of House Concurrent Resolution 108 (67 Stat. B132, otherwise referred to as the "Termination Act") in June of 1953. Predictably, the federal dissolution of American Indian nations such as the Klamath and Menominee so tarnished the U.S. image that implementation of the policy was shortly suspended (albeit the law remains on the books).

4. The best overview of the IRA process may be found in Deloria and Lytle, 1984; on referenda fraud, see Chapter 11.

5. The author is an enrolled Juaneño, as is her eldest son. Her younger son, born after the closing of the Juaneño rolls, is not federally recognized as an Indian, depsite the fact that his genealogy, cultural background, etc., is identical to that of his brother. The "suggestions" mentioned in the text were made to the author by a federal employee in 1979. It is estimated that, by the middle of the coming century, no one recognized as being a Juaneño will still be living.

6. On the Trail of Broken Treaties challenge, see Akwesasne Notes, 1973:78. On VVAW naturalization, see Burnette and Koster, 1974:238.

7. *Zarr v. Barlow, et al.*, No. 85-2170, U.S. Ninth Circuit Court of Appeals, District Court for the Northern District of California, Judge John P. Vukasin presiding.

8. These have included Austria, Cuba, Nicaragua, Poland, East Germany, Hungary, Rumania, Switzerland, Algeria, Grenada, El Salvador, Columbia, Tunisia, Libya, Syria, Jordan, Iran, the Maori of New Zealand, New Aotara (Australia), Belize, Mexico, Costa Rica, Guinea, Kenya, Micronesia, the U.S.S.R., Finland, Norway, Sweden, Canada, Great Britain, Netherlands, France, Belgium, Japan, West Germany, Bulgaria, Yugoslavia, and Papua (New Guinea). The list here is undoubtedly incomplete.

PART VII ———————————

Some Comparisons: The Fourth World

INTRODUCTION

The "fourth world" is a term generally used to describe the situation of minority Indigenous peoples living within contemporary nation states. Although they may be the original inhabitants of the territories in which they live, Aboriginal people in many countries throughout the world now find themselves engaged in a struggle to retain their traditional lands, or to retain an ethnic and political independence in the face of increasing governmental administration and intervention in their affairs. Unlike many third world populations, the people of the fourth world make up *minority* populations or territories within the nation states that have usurped their lands, and face special problems and a different, sometimes difficult future because of this. Like their counterparts in North America, Aboriginal peoples in the rest of the world have had the indignity of inappropriate and outside conceptions of identity forced upon them. We close this volume with two examples, one from Australia and one from Norway.

In many ways, the Australian Aborigines offer a striking parallel to Canada. For years they were defined either in government or White terms, and only now are attempting to construct their own definition of Aboriginal. Like Canadian Native peoples, they are struggling between an identity as a collective ("Aboriginal") versus their separate ethnicities (nations or "tribes"). As in Canada, there are two levels of government for them to deal with — state (provincial) and federal.

Jordan portrays the "symbolic universe" within which Aboriginal people were located by mainstream society through legislation and policies in Australia. As in other parts of the world, the Aboriginal peoples were conceived of as inferior, and they were segregated from the rest of society through reserves. By the 1950s the official government policy was that of assimilation, similar to policies found in the U.S.A and Canada. Like Canada, Australia pursued an official policy of multiculturalism in the 1970s and 1980s; the catch words being "integration, not assimilation." But for the most part, Aborigines were excluded from the newly emerging multi-cultural identity. By contrast, Canadian Native peoples were able to use many of the multiculturalism programmes of the Canadian federal government to their advantage; for example, the Secretary of State funded Native political organizations for years, which played an important part in forging political and national identities. However, in Australia, Jordan feels that Aborigines were actually helped in the construction of an Aboriginal identity of their own by their *exclusion* from the multicultural programmes. Being the original Australians, they were different from all immigrants, and saw themselves as such. This separation helped disparate groups of Aboriginal people became more cohesive, and they began constructing a framework for building a positive and national identity.

In the final paper, Steinlien, himself a Sami, gives us a review of the major trends in Sami law in Norway from 1850 to the present. Like similar laws in Canada, the United States and Australia, Sami law has gone through several stages, affected both by international trends and national interests. The first stage, "Norwegianization" (1850-1959) is clearly related to the assimilationist practices found in both Canada and the U.S.A in the same time period. At this time, there were restrictions placed on the use of the Sami language, and efforts made to encourage the Sami to abandon all aspects of their culture in favour of that of the nation state. For example, an act of Parliament in 1902 made it illegal for an individual to buy land unless he/she could read and write Norwegian. Later there were other trends, such as economic integration, but the government continually determined the parameters of the Sami; for example by restricting certain regulations and trade concessions to "Sami-speaking persons" rather than to Sami people. This allowed the Norwegian government to avoid recognizing those people who identified themselves as Sami, but were no longer able to speak the language. But the *government itself* was responsible for Sami being unable to speak their language, having actively discouraged the use of Sami for years. Thus, the Norwegian government, after having almost eradicated the language, then used the ability to speak that language as an identifying feature of the people in question! In effect, it legislated the people out of existence — or at least a goodly portion of them.

Steinlien shows that things may have improved somewhat; a "Sami Act" was passed in 1987, which among other things, recommended a separate Sami Parliament with advisory powers, and protection of the Sami language. But again, the criteria of who, when and what constitutes the Sami people is determined by the state. Thus the Sami must still submit to premises held by another people — non-Sami Norwegians — in order to secure legal protection, and any Sami sovereignty they may negotiate only comes about through the sufferance of the dominant majority.

ABORIGINAL IDENTITY: THE MANAGEMENT OF A MINORITY GROUP BY THE MAINSTREAM SOCIETY

Deirdre F. Jordan

The thing at issue is the ruin of a frame of reference, a culture, and the consequent devaluation of individuals. Yet we can see the start of some slight search for 'Aboriginality'. But what is Aboriginality? Is it being tribal? Who is an Aboriginal? Is he or she someone who feels that other Aboriginals are somehow dirty, lazy, drunken, bludging? Is an Aboriginal anyone who has some degree of Aboriginal blood in his or her veins and who has been demonstrably disadvantaged by that? Or is an Aboriginal someone who has had the reserve experience? Is Aboriginality institutionalized gutlessness, an acceptance of the label 'the most powerless people on earth'? Or is Aboriginality when all the definitions have been exhausted a yearning for a different way of being, a wholeness that was presumed to have existed before 1776? (Watson, 1977:184).

The Aboriginal search for identity grows out of confusion and a need to come to grips not merely with the question of "identifying" as an Aboriginal person, but seeking to know, to understand, what can be the components of an Aboriginal identity, credible to individuals, which they can select out of the many Aboriginal identities offered them, and which they can build upon in order to attain a personal identity.

It is a problem which has not been addressed to any great extent in Australia by researchers from the White world. Current research literature in anthropology, if it touches at all on identity, is centred on changes taking place in the structures of tradition-oriented people (Elkin, 1932a; 1932b; 1953; 1959a; 1959b; 1960; C.H. Berndt, 1961; R.M. Berndt, 1959; 1961; 1972; 1981; Chase, 1980; Fink, 1955; Tonkinson, 1974; Berndt and Phillips, 1973). Research literature in psychology, until very recently, sought either to provide data on concepts which parallel those of studies of mainstream society, or had a "mental health" approach to the problems of assimilation, examining "problems" of adjustment to White society (Dawson, 1969; de Lacey, 1971; de Lemos, 1969; Douglas, 1968; Duncan, 1969; Gault, 1969; Kearney, 1966; McElwain, 1969; Milliken, 1969; Nurcombe and Moffitt, 1970; Seagrim, 1971; Teasdale and Katz, 1968). Research literature, still the work of the White world, by its very nature is generated by and defined within a White framework of thought. It has focussed, by and large, on the assimilation of Aboriginal people into a White world of culture, of motivation, of learning, a world where Aboriginal identity is absorbed (Berry, 1970; Cawte, Bianchi and Kiloh, 1968; Nurcombe and Cawte, 1967).

The analysis by Aboriginal people themselves of the problem of *loss of identity and anomie* is taking a different point of departure; it is focussing on*identity construction*. Stewart (1976:26), for example, spoke of "embarking upon a long, difficult and in some cases a traumatic journey to establish our identities". Anderson (1975:19) projected a time when "Aboriginal people and Aboriginal teenagers would start grabbing hold of their identity themselves" (see for example, Elphick, 1977; Gilbert, 1973; 1977; Perkins, 1975; personal communication during field work, 1980/81).

THE THEORY

The Aboriginal people, in voicing the need to "grab" or "build" their identity, place themselves unconsciously within the theoretical framework provided by the sociology of knowledge. Within this framework, the society into which one is born is conceptualized as a social construct, and identity is the result of social processes within that construct. The Australian Government's "working definition" of aboriginal identity may also be located within this context.

> An Aboriginal or Torres Strait Islander is a person of Aboriginal or Torres Strait Islander descent who identifies as an Aboriginal or Torres Strait Islander and is accepted as such by the community in which he lives (Australian Department of Aboriginal Affairs, 1981).[1]

This basis for identification reflects the sociological dimension of the following definition of identity developed as part of a larger study on

Aboriginal identity (Jordan, 1983), and proposed as a reference point for the rest of this article.

> Identity is defined as location of the self in a particular world of meaning both by the self and others. It is a product of interactions between individuals and social structures, and individuals and others. Through this location of the self, individuals recognize their self-sameness and continuity in time and perceive that others recognize their self-sameness and continuity.

The problems associated with assimilation grew out of a lack of success on the part of the White world in locating Aboriginal people in that world. White people "theorized" about assimilation, but they also predicted that Aboriginal people would always be resistant to civilizing influences: "it was not so much a matter of the colour of the skin as the colour of the mind" (Bleakley, 1961:314). Aboriginal people who tried to locate themselves in the White world met with hostility and rejection:

> On the street there are the eyes, staring at black skin (Gilbert, 1973:41).

> I'd walk into a town. You walk down the street and you're black and the white man doesn't have to say a word to you. He steps around you, you're shit, you're nothing. And they cut you down with this sort of concept and you get that way, you feel it, you feel inferior (Dixon, 1975:49).

Aboriginal people in the past have been thwarted and frustrated in their efforts to respond to the (White) policy of assimilation. If they now wish to follow a different path and locate themselves in an *Aboriginal* world, then, in terms of the definition proposed above, they must locate themselves in a world of meaning that has characteristics that are specifically Aboriginal, a world which is legitimated, made credible to the self, at all levels of "theorizing".[2] It is not enough, for the construction of identity, for individuals to locate themselves unilaterally within a particular "world". Identity is a social construct; its maintenance depends not only upon the individual, but upon the readiness of others to confirm the chosen identity of the individual.

The construction of an Aboriginal identity may lead to a conflict situation as the theorizing of Aboriginal people about an "Aboriginal" world of meaning within which an Aboriginal identity may be found may well be at variance with that of mainstream theorizing. The maintenance of the "world" of meaning of the mainstream group may then be threatened by a version of a deviant world, held by a visible group that is not assimilated into the mainstream. The Aboriginal "world", as a site for the location of identity, must therefore be studied not in isolation, but in relation to mainstream Australian society.

An understanding of this "objective reality" for Aboriginal people, that is, knowledge about an Aboriginal world which is objectivated and taken for granted, demands an understanding, therefore, at the conceptual level, of the machinery by which the world of Aboriginal society has been managed in the past, and is being managed in contemporary society by the dominant group. A discussion of various forms of conceptual machinery used to exercise control over a minority group by a dominant group may be found in Berger and Luckmann (1966:122-134). Two relevant forms of such "machinery" are those of therapy and nihilation. *Therapy* entails processes directed towards keeping deviants within the universe of meaning of the dominant group. Examples are available from those schools of psychiatric treatment and of classroom practice which are aimed at "adjusting" the individual to society. Therapy is employed to return the deviant individual to the norms of the mainstream group. *Nihilation* acts in the opposite way and is brought into play to protect a universe of meaning by liquidating conceptually all alternative systematizations of meaning. For example, the right-wing governments of South America set out, in the sixties and seventies, to silence the ideological stirrings of the oppressed groups in their countries. To attain this end, the world of meaning of the poor (who might seek justice) and of those religious who cast their lot with the poor, was nihilated by the dominant group by being categorized as "communist".[3] As the power base of the military governments was secure, the conceptual nihilation of the "world" of those critical of the government could be consummated in physical nihilation; the facts of the "dirty wars" of the sixties and seventies in Argentina, for example, are now widely known; the same processes continue still in Chile.

The situation in South America represents an extreme contemporary example of the way in which a dominant group has acted to control a minority group. I intend to argue a somewhat less extreme case, namely that the history of the Aboriginal people in Australia also shows evidence of the nihilation of the Aboriginal world (and therefore of Aboriginal identity) by mainstream society, a nihilation which tolerated – until the turn of the century the physical nihilation of the people.

The following propositions will be examined:

that the "world" of Aborigines was controlled by means of legislation and policy which employed nihilation as the conceptual machinery to protect and maintain the "world" of the dominant group;

that such nihilation was supported by appropriate forms of legitimation;

that legislation and policy promoted negative typifications;

that the boundary constructed for Aboriginal society, within which Aboriginal people found identity, was a boundary from without, imposed not by Aborigines themselves, but by the dominant society.

LEGISLATION AND NIHILATION - AN HISTORICAL REVIEW FROM A SOCIOLOGICAL PERSPECTIVE

One of the most important sources of mainstream theorizing with relation to the world of Aborigines is that found in legislation. A watershed in this "theorizing" is marked by a referendum held throughout the commonwealth of Australia in 1967. As a result of the referendum, the Commonwealth Government was given power, formerly held by the states, to legislate for the welfare of Aboriginal people.

I propose to examine the symbolic universe within which Aboriginal people were located by mainstream society as it can be found in Government legislation, policy and practice in two areas: in one particular state, South Australia, held to be one of the more enlightened states in its treatment of the Aboriginal people (Gale, 1972:42; Rowley, 1971a:409), and at the Federal level, after the referendum, when the Commonwealth Government assumed responsibility for Aboriginal people.

In order to appreciate the context within which theorizing about Aborigines took place, a brief historical outline is required. South Australia was established as a colony in 1836; the first legislation relating to its foundation was the Foundation Act of 1834, enacted by the British Parliament. This Act categorized all land in the colony as public land, a decision legitimated by the fact that, in the preamble to the Act, the area to be settled was declared waste and unoccupied (Jenkin, 1979:25).

Jenkin (1979:34ff) points out that in 1835, Lord Glenelg, the British Secretary of State for the Colonies, prevailed upon the founders of South Australia before they left England to insert a clause in the Letters Patent intended to protect the land rights of the indigenous people of Australia. The proviso, however, was worthless, as, *vis-à-vis* the 1834 Act of Parliament, it had no legal status. Glenelg's representations were heeded by only one colonist, a Quaker, who insisted on paying the Aborigines the interest on the amount of money used in purchasing his land from the government.[4]

Despite action taken by Gawler to protect some land for the use of Aborigines, Jenkin concludes that the 1842 Waste Lands Act,

...by mentioning the two things that *could* be done for them [setting aside money for Aboriginal welfare, recovering land for the use of Aboriginal inhabitants of the country] without accepting that they had any *rights* at all to land or finance, effectively ossified the position of Aborigines as a mendicant, pauper class, completely at the mercy of a foreign authoritarian government which might or might not be benevolent in ensuing years.

Gale (1972:52) points out a further effect of the 1842 legislation. While the Act gave the *possibility* of land being put aside for the Aboriginal people, at the same time all land not already surveyed was declared waste and unoccupied. The Aborigines were thus, officially and legally, dispossessed of their land. In those cases where land was put aside for the use of Aborigines, the area was too small to be of any use for the production of food.

Apart from the injustices perpetrated by the Acts, they resulted in two outcomes leading to the destruction of the Aboriginal world. Being deprived of their land, the people were also deprived of the means of gaining food. The result was that they were made dependent in that regard on White society. More especially, through dispossession of their traditional lands to which their "Dreaming", their source of spiritual life is inextricably bound, they were prevented from maintaining a world of meaning encompassed by their Law which touched on every aspect of their life and provided a framework for their cultural identity.

What were the processes at work which permitted this situation to be legitimated?

In order to make the oppression of a minority group seem to be natural and justified, and in order to protect its own universe of meaning, a dominant group must build up a coherent body of theorizing which nihilates the world of the "deviant group" while supporting the actions of mainstream society. In Nazi Germany, for example, the conceptual nihilation of the "world" of Jewish people was based on a body of "theorizing" about the purity of race. In the case of the indigenous inhabitants of Australia, there were several strands of theorizing based upon a White world of meaning which countenanced the nihilation of the Aboriginal world, and indeed permitted the physical nihilation of Aborigines. The initial denial of existence of the people, found in the Land Acts, was legitimated in a different form at the turn of the century by a theorizing that claimed that Aborigines were not fully human.

Archbishop Polding, appearing in 1845 before a Parliamentary Committee on the *Condition of Aborigines,* gave, as his opinion concerning the reasons for the great decrease in the numbers of the Native people, "the aggressive manner of taking possession of their country."

> I myself have heard a man, educated and a large proprietor of sheep and cattle maintain that there was no more harm in shooting a native than in shooting a wild dog. I have heard it maintained by others that it was in the course of Providence that the blacks should disappear before the white, and the sooner the process was carried out the better for all parties. I fear such opinions prevail to great extent. Very recently, in the presence of two clergy-men, a man of education narrated as a good thing that he had been one of a party who had pursued the blacks in consequence of the cattle having been rushed by them and that he was sure they had shot upward of a hundred. When expostulated with he maintained there was nothing wrong with it, that it was preposterous to suppose that they had souls (Thorpe, 1950:262).

"Theorizing" by the general populace that Aborigines had no souls and were therefore less than human provided a pseudo-theological view which meshed well with widespread beliefs that primitive peoples in general were sub-human. These beliefs were transferred to Australian Aborigines and strengthened at the turn of the century, even in the face of contrary evidence, by a pseudo-scientific version of Darwin's theories which allowed the nihilation of the Aboriginal world at the cognitive level. Evolutionists conveniently found in Aborigines the missing link between apes and men.

Popular theorizing that Aborigines were less than human, that they had no "souls", permitted the massacre of Aboriginal people on a scale wide enough to see their extermination as being, at the very least, countenanced on the part of the policy makers, who remained passive in the face of wide-scale killings. The earlier conceptual nihilation of the existence of Aborigines was thus carried to an ultimate conclusion in their physical nihilation. This was brought about by such measures as giving people damper poisoned with corrosion sublimate, driving them from waterholes (Report of the Commissioner of Police, 5 June 1885 quoted in Jenkin, 1979:63), and murder by the police themselves (Horner, 1972:211-227).

The "scientific" view that Aborigines were less than human was rejected by South Australia in an Adelaide newspaper through the publication of "scientific" findings which came to the conclusion that the Aboriginal people were human after all!

The Register of 17th June, 1914, made the following startling announcement:

The native tribes of Australia are generally considered to be at the bottom of the scale of humanity...and probably to be inferior in mental development to many of the stone-age inhabitants of Europe in prehistoric ages. Yet they have every right to be considered man.

HUMAN AFTER ALL

Though infantile in intellectual development, the Australian natives are thoroughly human, as can readily be seen by the cubic measurement of their brains, 99.35 inches compared with that of a gorilla 30.51 inches (quoted in Jenkin, 1979:248).

The statement itself is absurd. Even more absurd is the arrogance of the dominant group recognizing as "human after all", or "thoroughly human", the Aboriginal people of South Australia, people such as those from Port McLeay who, in 1914, were well educated in comparison with White people of those times.[5] They read the newspaper (Jenkin, 1979:240; photographs, South Australian Archives), and would have been well aware of the "scientific" decisions being made about them; indeed, well aware that though now considered "human", they were still held to be at the "bottom of the scale of humanity".

Once the accepted knowledge of the time declared that Aborigines were human, one would have thought that it was no longer possible to legitimate their physical nihilation on the grounds of their supposed affinity with the animal world. Nevertheless, knowledge about the inherent inferiority of the Aboriginal people became accepted as "sedimented knowledge"[6] of mainstream society – that is as everyday knowledge, what everyone knows without having to examine it. This sedimented knowledge was a form of theorizing which legitimated the widespread incidents of extermination which continued well into this century.[7] Ted Docker documents the attitudes of the White population to Aborigines in connection with murders by police in what was at that time a territory administered, for certain purposes, by South Australia:

> In 1928 a trooper of the Northern Territory Mounted Police cold-bloodedly shot down more than seventeen natives (his own admission) in what was supposed to be a round up of witnesses for criminal investigation. He was compared in an Adelaide newspaper to the Canadian mountie: "always rides alone, always gets his man" (Docker, 1964:9-10).

Sedimented "knowledge" about the inferiority of the Aboriginal world also permitted social legislation which, in its turn, was instrumental in destroying the social structures of the Aboriginal people and therefore the locus of identity. Such legislation was an unintended consequence of activities carried out by Church groups. These groups recognized that the Aboriginal people had "souls" to be saved. But they also believed that the Aboriginal people were infantile. The policies of missionaries, almost without exception, were of a paternalistic nature, denying the people autonomy. The symbolic world[8] which the churches had to protect differed from that of mainstream society. Nevertheless, the same conceptual mechanisms were used to nihilate the Aboriginal world of culture. The rites of initiation, the marriage customs, indeed, the total spiritual and social world of the Aborigines was categorized as pagan and hence eligible for nihilation.

While on the one hand the churches supported with all their power the "sanctity of the (White) family", at another level of theorizing they implemented practices designed to destroy the family and the authority structures of the Aboriginal people. For example, in many places, until a decade ago, the dormitory system for educating children continued, children were removed from parental control and traditional education, and the authority and autonomy of the people was over-ridden.

Structures set up by missions were progressively taken over by the government, and practices established by church groups, whereby all autonomy was removed from the people, were codified in law.[9] Under the South Australian Aborigines Act (1911), for example, Aborigines became minors, and their children could be taken from them. The Chief Protector appointed under the Act became the "Guardian of every Aboriginal and half-caste child", a not unexpected corollary of a situation where policy separated families.

On the reserves, in the personal sphere, codes of conduct were no longer subject to tribal authority. They were made the subject of White legislation which invented a deviancy and a delinquency for Aboriginal people. A "criminal class" was established by the definition of new "crimes" specific to Aboriginal people. The Protector was entitled to

> ...inflict summary punishment by ways of imprisonment not exceeding fourteen days, upon Aborigines and half-castes living upon a reserve or within the district under his charge, who, in the judgement of such protector are guilty of any crime, serious misconduct, neglect of duty, gross insubordination or wilful breach of any regulation (South Australia, Aborigines Act, 1911:Section 10).

Managers of reserves had immense power which could be used quite capriciously to categorize activities as criminal and to punish the offenders. Regulations under the Act, promulgated in 1917 and 1919, added further "crimes" specific to Aborigines. Under the regulations, Aborigines could be summarily fined for not closing a gate or for being untidily dressed: the time of rising in the morning was stipulated. For failing to obey an order an Aborigine could be fined ten pounds or gaoled, with or without hard labour, for two months. The Chief Protector could cause any Aboriginal to be moved to a reserve or Aboriginal institution (Sections 17-21) and he could assume control of the property of any Aboriginal (Sections 35). There were penalties to be imposed upon people who unlawfully entered a reserve (Sections 20) or who caused an Aboriginal to leave one (Sections 21).[10] Section 34a made it an offence for a male, not of Aboriginal descent, to associate with a female who had any aboriginal ancestry. Successive Aborigines Acts gave power to segregate the "deviant" Aboriginal population from mainstream society.

SEGREGATION

The power to segregate Aborigines in South Australia was contained in the 1842 Act, the 1911 Act, and the 1933 Aborigines Act which remained in force until the more enlightened legislation of the 1962 Aborigines Act. Segregation, involving the removal of those deviating from mainstream norms from the sight of the dominant group, was a form of denial and nihilation. It may be seen as a form of physical nihilation which was less extreme than that of extermination.[11]

Under the 1911 Act, Aborigines could be subject to curfews and to restriction of movement in towns. These restrictions were confirmed in the 1939 Act, in South Australia, which

> ...gave the Board power to remove Aborigines to reserves and keep them there, prevented entry by unauthorized persons and made it an offence to assist or entice them to escape. It enabled the Board to remove camps from the vicinity of towns and to remove individuals for 'loitering' or being improperly clothed. *Towns could be proclaimed prohibited areas* (emphasis added).

Certainly, for later generations in South Australia the Aboriginal people were allowed to impinge very little on White society (Rowley, 1971a:passim; 1971b:22). In South Australia before the 1950s and even into the 1960s, many, if not most urban people had never seen an Aboriginal person. They, like the Government officials, were, stoutly and with clear conscience, able to deny racism in Australia.

Perkins relates his own experience in Alice Springs:

> We had to stay there. We were not allowed in Alice Springs after dark, only for the pictures on Saturday night. That rule has relaxed a little over the years...But before the idea was simple:

'Keep the street clean of Aborigines.' That was the way we had to live as scum, the unwanted (Perkins, 1975:17).

Aborigines were separated spatially by the location of their housing: they were separated socially from those with whom they worked or played sport.

Perkins relates:

> I would go into a pub with the cricket team and the barman would say, "Listen darkie, you know you don't belong in here. If you don't get out, I'll get the copper on to you" (Perkins, 1975:55-56).

The construction by mainstream society of a criminal identity creating "crimes specific to Aborigines" is clear. Behaviour typified as "normal" for White citizens — being within town precincts, drinking in a pub — was typified as criminal for black people (Jenkin, 1979:246).

Through policies of segregation, Aboriginal people were not only excluded from White society; they were located in a negative world by mainstream society. Hasluck (1970:160-161) commented that the system confined "the native within a legal status that has more in common with that of a born idiot than of any other class of British citizen." The Aborigine was stereotyped as "idiot", of low intelligence, as a child who must be protected, his movements restricted, his liberty curtailed, a person socially unacceptable. Jenkin (1979:246) notes that the only other people who could be treated in this way were lunatics or criminals (and even they had to be proven to have committed an offence). As Perkins (1975:188) put it poignantly, "It is a crime to be an Aborigine in Australia". Having black skin was sufficient to draw down punishment for anything "defined" as a crime, without any recourse to the courts.

The institutionalization of negative typifications for Aborigines is shown by the fact that one of the amendments to the 1939 Act in South Australia provided for exemption from the Act for some who could meet certain qualifications.

> In any case where the Board is of the opinion that any Aborigine by reason of his character and standard of intelligence and development should be exempted from the provisions of this Act, the Board may, by notice in writing, declare that the Aborigine may cease to be an Aborigine for the purpose of this act (South Australia, Aborigines Act, 1934 and 1939:Section IIA).

Therefore, there was no possibility of a positive identity for Aboriginal people, as those who, in White terms, successfully appropriated an identity offered by White society, were no longer Aborigines. They were exempted from the penalties attached to Aboriginal identity. Clearly, legislation for Aborigines in general was intended to be seen as articulated for people who did not fulfill the requirements for exemption, that is, people of bad or indifferent character, of low standard of intelligence and development. By derivation, all Aborigines had these characteristics, as those who were considered not to possess these negative traits could be declared exempt from being Aborigines. The legislation thus located Aboriginal identity within a negative world of meaning.

Those Aborigines who wished to be part of White society after the Act of 1939 were forced to carry a certificate of exemption. Perhaps the most destructive aspect of the legislation was the requirement that if, "in order to be treated like a human being" (the phrase recurs again and again in conversation with Aboriginal people, and is interchangeable with "being treated like a White"), individuals applied for and were granted an "exemption", they had to cut themselves off from their family, their kin, their place of birth, their culture, and indeed, their Aboriginal identity.

All of the forces discussed produced a new conceptualization of the "Aboriginal problem" in the 1940s. The assumptions underlying the Land Acts legislation (namely that Aborigines did not exist), the active extermination of Aborigines, their removal from sight by the enforcement of segregation, the high death rate due to disease and malnutrition, all this led with ease to a promotion of theorizing that Aborigines were a dying race. This theorizing, in turn, was used as a basis for different forms of segregation: policies of *isolation* and *dispersal* were advocated, the former legitimated by prospects of economic advantage to the dominant group.

ISOLATION

Tindale, summarizing his research (in part supported by the Government), talked of the full-blood Aborigines of South Australia as a dying remnant. He noted that

> The full bloods in the settled districts are a diminishing group and will soon be extinct. Isolation of the surviving desert tribes which have not yet completely lost their old ways of living would be an economic advantage to the State of South Australia. It *would enable the control of faunal pests and the effective occupation of a desert area which is a menace to the pastoral areas* (emphasis added) (Tindale, 1941:68).

Tindale would have thought of himself as humanitarian. Yet his proposal for the tribal people did little to differentiate them from trained dogs, or some native animal promoting a balance in the wild – much as, in game parks, a mingling of animals preserves a balance. His solution of isolation was based on a widely held assumption (or wish) that Aborigines were dying out. He unashamedly posited the economic advantage of White people as a basis for the banishment, or, in effect, the physical nihilation of Aboriginal people.

DISPERSAL

A different solution, that of dispersal, was proposed for "half-castes" Tindale made the following observation:

> The problem of how to deal [with the half-castes who replace tribal people] is a difficult but not insoluble one. They are faced with the same problems as we are in nurturing their families, securing education and finding a place in the community. They should not be treated as if they were a highly developed species of animal, to be viewed only as though they were inhabitants of a zoological garden. They should not be shut away in segregated (almost caged) communities (Tindale, 1941:67).

The last two sentences are most revealing of the perception and treatment of Aborigines in the early forties when Tindale was writing: categorization as animals, inhabitants of zoological gardens, echoes the stereotype of sub-human, a stereotype based on the "scientific" findings of the "followers" of Darwin, which had been sedimented into the thinking of a racist population.

Despite his desire to be humanitarian, Tindale was a man of his times in that he saw the "Aboriginal problem" not as one caused by White people, but one to be solved by White people, and solved by an act as inhuman as the treatment already accorded the Aboriginal people. He put forward a solution of dispersal:

> It would appear that the more ready means of bringing about a process of physical and social assimilation of the Australian mixed bloods into the community would be by the simple device of ensuring that a maximum dispersal or spread of the minority group will take place (Tindale, 1941:119).

Assimilation as a policy in this particular formulation (one of dispersal) was also a form of nihilation of the Aboriginal world of meaning: the Aboriginal people, as a group, were to disappear from sight. This would occur because Aborigines would either become extinct or completely absorbed into the population by compulsory, "maximum" dispersal. Such dispersal would lead to total assimilation.

ASSIMILATION

By the 1950's, assimilation had become official policy for all of Australia. For the first time, the states gathered to discuss the "Aboriginal problem". In 1951 Hasluck, then Minister for Territories, reported to Parliament that the Native Welfare Conference held in Canberra:

> ...agreed that assimilation is the objective of native welfare measures. Assimilation means, in practical terms, that, in the course of time, it is expected that all persons of Aboriginal blood or mixed blood in Australia will *live like White Australians do* (emphasis added) (Hasluck, 1953:13).

The policy of assimilation, spelled out by Hasluck in 1951, was confirmed in 1963 when a further conference of Commonwealth and State Ministers was held in Darwin and resulted in a more detailed statement on the meaning of the policy of assimilation

> The policy of assimilation means that all Aborigines and part Aborigines will attain the same manner of living as other Australians and live as members of a single Australian community enjoying the same rights and privileges, accepting the same responsibilities, observing the same customs and influenced by the same beliefs, hopes and loyalties as other Australians (Commonwealth of Australia Parliamentary Papers, 1963:651).

The statement went on to acknowledge the conflict between such a policy and the existing legislation referring to Aborigines. It adverted to the fact that there was specific (restrictive) legislation for Aborigines and noted the "rather loose use of the term 'citizenship'", as Aboriginal people in most states were not permitted to vote at that time. This anomaly, however, was easily dismissed with a meaningless phrase:

> ...such statutes can in no sense derogate from their citizenship in the sense of their status as Australian citizens.

Thus on the one hand, Aboriginal people in 1963, in most states, were not entitled to vote. On the other hand, this was not to be seen as derogating from their status as Australian citizens. Nevertheless, there was a difference in the status accorded Aboriginal people. As late as 1964, Beazley, the member for Fremantle, was pleading for all Commonwealth instrumentalities, including the armed services, to pay Aborigines employed by them a wage at least equivalent to the award rate as fixed by the Arbitration Commission for a worker similarly employed who was covered by awards, and for the need for the extension of the protection of Australian Commission awards to Aborigines employed privately in the Northern Territory (Commonwealth of Australia Parliamentary Debates, 1964:821-822). Differences and differential treatment did exist even at the official level.

Other White voices supported Beazley's pleas for the injustices suffered by Aboriginal people to be redressed; there was also a growing insistence on the part of the Aboriginal people to have their voice heard. Once policies of assimilation of Aborigines were projected, and their status as citizens having some rights and some status was acknowledged (if only at the level of rhetoric), a change had to be made in the conceptual machinery seen as appropriate for their control by the dominant group. Aboriginal people became eligible for a form of control different from that of nihilation. A new conceptualization of Aboriginal identity by the White world was to be articulated at the Federal level, requiring a new form of control. Therapy, that is "treatment", of a deviant group designed to integrate their world within that of mainstream society, became more appropriate.

The crucial issue in the politics of assimilation became that of the necessity of devising machinery to absorb the hitherto rejected minority group. It required the glossing over of differences and the elimination of the more vital elements of the culture of the minority group.

Parliamentary debate henceforth addressed this problem. Whereas, until the mid-1960s, governments had created differences between White society and Aborigines, erecting boundaries to exclude the latter, now differences could not be tolerated. Formerly, the total world of meaning of Aboriginal people was nihilated; in changed circumstances, operating under a policy of assimilation, Aboriginal people were to be recognized as citizens. If, however, they attempted to assert their rights as "human beings", such activity called into question the theory and practice, the world of meaning of the dominant group, and could not be tolerated. "Political" activity of Aboriginal people (that is, activity to bring about change in their circumstances) had to be nihilated, while at the same time, as individuals, Aboriginal people were to be assimilated.

Instances of this particular focus for nihilation may be found, for example, in speeches made in Parliament. In 1967, a referendum addressed to the people of Australia relating to the transfer of responsibility concerning Aboriginal Affairs from the states to the Federal sphere was supported. The year following the referendum, W.C. Wentworth, at that time Minister for Social Services and Aboriginal Affairs, was posed a question in Parliament relating to the activities of Aborigines seeking their rights;

these activities were categorized negatively as "black power". Wentworth repudiated the possibility of Aboriginal options different from those of White society:

> I am aware of the disruptive attempts of certain people to create differences of opinion and outlook between our Aboriginal people and the people of white descent. I deplore these efforts. I deplore entirely the efforts of certain people to create in Australia as they have succeeded in creating in the United States, differences that could lead to violence. I assure the Honourable Member and the House that the Government will do everything in its power to provide for the advancement of our Aboriginal people, and to ensure that they receive justice in every way and to prevent the emergence of conditions that could be used as an excuse for creating differences in the Australian community. The government regards the Aboriginals as Australians in the same sense as all other Australian citizens (Commonwealth of Australia Parliamentary Debates, 1968, 58:886).

The fact that Wentworth needed to make the statement – "The government regards the Aboriginals as Australians in the same sense as all other Australian citizens" – shows two things:

1. The Aborigines had previously **not** been regarded in this way.

2. The Aborigines were now **not** to be different. They were to be assimilated. But they were to be assimilated on White terms. (It is revealing that Wentworth twice used the possessive "our" when referring to Aborigines.)

From such an assimilationist perspective, it is not surprising that the assertion of Aboriginality, manifested in the setting up of a Black Embassy in Canberra in 1972, was seen as threatening the dominant group as it went counter to the mechanisms of therapy. The exercise of rights by the minority group had to be redefined in negative terms by the dominant group so that it could be rejected. This was achieved by categorizing the setting up of the Aboriginal embassy as evidence of black power, a concept which was raised as a spectre, and condemned; assimilation was proposed as an antidote. That is, Aboriginal stirrings would be contained within mainstream society. Those who continued to seek human rights would have their world of meaning nihilated, by being categorized negatively by the dominant group. Mackay, speaking on this issue in Parliament, made it clear that those Aborigines who demanded rights were no longer to be "Aborigines", but were given a new, negative redefinition. Their activity was deemed to originate from "apostles of class hatred" (i.e. communists).[12]

> ...at our very doors the apostles of class and race hatred have stirred up many good people to support a cause which is aimed at the creation of apartheid and race friction.
>
> The government is not prepared to see a separate race within a race developed in Australia with an embassy from the Aborigines to the Government of Australia as though this were a foreign power.
>
> Like all other groups within our widening society, we welcome their participation and their political aspirations as part of a family, not as aliens holding the nation to ransom (Commonwealth Hansard, 1972).

Assimilation now meant the assimilation of political, as well as cultural, activity. The Aboriginal people were to be "part of a family". Any activity which questioned the values of the dominant society was "alien". To accomplish the therapeutic intent of incorporation into the White family, political activity had to be nihilated. In the instance quoted, the credibility of the Aborigines' grievances was further destroyed by aligning them, not only with Communist-inspired apostles of class and race hatred, but with Labor party politicians. Mackay continued his speech.

> But once again Labour stands, in most of its expressions, with the apostles of radical and even violent action to divide and denigrate this nation in our own eyes and in the esteem of the world (Commonwealth Hansard, 1972).

In sum, the notion of the exercising of human rights by Aborigines as a group was nihilated. Therapy was proposed as the appropriate conceptual machinery to control Aborigines. The form of therapy was to assimilate the Aboriginal people "into the same customs, beliefs, hopes and loyalties" (Commonwealth of Australia Parliamentary Papers, 1963:25). The beneficiaries were to be the majority group who would thus be freed of the criticism of an outgroup. It can be argued that physical assimilation and political assimilation are aimed at achieving the same ends.

The seeking of rights was offensive in that it called into question the policies and practices of mainstream society. Nevertheless, the very seeking of rights had led to a transformation of policy. Aborigines were no longer to be segregated, but were to be contained by becoming "part of a family". However, as a family has rights by ascription, not by achievement, the seeking of rights by Aboriginal people in the political arena demonstrated clearly that, over a period of two hundred years, such rights had been denied by mainstream society. It was an affront to White society for Aboriginal people to demonstrate this openly by claiming such rights.

The incorporation of Aborigines into mainstream society was predicated upon the nihilation of the world of meaning of Aborigines. The same strategy may be observed in the assimilation of Aboriginal activists into Government positions where activism can be contained.[13] Rowley (1971a:35) gave it as his view that assimilation in practice was an "effort to train the Aboriginal to make him less offensive to whites". He could have added that it was a mechanism for absorbing any criticism or opposition which might call into question the world of the dominant society.

SOUTH AUSTRALIA

> South Australia is the best state in Australia. Don Dunstan's the one that helped us up the ladder, our Premier. He's put us on the map, mate. We's Kangaroos and emus, before that. We got counted since then. They counted every bullock and sheep in Australia but they never counted Aborigines. See? (Elphick, 1977:100).

The sixties began in South Australia with a reversion to earlier policies of segregation. New reserves were established (Amata in 1961: Davenport in 1963); missions were transferred to government control (Gerard in 1961; Koonibba in 1963). Gale (1972:48) asserted that this development mirrored the policies of segregation developed in the first years of settlement. It may also be argued that the focus on reserves, seen as a return to the former policies of "apartheid", constituted an alarmed response on the part of mainstream society to the discernment of an emerging consciousness of Aboriginal identity on the part of the Aboriginal people.

We have seen that, at the Federal level, when the consciousness of Aboriginal identity began to crystallize and form a basis for action, the policies and practices of two centuries were re-examined, and new policies of assimilation projected, together with legitimating theorizing. In this developing situation, the government of South Australia opted initially for a policy of retrogression. It did not seek to defend the world of mainstream society by embracing the machinery of therapy with its corollary of assimilation, and the consequent need to deemphasize differences. Instead, in order to protect the world of meaning of mainstream society, South Australia chose to establish further reserves and to continue the segregation of the Aboriginal people. This form of control was, however, to be abruptly terminated in the mid-1960s. A newly elected Labor Government set Aboriginal affairs on an entirely new path. Rowley (1971a:409) saw the policies of this government as the most daring and positive innovations of any Australian government.

Legislation in South Australia before the 1960s had, in general, codified and legitimated practice. In the mid-1960s legislation was introduced not to legitimate, but to change practice. Laws were passed regarding land rights for Aborigines (South Australia, Aboriginal Lands Trust Act, 1966b). Antidiscrimination laws were aimed at changing the practices, if not the attitudes, of the White population towards Aborigines (South Australia, Prohibition of Discrimination Act, 1966b). For the first time, there was a move away from policies aimed at the control and containment of the Aboriginal people towards policies requiring consultation and negotiation. Auntie Glad Elphick recounts how Don Dunstan, who later became Premier of the State, was instrumental in setting up a Legal Aid Service for the Aboriginal people. He was the first White person, in all her long life, who directed discussion about Aboriginal affairs by suggesting the need, and appropriateness, for consultation with Aboriginal people. "Why don't we ask the Aboriginal people themselves what they think?" At that time, to Aboriginal ears, this was the most incredible, extraordinary response (Elphick, personal communication). A new era had begun wherein Aboriginal people were seen as adults who had opinions worth consulting, who had a right to autonomy over their lives. For the first time, theorizing about a positive Aboriginal identity was offered by government.

By the seventies, a new policy towards Aborigines had been established. King, the South Australian Minister for Aboriginal Affairs in Dunstan's government, issued a statement in 1971 entitled *The Shaping of a New Aboriginal Policy in South Australia.* He repudiated the official policies of assimilation held by the previous Liberal governments and maintained that,

> The final wrong would be to attempt to destroy the Aborigine's racial and cultural identity and to turn him into a pseudo-white man. A most encouraging sign is the development among Aborigines of the desire to identify with their own people and to be proud of their race and its culture.

> This desire of educated Aborigines to be with their own people, rather than escape from their environment into the white community, is a most hopeful indication of the rapid recovery of self-respect of the Aboriginal people (King, 1971:756-759).

To make it possible for the Aborigines to "identify with their own people"[14], but yet remain within White society, King proposed a policy radically different from that operating at the Federal level. Assimilation was to give way to integration. He defined the policy of integration as

...the right of the Aboriginal people to live in our community on fully equal terms but retaining, if they so desire, a separate and identifiable[15] Aboriginal heritage and culture (King, 1971:756).

King's statement supported the politicization of Aborigines, a stance totally at variance with the policy of the Federal (Liberal) Government. He advocated that there should be active encouragement of a "sophisticated and articulate Aboriginal public opinion." He looked to the development of autonomous government on reserves, and to the participation of Aborigines in the political community.

The policy of integration put forward by King was a policy that, at the conceptual level, neither nihilated the Aboriginal world of meaning nor employed therapy to assimilate this world. Rather, such policy provided the possibility for the recognition of an alternative Aboriginal identity located within mainstream society.

The policy made a major impact on "official" theorizing about Aborigines; for the first time mainstream society projected a positive psychological world with which Aboriginal people could interact and which they could appropriate. They now had the possibility of locating themselves, and being located by the White world, within a positive Aboriginal identity.

INTO THE SEVENTIES – THE FEDERAL LEVEL

When the Labor Party came into power at the Federal level in 1973, policies which had been developed in South Australia concerning Aboriginal affairs became official party policy. The platform statement of the Federal Labor Party proposed legislation against all forms of discrimination and the promotion of the rights of Aborigines with regard to social services, land rights and health – all new policies:

> ...Aboriginal people were to receive the *standard rate of pay* for employment and the same industrial protection as other Australians, a dramatic departure from practice.

> ...*Educational opportunities* were to be provided that were in no way inferior to those of the general community. Pre-school and adult education were to be provided as broadly as possible.

> ...The philosophy underlying these programmes was that of *self-determination* for the Aboriginal people, and the exercise of a *greater autonomy* in all areas of their lives.

In one sense, such a policy was integrated into the overall thrust of Labor policy, which was one of providing equality of opportunity for all those in society who were disadvantaged in one form or another. However, the policy for Aborigines went beyond this. It recognized the need for positive discrimination. For example, special provision for employment was to be provided in regions where there was a concentration of Aboriginal people. Above all, the policy recognized in positive terms the right of Aboriginal people to find their identity within an Aboriginal world of meaning. Every Australian child was to be taught the history and culture of Aboriginal Australians, as an integral part of the history of Australia. The Labour Party, although in office only a short time, introduced massive legislation at the Commonwealth level. This legislation objectivated a world of meaning about Aboriginal identity, laying down guidelines which were inherited by the Liberal/National Country Party Coalition in 1975. The policy of self-determination initiated by the Labor Party was modified by the Liberal/National Country Party Coalition to one of self-management in its platform policy of 1975.[16] There was no emphasis in this policy, as there was in the South Australian policy, on the active encouragement of the politicization of Aboriginal groups. The possibility of structural differentiation was not entertained. Nevertheless there was a statement that recognized differences in the life-style of different groups of Aboriginal people.

The preamble noted that:

> ...the life styles of Aborigines will, of necessity, vary between those living a more tribalized state in or near their traditional lands and those living in or near towns or cities. Policies must therefore reflect this fact (Guidelines, Liberal/National Party Policy, 1975).

As in the case of the Labour Government, there was positive support for the retention of Aboriginal values and Aboriginal culture.

> Aboriginal values are an intrinsic part of Australia's culture and heritage. We are part of each other. Without mutual respect and support for each other's cultural integrity, we cannot secure our personal identities (Guidelines, Liberal/National Party Policy, 1975).

The theorizing was positive in its tone. The identity offered to Aboriginal people, within the limitations of the conceptualization of the policies, was not one of socialization into negative identity. There was recognition, as in the case of the Labor Party, that Aborigines are not a monolithic group; there was recognition of the need to leave options open so that the people might choose an identity. Thus, the policy statements of both political parties in the 1970s represented a new era for Aboriginal people insofar as government policy and legislation was concerned.

The question must be asked whether the statement in the Liberal Party Platform "we are part of each other" was merely a sentiment, or whether it is possible to establish that it is integrated into overall theorizing. In particular, is the notion of differentiation of Aborigines into worlds where they "retain their racial identity and traditional life-style, or where desired adopt partially or wholly a European life-style" supported by other theorizing?

The possibility of testing whether such a policy may be seen as rhetoric rather than reality may be found in examining whether or not the assumptions made, and the policies projected, can be meshed into overall policy without losing credibility. The application of such a test is provided for by the fact that at the same time as positive "theorizing" was incorporated into party policies, a new emphasis was being projected relating to the conceptualization of Australian society; Australia was about to take on a new identity as a multicultural society.

By the early 1970s many different immigrant groups had attained their particular ethnic identity. This occurred for various reasons, some connected with language, some with religion, some with political affiliation, some with social moodity, giving higher status to individuals within the group which allowed them to set themselves up as definers of reality over and against mainstream society. The promotion of ethnic identities, added to a vigorous ethnic press, led politicians to believe that the "ethnic vote" would have considerable power at the ballot box. Politicians in certain "ethnic" areas decided that, in order to retain their seats, it was imperative to recognize ethnic groups and support their causes.[17] Thus a change in the conceptualization of Australian society to accommodate immigrants as an integral part of the "world" of Anglo-Saxons[18] society was forced upon politicians. Changes in government attitudes were attributed unashamedly

> ...to growing awareness within all major political parties in recent years of the needs of migrant communities and of the importance of the migrant vote, particularly in marginal electorates (Commonwealth Education Portfolio, 1978).

Australian society was to be reconceptualized as a multicultural society where immigrants were not to be marginalized as the "strangers" outside mainstream society. New theorizing would integrate them within this society. But how were Aboriginal people to be located in this multicultural society?

CONTEMPORARY POLICY – AUSTRALIA AS A MULTICULTURAL SOCIETY

As was the case with Aborigines, policy towards immigrants was initially one of assimilation. By 1972, however, at the same time that King was announcing integration as policy for Aborigines in South Australia, Lynch, the then Minister for Immigration in the Federal Liberal Government, also announced integration as a new policy for immigrants:

> The earlier desire to make stereotype Australians of the newcomers has been set aside. The use of integration instead of assimilation is not mere semantics; it is the outward sign of a fundamental change in the attitude of the Australian Government and people (Lynch, 1972:10).

What Lynch did not state was that the fundamental change in the attitude of the Australian Government was due to a perception that political pressure could be brought to bear on the government by migrant groups. The policy was a legitimation of a *de facto* situation brought about by immigrant groups constructing an ethnic identity. While policy, however, could be reformulated and restated at the government level, Lynch's proclamation that the policy of integration of immigrant groups also showed a change of attitude on the part of Australian people was utopian in the extreme. Changes in practice can be legislated for example, practices of discrimination can be penalized. It is not possible to legislate for changes of attitude. It is even less realistic to speak of changes in the attitudes of people simply following government reconceptualization of particular issues. Nevertheless, from this date, policies regarding immigrant communities (redefined as ethnic groups) must be considered within the framework of a multicultural Australia, a notion that was stressed again by the Liberal Party when it returned to power in 1975.

In 1978, the Prime Minister (Malcolm Fraser), tabling in Parliament the Galbally Report on post arrival services for immigrants, made the following pronouncement:

> Australia is at a critical stage in developing a cohesive, united, multicultural nation. Further steps to encourage multi-culturalism are needed...[the government] will foster the retention of the cultural heritage of different ethnic groups and promote inter-cultural understanding (Fraser, 1978:2728).

It was Fraser's view (1978:2731) that schools were "the key element in achieving such a goal".

Recognition of an emerging Aboriginal identity did not have its origins (as did that of immigrant identity) in a response to the political realities of the time. At the Federal level, Aborigines had no vote in most states until the referendum. It had been advantageous to a mainstream society to exclude them from a common framework; Aboriginal people were a group without power in every sense—unlike the immigrant groups many of which were coherent and highly politicized.

In order to investigate how theorizing on the part of government about multicultural attitudes found issue in practice, it is proposed to examine the particular "world" in which the effect of the policy of multiculturalism can be clearly discerned, namely the "world" of education which Fraser saw as the key element in achieving policies of multiculturalism, and to put into context theorizing about Aboriginal identity within the development of this world.

GOVERNMENT POLICY ON MULTICULTURALISM IN EDUCATION

The urgency of promoting multiculturalism in education is shown by the number and status of the committees appointed and the speed with which they presented reports and with which their recommendations were implemented. These general issues will not be surveyed here. Rather, the focus will be on whether or not the policy of integration for Aborigines was itself subsumed, in its initial formulations, into overall policy for a "new" Australia.

One source of government theorizing, against which policy towards Aborigines may be tested, is found in the Commonwealth Education Portfolio discussion paper of 1978. This paper set out to adumbrate the means of establishing formal machinery to implement the recommendations of the Galbally Report (Galbally, 1978), particularly with regard to its recommendations for education. The paper devoted one page (page 4) to a description of the Aboriginal situation, but then was able to ignore the participation of the Aboriginal people in a multicultural society as "the Government has acknowledged the unique position of the Aboriginals by the establishment of the Department of Aboriginal Affairs".

On page 8, the statement was made:

> The conceptual framework for education for a multicultural society must include *all groups* in Australian society. There is a popular tendency to think of multicultural education as relating only to immigrants (emphasis added).

Mention of "all groups" in society did not refer to Aborigines but to established Anglo-Saxon groups who were to be encouraged to appreciate the culture and customs of the immigrants, as is made clear by the footnote:

> The Government has accepted that special educational provisions are necessary for the Aboriginal group.

Aborigines were to be given special help, placed in a unique position; at the same time they were placed outside the conceptual framework of a multicultural society in a footnote. They were prevented from locating themselves within mainstream society by a boundary-from-without.[19] Furthermore, they were excluded as a single, monolithic group in contra-distinction to the official government policy, which, at the level of theorizing, offered various possibilities for the location of Aboriginal identity within the total framework of Australian society. There is no doubt that some tradition-oriented Aboriginal people did reject the values of White society, and by their own volition excluded themselves from a multicultural society. There is also no doubt that some Aboriginal people wished to include themselves in mainstream White society, but were prevented from doing this by the way in which this new society was conceptualized.[20] Watts (1981:56-57), in a study of 900 students receiving Aboriginal Study Grants, found that 54 per cent preferred to identify themselves as Aboriginal and Australian (despite the fact that grants are given only to those who identify themselves as Aborigines). Aboriginal leaders in the 1970s opted for a nomenclature which would integrate Aboriginal people within the wider group. In 1973, when a Central Australian Aborigines Congress was established, Neville Perkins outlined the reasons for adopting the term "Aboriginal Australian", which he saw both as promoting the notion of uniqueness, and of allowing "for people of Aboriginal descent to identify broadly as both Aboriginal and Australians within the context of modern Australian society".

In the same year as the publication of the Commonwealth Education Portfolio discussion paper (1978), a ministerial committee was appointed to make recommendations on the distribution of funds for multicultural education.

This committee, in presenting its report, stated:

> Australia has always been a multicultural society. Even before the European settlement the continent was inhabited by the Aboriginal groups each with their own distinct and different languages and cultures (Committee on Multicultural Education, 1979:5).

With these few words, which can only be seen as pure rhetoric (the use of the word multicultural in the quote bears no resemblance to the use of the word throughout the rest of the text), Aborigines were dismissed from inclusion in the "new" multicultural society.[21]

Manifestly, the situation of the Aboriginal people, their loss of culture and their loss of identity, places them in a category quite different from that of immigrants to Australia. Aborigines recognize this; they see their case on all counts as different from that of immigrants. (They are not "New Australians"; they are the *original* Australians). In a paradoxical way, the report of the ministerial committee pointed to the unique position of the Aboriginal people but recognized it by excluding Aborigines from further mention!

Nevertheless, if Aborigines are to be seen as part of a multicultural society, if policies of integration for Aborigines advanced by the government in power are not to be mere rhetoric ("we are part of each other"), then efforts must be made to conceptualize Australian society in a way that does not exclude Aborigines.

In sum, Aboriginal people were excluded from the conceptualization of mainstream society at the same time that they were presented with an ideology of self-identification/self-management; it must be judged that the Party Platform of the Liberal Governments concerning multiculturalism in the 1970s, in seeking to integrate *immigrant* groups in the newly emerging multicultural Australia, at the same time had the consequences of working against the integration of *Aboriginal* people.

A further reflection of contemporary theorizing may be found in the influential report of the Ethnic Affairs Commission of New South Wales, also published in 1978. The Ethnic Affairs Commission related the promotion of multiculturalism to the maintenance of a secure identity:

> The long search for an Australian identity is taking a new turn. A new identity is now emerging through huge shifts in community values, taste, style, norms (Ethnic Affairs Commission of New South Wales, 1979:1).

The Commission, too, did not see Aboriginal people as part of this newly emerging Australian identity.

> Regarding the Australian Aborigines the Commission felt during its first year of operation, that it had neither the competence nor the resources even to start tackling the first issue; — that is, whether the Aborigines would like to be included in the work of the Commission (Ethnic Affairs Commission of New South Waltes, 1979:5).

In this document, once again Aborigines were not seen as part of a multicultural Australia. The Commissioners, like so many before them, felt they were faced with an intractable problem. Their reaction reflected so many other stances towards Aborigines; Aborigines are Aborigines, not really Australians.

A further institution which has the potential to be a powerful "reality definer" for immigrants and for Aborigines alike is found in the Australian Institute of Multicultural Affairs, established in 1979. The Institute addressed education as its first major issue. It came to the conclusion that the maintenance of aspects of ethnic culture was not incompatible with identification as an Australian. The stated aims of its document were to promote a cohesive Australian society by developing among Australian people an awareness and understanding of the diverse cultures resulting from the immigration of various ethnic groups. By using a conceptualization of society which focussed on ethnic groups as immigrants it was not possible for the Institute to include Aborigines in its concern. It declared itself ready to co-operate with Aboriginal groups. It is not surprising however, that the latter, as they were **not** immigrants, and because the conceptualization of the 1970s separated them out of the newly developing cohesive society, Aborigines were forced into a separate identity.

As, by general consensus of policy makers in multicultural Australia in the 1970s, Aborigines were not part of the new multicultural "Australian" identity, the logical deduction was that they had to find a separate Aboriginal identity. Policies which act to exclude, either by omission or commission, must be seen to erect a boundary-from-without. The conclusion must be reached that, except for the brief period when a Labour Government was in power, despite the granting of citizenship to Aborigines, they were nevertheless not seen in the theorizing of government or of official organizations as eligible for therapy and appropriate subjects for full integration into a multicultural society.

The exclusion of Aborigines from the newly emerging multicultural identity was cemented by the decisions about the locus of administration for Aboriginal affairs. The Department of Aboriginal Affairs was initially set up to further Aboriginal interests. Bureaucracies, however, once established, take on a life of their own. It can be argued that Aborigines were separated from mainstream multicultural Australia not only because of their "uniqueness", but because their conceptual exclusion was necessary to the maintenance of the operations of a government department.

> Separate administrative arrangements apply to those areas and as the Minister for Immigration and Ethnic Affairs made clear in November 1979, in his second reading speech on the Bill to establish the Institute (of Multicultural Affairs) it would not overlap the functions of the Department of Aboriginal Affairs or the Australian Institute of Aboriginal Studies (Australian Institute of Multicultural Affairs, 1980:v).

The basis for the exclusion of Aboriginal people may very well be traced to the (unintended) consequences of policies concerning other ethnic groups and to the consequences of the reification of the activities of government departments.[22] All three contributing factors discussed lead to the conclusion that, in the early theorizing of those involved in multicultural education, the Aboriginal people were not located within the conceptualization of a multicultural Australia.

The exclusion of Aboriginal people in the 1970s through a "boundary-from-without," nevertheless paradoxically worked to the advantage of Aboriginal people in the construction of Aboriginal identity, as the possibility of disparate groups of Aboriginal people becoming more cohesive and constructing a framework for building positive identity was facilitated by policies which acted to exclude Aborigines, while "theorizing" about them positively. Indeed, the very fact that mainstream theorizing about Aborigines since the 1970s has been positive, has further acted to separate Aboriginal people. This consequence is inherent in the conceptualization of policies of self-management/self-determination projected by government because, if the "uniqueness" of Aborigines is accepted, and the framework of a multicultural society excluding Aborigines is also accepted, then Aborigines are forced into exercising their autonomy outside this framework. As a consequence, the grounds for declaring Aboriginal activities aimed at promoting their autonomy (formerly designated as creating a "race within a race") are removed.

Certainly, Aboriginal people seized the concept of self-determination and interacted with it to build a new, positive world of meaning for themselves. The tradition-oriented people express this by saying "The marrngu are the boss! "This is used both as a rallying cry, and as a firm basis for building a world of meaning in which Aboriginal people exert autonomy (Jordan, 1983:181ff).

On all sides, Aboriginal people at every level in society and in every sphere of action, such as health care, legal rights, and educational policy-making, are asserting "We will do it ourselves". It is no longer accepted without question that White people will work for Aboriginal people as before. Rather, today the meaning of working for Aboriginal people has changed. Aboriginal people *employ* White staff to "work for" them – in Aboriginal independent schools, in legal services, in health care. The role of the non-Aboriginal is to implement the policy of the Aboriginal people; White people work for Aboriginal people, or with Aboriginal people to further the aims of the latter.

In sum, while Aboriginal people are physically located within a multicultural society, more and more they are entering into situations which are structurally alternative, and within which they have greater control of their futures. While this was not by choice originally, social interactions have produced a situation where the Aboriginal voice, expressing political, cultural, physical and educational needs, is heard.

The legislation noted in South Australia in 1834 has turned full circle. The Federal Government *Land Rights Act* was proclaimed in 1977; instead of Land Acts dispossessing the people, legislation returning territory to the Aboriginal people is currently, in the mid-1980s, under consideration: in most states this is favourable to Aboriginal wishes. Aboriginal people are in positions of leadership in Aboriginal organizations;[23] positions within government, within the Public Service, have been identified as appropriately filled by Aboriginal people.

The positive theorizing of the governments in the 1970s has borne fruit in the 1980s as the Aboriginal people have been given, and have taken, responsibility for their own development, and incipient, rudimentary theorizing has become fact – "We will do it ourselves".

One example, appropriate to the present discussion, is the role played in education.

NATIONAL ABORIGINAL EDUCATION COMMITTEE

The Minister for Education, Senator Carrick, in announcing the establishment of the NAEC in 1977, outlined the role of the committee as giving advice to the Department of Education on Aboriginal needs, and ways of meeting these needs, and advising the Department of Aboriginal Affairs and indeed all instrumentalities concerned with education. The Committee was to assist the Department in monitoring existing programmes and researching and proposing new programmes.

The Committee has more than fulfilled these expectations; it has carried out a series of evaluations on existing projects (e.g. the Black community school in Townsville, the Aboriginal Community College in Adelaide etc.). In 1979, it researched the need for Aboriginal teachers and the opportunity for teacher training for Aboriginal people in response to the National Inquiry into Education; it articulated and disseminated NAEC policy in the area.[24] It has clearly stated its Aims and Objectives for Aboriginal Education in a widely disseminated policy statement. It researched the involvement and needs of Aboriginal people in higher Education, and produced a comprehensive document to guide the government in the allocation of funds for the 1985-1987 triennium (Aborigines and Tertiary Education – A framework for the 1985-87 triennium). Together with the Commonwealth Tertiary Education Commission it mounted a review of support systems for Aboriginal students in higher Education (Jordan, 1984).

Government Departments have heeded and implemented NAEC policy. It is undeniable that great steps, indeed leaps, have been made in self-management for Aboriginal people since the 1970s in the area of education.

Nevertheless, one issue still remains: the Schools Commission (1982) advocated that Aboriginal people take full responsibility not only for policy making in education but also for funding. This has not yet happened. Clearly the "golden rule" applies – "He who has the gold, makes the rules". This is true of most situations in the White world; research is carried out in those areas *which are funded,* and therefore which, by definition, meet the needs of the funding group. Aboriginal progress towards self-management, self-determination, will always be controlled, in the final analysis, by those who control the funds.

Hence, while lauding the progress made, from a sociological viewpoint we must return to the notion of how minority groups are managed by mainstream groups. In education, the consultation of Governments with Aboriginal people is real; the Aboriginal voice is clear and coherent and it is heard. Alternative structures exist for policy making, alternative schools to meet the needs of Aboriginal people are encouraged and are flourishing. There is, then, evidence of structural differentiation. Until, however, funding is controlled by Aboriginal people, the issues discussed above relating the mechanism of therapy as a form of control of minority groups by the dominant groups in society must be addressed.

It will be recalled that Rowley saw assimilation as a means of controlling Aboriginal people and making them more acceptable to Whites. The question must be asked whether the assimilation of Aboriginal leaders into government instrumentalities without the power of funding to implement their policies is not also acting as a form of therapy, a means of controlling[25] a minority group, so that, while they are given (limited) powers of self-management, their radicalism[26] is at the same time absorbed, and, paradoxically, Aboriginal people and their alternative structures are integrated into Australian multicultural identity.

NOTES

1. The census has never operated to reflect the second part of this definition (namely that a persons's self-identification must be legitimated by others).

2. 'Theorizing", as the concept is used here, occurs at various levels. Berger and Luckmann (1966:110ff) discuss the process of legitimation as a form of theorizing.

    Legitimation is best described as a "second order" objectivation of meaning. Legitimation produces new meanings that serve to integrate the meanings already attached to disparate institutional processes. The function of legitimation is to make objectively available and *subjectively* plausible the first order objectivations that have been institutionalized. The lowest form of legitimation is contained in, and transmitted through, language.

Berger and Luckmann (1966:122) call this incipient theorizing. C. Wright Mills (1963:441) refers to vocabularies of motives that canalize thought.

Rudimentary forms of theorizing, according to Berger and Luckmann (1966:122), "are highly pragmatiç explanatory schemes relating to concrete actions."

Such rudimentary forms of theorizing may be found in every day statements of belief, of "recipe" knowledge (Schutz, 1971:72ff).

Explicit theories characterize a third level of theorizing. The highest level of theorizing is found in the construction of a symbolic universe, the latter defined by Berger and Luckmann (1966:113) as

> ...bodies of theoretical tradition that integrate different provinces of meaning and encompass the institutional order in a symbolic totality.

The identity of individuals is dependent upon their ability to locate themselves within a world of meaning wherein they recognize their self-sameness and continuity and perceive that others affirm this recognition. If the Aboriginal person wishes to locate himself in an Aboriginal world, then the legitimation of this world, at all the levels of theorizing, must make this world plausible to him, so that it offers a real possibility of identity, that is, location in a world of meaning that has characteristics that are specifically Aboriginal.

3. Parallel examples may be found in Australia. For example, in the early eighties, the unemployed were categorized as dole bludgers. The world of meaning of the *employed* was threatened by the world of the unemployed; the latter was then given negative connotations by the dominant (employed) group.

4. Contrary to popular mythology, the Aboriginal people were not passive; they resisted the usurpation of their land. A correspondent to the *South Australian* of June 16, 1838, observed that:

    > ...the whole of the districts surveyed under the Act of Parliament and allotted without any reserve to the colonists were occupied by the natives; indeed, the more intelligent part of the natives themselves have often asserted, that the land, for instance, on which Adelaide is situated, belongs to the "blackfellow" (Jenkin, 1979:3).

5. *The Advertiser,* Adelaide 13 December 1909 commented on the speech of David Ngunaitponi, one of the Port McLeay Aborigines in Adelaide, in the following way:

But it was when the "adult" David took the platform and spoke of the tradition of his people, of their knowledge of astronomy, their intimacy with the science of botany, their bushcraft and folklore that the audience gave most attention...this civilized native spoke of the similarity of Greek mythology and the Aboriginal fiction (quoted in Jenkin, 1979:226).

David has astonished the professors of Sydney and Melborne by the breadth of his intelligence and his capacity for absorbing knowledge, and he has been a recognized authority on that branch of knowledge known as ballistics. . . He has always been interested in mechanics. He made an improvement on ordinary sheep shears which proved very promising (quoted in Jenkin, 1979:234-5).

Ngunaitponi was not alone in his achievements.

6. Berger and Luckmann (1966:85-89) discuss the process of "sedimentation" of knowledge, whereby particular experiences become "part of the common stock of knowledge. Language becomes the depository of a large aggregate of collective sedimentations, which can be acquired monothetically, that is, as cohesive wholes and without reconstructing their original process of formation."

The lack of blame attached to killing Aboriginal people thus continued into this century as exemplified by public statements which treated Aborigines as less than human. A certain Miss Cantle (1978:1) a missionary working at Port Augusta, relates how, at a town council meeting in Port Augusta in 1937, "one councillor stood up and gave his opinion that the best thing to do was to turn a machine gun on the whole camp and wipe it right out, people and all". The contemporary sedimentation of theorizing about Aborigines as less than human may be seen also as late as the seventies in an anecdote related by Turnbull, (1972:233):

People selling buttons in Melbourne streets for an Aborigine cause not long ago were astounded by the savagery of the answers given by some of those asked to buy – "I'd rub the lot out", "Give 'em bait" and so on, and these people who had probably never seen an Aborigine.

The very use of the word "bait" categorizes Aborigines as animals. The comments reveal that extermination, as a permitted activity, and the typification of Aborigines as less than human, has been sedimented into the common stock of knowledge of people far removed from those who actually did give Aboriginal people "bait". The force of racist policies of extermination and the stereotypes which supported them may be shown in their persistence throughout Australia, and may be found even in the deliberations of the Federal Parliament. As late as 1969, W.C. Wentworth, then Minister for Social Services and Aboriginal Affairs, replying in Parliament to a question concerning statements made by a member of the Government, the member for Capricornia, was forced to admit that, while he believed the Government would not support the statement, the member had in fact stated that Aborigines were second-class citizens, and that therefore they should submit to sterilization, and that moral compulsion should be applied to make the people submit (Wentworth, 1969). It is not extravagant to categorize sterilization as a latter day form of extermination.

7. Aboriginal people interviewed at Strelley as part of a research project on the construction of Aboriginal identity (Jordan, 1983) remember graphically being present at incidents of mass killings. The people there believe that the giving of grog was also part of a government policy of extermination (see also Rowley, 1971a).

8. Berger defines a symbolic universe as "the matrix of all socially objectivated and subjectively real meanings". He goes on to say "The entire historic society and the entire biography of the individual are seen as events taking place *within* this universe...The symbolic universe provides order for the subjective apprehension of biographical experience (Berger and Luckmann, 1966:114ff).

9. Gale (1972:61) states: The contemporary situation whereby Aborigines were isolated in the precincts of Christian missions appeared at the time to be workable and useful. It was therefore natural that it should have become codified and perpetuated by the 1911 Aborigines Act. Indeed, the idea of the maintenance of Aborigines on reserves lay at the very core of this Act, the effect of which was to set Aborigines apart as a separate group in the community and, in contrast to the earlier attitudes of *laissez-faire*, to legislate for them in a rigid and paternalistic way.

10. An Aborigine who had been declared "exempt" could not visit a reserve without permission. Mrs. Elphick, an "important woman", states that she had to obtain permission to attend her mother's funeral; another family negotiated for three days to take their mother to a reserve for burial.

11. Nihilation by banishment has been used consistently to manage the problems of those having some form of stigma. Usually this stigma is allied to physical attributes. However, in Western Australia in the

1930s, the unemployed were seen as being stigmatized and were removed from sight into camps outside the city boundaries.

12. Similarly, in the forties, marches in the streets by Aborigines seeking recognition of their rights were categorized as Nazi inspired.

13. Tradition-oriented people make this very point. They claim that marta-marta (part-European people) cannot make a treaty on their behalf with the government. Marta-marta working in Government agencies are *part* of the government.

14. It is interesting (and revealing, as an example of sedimentation of knowledge) to note that, despite King's enlightened attitude, he still thought of Aborigines as identifying with "their own people". The Aborigines to whom he referred were part-Aborigines, and therefore also part-European. It is a commentary on the perceptions of White society that contemporary theorizers, even the most enlightened, assume that Aborigines should identify with the race of their black parent rather than their White parent.

15. It should be noted that King made the assumption that the urban Aboriginal people possessed a "separate and identifiable Aboriginal heritage and culture" that they could maintain. This assumption must be questioned. Rather it is an identity that must be *reconstructed*.

16. In the major guidelines of the Liberal/National Party policy 1975, self-management was outlined in the following way:

> The Liberal and National Country Parties recognize that if a policy of self-management is to be effective, Aborigines must play a leading role in their affairs. This will include Aborigines playing a significant role:
>
> > (a) in setting long term goals and objectives which the government should pursue and the programmes it should adopt in such areas as Aboriginal education, housing, health, employment and legal aid;
> >
> > (b) in setting the priorities for expenditure on Aboriginal affairs within the context of overall budget allocations, and
> >
> > (c) in evaluating existing programmes and formulating new ones.
>
> The following statements detailed the assumptions and aims in recognizing and promoting an Aboriginal identity:
>
> > - We recognize the fundamental right of Aborigines to retain their racial identity and traditional life-style or where desired to adopt partially or wholly a European life-style;

- We will, within the limits of available finances fund programmes which develop Aboriginal self-sufficiency and which represent initiatives that Aborigines themselves believe will enhance their dignity, self-respect and self-reliance;

- We will promote cross-cultural understanding and co-operation by a continuing process of community education for all age groups to ensure a higher level of mutual toleration, trust and enterprise than has so far marked our history.

- A special obligation is also imposed upon us all to provide opportunities for Aborigines to preserve their traditions, languages and customs from further encroachment and destruction.

17. It is not asserted here that ethnic groups either had the power, or exerted the power to elect particular individuals or groups to Parliament: it is merely recorded that politicians believed this way a factor at the time.

18. It must be noted that the dominant group in society has, in the 1980s, reconceptualized its own composition. The categorization of White/Anglo/Saxon/Protestant has given way to Anglo/Saxon/Celtic, to include the once despised Irish group. Clearly the ingroup has redefined itself over and against the minority group.

19. Isajiw (1974:122) highlights the importance of the notion of a boundary which excludes certain ethnic groups.

> Ethnicity is the result of a double boundary, a boundary from within, maintained by the socialization process, and a boundary from without established by the process of intergroup relations ...the basic difference lies in the external boundaries. It is not so much a matter of faster or slower assimilation or non-assimilation. More significantly, it is a matter of how the various ethnic groups are perceived and identified by the power-holding, policy-making and influence-exerting bodies of the two societies.

Barth (1969) saw the very existence of ethnic groups dependent upon boundaries, rather than cultural features.

> The cultural features that signal the boundary may change and the cultural characteristics of the members may likewise be transformed, indeed even the organizational form of the group may change. Yet the continuing dichotomization between members and outsiders allows us to specify the nature of

continuity and investigate the changing cultural form and context (Barth, 1969:14).

20. It must be noted that, with regard to *funding*, a different source already existed for Aborigines. The question here is that of inclusion of Aboriginal people in *theorizing* about a multicultural society. The problem posed by separate funding is taken up later in this paper.

21. The commitment of Australia's ethnic groups to maintaining aspects of their cultural heritage is clear, and this is not only compatible with, but supportive of identification with Australia...To fully realize Australia's potential, meet the responsibilities and reap the benefits inherent in the composition of our population, it is necessary that all Australians be afforded equality of opportunity to participate in the life of the nation and maintain their ethnic and cultural heritage within the law and accepted political framework...Education in Australia should embrace the teaching of English as a second language, the teaching of community languages and studies of ethnic and cultural diversity in Australia" (Australian Institute of Multi-Cultural Affairs, 1980:vii, 7).

22. The term reification is used here to describe social constructs which, once established, take on a life of their own and act back upon society to constrain action.

23. See Watts (1981:58ff) for a full list of Aboriginal bodies, the date of establishment, their roles and functions, and the work carried out by them.

24. The acceptance of this policy was reaffirmed by the minister for Education, Senator S. Ryan, in allocating funding in 1984.

25. It is not suggested that government instrumentalities *formulate* a policy intended to control but rather that, as discussed earlier, when the world of the dominant group is threatened by another "world of meaning" it must take steps to preserve its own world — usually either by nihilation or therapy.

26. Radicalism here is used in the same sense of "returning to the roots"; in this case returning to the root causes of Aboriginal disadvantage in society.

THE SAMI LAW: A CHANGE OF NORWEGIAN GOVERNMENT POLICY TOWARD THE SAMI MINORITY?

Oystein Steinlien

INTRODUCTION

Norwegian government policy towards the Sami has changed through the centuries, both in accordance with international trends, and in terms of national interests. This paper will review the situation from 1850 up to the present. I will discuss the different policies over time with an eye to the concepts of formal and real equality, and the fact that formal equality does not automatically create real equality.

Norwegian government policy was built on an ideology that does not clearly distinguish between these two concepts. Rather it was built upon an assumption that formal equality creates real equality. This kind of thinking does not take cultural factors into account, or the fact that rights and duties are not evenly distributed in a population, especially in majority/minority societies or in a majority/minority context.

The nature of minority cultures in this context is related to the assumption that the minority cultures will remain in a permanent dilemma unless a certain degree of self-determination is granted. The dilemma can be posed as follows: What is the point in learning language and culture, and of teaching children cultural skills, if the majority is going to go on defining the conditions for the future development of the culture?

STAGES IN NORWEGIAN SAMI POLICY

To provide a context I will sketch some major trends in Norwegian government policy towards the Sami minority since 1850.

At that time, there was a change in the policy with the introduction of the so-called Norwegianization policy. This policy was active until 1959, when the government-appointed Sami Committee presented their report. Following some major trends, I will divide governmental policy into three stages: (1) Norwegianization/assimilation, 1850-1959; (2) economic and cultural integration, or integrated pluralism, 1959-1984; and (3) cultural pluralism, 1984 to the present.

NORWEGIANIZATION/ASSIMILATION, 1850-1959

The Transition Period: 1850-1880

In the period preceding 1850, policy developed on the basis of cultural pluralism, a model corresponding to such European concepts as "nation", "justice" and "liberty". According to these principles, all people have both the right and the obligation to secure and develop their language and nationality.

In the late 1840s this cultural policy was much debated. In 1851 the first sign of a changing policy came with the introduction of the *Finnefondet* by the Norwegian parliament, a sort of foundation for the promotion of the Norwegian language in Sami areas.

Even if the principle of Norwegianization can be considered as having been decided upon in 1851, the period up to 1880 was really a transition phase. It was still permissible to use the Sami language in religious teaching, and local school boards were still allowed to decide whether Norwegian, both Norwegian and Sami, or only Sami, were to be used for instruction. During this transition phase, both regional and local variations were allowed as far as language was concerned, because of the high frequency of Sami monolinguals. However the tendency during this period was clearly one of *restricting* the use of the Sami language.

Establishment Of An "Infrastructure": 1880-1905

In 1880 the implementation of cultural policy was centralized and what might be called the "hard" Norwegianization period started. Now policy was determined by a "Directive for teaching in Sami and Kvaen [Finnish-speaking immigrants] districts". This directive put restrictions on the use of Sami and Finnish. The earlier policy, which allowed children to learn their mother tongue, was accordingly abandoned.

This policy was confirmed by an act of 1889 concerning primary schools. This legislation required that the Language of Instruction in schools was to be Norwegian, with certain exceptions for a few regions where Sami was to be allowed as a language for assistance only.

This was further confirmed by new directives in 1898, *Wexelsenplakaten*, that turned out to be almost identical to the ones mentioned. These three statements formed the central documents in the Norwegianization policy. In spite of many changes of government over the years and regardless of major changes in political trends throughout Europe to recognize and affirm the cultural rights of minorities, there was a general political agreement on, and acceptance of, this policy in Norway until 1959. In addition to these directives, there was an Act of Parliament in 1902 concerning agriculture which required an individual to be able to read and write Norwegian in order to buy land.

By 1905 the legal infrastructure for the ideology had been fully established and the different kinds of efforts towards Norwegianization were being implemented. In this period we can also see the first tendencies to integrate these notices of cultural policy into a general governmental policy in the northern part of Norway. In that way Norwegianization was attached to policies and initiatives in other sectors of life, especially security and defence policy.

The Security And Defence Policy Argument: 1905-1930

By 1905, Norway was a "young" nation-state with the termination of union with Sweden. The increasing Norwegian nationalism which had developed during the union gave no room for cultures other than Norwegian.

This nationalism provided the ideological basis for the security and defence policy argument, but there was also an argument of a more practical type. The Kvaen immigration into the northern part of Norway was looked upon as a problem of defence. The main weapon in attempts to try to diminish this threat was Norwegianization. As the authorities found it difficult to differentiate between the two groups, Sami and Kvaen, the solution was a concerted Norwegianization policy directed against both of these people, a policy which was explained as necessary for the security and defense of the young independent Norwegian state.

The Post War Period: 1945-1959

The post war period is characterized by a more liberal attitude towards Sami culture, fuelled in part by the experiences of the Second World War. The Act of 1898, the *Wexelsenplakaten*, however, was still in force.

In 1949 a government committee on school policy (*Samordningsnemda for skoleverket*) launched a proposition which lent some support to the recognition of Sami culture and language. This was sent to local schoolboards for comments, but all of the replies returned were negative. This clearly demonstrated, for the first time, that the Norwegianization policy had actually been effective in that it had made the Sami population look unfavourably upon their own culture. In general, Sami people wanted the existing system of Norwegianization to continue.

But after all, a change in the policy was evident in that the leader of the committee, Boyesen, stated that a new attitude towards Sami culture had developed recently. Instead of denying the Sami people their cultural heritage, he noted the duty the Norwegian state had to treat the Sami people respectfully. He also stated that the authorities were prepared to revise the Norwegianization policy, and to work instead in the best way possible to arrange for Sami cultural vitality in Norway.

ECONOMIC AND SOCIAL INTEGRATION, 1959-1984

The Sami Committee: 1956

The Sami Committee was appointed by government in 1956, and the report was presented in 1959. In many ways its proposals can be characterized as the beginning of a new era. The report resulted in a broad debate on Sami questions and it marked a new will on the part of Norwegian authorities to end the earlier Norwegianization policy.

This policy has often been characterized as cultural integration or intergrational pluralism. The manner in which the Committee tried to solve the "Sami question", would however seem to be both contradictory and impossible. One major aim was Sami integration into the economic and social structure of the country to further economic and social equality. On the other hand, another goal was the consolidation of Sami areas through cultural and administrative efforts to prevent assimilation. The idea was to make it possible for the Sami population in Norway to maintain its integrity as a viable culture.

Accordingly, when the report talks about special efforts to maintain Sami culture, they are basically concerned with the language. A further characteristic of the proposal is that it stresses the importance of the welfare and educational sectors, noting that:

> The main efforts from the authorities are efforts concerning all people in the country. The building of schools, social welfare programs, health services, social housing and general economic development of the nation provides better living condi-

tions for the individual. Special efforts are connected to the language situation....Equality and economic development under social stability will enable the Sami-speaking people to maintain Sami culture in our country. It will then depend upon the individual, if this is going to happen.... (p.4 in the proposal, author's translation).

The Committee pointed out that equal rights do not necessarily create identical rights, and stated that cultural policy in the future had to be pluralistic. Unfortunately, the committee did not seem to be fully aware of the consequences of this statement.

Accordingly, the responsibility of the government concerning the Sami people was to be carried out through a combination of general national welfare policy and special regional political remedies. The official policy towards the Sami people was defined as cultural and political efforts to be launched in the education and language sectors only.

There was one exception to this program, the reindeer herders. The Norwegian government felt the reindeer herders to be of special concern to them, because they were all Sami-speaking and the technology and concepts of their culture were expressed in Sami only. Therefore they developed special regulations concerning trade concessions and expropriation for reindeer herding as a special Sami sphere.

Unfortunately, the committee clearly used the term "Sami-speaking persons". The policy was clearly guided by the idea that the people concerned were only a group of Sami-speaking Norwegians, requiring special efforts to be able to continue to be Sami-speaking, rather than a Sami people who should have the option of continuing to be Sami people living in Norway.

Thus the Committee avoided many tricky questions by using the term "Sami-speaking persons", and not recognizing them as a separate ethnic group. A further consequence of this policy was that it completely excluded all Sami who did not speak Sami, that is people who, as a consequence of the Norwegianization policy up to 1959, had lost their language. This applied especially to the south Sami areas and to the coastal Sami areas. It should be pointed out that the major part of the total Sami population lives in the coastal areas.

In sum, the Committee's report was first and foremost a very pragmatic document, where questions of principle were largely avoided in order to permit solutions for more practical issues. In general terms, however, the report can be recognized as the end of the earlier Norwegianization policy.

The Implementation Of The Recommendations

The implementation of the recommendations of the Sami Committee took place only very slowly. One reason was that many Sami rejected the recommendations. Very clearly, the Norwegianization policy had been effective. For example, a Sami meeting in Karasjok declared: "We strongly protest upon use of Sami, except as a subsidiary language" (Paskersolusjonen, 1960).

Delay was also a result of lack of coordinating administrative bodies to assist in the implementation of the recommendations. It was assumed that existing government departments could handle the recommendations. The problem was that these were sectorized while the proposals were holistic, affecting many professions. The Committee did not itself propose an administrative body to coordinate the implementation of their program. It proposed that the Norwegian Sami Council, a Government appointed body, would do the job, but not only was that group not strong enough, it was not designed for that purpose.

How does this summary of the first two periods tie up with my point of departure, that of formal vs. real equality? The Sami Committee seemed to be aware of these two distinctions in that they talked about equal and identical rights, but their report did not seem to take into account the consequences of their recommendations.

There are two reasons for my conclusion. The first is that the Committee was not willing to use the term "Sami" which would imply that the Sami were perceived as a separate ethnic group. Instead they consistently used the term "Sami-speaking persons". Accordingly, the policy was intended to address only the concerns of a group of Norwegians who also happened to speak Sami.

The other reason, perhaps a more basic one, is that with these recommendations the authorities defined Sami interests first and foremost as cultural, and in so doing neglected the trickier questions, those which were territorial and political.

CULTURAL PLURALISM, 1984–PRESENT

The Establishment Of Two Commissions: 1980

As pointed out earlier, the implementation of the recommendations from the Sami Committee was only slowly taking place. Attention to Sami issues was again brought into focus during demonstrations against a new hydro-electric power plant in Alta, in the middle of Samiland. Early in the 1970s, the government launched plans to build a dam on the Kautokeino-Alta river, which runs through what is considered to be the "core Sami area". The first plans were very extensive, and would have resulted in flooding a whole Sami community, Masi, half way between Kautokeino and Alta.

The first plans for a dam from 1979, were reduced and Masi was no longer directly effected. Nonetheless, the decision resulted in large-scale demonstrations, both in Alta and in the capital, Oslo. Norwegian environmentalists from all over the country, as well as Sami took part, and the demonstrations created international attention.

As a result of the demonstrations, two public commissions were created in 1980: the Sami Rights Commission and the Sami Cultural Commission.

The Sami Rights Commission

The mandate of the Sami Rights Commission was wide, including a duty to "examine questions concerning Sami rights to land and water and some other juridical questions" (author's translation).

The political events in Alta resulted in a meeting between governmental representatives and Sami politicians in Kautokeino in 1981. It was decided to accelerate the work, and it was decided to give priority to the draft of a constitutional provision and an Act concerning a Sami parliament. It was also agreed that these provisions should formulate a statement of principle, and not, as originally intended, incorporate specific rights into the Constitution. The reason for this was that the commission could not put forward radical proposals for a constitutional provision dealing with any form of actual title to land and water, unless it had laid down its position on the question of rights to natural resources.

From a Sami point of view it was important to accelerate the work on the constitutional provision, because this would imply the strongest possible emphasis on the responsibilities of the Norwegian authorities for Sami culture.

The first report from the Sami Rights Commission came in 1984 (NOU, 1984:18). The parliamentary report which followed (Ot.prop nr.33, 1986-1987) and the guidelines established were later accepted by the Norwegian parliament in May of 1987.

The Sami Cultural Commission

The other commission, the Sami Cultural Commission, had the following mandate: "the Commission shall consider principal sides of the Sami cultural and educational policy, and discuss initiatives that can promote Sami culture and strengthen the use of Sami language" (author's translation). In 1982 the mandate was extended to consider Sami secondary education as well. The commission completed its work in 1985, *Sami Culture and Education* (NOU, 1985:14).

Provisions

The report of the Sami Rights Commission, which passed Parliament in 1987, contained two provisions. One was a constitutional provision, the other "The Sami Act", an Act considering a Sami parliament.

The constitutional provision read: "It is incumbent upon the government authorities to take the necessary steps to enable the Sami population to safeguard and develop their language, their culture and their societal life" (NOU, 1984:18:599, author's translation).

The Sami Act recommends a Sami parliament with advisory powers. The Act opens with a preamble: "The purpose of this Act is to provide for steps to be taken to enable the Sami population in Norway to safeguard and to develop their language, their culture and their societal life" (NOU, 1984:18:599, author's translation).

The Act was designed to enable other juridical provisions concerning the Sami people to be incorporated at a later date through future legislation.

The Sami Cultural Commission put forward a proposition for a language Act which states that: "Sami and Norwegian are equal languages and must have equal status as official languages under the regulations of this Act" (NOU, 1985:14:29, author's translation).

Basic View

One of the most important principles in the constitutional proposal is that the Sami people are a separate ethnic group, a separate people, in certain respects different from the rest of the Norwegian people. It also notes that Sami culture is a threatened culture, and that the Norwegian government is responsible for maintaining the Sami culture and providing the Sami with opportunities for their development as *Sami.*

It also states that it is important that the maintenance and further development of Sami culture in Norway be recognized as a *national* task and a national responsibility. The financial burdens imposed by the special measures called for in this initiative should be born first of all by the state, not by the individual municipality or community.

It is also made clear that the further development and maintenance of Sami culture is dependent upon special measures. Such a deviation from formal equality is necessary to secure a real equal worth between Sami culture and other cultures in Norwegian society.

And, lastly, the proposition notes that the Norwegian state has an obligation to ensure that the rules of international law are implemented by the Norwegian authorities, and the Norwegian state is obligated under international law for the implementation of special positive measures — that is, positive discrimination — towards the Sami people in Norway, to the extent that this is necessary to ensure that Sami culture is maintained.

International Law

The most effective defence of minority rights is found in Article 27 of the United Nations International Covenant of 1966 on Civil and Political Rights. It states:

> In those states in which ethnic, religious or linguistic minorities exist, persons belonging to such minorities shall not be denied the right, in community with the other members of the group, to enjoy their own culture, to profess and practice their own religion, or to use their own language.

There was discussion in the Sami Cultural Commission on the interpretation of culture. The question concerned whether culture was to be perceived as "ideal" forms of expression, such as books, newspapers and radio, or if it was also to embrace the material prerequisites for the "ideal" (spiritual) culture.

The Commission interpreted culture in the widest sense. This interpretation has certain implications for the right of the Sami to carry on their traditional economic activities and for rights to land and water. According to this, the ethnic minority is entitled to a certain degree of autonomy (non-intervention on the part of the state), to governmental support for the maintenance of their cultural activities (positive rights) and to be allowed to participate in the rest of community life on an equal footing with the majority population (the principle of non-discrimination).

CONCLUSIONS

To sum up, I will return to the two concepts of *formal* equality and *real* equality. The report of the Sami Commission is based upon a view which recognizes that a deviation from formal equality is necessary to secure real equality. The question I wish to consider is whether or not the recommendations proposed by the Commission are enough to create real equality — and thus equal worth — between Sami people and people of other cultures in Norwegian society.

I am not sure this is going to happen, and I am going to point to a discrepancy in the proposed measures that in my opinion shows that there is a deviation between principles and implementation.

Article 1 in the United Nation International Covenant of 1966 states that all people have the right of self-determination. The question for the Sami Rights Commission was whether the Sami minority, as an ethnic minority within a nation state, was embraced by the concept of "peoples" as it was used in this context. The Commission interpreted the article in such a way that the Sami minority in Norway cannot invoke any of the principles of rights to self-determination in the current conventions. And the crucial argument as far as I can see it, from the Commission, was that they would not recognize the Sami people as a colonized people:

> In this respect, the position of the Sami people is quite different from that of the Inuit population from Greenland – where the area and its population are distinctly separate, geographically, historically, and culturally, from the "mother country", and where the area has, moreover, for many years had the explicit status of a colony – even though there are points of resemblance between the Sami and the Inuit in other respects. Meanwhile, it may be maintained that Article 1 supports a broad interpretation of Article 27, so that the latter, through the wording "enjoy their own culture", authorizes a certain inner autonomy in the cultural sector of community life (NOU,1984:18:18, author's translation).

I would argue that this interpretation is not in accordance with the basic position of the Commission on the basis of the above quotation. They recommend a Sami parliament with, in principle, only advisory power. This I would argue is not in accord with a statement elsewhere in the report:

> as a political principle, the right of all people to self-determination is a bearing principle both in Europe and elsewhere in the world – and the aim is to give minorities better protection (NOU, 1984:18:342, author's translation).

On the one hand the Sami are considered to be an ethnic minority, a separate people, while on the other hand they are recognized as a minority in numerical terms only. They must also, according to the Sami Commission, submit to premises held by another people – non-Sami Norwegians – in order to secure any legal protection for their cultural ideals. Thus any Sami sovereignty comes about only through the dominant majority in Norway.

Territorial Rights

Through political channels available to them, the Sami people have repeatedly tried to focus on the colonial situation. They have done this by raising, as a political issue, not only rights to language and culture, but also rights to land and water. These issues arose because the Sami people felt them to be a threat to their cultural survival, as they saw the Norwegian state gradually taking possession of what they considered to be their original areas. The state sees themselves as property owner of about 90% of Finnmark, the northernmost county of Norway, and a major Sami area, without any formal session.

The claim of territorial rights has first and foremost been formulated as a claim that Sami livelihood interests are going to be decisive in terms of exploitation of resources and intervention in what are considered Sami areas. And further, Sami feel that if there are diverging interpretations in the future concerning the administration of these areas, they must be settled by a representative body where Sami representatives are in a majority.

In their basic view, the Sami Rights Commission recognizes the Sami people as an indigenous people. The key characteristics for this are:

1) it is a population group with historical continuity in relation to all or parts of a nation-state, from before the establishment of the territory in relation to all or parts of the state, without necessarily being the original population;

2) that the population constitutes a minority in the state, or that it is not politically dominant for other reasons; and

3) that it has its own culture, and that this culture is still especially closely linked to traditional primary industries (NOU, 1984:18:342, author's translation).

As a result of the meeting in Kautokeino in 1981, the Sami Rights Commission first report does not deal with these questions. They are to be brought up in a second report. However, the aim of the propositions in the report is to create real equality of worth between Sami culture and other cultures in Norwegian society. I do not think that this can be obtained before the issues of territorial rights and the transfer of authority to the Sami parliament are considered. In the first report, the Sami Rights Commission does not consider territorial rights, or a transfer of authority, either on a cultural or a territorial basis.

So once again, real equality, that is equal worth between non-Sami Norwegian people and the Sami population in Norway, cannot be achieved unless the government also confers political and territorial rights, along with the right to self-government.

Map 1: Finnmark (some key place-names)

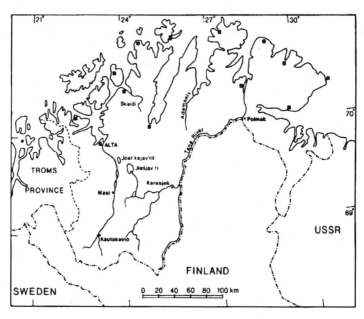

Legend

■   principal Norwegian urban centres
—·—· international boundary
----- provincial boundary

Source: Reproduced from Robert Paine: *Dam A River, Dam a People?*
Saami (Lapp) Livelihood and the Alta/Kautokeino Hydro Electric Project and
the Norwegian Parliament. IWGIA Document 45, Copyright Copenhagen,
1982 by International Work Group for Indigenous Affairs.

But there are also some bright spots concerning the transfer of authority
and cultural and territorial rights. Although the Commission noted that, in
principle, the representative body will have only advisory authority, their
report adds: "it also shall have the authority to make decisions in well-de-
fined areas" (NOU, 1984:18:516, author's translation). The parliamentary
bill that followed the report clarified this further by stating: "The Sami
parliament has decisive power where this follows the provisions in this law,
or is decided otherwise" (Ot.prop. nr 33, 1986-87:123, author's translation).

The report also comments elsewhere in the report upon the power of the parliament. Thus it states: "Principally the power of the [Sami Parliament] should not be decided upon once and for all, but should be extended according to the [Parliament's] own interpretation..."(Ot.prop nr 33, 1986-87:154, author's translation).

More specifically, concerning cultural and territorial questions, the report notes:

> meanwhile, it may be maintained that Article 1 supports a broad interpretation of Article 27, so that the latter, through the wording "enjoy their own culture", authorizes a certain inner autonomy in the cultural sector of community life (NOU, 1984:18:18, author's translation).

And finally, on territorial questions, the report notes that the interpretation of culture in Article 27 of the United Nations International Covenant of 1966 as also involving a national foundation for "ideal" culture is actually in favour of Sami rights and has consequences for traditional trade and for rights to land and water (NOU, 1984:18:272).

REFERENCES

AAPS (Assembly of Aboriginal Peoples of Saskatchewan)
1989   Submission to Secretary of State, 16 March 1989 for fiscal year 01 April 1989 to 31 March 1990.

Abercrombie, N. et al
1984   The Penguin Dictionary of Sociology. London: Allen Lane.

Acheson, A.W.
1981   Old Crow, Yukon Territory pp. 694-703, in J. Helm (Editor): Handbook of North American Indians, Volume 6: Subarctic. Washington: United States Government Printing Office.

Acoose-Pelletier, Janice
1985   The Land Commission. New Breed 16(3):14-15.

Adams, E.C.
1946   American Indian Education: Government Schools and Economic Progress. New York: King's Crown Press.

Adams, Howard
1975   Prison of Grass: Canada from the Native Point of View. Saskatoon: Fifth House Publishers.

Ahenakew, David
1976   Address given to the General Assembly of the Federation of Saskatchewan Indians. Saskatoon: October.

1984   Aboriginal Title and Aboriginal Rights: The Impossible and Unnecessary Task of Identification and Definition.

Akwesasne Notes
1973   I'm Not Your Indian Any More. BIA. Mohawk Nation.

1977   A Basic Call to Consciousness: The Hau de no sau nee Address to the Western World. Rooseveltown, New York: Akwesasne Notes.

American Friends Service Committee
1970   Uncommon Controversy: Fishing Rights of the Muckleshoot, Puyallup, and Nisqually Indians. Seattle: University of Washington Press.

American Indian Policy Review Commission
1977   Final Report, Volume 1 (submitted to Congress on 17 May 1977). Washington, D.C.: U.S. Government Printing Office.

AMMSA (Aboriginal Multi-Media Society of Alberta)
1984   MAA to have local voting. 24 August.

Andersen, W.
   1986   LIA Submission. *Federal Environmental Assessment Review Panel Review of Military Flying Activities in Labrador and Quebec.* Nain, Labrador 14:1645.

Anderson, M.
   1975   in C. Tatz (Editor): *Black Viewpoints: The Aboriginal Experience.* Sydney: Australia & New Zealand Book Co.

Anonymous
   1990   *Human Rights Newsletter,* 3(4) October.

Arendt, Hannah
   1958   What Was Authority?, in Carl J. Friedrich (Editor): *Authority.* Cambridge: Harvard University Press.

Armstrong, Virginia I.
   1975   *I Have Spoken: American History Through the Voices of Indians.* New York: Pocket Books.

Asch, M.
   1983   Native Research and the Public Forum: Implications for Ethnological Theory, in F. Manning (Editor): *Consciousness and Inquiry: Ethnology and Canadian Realities.* Canadian Ethnology Service Paper Number 89E. Ottawa: National Museums of Canada.

   1984a   Personal Communication.

   1984b   *Home and Native Land: Aboriginal Rights and the Canadian Constitution.* Toronto: Methuen.

Assembly of First Nations
   1982   Memorandum Concerning the Rights of First Nations and the Canadian Constitution. 16 June.

   1983   Opening Remarks for Presentation by David Ahenakew, National Chief, Assembly of First Nations to the First Ministers' Conference on Aboriginal Rights. 15 March.

Association of Iroquois and Allied Indians
   1971   *Position Paper.* 27 November.

Australian Department of Aboriginal Affairs Constitution Section
   1981   *Report on a Review of the Administration of the Working Definition of Aboriginal and Torres Strait Islanders.* Canberra: A.G.P.S.

Australian Institute of Multicultural Affairs
   1980   *Review of Multicultural and Migrant Education.* Chairman F. Galbally.

Bagley, Christopher
    1991   Adoption of Native Children in Canada: A Policy Analysis and
            a Research Report, pp. 56-79 in H. Alstein and R. Simon
            (Editors): *Intercountry Adoption: A Multinational Perspective.*
            New York: Praeger.

Bailey, F.G.
    1981   Dimensions of Rhetoric in Conditions of Uncertainty, in Robert
            Paine (Editor): *Political Speaking: Cross-Cultural Studies of
            Rhetoric.* Newfoundland: ISER.

Bakvis, Herman
    1981   *Federalism and the Organization of Political Life: Canada in
            Comparative Perspective.* Kingston: Institute of Intergovern-
            mental Relations, Queen's University.

Banotti, Mary
    1990   *Report on European Parliament Visit to Canada From February
            18th to 26th, 1990.* European Parliament document PE
            140.099.

Barger, W.K.
    1979   Inuit-Cree Relations in the Eastern Hudson Bay Region. *Arctic
            Anthropology* 16(2):59-75.

Barker, Sir Ernest
    1951   *Principles of Social and Political Theory.* Oxford: Clarendon
            Press.

    1960   *Essays on Government.* Second Edition. Oxford: Clarendon
            Press.

Barkwell, Lawrence J., David N. Gray, David N. Chartrand, Lyle N.
Longclaws and Ron Richard
    1989   Devalued People: The Status of the Métis in the Justice System.
            The Canadian Journal of Native Studies 9(1):121-150.

Barkwell, Lawrence J., Lyle N. Longclaws and David N. Chartrand
    1989   Status of Métis Children Within the Child Welfare System. *The
            Canadian Journal of Native Studies* 9(1):33-53.

Barnett, Leroy
    1979   Buffalo Bone Industry in Canada. *Alberta History* 27(1) and
            27(2):6-13.

Barth, Frederik (Editor)
    1969   *Ethnic Groups and Boundaries: The Social Organization of
            Culture Difference.* Boston: Little, Brown and Company.

Beatty, Bonita
    1984   Constitutional Update. *New Breed* 15(10):6.

Becker, Howard S.
1960   Notes on the Concept of Commitment. *American Journal of Sociology* 66:32-40.

Bell, Wendell
1964   *Jamaican Leaders: Political Attitudes in a New Nation*. Berkeley: University of California Press.

1967   *The Democratic Revolution in the West Indies: Studies in Nationalism, Leadership and the Belief in Progress*. Cambridge: Schenkman.

1975   New States in the Caribbean: A Grounded Theoretical Account, in S.N. Eisenstadt and Stein Rokkan (Editors): *Building States and Nations: Analysis by Region*, Volume 2. Beverly Hills: Sage.

1980   Equality and Social Justice: Foundations of Nationalism in the Caribbean. *Caribbean Studies* 20:5-36.

Berger, Mr. Justice Thomas
1977   *Northern Frontier, Northern Homeland: The Report of the Mackenzie Valley Pipeline Inquiry, Volume One*. Ottawa: Supply and Services Canada.

Berger, P.L. and T. Luckmann
1966   *The Social Construction of Reality*. London: Allen Lane.

Berndt, C.H.
1961   The Quest for Identity. *Oceania* 32(1):16-35.

Berndt, R.M.
1959   Current Misconceptions About the Australian Aborigines. *UNESCO Courier* April:28-32.

1961   Problems of Assimilation in Australia. *Sociologus* 2(1):34-51.

1972   Problems of Development of Personal Identity, in R. J. Hunt (Editor): *Socialization in Australia*. Australia: International Press and Publications Ltd.

1981   The Australian Experience. *Optima* 30(1):2-13.

Berndt, R.M. and E.S. Phillips (Editors)
1973   *The Australian Aboriginal Heritage: An Introduction Through the Arts*. Ure Smith in association with the Australian Society for Education Through the Arts.

Berry, J.W.
1970   Marginality, Stress and Ethnic Identification in an Acculturated Aboriginal Community. *Journal of Cross-Cultural Psychology* 1(3):239-252.

Bjorklund, Ivar and Terje Brantenberg
1981   *Samisk Reindrift - Norske Inngrep*. Tromso-Oslo, Bergen.

Bleakley, J.W.
1961   *The Aborigines of Australia.* Brisbane: Jacaranda Press.

Bloch, Maurice
1971   The Moral and Tactical Meaning of Kinship Terms. *Man* 6:79-87.

Block, Fred
1980   Beyond Relative Autonomy: State Managers as Historical Subjects, in Ralph Miliband and John Saville (Editors): *The Socialist Register 1980.* Merlin Press.

Boldt, Menno
1981a   Enlightenment Values, Romanticism and Attitudes Toward Political Status: A Study of Native Indian Leaders in Canada. *Canadian Review of Sociology and Anthropology* 18:545-565.

1981b   Philosophy, Politics and Extralegal Action: Native Indian Leaders in Canada. *Ethnic and Racial Studies* 4:205-221.

1981c   Social Correlates of Romanticism: A Study of Leadership in an Internal Colony. *Ethnic Groups* 3:307-332.

1982   Intellectual Orientations and Nationalism Among Indian Leaders in an Internal Colony: A Theoretical and Comparative Perspective. *British Journal of Sociology* 33:484-510.

Bone, R., E. Shannon and S. Raby
1973   *The Chipewyan of the Stony Rapids Region.* Saskatoon: Institute for Northern Studies.

Bradbury, P.
1985   Luftwaffe over Labrador. *This Magazine* 19(3):9-11.

Brantenberg, Terje
1977   Ethnic Commitments and Local Government in Nain, 1969-76, pp. 376-410 in R. Paine (Editor): *The White Arctic: Anthropological Essays in Tutelage and Ethnicity.* Newfoundland Social and Economic Papers No. 7. St. John's: Institute of Social and Economic Research, Memorial University of Newfoundland.

Brantford Expositor
1971a   Letter to the Editor from "Forbidden Voice." 14 September.

1971b   Letter to the Editor from "Not Quite White." 14 September.

1971c   Editorial. 14 September.

Braroe, N.W.
1975   *Indian and White: Self-Image and Interaction in a Canadian Plains Community.* Stanford: Stanford University Press.

Brass, P.
1985   Ethnic Groups and the State, pp. 1-56 in P. Brass (Editor): *Ethnic Groups and the State.* Beckenham: Croom Helm Ltd.

Brightman, R.
1984   Personal Communication.

Brown, C.H.
1980   *Agents of Manifest Destiny: Lives and Times of the Filibusters.* Chapel Hill, North Carolina: University of North Carolina Press.

Brown, Jennifer S.H.
1983   Woman as Centre and Symbol in the Emergence of Métis Communities. *The Canadian Journal of Native Studies* 3(1):39-46.

Burnette, Robert and John Koster
1974   *The Road to Wounded Knee.* New York: Bantam Books.

Campbell, Maria
1973   *Halfbreed.* Toronto: McClelland and Stewart.

Campbell, Robert M. and Leslie Pal
1991   *The Real Worlds of Canadian Politics: Cases in Policy and Process.* Second Edition. Peterborough: Broadview Press.

Canada, Department of Interior
1921-22 *Annual Report.*

Canada, Department of Justice
1932a   Report from Hugh Guthrie (Minister of Justice). Ottawa: 22 July.

1932b   H.H. Rowatt (Deputy Minister of Justice) to Philip Bill (Acting Minister of Justice). 22 July.

1933   Charles Lanctot (Deputy Attorney General of Quebec) to H.H. Rowatt. 03 August.

1934a   Assistant Deputy Minister of Justice to Plaxton (Deputy Minister of Justice). 09 August.

1934b   James McGregor Stewart to Plaxton. 15 September.

1934c   McGregor to Plaxton. 18 September.

1935   Edwards (Deputy Minister of Justice) to Ralph Parsons (Fur Trade Commissioner, Hudson's Bay Company, Winnipeg). 30 November.

Canada, Federal Court of Appeal
1971   *Lavell v. Attorney General of Canada.* Judgement. 08 October.

Canada, Government of
1869   *An Act for the Gradual Enfranchisement of Indians, the Better Management of Indian Affairs, and to Extend the Provisions of the Act.* 32 and 33 Victoria, Chapter 6, Section 6.

1876   *An Act to Amend and Consolidate the Laws Respecting Indians.* 39 Victoria, Cap. 18 (The *Indian Act,* 1876).

1970   *Report of the Royal Commission on the Status of Women in Canada.* Ottawa: Supply and Services.

1976   *Native Policy: A Review With Recommendations.* A confidential unpublished memorandum to Cabinet, dated 27 May.

1983   Opening Statement by the Prime Minister of Canada, The Right Honourable Pierre Elliott Trudeau to the Constitutional Conference of First Ministers on the Rights of Aboriginal Peoples. 15 March.

Canada, House of Commons
1983a   *Indian Self-Government in Canada.* Report of the Special Committee on Indian Self-Government. Ottawa: Supply and Services. 20 October.

1983b   Report of the Special Committee on Indian Self-Government in Canada. *Minutes of Proceedings.* 12 and 20 October. Issue No. 40 (commonly referred to as the "Penner Report").

1985   *Bill C-31, An Act to Amend the Indian Act.* 1st Session, 33rd Parliament, 33-34 Elizabeth 11, 1985-1985.

Canada, Province of
1850   *An Act for the Better Protection of the Lands and Property of the Indians in Lower Canada.* 13 and 14 Victoria, Cap. 42.

1857   *An Act to Encourage the Gradual Civilization of the Indian Tribes in this Province and to Amend the Laws Respecting Indians.* 20 Victoria, Chapter 26, Section 1.

Canada, Supreme Court
1938a   *Case on Behalf of the Attorney General of Canada* (also known as the *Canada Case*). Ottawa: King's Printer.

1938b   *Case on Behalf of the Attorney General of the Province of Quebec* (also known as the *Quebec Case*). Ottawa: King's Printer.

1938c   *Factum,* Canada.

1938d   *Factum,* Quebec.

1939   *Decisions.* 05 April:104-124.

1973   *Isaac et al v. Bedard* and *Attorney General of Canada v. Lavell.* Judgement. 27 August.

Canadian Press
1991   Tarnished Image Gets Cleaned Up. *Calgary Herald* 20 February:B8.

Canadian Public Health Association
1987   *Final Report of the CPHA Task Force on the Health Effects of Increased Flying Activity in the Labrador Area.* Ottawa: Canadian Public Health Association.

Cantle, M.
1978   *The Umeewarra Story.* Port Augusta: Mimeo.

Card, B.Y.
1964   *Alberta Improvement District 124: A Case Study.* Edmonton: Faculty of Education, University of Alberta.

Card, B.Y., G. Hirabayashi and C. French
1963   *The Métis in Alberta Society.* Edmonton: Alberta Tuberculosis Society.

Cardinal, Harold
1977   *The Rebirth of Canada's Indians.* Edmonton: Hurtig.

Carstens, Peter
1971   Coercion and Change, pp. 126-145 in Richard J. Ossenberg (Editor): *Canadian Society: Pluralism, Change and Conflict.* Scarborough: Prentice-Hall of Canada.

Catlin, George
1959   in M. Ross (Editor): *Episodes From Life Among the Indians and Last Rambles.* Norman, Oklahoma: University of Oklahoma Press.

Cawte, J.E. and G.N. Bianchi and L.G. Kiloh
1968   Personal Discomfort in Australian Aborigines. *Australia and New Zealand Journal of Psychiatry* 2(2):67-79.

Centre for Human Rights
1990   *Human Rights: The Rights of Indigenous Peoples — Fact Sheet #9.* Geneva: United Nations.

Chartrand, Paul
1991   "Terms of Division": Problems of Outside Naming for Aboriginal Peoples in Canada. *Journal of Indigenous Studies* 2(2):1-22.

Chase, A.K.
1980   *Role of 'Tradition' and 'Identity' in the Social Dynamics of Modern Aboriginal Communities.* Unpublished Ph.D. Thesis, University of Queensland.

Churchill, Ward
1986   American Indian Lands: The Native Ethic Amid Resource Development. *Environment* 28(6):13-34.

Churchill, Ward (Editor)
1984   *Marxism and Native Americans.* Boston: South End Press.

Churchill, Ward and Winona LaDuke
  1985   Native America: The Political Economy of Radioactive Coloni-
          zation. *Journal of Ethnic Studies* 13(3):107-140.

Clark, W. Leland
  1983   The Place of the Métis within the Agricultural Economy of the
          Red River During the 1840s and the 1850s. *The Canadian
          Journal of Native Studies* 3(1):69-84.

Cohen, Abner
  1974   *Two-Dimensional Man*. Berkeley: University of California Press.

Cohen, Abner (Editor)
  1974   *Urban Ethnicity*. London: Tavistock Publications.

Cohen, Fay G.
  1986   *Treaties on Trial: The Continuing Controversy over Northwest
          Indian Fishing Rights*. Seattle: University of Washington Press.

Cohen, Ronald
  1962   *An Anthropological Survey of Communities in the Mackenzie-
          Slave Lake Region of Canada*. Ottawa: Department of Northern
          Affairs and Natural Resources, Northern Co-ordination and
          Research Centre.

  1978   Ethnicity: Problem and Focus in Anthropology. *Annual Review
          of Anthropology* 7:379-403.

Cole, Douglas and Chaikin
  1990   *An Iron Hand Upon the People: The Law Against the Potlatch
          on the Northwest Coast*. Vancouver: Douglas and McIntyre.

Collier, John
  1934   *Memorandum, Hearings on H.R. 7902 before the House Com-
          mittee on Indian Affairs* (73rd Congress, 2nd Session) U.S.
          Department of the Interior, Washington, D.C.

Colson, Elizabeth
  1971   Indian Reservations and the American Social System. *North-
          west Anthropological Research Notes* 5:7-11.

Committee on Multicultural Education
  1979   *Education for a Multicultural Society*. Reports to the Schools
          Commission. Canberra.

Commonwealth Education Portfolio
  1978   *Discussion Paper on Education in a Multi-Cultural Australia*.
          Canberra: A.P.G.S.

Commonwealth Hansard Appropriation Bill No. 1
  1972   Mackay, Debate, Senate, 23 August 1972. Canberra.

Commonwealth of Australia Parliamentary Debates
1964   House of Representatives. 25 February - 16 April 1964. Volume H. of R. 41:821-822. Canberra.

1968   House of Representatives. Volume H. of R. 58, Wentworth Debate. Canberra.

Commonwealth of Australia Parliamentary Papers, III
1963   *Aboriginal Welfare*. Report of Conference of Commonwealth and State Ministers, Darwin, July. Canberra.

Connor, Walker
1970   Ethnic Nationalism as a Political Force. *World Affairs* 35:91-97.

1972   Nation-Building or Nation-Destroying. *World Politics* 24:319-355.

1978   A Nation is a Nation, is a State, is an Ethnic Group is a ... *Ethnic and Racial Studies* 1:377-400.

Copi, I.M.
1961   *Introduction to Logic*. New York: The MacMillan Company

Corrigan, Samuel W. and Lawrence J. Barkwell (Editors)
1991   *The Struggle for Recognition: Canadian Justice and the Métis Nation*. Winnipeg: Pemmican Publications Inc.

Crawford, John
1981   What Sort of Thing is Michif? Paper presented to Conference on the Métis in North America, Chicago.

1983   Speaking Michif in Four Communities. *The Canadian Journal of Native Studies* 3(1):47-55.

Cumming, P.A. and H.H. Mickenberg
1972   *Native Rights in Canada*. Second Edition. Toronto: General Publishing.

Curran, Peggy
1991   Natives Will Suffer Death of Meech Accord. *Calgary Herald*. 01 February:B6 (copyright *Montreal Gazette*).

Daes, Erica-Irene A.
1990   *Discrimination Against Indigenous Peoples: Report of the Working Group on Indigenous Peoples on Its Eighth Session*. Geneva: United Nations ECOSOC document E3/cn.4/Sub.2/1990/42.

Daniels, Harry (Editor)
1979   *The Forgotten People: Métis and the Non-Status Indian Land Claims*. Ottawa: Native Council of Canada.

Daniels, Robert E.
1970   Cultural Identities Among the Oglala Sioux, pp. 198-245 in Ethel
        Nurge (Editor): *The Modern Sioux: Social Systems and Reser-*
        vation Cultures. Lincoln: University of Nebraska Press.

Davis, A.K.
1968   Urban Indians in Western Canada: Implications for Social The-
        ory and Social Policy. *Transactions of the Royal Society of*
        Canada 6:217-228.

Dawes, Charles E.
1986   Tribal leaders see danger in use of blood quantum as eligibility
        standard. *The Uset Calumet*, Nashville, Tennessee. Febru-
        ary/March.

Dawson, J.L.M.
1969   Attitude Change and Conflict Among Australian Aborigines.
        Australian Journal of Psychology 21(2):101-116.

DeCora (Means), Lorelei
1986   Statement on radio station KILI. Porcupine, South Dakota: 12
        October.

de Lacey, P.R.
1971   Classification, Ability and Verbal Intelligence Among High-Con-
        tact Aboriginal and Low Socio-Economic White Australian Chil-
        dren. *Journal of Cross-Cultural Psychology* 2(4):393-396.

de Lemos, M.M.
1969   Conceptual Development in Aboriginal Children: Implications
        for Aboriginal Education, in S.S. Dunn and C. Tatz (Editors):
        Aborigines and Education. Melbourne: Sun Books.

Deloria, Vine Jr.
1976   The Place of Indians in Contemporary Education. *American*
        Indian Journal 2(21).

Deloria, Vine Jr. and Clifford M. Lytle
1983   *American Indians, American Justice*. Austin: University of
        Texas Press.

1984   *The Nations Within: The Past and Future of American Indian*
        Sovereignty. New York: Pantheon.

Deshaies, G.
1986   La bataille de Goose Bay. *L'Actualité* 11(11):50-58.

de Tremaudan, A.H.
1982   *Hold High Your Heads: History of the Métis Nation in Western*
        Canada. Translated by Elizabeth Maguet. Winnipeg: Pemmican
        Publications.

Dickason, Olive Patricia
1981 "One Nation" in the Northeast to "New Nation" in the Northwest: A Look at the Origins of the Métis. Paper presented to Conference on the Métis in North America, Chicago.

Dixon, C.
1975 Chicka Dixon, in C. Tatz (Editor): *Black Viewpoints: The Aboriginal Experience*. Sydney: Australia and New Zealand Book Co.

Dobbin, Murray
1981 *The One-And-A-Half Men*. Vancouver: New Star Books.

Docker, T.
1964 The Popular Image: Aborigines and the Newspaper, in M. Reay (Editor): *Aborigines Now*. Sydney: Angus & Robertson, Ltd.

Dorris, Michael
1979 Twentieth Century Indians: The Return of the Natives, in Raymond L. Hall (Editor): *Ethnic Autonomy, Comparative Dynamics: The Americas, Europe and the Developing World*. New York: Pergamon Press.

Dosman, Edgar J.
1972 *Indians: The Urban Dilemma*. Toronto: McClelland and Stewart.

Douglas, Jack D.
1974 *Understanding Everyday Life*. London: Routledge and Kegan Paul.

Douglas, W.H.
1968 *The Aboriginal Languages of South-West Australia: Speech Forms in Current Use and a Technical Description of Nyungar*. Canberra: Australian Institute of Aboriginal Studies.

Driben, P.
1986 *Aroland in Our Home: An Incomplete Victory in Applied Anthropology*. New York: AMS Press.

Drinnon, R.
1980 *Facing West: The Metaphysics of Indian-Hating and Empire Building*. Minneapolis: University of Minnesota Press.

Drucker, Philip
1963 *Indians of the Northwest Coast*. Garden City, New York: Natural History Press.

Duncan, A.T.
1969 Motivation for Achievement in an Industrial Society, in S.S. Dunn and C.M. Tatz (Editors): *Aborigines and Education*. Melbourne: Sun Books.

Dunning, R.W.
   1959a Ethnic Relations and the Marginal Man in Canada. *Human Organization* 18(3):117-122.

   1959b *Social and Economic Change Among the Northern Ojibway.* Toronto: University of Toronto Press.

Dyck, N.
   1970   The Administration of Indian Aid in the North-West Territories, 1878-1886. Unpublished Master of Arts Thesis, University of Saskatchewan, Saskatoon.

   1980   Indian, Métis, Native: Some Implications of Special Status. *Canadian Ethnic Studies* 12(1):34-46.

   1986   Negotiating the Indian "Problem." *Culture* 6(1):31-41.

Dyck, Noel (Editor)
   1985   *Indigenous Peoples and The Nation State: Fourth World Politics in Canada, Australia and Norway.* St. John's: Institute of Social and Economic Research, Memorial University of Newfoundland.

Easton, David
   1958   The Perception of Authority and Political Change, in Carl J. Friedrich (Editor): *Authority.* Cambridge: Harvard University Press.

Eidheim, H.
   1971   *Aspects of the Lappish Minority Situation.* Oslo: Universitetsforlaget.

Eidheim, H., G. Henriksen, P. Mathiesen and T. Thuen
   1985   Samenes Rettstilling et Sporsmall om Likeverd og Rettferdighet? *Nytt Norsk Tidskrift #2.* Oslo.

Elkin, A.P.
   1932a Cultural and Racial Clash in Australia. *Morpeth Review* 21:35-45.

   1932b *The Australian Aborigines.* Australia: Angus & Robertson.

   1953   *Native Reaction to an Invading Culture and its Bearers—with Special Reference to Australia.* Pacific Science Association 7th Congress Proceedings Volume 7:37-42.

   1959a The Australian Aborigines: Today and Tomorrow. *Extrait de Scientia.* 6e Ser., October.

   1959b The Foundation—A Light Along the Way. *Dawn* 14(10):9-10.

   1960   Aborigines and Citizenship. *Dawn* 9(5):6-19.

Elmendorf, William
1960 *The Structure of Twana Culture.* Research Studies, Mono-graphic Supplement 2. Pullman: Washington State University Press.

Elphick, G.
1977 Gladys Elphick in K. Gilbert *Living Black: Blacks Talk to Kevin Gilbert.* Melbourne: Allen Lane, The Penguin Press.

Emerson, Rupert
1971 Self-Determination. *American Journal of International Law* 65:459-475.

Ens, Gerhard
1983 Métis Lands in Manitoba. *Manitoba History* 5:2-10.

Eriksen, K.E. and E. Niemi
1981 *Den Finske Fare. Sikkerhetspolitikk og Minoritets: Politikk i Nord 1860-1940.* Oslo.

Ethnic Affairs Commission of New South Wales
1979 *Participation.* New South Wales: Government Printer.

European Parliament
1989 Position of the World's Indians (Doc. A2-44/89). *Official Journal of the European Communities.* 16 May.

Evening Telegram
1986 29 April; 31 May:6.

Fanon, Frantz
1963 *The Wretched of the Earth.* New York: Grove Press.

Federation of Saskatchewan Indians
1977 Indian Nationhood and Indian Government.

Fink, R.A.
1955 *Social Stratification: A Sequel to the Assimilation Process in a Part Aboriginal Community.* Unpublished Master of Arts Thesis, Sydney University.

Fisher, A.D.
1976 The Dialectic of Indian Life in Canada. *Canadian Review of Sociology and Anthropology* 13(4):458-464.

Flanagan, Thomas
1979 The Political Thought of Louis Riel, pp. 111-127 in Antoine S. Lussier (Editor): *Louis Riel and the Métis.* Winnipeg: Pemmican Publications.

1983a The Case Against Métis Aboriginal Rights. *Canadian Public Policy* 9(3):314-325.

1983b *Riel and the Rebellion: 1885 Reconsidered.* Saskatoon: Western Producer Prairie Books.

1985 The Sovereignty and Nationhood of Canadian Indians: A Comment on Boldt and Long. *Canadian Journal of Political Science*
18(2):367-374.

1990 The History of Métis Aboriginal Rights: Politics, Principle, and
Policy. *Canadian Journal of Law and Society* 5:71-94.

FMS (Federation of Métis Settlements)
1982 *Métisism: A Canadian Identity.* Edmonton, Alberta: Federation
of Métis Settlement Associations.

Forbes, J.D.
1964 *The Indians in American Past.* Englewood Cliffs: Prentice-Hall.

Foster, John Elgin
1978 The Métis: The People and the Term. *Prairie Forum* 3(1):79-90.

Fraser, J.M.
1978 Ministerial Statement: Review of Post-Arrival Programmes and
Services for Migrants. *Hansard.* Canberra: 30 May 1978.

Frideres, J.S.
1974 *Canada's Indians: Contemporary Conflicts.* Scarborough: Prentice-Hall.

Frideres, J. and S. Goldenberg
n.d. Ethnic Identity in Western Canada: Myth and Reality. Unpublished manuscript.

Fried, Morton
1975 *The Notion of Tribe.* Menlo Park, California: Cummings Press.

Friedrich, Carl J.
1958 Authority, Values, and Policy, in Carl J. Friedrich (Editor): *Authority.* Cambridge: Harvard University Press.

Gale, F. with A. Brookman
1972 *Urban Aborigines.* Canberra: A.N.U. Press.

Garfinkel, Harold
1967 *Studies in Ethnomethodology.* Englewood Cliffs, New Jersey:
Prentice-Hall Inc.

Gault, E.
1969 Attitudes of Aboriginal Adolescents in Victoria: A Preliminary
Study, in S.S. Dunn and C.M. Tatz (Editors): *Aborigines and
Education.* Melbourne: Sun Books.

Ghostkeeper, Elmer
1982 *Métism: A Canadian Identity.* Edmonton: Alberta Federation of
Métis Settlement Associations. June.

Giago, Tim
  1984   Blood Quantum is a Degree of Discrimination, *Notes from Indian Country, Volume 1*, Pierre, South Dakota: State Publishing Co.

Gilbert, K.
  1973   *Because a White Man'll Never Do It*. Sydney: Angus and Robertson.

  1977   *Living Black: Blacks Talk to Kevin Gilbert*. Melbourne: Allen Lane, The Penguin Press.

Giraud, M.
  1945   *Le Métis canadien*. Paris: Institut d'Ethnologie:384-428.

  1954   Métis Settlement in the Northwest Territories (translation). *Saskatchewan History* 7(1):1-16.

Gitlin, Todd
  1980   *The Whole World is Watching: Mass Media in the Making and Unmaking of the New Left*. Berkeley: University of California Press. Excerpted in Ralph H. Turner and Lewis M. Killian, *Collective Behavior* (Third Edition). Englewood Cliffs, New Jersey: Prentice Hall (1987):213-216.

Glazer, Nathan and Daniel P. Moynihan
  1975   *Ethnicity: Theory and Experience*. Cambridge, Massachusetts: Harvard University Press.

Globe and Mail
  1983   02, 09 March.

  1986   22 September.

  1990   17, 21, 27 July.

  1992   Métis Threaten Legal Action if Excluded at Negotiations. 02 March.

Globe and Mail Staff
  1990   Chief Issues Warning: Crees can stop power projects. *Globe and Mail*. 11 August.

Goffman, Erving
  1974   *Frame Analysis: An Essay on the Organization of Experience*. Cambridge: Harvard University Press.

Guemple, Lee
  1979   *Inuit Adoption*. Canadian Ethnology Service Paper Number 47. Ottawa: National Museums of Canada.

Gulliver, P.H. (Editor)
  1969   *Tradition and Transaction in East Africa: Studies of the Tribal Element in the Modern Era*. London: Routledge and Kegan Paul.

Gusfield, J.R.
1981   *The Culture of Public Problems: Drinking-Driving and the Symbolic Order.* Chicago: University of Chicago Press.

Gutkind, Peter C.W. (Editor)
1970   *The Passing of Tribal Man in Africa.* Leiden: E.J. Brill.

Haida Constitution
1982   Draft, *Haida Constitution,* circa 1982. Xerox copy provided to the author by Ms. Pam Colorado.

Hamilton, C.E.
1950   *Cry of the Thunderbird: The American Indian's Own Story.* New York: Macmillan.

Handelman, Don
1977   The Organization of Ethnicity. *Ethnic Groups* 1:187-200.

Hara, H.S.
1980   *The Hare Indians and Their World.* Canadian Ethnology Service Paper Number 63. Ottawa: National Museums of Canada, Mercury Series.

Hasluck, P.
1953   A Report on the Native Welfare Conference held in Canberra, September 1951, in *Native Welfare in Australia.* Speeches and Addresses by the Honourable Paul Hasluck, M.P. Perth.

1970   *Black Australians: A Survey of Native Policy in Western Australia, 1829-1897.* Second Edition. Carlton, Victoria: Melbourne University Press.

Hatt, Fred K.
1971   Social Science and the Métis: Recent Perspectives. Unpublished paper presented to the Western Association of Sociologists and Anthropologists. Calgary, Alberta: December 28-30.

Hauser, Rita E.
1971   International Protection of Minorities and the Right of Self-Determination. *Israel Yearbook on Human Rights* 1:92-102.

Hawthorn, H.B. (Editor)
1966   *A Survey of the Contemporary Indians of Canada: A Report on Economic Political and Educational Needs and Policies, Volume One.* Ottawa: The Queen's Printer.

Hedican, Edward J.
1991   On the Ethno-Politics of Canadian Native Leadership and Identity. *Ethnic Groups* 9:1-15.

Heinemann, L.
1984 *An Investigation into the Origins and Development of the Métis Nation, the Rights of the Métis as an Aboriginal People, and their Relationship and Dealings with the Government of Canada.* Research report prepared for the Association of Métis and Non-Status Indians of Saskatchewan, Gabriel Dumont Institute, Regina.

Helm, J. (Editor)
1981 *Handbook of North American Indians, Volume 6: Subarctic.* Washington: United States Government Printing Office.

Helm, June (Editor)
1968 *Essays on the Problem of Tribe: Proceedings of the 1967 Annual Spring Meeting of the American Ethnological Society.* Seattle: University of Washington Press.

Helm, June and Eleanor Burke Leacock
1971 The Hunting Tribes of Subarctic Canada, pp. 343-374 in Eleanor Burke Leacock and Nancy Oestreich Lurie (Editors): *North American Indians in Historical Perspective.* New York: Random House.

Hietala, T.R.
1985 *Manifest Design.* Ithaca: Cornell University Press.

Hiller, Susan
1991 *The Myth of Primitivism: Perspectives on Art.* London: Routledge.

Hinsley, Frances F.
1966 *Sovereignty.* London: C.A. Walls.

Hofstadter, R. and S.M. Lipset (Editors)
1968 *Turner and the Sociology of the Frontier.* New York: Basic Books.

Honigmann, John J.
1946 Ethnography and Acculturation of the Fort Nelson Slavey. *Yale University Publications in Anthropology 33.* New Haven: Yale University Press.

1952 Intercultural Relations at Great Whale River. *American Anthropologist* 54(4):510-522.

1957 Interpersonal Relations and Ideology in a Northern Canadian Community. *Social Forces* 35(4):365-370.

1962 Social Networks in Great Whale River: Notes on an Eskimo, Montagnais-Naskapi, and Euro-Canadian Community. *National Museum of Canada Bulletin 178*, Ottawa.

1975   Five Northern Towns. *Anthropological Papers of the University of Alaska* 17(1).

Horner, J.
1972   In F.S. Stevens (Editor): *Racism, the Australian Experience.* Volume 2. Sydney: Australia and New Zealand Book Co.

Horsman, R.
1981   *Race and Manifest Destiny.* Cambridge: Harvard University Press.

Hourie, Audreen
1991   Unpublished Letter to the Aboriginal Justice Inquiry: Métis Adoptions. Winnipeg.

Hundley, Norris C. Jr.
1979   The Dark and Bloody Ground of Indian Water Rights, in Roxanne Dunbar Ortiz (Editor) *Economic Development in Indian Reservations.* University of New Mexico Press.

Inglis, Gordon B.
1971   Canadian Indian Reserve Populations: Some Problems of Conceptualization. *Northwest Anthropological Research Notes* 5:23-36.

Innis, Harold A.
1956   *The Fur Trade in Canada.* Second Edition. Toronto: University of Toronto Press.

Innstilling O.nr.79
1986/87 Innstilling fra justiskomiteen om lov om sametinget og andre samiske rettsforhold (Sameloven). Oslo.

International Labour Organization
1989   Convention Concerning Indigenous and Tribal Peoples in Independent Countries. *International Legal Materials* 28:1382-1392.

Isajiw, W.W.
1974   Definitions of Ethnicity. *Ethnicity* 1:111-124.

Jamieson, Kathleen
1978   *Indian Women and the Law in Canada: Citizens Minus.* Ottawa: Supply and Services.

Jarvenpa, R.
1980   *The Trappers of Patuanak: Toward a Spatial Ecology of Modern Hunters.* Canadian Ethnology Service Paper Number 67, Ottawa: National Museums of Canada.

1982a   Symbolism and Inter-Ethnic Relations Among Hunter-Gatherers: Chipewyan Conflict Lore. *Anthropologica* 24:43-76.

1982b   Intergroup Behavior and Imagery: The Case of the Chipewyan and Cree. *Ethnology* 21(4):283-299.

1984   Personal Communication.

Jenkin, G.
1979   *Conquest of the Ngarrindjeri.* Adelaide: Rigby.

Jenness, Diamond
1932   The Sarcee Indians of Alberta. *National Museum of Canada Bulletin.* Ottawa.

1964   *Eskimo Administration: II, Canada.* Arctic Institute of Canada, Technical Paper Number 14.

Jennings, F.
1979   Sovereignty in Anglo-American History, in W.R. Swagerty (Editor): *Indian Sovereignty: Proceedings of the Second Annual Conference on Problems and Issues Concerning American Indians Today.* Chicago: Newberry Library.

Johnston, Basil H.
1989   *Indian School Days.* Norman: University of Oklahoma Press.

Johnston, Patrick
1983   *Native Children and the Child Welfare System.* Toronto: James Lorimer and Company.

Jones, L.
1983   American as Poison Pie. *New Statesman.* 7 October:16-17.

Jones, R.
1984   *American Indian Policy: Selected Major Issues in the 98th Congress,* Issue Brief No. 1B83083, Library of Congress, Government Division, Washington, D.C.

Jordan, D.F.
1983   Identity, as a Problem in the Sociology of Knowledge. Unpublished Doctor of Philosophy Dissertation, London.

1984   Report to C.T.E.C. and the N.A.E.C. Support Systems for Aboriginal Students in Higher Education Institution. Mimeo.

Josephy, A.M., Jr.
1968   *The Indian Heritage of America.* New York: Bantam Books.

Judd, Carol
1983   Housing the Homeguard at Moose Factory. *The Canadian Journal of Native Studies* 3(1):25-37.

Kappler, Charles J. (Editor)
1973   *Indian Treaties, 1778-1883.* New York: Interland Publishing Co.

Kearney, G.E.
   1966   Aboriginal Ability. *Journal of Christian Education* 9(2).

Keller, A.S., O.J. Lissitzyn and F.J. Mann
   1958   *Creation of Rights of Sovereignty Through Symbollic Acts 1400-1800*. New York: Columbia University Press.

Kennedy, J.C.
   1982   Holding the Line: Ethnic Boundaries in a Northern Labrador Community. *Social and Economic Studies* 27. St. John's: Institute of Social and Economic Research.

   1987   Aboriginal Organizations and their Claims: the Case of Newfoundland and Labrador. *Canadian Ethnic Studies* 19(2):13-25.

Kew, J.E.M.
   1962   *Cumberland House in 1960*. Saskatoon: Centre for Community Studies.

Kimelman, Edwin
   1984   *File Review Report*. Report of the Review Committee on Indian and Métis Adoptions and Placements. Winnipeg: Manitoba Community Services.

King, A. Richard
   1967   *The School at Mopass: A Problem of Identity*. New York: Holt, Rinehart and Winston.

King, Commonwealth Hansard
   1971   *Senate Budget Debate* 1971-72:756-759.

Krauter, J.A. and M. Davis
   1978   *Minority Canadians: Ethnic Groups*. Toronto: Methuen.

LaDuke, Winona
   1984   Presentation at International Women' Week activities, University of Colorado at Boulder (tape on file): 13 March.

Lagasse, Jean H. (Editor)
   1959   *A Study of the Population of Indian Ancestry Living in Manitoba*. 3 Volumes. Winnipeg: Department of Agriculture and Immigration.

Larsen, Tord
   1977   Negotiating Identity: Ethnic Incorporation Among the Nova Scotia Micmacs. Unpublished Master of Arts Thesis in Social Anthropology, University of Oslo, Norway.

Laslett, Peter
   1963   The Face to Face Society, in Peter Laslett (Editor): *Philosophy, Politics and Society*. Oxford: Blackwell.

LaViolette, Forrest
    1961   *The Struggle for Survival: Indian Cultures and the Protestant Ethic in British Columbia.* Toronto: University of Toronto Press.

Leacock, Eleanor Burke and Nancy Oestreich Lurie (Editors)
    1971   *North American Indians in Historical Perspective.* New York: Random House.

League of Women Voters
    1977   *Indian Country.* Publication Number 605, Washington, D.C.

Leiter, Kenneth
    1980   *A Primer on Ethnomethodology.* Oxford: Oxford University Press.

Levin, M.B.
    1971   *Political Hysteria in America.* New York: Basic Books.

Levine, Robert and Donald Campbell
    1972   *Ethnocentrism: Theories of Conflict, Ethnic Attitudes and Group Behavior.* New York: John Wiley and Sons.

Limerick, Patricia Nelson
    1987   *The Legacy of Conquest: The Unbroken Past of the American West.* New York: W.W. Norton & Co.

Lowie, Robert H.
    1943   Property Rights and Coercive Powers of Plains Indians. *Journal of Legal and Political Sociology* 1:59-71.

Lurie, Nancy Oestreich
    1971   The Contemporary American Indian Scene, pp. 443-446 in Eleanor B. Leacock and Nancy Oestreich Lurie (Editors): *American Indians in Historical Perspective.* New York: Random House.

Lussier, Antoine S. and D. Bruce Sealey (Editors)
    1978   *The Other Natives: the-les Métis.* Volume One - Tome Premier, 1700-1885. Winnipeg: Manitoba Métis Federation Press.

Lyman, Stanford M. and William A. Douglass
    1973   Ethnicity: Strategies of Collective and Individual Impression Management. *Social Research* 40:344-365.

Lynch, P.
    1972   Australia's Immigration Policy, in H. Roberts (Editor): *Australia's Immigration Policy.* Perth: University of Western Australia Press.

Lysyk, Kenneth
    1967   The Unique Constitutional Position of the Canadian Indian. *Canadian Bar Review* 45:513-553.

1982 The Rights and Freedoms of the Aboriginal Peoples of Canada, in W.S. Tarnopolsky and G.A. Beaudoin (Editors): *The Canadian Charter of Rights and Freedoms*. Toronto: Carswell.

MAA (Métis Association of Alberta)
1977 Constitution of the Métis Association of Alberta (Revised 13 August 1977).

MacEwan, Grant
1981 *Métis Makers of History*. Saskatoon: Western Producer Prairie Books.

MacGregor, James G.
1972 *A History of Alberta*. Edmonton: Hurtig.

MacGregor, Roy
1989 *Chief: The Fearless Vision of Billy Diamond*. Markham: Penguin Books.

MacKenzie, J.B.
1896 *The Six Nations Indians in Canada*. Toronto: Hunter Rose.

MacLaine, Craig and Michael S. Baxendale
1990 *This Land is Our Land: The Mohawk Revolt at Oka*. Montreal: Optimum Publishing International.

Mannette, Joy A.
1990 Not Being a Part of the Way Things Work: Tribal Culture and Systemic Exclusion in the Donald Marshall Inquiry. *Canadian Review of Sociology and Anthropology*. 27(4):505-530.

Mannoni, O.
1956 *Prospero and Caliban: The Psychology of Colonization*. New York: Praeger.

Manuel, George and Michael Posluns
1974 *The Fourth World: An Indian Reality*. Toronto: Collier-Macmillan.

Martel, Gilles
1979 Les Indiens dans la pensée messianique de Louis Riel, in Thomas Flanagan (Editor): *Riel and the Métis*. Winnipeg: Manitoba Métis Federation.

Margetts, Jenny
1985 Indian Nations Stronger by New-Status Women. *Kainai News* July (1):2.

Martinez, Cobo, José R.
1986/87 *Study of the Problem of Discrimination Against Indigenous Populations*. Five volumes. Geneva: United Nations document #E/CN.4/Sub.2/1986/7 and Add. 1-4.

Martz, Ron
1986a Indians decry verification plan for federally-funded health care. *Cox News Service*. Pierre, South Dakota: 07 October.

1986b Indians maintain U.S. trying to erode tribal sovereignty: cultural insignificance said to be goal. *Cox News Service*. Pierre, South Dakota: 16 October.

Marule, Marie Small Face
1978 The Canadian Government's Termination Policy: From 1969 to the Present Day, pp. 103-116 in Ian A.L. Getty and Donald B. Smith (Editors): *One Century Later: Western Canadian Reserve Indians Since Treaty 7*. Vancouver: University of British Columbia Press.

Marx, Gary
1982 External Efforts to Damage or Facilitate Social Movements: Some Patterns, Explanations, Outcomes and Complications, pp. 181-200 in James L. Wood and Maurice Jackson (Editors): *Social Movements: Development, Participation, and Dynamics*. Belmont, California: Wadsworth.

Mason, John Alden
1946 Notes on the Indians of the Great Slave Lake Areas. *Yale University Publications in Anthropology 34*. New Haven: Yale University Press.

Mattson, V.E. and W.E. Marion
1985 *Frederick Jackson Turner: A Reference Guide*. Boston: G.K. Hall and Company.

Maybury-Lewis, D.
1985 A Special Sort of Pleading: Anthropology at the Service of Ethnic Groups, pp. 130-148 in R. Paine (Editor): *Advocacy and Anthropology: First Encounters*. St. John's: Institute of Social and Economic Research.

McElwain, A.W.
1969 Some Aspects of the Cognitive Ability of Aboriginal Children, in S.S. Dunn and C.M. Tatz (Editors): *Aborigines and Education*. Melbourne: Sun Books.

McFeat, Tom
1979 *Anthropology Changing*. Proceedings and Transactions of the Royal Society of Canada. Fourth Series, Volume XVII. Ottawa: Royal Society of Canada.

McGee, J.T.
  1961   Cultural Stability and Change Among the Montagnais Indians of the Lake Melville Region of Labrador. Washington: Catholic University of America Press.

McLean, D.
  n.d.   A Research Resource Book of Native History. Paper prepared for the Gabriel Dumont Institute, Regina.

McNab, David T.
  1983   Herman Merivale and Colonial Office Indian Policy in the Mid-Nineteenth Century, pp. 85-103 in A.L. Getty and Antoine S. Lussier (Editors): As Long as the Sun Shines and Water Flows. Vancouver.

McRae, Kenneth D.
  1979   The Plural Society and the Western Political Tradition. this Journal 12.

McRae, Kenneth D. (Editor)
  1974   Consociational Democracy: Political Accommodation in Segmented Societies. Toronto: McClelland and Stewart.

Means, Russell
  1983   The Same Old Song, in Ward Churchill (Editor) Marxism and Native Americans. Boston: South End Press.

  1985   Speech at the law school of the University of Colorado at Boulder (tape on file): 19 April.

Means, Ted
  1975   Statement before the South Dakota Indian Education Association. Pierre, South Dakota: 16 November.

Melody, Michael E.
  1980   Lakaota Myth and Government: The Cosmos as the State. American Indian Culture and Research Journal 4:1-19.

Memmi, Albert
  1967   The Colonizer and the Colonized. Boston: Beacon Press.

Merriam, Charles E., Jr.
  1968   History of the Theory of Sovereignty Since Rousseau. New York: AMS Press.

Métis National Council
  1984   Summary on Métis Rights in the Constitution. Working Group Three. Document No. 840-293/004. January.

Miller, James R.
  1989   Skyscrapers Hide the Heavens: A History of Indian-White Relations in Canada. Toronto: University of Toronto Press.

Miller, Walter B.
1955   Two Concepts of Authority. *American Anthropologist* 57:271-289.

Milliken, E.P.
1969   Social and Cultural Factors Influencing Achievement of Aboriginal Children, in S.S. Dunn and C.M. Tatz (Editors): *Aborigines and Education*. Melbourne: Sun Books.

Mills, C. Wright
1963   Power, Politics and People, in Irving Louis Horowitz (Editor): *The Collected Essays of C. Wright Mills*. New York: Oxford University Press.

Mitchell, J. Clyde
1970   Tribe and Social Change in South Central Africa: A Situational Approach, pp. 83-101 in Peter C.W. Gutkind (Editor): *The Passing of Man in Africa*. Leiden: E.J. Brill.

Moerman, Michael
1965   thnic Identification in a Complex Civilization: Who Are the Lue? *American Anthropologist* 67:1215-1230.

1968   Being Lue: Uses and Abuses of Ethnic Identification, pp. 153-169 in J. Helm (Editor): *Essays on the Problem of Tribe: Proceedings of the 1967 Annual Spring Meeting of the American Ethological Society*. Seattle: University of Washington Press.

Molohan, K.T.
1984   Personal Communication.

Moore, Robert G.
1978   The Evolution of the Indian Act in Canada. Ottawa: Government of Canada, Department of Indian Affairs, Policy Research and Evaluations Branch.

Morse, Brad
1984   *Aboriginal Self-Government in Australia and Canada*. Kingston: Institute of Intergovernmental Relations, Queen's University.

Morton, A.S.
1938   *History of Prairie Settlement*. Frontiers of Settlement Series. W.A. Mackintosh and W.L.G. Long (Editors). Toronto.

1975   *The Métis: Canada's Forgotten People*. Winnipeg: Manitoba Métis Federation Press.

1978   The New Nation, the Métis, pp. 27-37 in Antoine S. Lussier and D. Bruce Sealey (Editors): *The Other Natives: the-les Métis*. Volume One - Tome Premier, 1700-1885. Winnipeg: Manitoba Métis Federation Press.

Morton, William L.

1967a   *Manitoba: A History*. Toronto: University of Toronto Press.

1967b   *Manitoba, The Birth of a Province*. Manitoba Record Society.

Nagler, Mark

1970   *Indians in the City*. Canadian Research Centre for Anthropology. Ottawa: St. Paul University.

1975   *Natives Without a Home*. Don Mills, Ontario: Longmans Canada Ltd.

National Indian Brotherhood

1979   *Proceedings of the Indian Government Development Conference*. Ottawa: National Indian Brotherhood.

Native American Consultants Inc.

1980   *Indian Definition Study* (contracted pursuant to P.L. 95-561, Title IV, Section 1147, submitted to the Office of the Assistant Secretary of Education). Washington, D.C.: U.S. Department of Education.

Native Issues

1984   4(1):19.

Native Press

1971   18 March.

1976   26 November.

New Breed Journal

1983   Métis Organization Wins Ear of Provincial Organization. 14 May:5.

1984a   AMNSIS Remains United. 15 December (12):8.

1984b   Feature Interview: Clem Chartier, Vice-President, AMNSIS. August:22.

1984c   Sinclair Steps Down and Chartier Takes Over. 15 November (11):8-9.

1984d   Sinclair Upset at Racist Remarks at Annual Assembly. August :20.

1985   AMNSIS Members Prepared to Work. 16 January (1):8-9.

News of the North

1956   02 June.

1968   01 August.

1970   10 September.

Nicholas, R.W.
  1965   Factions: A Comparative Analysis pp. 21-61, in M. Banton
          (Editor): *Political Systems and the Distribution of Power*. A.S.A.
          Monographs 2. London: Tavistock.

  1966   Segmentary Factional Political Systems pp. 49-59, in M.J.
          Schwartz, V.W. Turner and A. Tuden (Editors): *Political Anthro-
          pology*. Chicago: Aldine.

Nisbet, Robert A.
  1962   *Community and Power*. New York: Oxford University Press.

Northern Reporter
  1985   13 September:7.

  1986   11 June; 06 August.

Northwest Territories, Government of
  1971   *Goals and Objectives*. Department of Local Government, De-
          velopment Division.

NOU
  1984   *Om samenes rettstilling*. Oslo.

  1985   *Samisk kulture og utdanning*. Oslo.

Norske Samers Riksforbund
  1985   Horingsuttalelse om NOU 1985-18. Om samenes rettsstilling.
          Karasjok.

Nurcombe, B. and J.E. Cawte
  1967   Patterns of Behaviour Disorder Amongst the Children of an
          Aboriginal Population. *Australia & New Zealand Journal of
          Psychiatry* 1(3):119-133.

Nurcombe, B. and P. Moffit
  1970   Cultural Deprivation and Language Deficit. *Australian Psychol-
          ogist* 5(3):249-259.

Ontario, Supreme Court
  1971   *Record* of case between *Yvonne Bedard and Richard Isaac et
          al*.

Ortiz, Alfonso
  1979   Summary, in W.R. Swagerty (Editor): *Indian Sovereignty: Pro-
          ceedings of the Second Annual Conference on Problems and
          Issues Concerning American Indians Today*. Chicago: New-
          berry Library.

Ossenberg, Richard J. (Editor)
  1971   *Canadian Society: Pluralism, Change and Conflict*. Scarbor-
          ough: Prentice-Hall of Canada.

Ot.prop nr.33
1986/87   Om lov om sametinget og andre samiske rettsforhold meloven).
          Oslo.

Owen, Roger
1968   Variety and Constraint in Cultural Adaptation, in W. Buckley
          (Editor): *Modern Systems Research for the Behavioral Scien-
          tist.* Chicago: Aldine.

Paine, R.
1957   *Coast lapp Society.* Tromso: Tromso Museum.

1977   Tutelage and Ethnicity, a Variable Relationship, pp. 249-263 in
          R. Paine (Editor): *The White Arctic.* St. John's: Institute of Social
          and Economic Research.

1981   When Saying is Doing, pp. 9-23 in R. Paine (Editor): *Politically
          Speaking: Cross-Cultural Studies of Rhetoric.* St. John's: Insti-
          tute of Social and Economic Research.

1985   Ethnodrama and the "Fourth World": The Saami Action Group
          in Norway, 1979-1981, pp. 190-235 in N. Dyck (Editor): *Indige-
          nous Peoples and the Nation State: "Fourth World" Politics in
          Canada, Australia and Norway.* St. John's: Institute of Social
          and Economic Research.

Paine, Robert
1974   *Second Thoughts About Barth's Models.* London: Royal Anthro-
          pological Institute, Occasional Paper No. 32.

1982   *Dam A River, Dam A People?* Copenhagen: International Work
          Group for Indigenous Affairs.

Perkins, C.
1975   *A Bastard Like Me.* Sydney: Ure Smith.

1980/81   Personal communication during field work.

Peterson, Jacqueline
1978   Prelude to Red River: A Social Portrait of the Great Lakes Métis.
          Ethnohistory 25(1):46-47.

1981   Ethnogenesis: Settlement and Growth of a New People in the
          Great Lakes Region, 1702-1815. Paper presented to Confer-
          ence on the Métis in North America, Chicago.

Plano, Jack C. and Ray Olton
1969   *The International Relations Dictionary.* New York: Holt, Rinehart
          and Winston.

Policy Development Group
1983   *The Government of Aboriginal Peoples.* Ottawa: Minister of
          Supply and Services.

Pollner, Melvin
1974a Mundane Reasoning. *Philosophy of the Social Sciences* 4:35-54.

1974b Sociological and Common-Sense Models of the Labelling Process, pp. 27-40 in Roy Turner (Editor): *Ethnomethodology: Selected Readings*. Harmondsworth: Penguin.

Ponting, J. Rick (Editor)
1986 *Arduous Journey: Canadian Indians and Decolonization*. Toronto: McClelland & Stewart.

Ponting, J. Rick and Roger Gibbins
1980 *Out of Irrelevance: A Socio-Political Introduction to Indian affairs in Canada*. Scarborough: Butterworth.

Préfontaine, René
1978 Le parler métis, pp. 162-170 in Antoine S. Lussier and D. Bruce Sealey (Editors): *The Other Natives: the-les Métis*. Volume One - Tome Premier, 1700-1885. Winnipeg: Manitoba Métis Federation.

Public Archives of Canada (PAC)
1939 Record Group 10, Department of the Interior Memo to Deputy Commissioner, Northwest Territories. 28 September.

Raunet, D.
1984 *Without Surrender Without Consent*. Vancouver: Douglas and McIntyre.

Rees, W.J.
1963 The Theory of Sovereignty Restated, in Peter Laslett (Editor): *Philosophy, Politics and Society*. Oxford: Blackwell.

Reeves, William J.
1986 Native Societies: The Professions as a Model of Self-Determination for Urban Natives, pp. 342-358 in J. Rick Ponting (Editor): *Arduous Journey*. Toronto: McClelland & Stewart.

Reid, D.
1984 Identity and Adaptation to Community and Economic Change Among the Southend Cree. Unpublished Master of Arts Thesis, University of Saskatchewan.

Report of Royal Commission on Rehabilitation of the Métis
1936 Edmonton: 15 February.

Richards, Audrey I.
1969 *The Multicultural States of East Africa*. Montreal: McGill-Queen's University Press.

Richmond, Sarah
1970 Cognitive and Structural Bases for Group Identity: The Case of the Southern Arctic Drainage Dene. *The Western Canadian Journal of Anthropology* 2:140-149.

Ridington, Robin
1971 Beaver Dreaming and Singing. *Anthropologica* 13:115-128.

Roberts, H.
1972 *Australia's Immigration Policy*. Perth: University of Western Australia Press.

Rowley, C.D.
1971a Aborigines in Australian Society Number 6. *Outcasts in White Australia, Aboriginal Policy and Practice*. Volume II. Canberra: A.N.U. Press.

1971b Aborigines in Australian Society Number 7. *Outcasts in White Australia, Aboriginal Policy and Practice*. Volume III. Canberra: A.N.U. Press.

Ryan, Frank A.
1979 *A Working Paper Prepared for the National Advisory Committee on Indian Education*, Paper No. 071279, Harvard American Indian Education Program. Cambridge: Harvard University Graduate School of Education: 18 July.

Sacerdoti, Giorgio
1984 New Developments in Group Consciousness and the Protection of the Rights of Minorities. *Israel Yearbook on Human Rights* 13:116-124.

Sanders, D.
1972 The Bill of Rights and Indian Status. *U.B.C. Law Review* 7:81-105.

Sanders, Douglas E.
1979 Métis Rights in the Prairie Provinces and the Northwest Territories: A Legal Interpretation, in Harry W. Daniels (Editor): *The Forgotten People: Métis and the Non-Status Indian Land Claims*. Ottawa: Native Council of Canada.

1981 Aboriginal Peoples and the Constitution. *Alberta Law Review* 19(3):410-434.

Saskatchewan History
1970 Louis Riel's Petition of Rights, 1884. *Saskatchewan History* 22(1):16-16.

Sawchuk, J.
1978 *The Métis of Manitoba: Reformulation of an Ethnic Identity*. Toronto: Peter Martin Associates.

1983   Métis Politics and Métis Politicians: A New Political Arena in Canada. Unpublished Ph.D. Dissertation (Anthropology). University of Toronto.

1985   The Métis, Non-Status Indians and the New Aboriginality: Government Influence on Native Political Alliances and Identity. *Canadian Ethnic Studies* 17(2):135-146.

Sawchuk, Joe, Patricia Sawchuk and Theresa Ferguson
1981   *Métis Land Rights in Alberta*. Edmonton: Métis Association of Alberta.

Schmeiser, D.
1974   *The Native Offender and the Law*. Ottawa: Information Canada.

Schools and Commission
1982   *Report for the Triennium 1982-1984*. Canberra: A.G.P.S.

Schutz, Alfred
1971   *Collected Papers, Volume II: Studies in Social Theory*. The Hague: Martinus Nijhoff.

Seagrim, G.
1971   The Cognitive Development of Aboriginal Children, in B.H. Watts (Editor): *Report of the National Workshop on Aboriginal Education, Priorities for Action and Research*. University of Queensland: Department of Education.

Sealey, D. Bruce
1978a   One Plus One Equals One, in Antoine S. Lussier and D. Bruce Sealey (Editors): *The Other Natives: the-les Métis*. Volume One - Tome Premier, 1700-1885. Winnipeg: Manitoba Métis Federation.

1978b   Statutory Land Rights of the Manitoba Métis, pp. 1-30 in Antoine S. Lussier and D. Bruce Sealey (Editors): *The Other Natives: the-les Métis*. Volume One - Tome Premier, 1700-1885. Winnipeg: Manitoba Métis Federation Press.

1979   The Metis Schools, Identity and Conflict, pp. 150-164 in Alf Chaiton and Neil McDonald (Editors): *Canadian Schools and Canadian Identity*. Toronto: Gage.

Shackleton, Phil
1947   Rehabilitation Experiment. *The Canadian Forum* 27 (November).

Sieciechowicz, K.
1984   Personal Communication.

Simon, Yves R.
1969   Sovereignty in Democracy, in W.J. Stankiewicz (Editor): *In Defense of Sovereignty*. New York: Oxford University Press.

Simpson, George E. and J. Milton Yinger
1972   *Racial and Cultural Minorities: An Analysis of Prejudice and Discrimination.* New York: Harper and Row.

Sindell, Peter S.
1968   Some Discontinuities in the Enculturation of Mistassini Cree Children, pp. 83-92 in Norman A. Chance (Editor): *Conflict in Culture: Problems of Developmental Change Among the Cree.* Ottawa: Canadian Research Centre for Anthropology, Saint Paul University.

Six Nations Agency Archives
1847   Six Nations Band Council Minutes. 23 March.

Slobodin, Richard
1971   The Indians of Canada Today: Questions of Identity, pp. 286-292 in W.E. Mann (Editor): *Canada: A Sociological Profile.* Second Edition. Toronto: Copp-Clark.

Smith, Anthony D.
1981   *The Ethnic Revival.* Cambridge: Cambridge University Press.

Smith, Anthony D. (Editor)
1976   *Nationalist Movements.* London: Macmillan.

Smith, D.M.
1981   Fort Resolution, NWT pp. 683-693, in J. Helm (Editor): *Handbook of North American Indians, Volume 6: Subarctic.* Washington, D.C.: United States Government Printing Office.

Smith, Donald B.
1974   *Le Sauvage.* Ottawa: National Museums of Canada.

Smith, J.G.E.
1975   Preliminary Notes on the Rocky Cree of Reindeer Lake pp. 171-189, in D. Carlisle (Editor): *Contributions to Canadian Ethnology.* Canadian Ethnology Service Paper Number 32, Ottawa: National Museums of Canada, Mercury Series,.

1978   The Emergence of the Micro-Urban Village Among the Caribou-Eater Chipewyan. *Human Organization* 37(1):38-49.

1981   Western Woods Cree pp. 256-270, in J. Helm (Editor): *Handbook of North American Indians, Volume 6: Subarctic.* Washington, D.C.: United States Government Printing Office.

1984   Personal Communication.

Smith, M.W.
1949   *Indians of the Urban North-West.* New York: Columbia University Press.

South Australia Legislation
  1834   *The Foundation Act.* 4 and 5 William IV C95 (British Parliament).
  1842   *An Act to Regulate the Sale of Waste Lands.* 5 and 6 Victoria C36 (British Parliament).
  1911   *The Aborigines Act.* No. 1048.
  1934   *Aborigines Act.* No. 2154.
  1939   *Aborigines Act Amendment Act.* No. 14.
  1962   *Aborigines Affairs Act.* No. 45.
  1966a *Prohibition of Discrimination Act.* No. 82.
  1966b *Aboriginal Lands Trust Act.* No. 87.

Spenger, G. Herman
  1978   The Métis Nation: Buffalo Hunting vs. Agriculture in the Red River Settlement, pp. 115-130 in Antoine S. Lussier and D. Bruce Sealey (Editors): *The Other Natives.* Winnipeg: Manitoba Métis Federation.

Sprague, D.N.
  1980a The Manitoba Land Question 1870-1882. *Journal of Canadian Studies* 15(3):74-84.
  1980a Government Lawlessness in the Administration of Manitoba Land Claims, 1870-1887. *Manitoba Law Journal* 10(4):415-441.

Stankewicz, W.J.
  1966   Sovereignty as Political Theory. *Political Studies* 24.

Stanley, George F.G.
  1936   *The Birth of Western Canada.* London: Longmans, Green.
  1972   *Manitoba 1870: A Métis Achievement.* Winnipeg: University of Winnipeg Press.
  1978a Alberta's Half-breed Reserve: Saint-Paul-des-Métis 1896-1909, pp. 75-107 in Antoine S. Lussier and D. Bruce Sealey (Editors): *The Other Natives: the-les Métis.* Volume One - Tome Premier, 1700-1885. Winnipeg: Manitoba Métis Federation Press.
  1978b Confederation - A Métis Achievement, pp. 63-86 in Antoine S. Lussier and D. Bruce Sealey (Editors): *The Other Natives: the-les Métis.* Volume One - Tome Premier, 1700-1885. Winnipeg: Manitoba Métis Federation Press.

Stevens, F.S.
  1972   *Racism, the Australian Experience.* Volume 2. Sydney: Australian and New Zealand Book Co.

Stewart, P.
1976 National Aborigines Day - A Personal Thing. *The Aboriginal Child at School* 4(5):25-26.

Stymeist, D.H.
1975 *Ethnics and Indians: Social Relations in a Northwestern Ontario Town*. Toronto: Peter Martin Associates.

Svensson, Frances
1980 Liberal Democracy and Group Rights: The Legacy of Individualism and Its Impact on American Indian Tribes. *Political Studies* 27:421-439.

Tatz, C.M. (Editor)
1975 *Black Viewpoints: The Aboriginal Experience*. Sydney: Australia & New Zealand Book Co.

Taylor, John L.
1983 An Historical Introduction to Métis Land Claims. *The Canadian Journal of Native Studies* 3(1):151-181.

Teasdale, A.R. and F.M. Katz
1968 Psycholinguistic Abilities of Children From Different Ethnic and Socio-economic Backgrounds. *Australian Journal of Psychology* 20(3):115-160.

Tekawennake (Six Nations Reserve Newspaper)
1971 13, 27 October; 08 December.

The Advertiser
1909 Adelaide. 13 December.

The Labradorian
1985 12 June:18; 27 November.

The Register
1914 Adelaide. 17 June.

The Sunday Express
1986 12 October.

1987 19 April:3.

The Liberal and National Country Parties
1975 *Aboriginal Affairs Policy*.

Thorpe, O.
1950 *First Catholic Mission to the Australian Aborigines*. Sydney: Pellegrini and Co.

Thuen, T. (Editor)
1980 *Samene-urbefolkning og minoritet*. Tromso-Oslo-Bergen.

Tindale, N.B.
  1941   Survey of the Half-caste Problem in South Australia. *Proc. R.G.-S.S.A.* 42:66-161.

Tobias, John L.
  1976   Protection, Civilization, Assimilation: An Outline History of Canada's Indian Policy. *The Western Canadian Journal of Anthropology* 6(2):13-30.

Tonkinson, R.
  1974   *The Jigalong Mob: Aboriginal Victors and the Desert Crusade.* Menlo Park, California: The Benjamin Cummings Publishing Co.

TREATY
  1982   *The Campaign of Russell Means for the Presidency of the Oglala Sioux Tribe.* Porcupine, South Dakota.

Tsigonde
  1972   Issue 6. Whitehorse.

  1973   Issue 6. Whitehorse.

Turnbull, C.
  1972   Tasmania: The Ultimate Solution, in F.S. Stevens (Editor): *Racism, The Australian Experience,* Volume 2, Black Versus White. Sydney: Australia and New Zealand Book Co.

Turner, Roy (Editor)
  1974   *Ethnomethodology: Selected Readings.* Harmondsworth: Penguin.

Union of British Columbia Indian Chiefs
  1980   Indian Nations: Determination or Termination. October.

Van Dyke, Vernon
  1974   Human Rights and the Rights of Groups. *American Journal of Political Science* 18:725-741.

  1975   Justice as Fairness: For Groups? *American Political Science Review* 69:607-614.

  1977   The Individual, the State, and Ethnic Communities in Political Theory. *World Politics* 29:343-369.

  1982   Collective Entities and Moral Rights: Problems in Liberal-Democratic Thought. *Journal of Politics* 44:21-40.

Vincent, Joan
  1974   The Structuring of Ethnicity. *Human Organization* 33:375-379.

Waddell, Eric
 1982   Cultural Hearth, Continental Diaspora: The Place of Quebec in
         North America, pp. 133-154 in L.D. McCann (Editor): *A Geog-
         raphy of Canada: Heartland and Hinterland.* Scarborough:
         Prentice-Hall.

Waldram, J.B.
 1980   Relocation and Political Change in a Manitoba Native Commu-
         nity. *Canadian Journal of Anthropology* 1(2):173-178.

 1986   The "Other Side": Ethnostatus Distinctions in Subarctic Native
         Communities pp. 270-295, in F.L. Barron and J.B. Waldram
         (Editors): *1885 and After: Native Society in Transition.* Regina:
         Canadian Plains Research Centre.

Watson, Graham
 1970   *Passing for White: A Study of Racial Assimilation in a South
         African School.* London: Tavistock.

 1979   On Getting Nothing Back: Managing the Meaning of Ethnicity in
         Canada's Northwest Territories. *Ethnos* 44:99-118.

 1981   The Reification of Ethnicity and its Political Consequences in
         the North. *The Canadian Review of Sociology and Anthropology*
         18(4):453-469.

Watson, R.
 1977   Ross Watson in K. Gilbert *Living in Black: Blacks Talk to Kevin
         Gilbert.* Melbourne: Allen Lane, The Penguin Press.

Watts, B.H.
 1981   *Aboriginal Futures: Reviews of Research and Developments
         and Related Policies in the Education of Aborigines.* E.R.D.C.

Weaver, Sally M.
 1971   Report on Archival Research Regarding Canadian Indian
         Women's Status, 1868-1869. Mimeo.

 1977   Segregation and the Indian Act: The Dialogue of 'Equality' vs.
         'Special Status', pp. 154-161 in W. Isajiw (Editor): *Identities: The
         Impact of Ethnicity on Canadian Society.* Canadian Ethnic
         Studies Association, Volume Five. Toronto: Peter Martin Asso-
         ciates.

 1978   Women's Rights vs. Indian Rights: The Legal Status of Indian
         Women in Canada. Unpublished paper presented to the Cana-
         dian Sociology and Anthropology Association. London: May
         29-June 1.

1983   *Towards a Comparison of National Political Organizations of Indigenous Peoples: Australia, Canada and Norway.* Lecture Series at the Institute of Social Sciences, University of Tromso, Tromso, Norway. October 19-26, 1983.

1985   Political Representivity and Indigenous Minorities in Canada and Australia, pp. 113-150 in Noel Dyck (Editor): *Indigenous Peoples and The Nation State.* St. John's: Institute of Social and Economic Research, Memorial University of Newfoundland.

Weber, Max
1968   *Economy and Society.* New York: Bedminster Press.

Wentworth, W.C.
1969   Commonwealth Parliamentary Debates. Hansard Volume H. of R. 65 *"Ministerial Statement"* 18 September (1561-1563).

Werhan, Keith W.
1978   The Sovereignty of Indian Tribes: A Reaffirmation and Strengthening in the 1970's. *Notre Dame Lawyer* 54:5-25.

White, L.
1949   *The Science of Culture: A Study of Man and Civilization.* New York: Farrar, Strauss.

Whiteside, Don
1972   The Necessity of Alliances in the Timeless Struggle by Amerindians For Freedom and Dignity. Unpublished Paper.

1977   A Good Blanket Has Four Corners: A Comparison of Aboriginal Administration in Canada and the United States, pp. 313-321 in C. Beattie and S. Crysdale (Editors): *Sociology Canada: Readings.* Second Edition. Toronto: Butterworth.

Wieder, D. Lawrence
1974a   *Language and Social Reality: The Case of Telling the Convict Code.* The Hague: Mouton.

1974b   On Meaning by Rule, pp. 107-135 in Jack D. Douglas (Editor): *Understanding Everyday Life.* London: Routledge and Kegan Paul.

Willis, Jane
1973   *Geniesh: An Indian Girlhood.* Toronto: New Press.

Winnipeg Free Press
1984   11 May:8.

Wintrob, Ronald M.
1968   Acculturation, Identification and Psychopathology Among Cree Indian Youth, pp. 93-104 in Norman A. Chance (Editor): *Conflict in Culture: Problems of Developmental Change Among the Cree*. Ottawa: Canadian Research Centre for Anthropology, Saint Paul University.

Wolf, Eric R.
1982   *Europe and the People Without History*. Berkeley: University of California Press.

Youngblood-Henderson, James
1979   Comment, pp. 71-72 in W.R. Swagerty (Editor): *Indian Sovereignty: Proceedings of the Second Annual Conference on Problems and Issues Concerning American Indians Today*. Chicago: Newberry Library.

Zaroulis, N.L. and G. Sullivan
1984   *Who Spoke Up?: American Protest Against the War in Vietnam, 1963-1975*. Garden City, New York: Doubleday.

Zimmerly, D.
1975   *Cain's Land Revisited: Culture Change in Central Labrador, 1775-1972*. St. John's: Institute of Social and Economic Research.